NATIONAL ACADEMIES *Sciences Engineering Medicine*

NATIONAL ACADEMIES PRESS
Washington, DC

Economic and Social Mobility

New Directions for Data, Research, and Policy

H. Luke Shaefer, Florencia Torche,
Malay K. Majmundar, and
David Johnson, *Editors*

Committee on a Research Agenda
for Improving Economic and Social
Mobility in the United States

Committee on Population

Committee on National Statistics

Division of Behavioral and Social
Sciences and Education

Consensus Study Report

NATIONAL ACADEMIES PRESS 500 Fifth Street, NW Washington, DC 20001

This activity was supported by a grant from the Gates Foundation (#INV-033351) to the National Academy of Sciences, with additional support from the National Academy of Sciences W. K. Kellogg Foundation Fund. Any opinions, findings, conclusions, or recommendations expressed in this publication do not necessarily reflect the views of any organization or agency that provided support for the project.

International Standard Book Number-13: 978-0-309-73039-6
Digital Object Identifier: https://doi.org/10.17226/28456
Library of Congress Control Number: 2025944749

This publication is available from the National Academies Press, 500 Fifth Street, NW, Keck 360, Washington, DC 20001; (800) 624-6242; https://nap.nationalacademies.org.

The manufacturer's authorized representative in the European Union for product safety is Authorised Rep Compliance Ltd., Ground Floor, 71 Lower Baggot Street, Dublin D02 P593 Ireland; www.arccompliance.com.

Copyright 2025 by the National Academy of Sciences. National Academies of Sciences, Engineering, and Medicine and National Academies Press and the graphical logos for each are all trademarks of the National Academy of Sciences. All rights reserved.

Printed in the United States of America.

Suggested citation: National Academies of Sciences, Engineering, and Medicine. 2025. *Economic and Social Mobility: New Directions for Data, Research, and Policy*. Washington, DC: National Academies Press. https://doi.org/10.17226/28456.

The **National Academy of Sciences** was established in 1863 by an Act of Congress, signed by President Lincoln, as a private, nongovernmental institution to advise the nation on issues related to science and technology. Members are elected by their peers for outstanding contributions to research. Dr. Marcia McNutt is president.

The **National Academy of Engineering** was established in 1964 under the charter of the National Academy of Sciences to bring the practices of engineering to advising the nation. Members are elected by their peers for extraordinary contributions to engineering. Dr. Tsu-Jae Liu is president.

The **National Academy of Medicine** (formerly the Institute of Medicine) was established in 1970 under the charter of the National Academy of Sciences to advise the nation on medical and health issues. Members are elected by their peers for distinguished contributions to medicine and health. Dr. Victor J. Dzau is president.

The three Academies work together as the **National Academies of Sciences, Engineering, and Medicine** to provide independent, objective analysis and advice to the nation and conduct other activities to solve complex problems and inform public policy decisions. The National Academies also encourage education and research, recognize outstanding contributions to knowledge, and increase public understanding in matters of science, engineering, and medicine.

Learn more about the National Academies of Sciences, Engineering, and Medicine at **www.nationalacademies.org**.

Consensus Study Reports published by the National Academies of Sciences, Engineering, and Medicine document the evidence-based consensus on the study's statement of task by an authoring committee of experts. Reports typically include findings, conclusions, and recommendations based on information gathered by the committee and the committee's deliberations. Each report has been subjected to a rigorous and independent peer-review process and it represents the position of the National Academies on the statement of task.

Proceedings published by the National Academies of Sciences, Engineering, and Medicine chronicle the presentations and discussions at a workshop, symposium, or other event convened by the National Academies. The statements and opinions contained in proceedings are those of the participants and are not endorsed by other participants, the planning committee, or the National Academies.

Rapid Expert Consultations published by the National Academies of Sciences, Engineering, and Medicine are authored by subject-matter experts on narrowly focused topics that can be supported by a body of evidence. The discussions contained in rapid expert consultations are considered those of the authors and do not contain policy recommendations. Rapid expert consultations are reviewed by the institution before release.

For information about other products and activities of the National Academies, please visit www.nationalacademies.org/about/whatwedo.

COMMITTEE ON A RESEARCH AGENDA FOR IMPROVING ECONOMIC AND SOCIAL MOBILITY IN THE UNITED STATES

H. LUKE SHAEFER (*Chair*), Hermann and Amalie Kohn Professor of Social Justice and Social Policy, University of Michigan
FLORENCIA TORCHE (*Vice Chair*), Edwards S. Sanford Professor of Public and International Affairs and Sociology, Princeton University
MARTHA J. BAILEY, Professor of Economics, University of California, Los Angeles
LAWRENCE M. BERGER, Vilas Distinguished Achievement Professor, University of Wisconsin–Madison
TYSON H. BROWN, W.L.F. Associate Professor of Sociology, Duke University
JOHNAVAE CAMPBELL, Manager of Child Welfare and Education, ICF International, Inc.
STEFANIE A. DeLUCA, James Coleman Professor of Sociology and Social Policy, Johns Hopkins University
SUSAN MARIE DYNARSKI, Patricia Albjerg Graham Professor of Education, Harvard University
DAVID B. GRUSKY, Edward Ames Edmond Professor of Sociology, Stanford University
KATHLEEN MULLAN HARRIS, James E. Haar Distinguished Professor of Sociology, The University of North Carolina at Chapel Hill
FABIAN T. PFEFFER, Professor of Sociology, Ludwig-Maximilians-Universität München, Germany
PATRICK SHARKEY, William S. Tod Professor of Sociology and Public Affairs, Princeton University
MARTA TIENDA, Maurice P. During '22 Professor in Demographic Studies, Princeton University
KENNETH R. TROSKE, Richard W. and Janis H. Furst Endowed Chair of Economics, University of Kentucky

Study Staff

MALAY K. MAJMUNDAR, Study Director
ILIYA GUTIN, Program Officer (until June 2024)
DAVID JOHNSON, Senior Program Officer (from April 2024 until April 2025)
ANTHONY S. MANN, Senior Program Associate

COMMITTEE ON POPULATION

ANNE R. PEBLEY (*Chair*), Distinguished Professor Emerita of Community Health Sciences, University of California, Los Angeles
EMILY M. AGREE, Research Professor, Johns Hopkins University
ALLISON E. AIELLO, James S. Jackson Healthy Longevity Professor of Epidemiology, Columbia University
RANDALL Q. K. AKEE, Associate Professor of Public Policy, University of California, Los Angeles
DEBORAH BALK, Professor, Baruch College of the City University of New York
COURTNEY C. COILE, William R. Kenan, Jr., Professor of Economics, Wellesley College
SONALDE DESAI, Distinguished University Professor, University of Maryland
KATHARINE M. DONATO, Donald G. Herzberg Professor of International Migration, Georgetown University
TOD G. HAMILTON, Professor of Sociology, Princeton University
SEEMA JAYACHANDRAN, Professor of Economics and Public Affairs, Princeton University
KENNETH LANGA, Cyrus Sturgis Professor of Medicine, University of Michigan
TREVON D. LOGAN, Hazel C. Youngberg Distinguished Professor of Economics, The Ohio State University
JENNA NOBLES, Professor of Demography, University of California, Berkeley
FERNANDO RIOSMENA, Professor of Sociology and Demography, The University of Texas at San Antonio
DAVID T. TAKEUCHI, Associate Dean for Faculty Excellence, University of Washington

Staff

MALAY K. MAJMUNDAR, Director

COMMITTEE ON NATIONAL STATISTICS

KATHARINE G. ABRAHAM (*Chair*), Distinguished University Professor of Economics, University of Maryland, College Park
MICK P. COUPER, Research Professor Emeritus, University of Michigan
WILLIAM (SANDY) A. DARITY, JR., Samuel DuBois Cook Distinguished Professor of Public Policy, Duke University
ROBERT M. GOERGE, Senior Research Fellow, NORC at the University of Chicago
ERICA L. GROSHEN, Senior Labor Market Advisor, Cornell University
ROEE GUTMAN, Professor of Biostatistics, Brown University
COLLEEN M. HEFLIN, Professor of Public Administration and International Affairs, Syracuse University
DANIEL E. HO, William Benjamin Scott and Luna M. Scott Professor of Law, Stanford Law School
HILARY W. HOYNES, Chancellor's Professor of Economics and Public Policy, University of California, Berkeley
HOSAGRAHAR V. JAGADISH, Edgar F. Codd Distinguished University Professor, University of Michigan
SHARON LOHR, Emeritus Professor, Arizona State University
LLOYD B. POTTER, Texas State Demographer, University of Texas at San Antonio
NELA RICHARDSON, Chief Economist, ADP Research Institute
ELIZABETH A. STUART, Frank Hurley and Catharine Dorrier Professor, Johns Hopkins Bloomberg School of Public Health
FLORENCIA TORCHE, Edwards S. Sanford Professor of International Affairs and Sociology, Princeton University
SALIL VADHAN, Vicky Joseph Professor of Computer Science and Applied Mathematics, Harvard University

Staff

MELISSA CHIU, Senior Board Director
CONSTANCE F. CITRO, Senior Scholar
BRIAN HARRIS-KOJETIN, Senior Scholar

Reviewers

This Consensus Study Report was reviewed in draft form by individuals chosen for their diverse perspectives and technical expertise. The purpose of this independent review is to provide candid and critical comments that will assist the National Academies of Sciences, Engineering, and Medicine in making each published report as sound as possible and to ensure that it meets the institutional standards for quality, objectivity, evidence, and responsiveness to the study charge. The review comments and draft manuscript remain confidential to protect the integrity of the deliberative process.

We thank the following individuals for their review of this report:

ANNA AIZER, Brown University
DIERDRE BLOOME, Harvard University
JENNIE E. BRAND, University of California, Los Angeles
ANNE CASE, Princeton University
SIWEI CHENG, New York University
MICK P. COUPER, University of Michigan
WILLIAM A. DARITY, Duke University
KATHRYN EDIN, Princeton University
MARGARET R. JONES, U.S. Census Bureau
KATHERINE MAGNUSSON, University of Wisconsin–Madison
STEFANIE MOULTON, The Ohio State University
XI SONG, The University of Pennsylvania

Although the reviewers listed above provided many constructive comments and suggestions, they were not asked to endorse the conclusions or recommendations of this report nor did they see the final draft before its release. The review of this report was overseen by **JUDITH A. SELTZER**, University of California, Los Angeles, and **ROBERT A. MOFFITT**, Johns Hopkins University. They were responsible for making certain that an independent examination of this report was carried out in accordance with the standards of the National Academies and that all review comments were carefully considered. Responsibility for the final content rests entirely with the authoring committee and the National Academies.

Contents

Preface   xvii

Summary   1

1   Introduction   17
    CHARGE TO THE STUDY COMMITTEE, 18
    DEFINITIONS: WHAT IS MOBILITY AND HOW IS IT
        MEASURED?, 19
    INTERGENERATIONAL MOBILITY AND ECONOMIC
        INEQUALITY, 27
    MOBILITY IS NOT WITHOUT RISKS, 29
    KINDS OF EVIDENCE ABOUT MOBILITY CONSIDERED
        IN THE REPORT, 29
    CONCEPTUAL FRAMEWORK FOR THE ANALYSIS OF
        MOBILITY, 32
    KEY DOMAINS, 39
    ORGANIZATION OF THE REPORT, 41

2   Early Life and Family   43
    THE CIRCUMSTANCES OF PREGNANCY, 45
    FAMILY CIRCUMSTANCES AT BIRTH AND SUBSEQUENT
        FAMILY EXPERIENCES, 47
    PARENTING, THE CAREGIVING ENVIRONMENT, AND
        CHILD DEVELOPMENT, 51

IMPLICATIONS OF SOCIOECONOMIC DIFFERENCES
    IN PARENTING, 54
EFFICACY OF EARLY LIFE AND FAMILY POLICIES AND
    PROGRAMS IN SHAPING THE DETERMINANTS OF
    ECONOMIC AND SOCIAL MOBILITY, 57
DATA LIMITATIONS AND OPPORTUNITIES, 64
SUMMARY, KEY CONCLUSIONS, AND
    RECOMMENDATIONS, 65

3   Space and Place   71
    SPACE AND MOBILITY, 72
    MECHANISMS LINKING SPACE AND ECONOMIC AND
        SOCIAL MOBILITY, 75
    IMPLICATIONS FOR SOCIAL POLICY, 82
    A FORWARD-LOOKING SCIENCE OF SPACE
        AND MOBILITY, 89
    SUMMARY, KEY CONCLUSIONS, AND
        RECOMMENDATIONS, 93

4   Postsecondary Education   99
    POSTSECONDARY ATTAINMENT IN THE UNITED
        STATES: TRENDS AND DISPARITIES IN ACCESS
        AND RETURNS, 101
    THE STRUCTURE OF POSTSECONDARY EDUCATION
        AND INTERGENERATIONAL MOBILITY, 113
    VARIATION ACROSS POSTSECONDARY INSTITUTIONS:
        RESOURCES, GOVERNANCE, AND GRADUATION
        RATES, 116
    THE FUNDING OF POSTSECONDARY EDUCATION
        IN THE UNITED STATES AND THE GROWING
        IMPORTANCE OF LOANS, 117
    POSTSECONDARY EDUCATON: BALANCING RISKS
        AND RETURNS, 119
    FROM DEMAND SIDE TO SUPPLY SIDE: RESEARCH ON
        IMPROVING COLLEGE QUALITY, 120
    ALTERNATIVE TRANSITIONS AND PATHWAYS TO THE
        LABOR MARKET, 122
    SUMMARY, KEY CONCLUSIONS, AND
        RECOMMENDATIONS, 126

5	Wealth, Credit, and Debt WEALTH, 136 CREDIT AND DEBT, 145 POLICY IMPLICATIONS, 152 SUMMARY, KEY CONCLUSIONS, AND RECOMMENDATIONS, 156	133
6	Data Infrastructure CURRENTLY AVAILABLE DATA RESOURCES, 162 DATA RESOURCES UNDER DEVELOPMENT, 170 REMAINING DATA SHORTFALLS, 173 DISSEMINATION AND ACCESS, 180 SUMMARY, KEY CONCLUSIONS, AND RECOMMENDATIONS, 183 ANNEX: GLOSSARY OF SELECTED TERMS, 198	161
7	New Directions for Research and Policy EARLY LIFE AND FAMILY, 203 SPACE AND PLACE, 205 POSTSECONDARY EDUCATION, 208 WEALTH, CREDIT, AND DEBT, 210 DATA INFRASTRUCTURE, 212 NATIONAL MOBILITY CENTER, 214 CONCLUSION, 216	201

References	217
Appendix Biographical Sketches of Committee Members	267

Boxes, Figures, and Tables

BOXES

1-1 Measuring Relative Mobility, 24

2-1 Child Support and Mobility, 61

4-1 PreK–12 Education and Economic and Social Mobility, 102
4-2 Linking Administrative and Survey Data to Track Educational Mobility in the United States, 109
4-3 What About Elite Colleges?, 114
4-4 Enlistment in the U.S. Military as a Pathway to Upward Mobility, 125

FIGURES

1-1 International comparisons of absolute upward mobility, 22
1-2 International comparisons of relative mobility (intergenerational income elasticity), 25
1-3 Status-attainment model of intergenerational mobility, 34
1-4 Life course–ecosocial framework to examine model of intergenerational mobility, 35

2-1 Lifetime determinants of economic and social mobility, 44

4-1 Cumulative change in real weekly wage of adults aged 16–64, United States, 1963–2017, 103
4-2 Trends in postsecondary educational attainment in the United States; cohorts born 1915–2001, 106
4-3a Proportion of students entering college by household income quartile and birth year, 108
4-3b Proportion of students graduating from college by household income quartile and birth year, 108
4-4 Percentage of 25- to 29-year-olds, by ethnoracial category, with some college completed or a bachelor's degree, 1972–2022, 111
4-5 Proportion of enrolled students by type of postsecondary institution, 2011–2012 and 2021–2022, 115
4-6 College attainment by cohort, by age, 124

TABLES

4-1 Proportion of College Students Who Worked, by Birth Cohort, 1940–2002, 123

Annex 6-1 Surveys Frequently Used for Mobility Research, 191
Annex 6-2 Illustrative Aggregate and Contextual Datasets, 194

Preface

The National Academies of Sciences, Engineering, and Medicine (National Academies) was solicited by the Gates Foundation to prepare a consensus study report on developing a research agenda for improving economic and social mobility in the United States. To carry out this task, the National Academies negotiated a statement of work and appointed the Committee on a Research Agenda for Improving Economic and Social Mobility in the United States. The study committee included 14 experts with backgrounds in areas such as economics, sociology, demography, statistics and methodology, public policy, and evaluation. The work of the study committee was carried out under the National Academies' standing Committee on Population and Committee on National Statistics in accordance with institutional procedures.[1] The committee began its work in April 2023. The bulk of the committee's information gathering and synthesis was completed by December 2024, and the final edits and revisions to the report were incorporated by June 2025.

This report would not have been possible without the contributions of many people. Special thanks go to the members of the study committee, who dedicated extensive time, thought, and energy to this task.

The committee received useful information and insights from presentations by outside experts at open sessions of committee meetings. We thank Gregory Acs (Urban Institute), Greg Duncan (University of California, Irvine), Kathryn Anne Edwards (economic policy consultant), Jacob Hacker (Yale University), Kristen Harknett (University of California, San

---

[1] https://www.nationalacademies.org/about/our-study-process

Francisco), Catherine Harvey (Urban Institute), Ariel Kalil (The University of Chicago), Leslie McCall (Graduate Center, City University of New York), Suresh Naidu (Columbia University), Claudia Solari (Urban Institute), Stefanie Stantcheva (Harvard University), Margery Austin Turner (Urban Institute), and Christina Weiland (University of Michigan). Thanks are also due to Arne Kalleberg (The University of North Carolina at Chapel Hill), who provided additional guidance to the committee on labor markets; and to Claire Daviss (Stanford University) and Hye Jee Kim (Stanford University), who provided valuable assistance conducting literature reviews and creating figures for the report.

Several staff members of the National Academies also made significant contributions to the report. Iliya Gutin provided valuable research and writing assistance and helped manage the committee's deliberation process. David Johnson made important contributions to the content of several report chapters and helped guide the report through the review process. Anthony Mann made sure that the committee meetings ran smoothly, assisted in preparing the manuscript, and provided key administrative and logistical support throughout the project. Thanks are also due to Kirsten Sampson Snyder for managing the report review process; Bea Porter for managing the report production process; and Melissa Chiu, director of the Committee on National Statistics, for providing overall guidance and oversight. Finally, we thank Allison Boman for her skillful editing.

H. Luke Shaefer, *Chair*
Florencia Torche, *Vice Chair*
Malay K. Majmundar, *Study Director*
Committee on a Research Agenda for Improving
Economic and Social Mobility in the United States

June 2025

Summary

Intergenerational mobility is a key measure of economic and social well-being. While economic growth and inequality measurements capture overall material prosperity and its distribution, mobility focuses on individuals' chances to succeed economically. Mobility is rooted in a shared belief that all individuals, regardless of their family circumstances, should have the chance to improve their economic status.

Intergenerational mobility can be assessed in both absolute and relative terms, capturing distinct dimensions of opportunity across generations. *Absolute mobility* measures whether individuals have a higher or lower standard of living than their parents, usually in terms of real income or earnings; absolute mobility is especially salient in public debates because it provides a tangible benchmark against which individuals gauge their economic success. *Absolute upward mobility* captures the probability that adult children will outearn their parents. Recent studies show that absolute upward mobility in the United States is no higher than in other affluent countries and that it has declined over time as inequality has grown. *Relative mobility* captures the persistence of socioeconomic status across generations, or the extent to which adult children's incomes (or another measure of socioeconomic status) depend on their parents' incomes; measures of relative mobility, such as intergenerational elasticity, are more abstract than those of absolute mobility. Relative mobility is closely related to equality of opportunity in a society: The stronger the association between parents' and adult children's income, the less equal economic opportunity is. While evidence on relative mobility trends over time in the United States is inconclusive, comparative studies indicate that relative mobility is lower in the United States than in other affluent democracies.

Higher relative mobility suggests a more open society, where success is less influenced by family background; unlike absolute mobility, measures of relative mobility require that for any upward move to happen, a downward move must "free up" a space in the socioeconomic hierarchy. A country can have high upward absolute mobility yet low relative mobility. For example, rapid economic growth may allow most adult children to earn more than their parents, but if growth disproportionately favors wealthy families, then the children of rich parents may still end up better off than children from poor families.

Limited absolute and relative intergenerational mobility in the United States compared with peer countries invites a research agenda to understand why mobility differs across places, people, and time. Developing this agenda requires a clear understanding of the changes in mobility patterns, factors that influence mobility, and how these factors are affected by policy interventions. To that end, the National Academies of Sciences, Engineering, and Medicine (National Academies) were solicited by the Gates Foundation to conduct a consensus study to identify key, actionable knowledge gaps in these areas; discuss promising conceptual, methodological, and data approaches; and make recommendations for policy-relevant research and evaluation. To carry out this study, the National Academies appointed a committee that included 14 experts with backgrounds in areas such as economics, sociology, demography, statistics and methodology, public policy, and evaluation.[1]

Addressing mobility requires considering economic inequality, especially given the increase in income inequality since the 1970s in the United States. Higher inequality could reduce intergenerational mobility through a variety of mechanisms, including disparities in parental investments, more unequal access to education, residential segregation, and growing political influence of the wealthy. While a full exploration of the causal links between inequality and mobility remains a target for future research, current levels of income inequality in the United States likely hamper intergenerational mobility. In addition, efforts to achieve upward mobility—such as taking out student loans or obtaining credit to start a business—necessarily carry some level of risk; the committee emphasizes the need to identify excessive levels of risk when pursuing upward mobility. The substantial individualization and privatization of some sources of risk in the United States might leave families vulnerable to the consequences of unexpected shocks or

---

[1] The descriptions of the roles and structures of federal and nonfederal activities—data, and policies relevant to improving economic and social mobility in the United States—were current as of June 2025.

unproductive investments. For example, increased reliance on loans to fund higher education may increase risk of economic shock for individuals pursuing mobility through educational investments, and economic risks may also be increased by changes such as privatization of retirement income and access to health care.

Mobility is a long-term intergenerational dynamic linking parents and their adult children. Measuring it is challenging because it requires tracking families over time to link parents' and children's economic well-being. This extended timeline makes it challenging to evaluate factors directly affecting mobility. Therefore, the evidence that the committee considered is mostly *indirect*. In this report, we focus on factors along the pathway connecting parental circumstances with adult children's outcomes, such as family environments, educational attainment, and access to income-generating resources. We consider diverse kinds of evidence, including descriptive, correlational, quasi-experimental, experimental, and qualitative, and explain which kind of claim each source of evidence supports throughout the report.

Important tasks of this committee included reviewing sources of available data (including administrative and survey sources), reviewing the plausibility of linking different data sources, and developing recommendations for building a data infrastructure to support continuous evaluation of intergenerational mobility. Understanding the determinants of mobility also requires considering economic, demographic, and institutional factors that shape opportunities available to each generation and the pathways linking parents' economic resources to their adult children's outcomes over the life course. This report focuses on key domains that shape mobility, including early life and family; the spaces and places where people live and work; postsecondary education; and wealth, credit, and debt. It also discusses the data infrastructure needed to support an extensive research agenda on economic and social mobility. Although labor markets play a key role in shaping intergenerational mobility, the committee, based on the available evidence, decided to focus on foundational "premarket" factors that feed into the labor market.

EARLY LIFE AND FAMILY

The family plays a critical role in the mobility process, serving as the primary institution through which investments are made in children, thus shaping human capital development from conception onward. Parents are central to this process, investing resources into their children's upbringing to directly affect their future economic and social prospects. Family environments are highly variable in the United States, largely based on families' socioeconomic resources and opportunities they afford.

The circumstances of pregnancy and childbirth are closely linked to the prenatal and childhood environment and parental investments in children. These circumstances are influenced by laws and policies, institutions, social norms, and social and economic conditions that shape opportunities for intergenerational mobility differently by race and ethnicity, immigration status, socioeconomic status, geography or state of residence, and other relevant characteristics. Populations of lower socioeconomic status are disproportionately likely to have unintended and nonmarital births, which are adversely associated with multiple determinants of upward mobility in domains such as infant and maternal health, cognitive and socioemotional development, human capital formation, and economic well-being (Conclusion 2-1).

Parents play a crucial role in shaping children's development and well-being in early life. Socioeconomic disparities in parental resources and parenting behaviors are associated with disparities in the social and economic well-being of children, thus providing a mechanism for the persistence of advantage and disadvantage across generations (Conclusion 2-2). Parental behaviors, including physical care, cognitive and emotional stimulation, opportunities for child autonomy and age-appropriate play, and activity arrangement, can require substantial investments of time and resources. Although racial/ethnic differences in parenting behaviors have been well documented, these relationships largely reflect disparities in parental socioeconomic resources and associated differential selection into parenthood, family formation, and subsequent child-rearing contexts, as well as by experiences with racism and discrimination (which are typically unobserved in existing quantitative studies).

Reproductive health policies and programs that increase access to contraception and abortion; early childhood education programs (e.g., Head Start); and economic support policies and programs that increase access to financial resources, food, and health care (e.g., the Earned Income Tax Credit, the Supplemental Nutrition Assistance Program, and Medicaid) have positive effects on the factors that link childhood experiences with adult health and economic and social well-being—including family resources, stress, parenting quality, and early childhood health and development; they also have direct positive impacts on adult health and economic and social well-being. As such, these programs and policies show promise for increasing upward intergenerational mobility. In contrast, the evidence on other pregnancy risk reduction, abstinence education, and parenting intervention programs is less encouraging (Conclusion 2-3).

Research to date offers limited evidence on whether associations among family context (e.g., pregnancy intendedness, family formation, family structure and stability), parenting behaviors and the caregiving environment, child development, and economic and social mobility are causal.

Research on the mechanisms through which these factors may operate, such as children's cognitive and socioemotional development and educational attainment, is also limited, although a growing body of work suggests causal effects of family resources on these intermediate factors. Future research should expand the use of existing longitudinal, administrative, and survey data, and further employ quasi-experimental and experimental approaches, when possible, to better understand the causal mechanisms through which family context, parenting behaviors, and child development affect economic and social mobility, as well as potential heterogeneity in such relations for demographic subpopulations (Recommendation 2-1).

Existing survey and administrative data are also not fully adequate for comprehensive research on malleable pathways through which social and economic (dis)advantages are transmitted within and across generations. The Panel Study of Income Dynamics and the Future of Families and Child Wellbeing Study are currently the only ongoing long-term U.S. panel studies to follow multiple generations of family members. These studies should be maintained and expanded to include detailed information on pregnancy intention and the circumstances of pregnancies, parenting, and child development for all children born to current sample members; in addition, the samples that support these surveys should be refreshed with respondents that represent the contemporary population, especially Latino/Hispanic and immigrant subgroups. The studies should follow children in utero onward and assess them regularly at key developmental stages of childhood, adolescence, and young adulthood. Also, these surveys should be linked to administrative data from the U.S. Census Bureau, the Internal Revenue Service, and state and federal agencies that administer core social welfare programs (Recommendation 2-2).

SPACE AND PLACE

While early quantitative research on the impact of residential environments faced methodological challenges associated with nonrandom selection into neighborhoods and cities, recent evidence has led to something close to a consensus suggesting that residential environments can have a causal impact on economic and social mobility (measured by income, earning, or occupation) and intermediate outcomes related to mobility, most notably academic achievement, cognitive skill, and physical and mental health. The link between place and individual outcomes has now moved beyond the question of whether neighborhoods matter and toward questions of when, where, why, and for whom residential contexts matter (Conclusion 3-1).

While scholarship on the effects of place has grown over time, less attention has been paid to the mechanisms that undergird these effects and the heterogeneity of these effects—vital considerations for improving policy and understanding the scalability of existing interventions. Evidence at the neighborhood level points to schools, community violence, and local social networks as examples of mechanisms linking the local residential environment with economic and social mobility. Evidence at larger levels of analysis—such as cities, counties, and commuting zones—points to segregation and local labor market conditions as examples of forces that influence economic and social mobility (Conclusion 3-2).

Broadly speaking, most spatial policy strategies are either *housing mobility policies*, which help relocate disadvantaged families to higher-opportunity areas, or *place-conscious investments*, which aim to bring opportunity and investment into disadvantaged communities. Housing mobility programs—such as the Gautreaux desegregation program and the Moving to Opportunity experiment—have shown positive impacts on academic outcomes, employment, and earnings, particularly for children moving to low-poverty neighborhoods. Place-conscious investment initiatives include programs such as New Hope, the Harlem Children's Zone, and Jobs Plus. These initiatives target residents of disadvantaged communities with employment opportunities, training, and support services and/or provide resources to foster job creation and economic development, and they have shown success in improving employment, earnings, and academic outcomes for participants. However, evidence on the effectiveness of place-based programs that have not targeted people in disadvantaged communities and have not provided a range of supports has been mixed (Conclusion 3-3).

A third approach emphasizes the importance of ending programs and policies that have historically amplified spatial and racial inequality and that continue to do so (Conclusion 3-4). Zoning, discriminatory housing practices, and some regressive federal housing programs (e.g., mortgage interest deduction, property tax deduction, exclusion of capital gains on the sales of homes) reinforce residential segregation and constrain residential mobility. While federal homeowner policies exist that assist low-income families (e.g., affordable mortgage programs and credit programs), many homeownership policies disproportionately benefit the most affluent communities and households, further entrenching economic segregation and the concentration of mobility-relevant resources in higher-income areas.

The committee identified seven research areas to fill gaps in the existing research on space mobility and to strengthen the connection between research and policy (Recommendation 3-1). First, more convincing evidence is needed on the central mechanisms underlying the link between place and mobility. Second, a more complete understanding of heterogeneity in the relationship between space and mobility will produce a better understanding of which groups are most likely to take advantage of and benefit from social policies designed to reduce spatial inequality or increase economic and social mobility. Third, qualitative research needs to play a larger role in illuminating the link between evidence and policy. Although quantitative research using survey and administrative data can powerfully identify patterns and relationships, qualitative research can help make sense of what is being seen and to apply the evidence to make more efficient policy investments. Fourth, while much of the research discussed by the committee is based on programs estimating the impact of residential moves, more needs to be known about the most effective ways of making place-based investments in communities or entire cities and regions. Fifth, policy discussions that focus on how to reduce spatial inequality typically take two approaches: moving people or investing in places. However, this discussion and the supporting evidence base should be expanded to include reassessing existing policies (e.g., federal housing policies, local land use policies) that exacerbate spatial inequality. Sixth, consideration should be given to the general equilibrium effects of social policies, to consider their system-wide impacts, as well as the feasibility and costs of different approaches. Seventh, there needs to be a greater focus on regions and areas that have received relatively little attention in the literature on neighborhood effects and mobility, including deeply disadvantaged rural areas, rural-adjacent small towns, and suburbs.

POSTSECONDARY EDUCATION

Elementary and secondary education (i.e., K–12) is a critical building block for cognitive and socioemotional development, which are essential for future academic and labor market success, both through and independent of postsecondary education. Indeed, K–12 is one of the most well-studied periods when it comes to understanding how education shapes mobility, as are interventions intended to identify core investments that improve and equalize mobility-relevant outcomes. The committee focused on the postsecondary stage not because it is the most important point at which to understand family-based inequities in education and training, but rather because it has received significantly less attention from research and policy.

Postsecondary educational attainment—and, especially, the attainment of a 4-year bachelor's degree—is central to the understanding of economic and social mobility in the United States. On the one hand, education is an avenue for intergenerational persistence, if advantaged families can afford more and better education for their children; on the other hand, postsecondary education can be the main vehicle for both absolute and relative mobility if attaining a degree detaches individuals from their social origins and provides a pathway to economic well-being.

The probability of attending and graduating from college, however, strongly depends on household income, and there are pronounced disparities by family income, residential location, and race and ethnicity in college attendance and, especially, college graduation. There is also a growing female advantage in college attainment, which requires further investigation and will likely have broader consequences for intergenerational processes involving fertility, children's educational opportunities, and growing gaps between families in which both parents have high versus low levels of schooling (Conclusion 4-1; Recommendation 4-1).

Existing data sources do not enable proper evaluation of current changes in the association between parents' income and bachelor's degree attainment—a critical factor in intergenerational mobility. One relatively low-cost strategy for addressing these data limitations is using existing sets of large, high-quality administrative data to supplement currently administered surveys (Conclusion 4-2).

The U.S. postsecondary system is heterogeneous, decentralized, and stratified. Colleges vary dramatically in their inputs (spending per student, student preparation) and their outcomes (graduation rates, economic payoff for graduates). The most disadvantaged students attend the institutions with the fewest resources and the worst outcomes. Although a college education can result in a large economic payoff, there is enormous variation around average payoff. Like any investment, education is not without risk. Risk is particularly salient in the sub-baccalaureate sector, which includes both public community colleges and private, for-profit schools; the students in this sector are the most disadvantaged. Addressing the key question about whether postsecondary education serves as an engine for upward economic mobility or as an intergenerational replicator of inequality requires considering variation across the vast and heterogeneous postsecondary sector, with broad-access universities playing a different role from that of selective institutions.

As tuition prices have risen, the federal government has stepped in to assist students and families. Some of this aid has taken the form of grants, but much has been in the form of student loans. Borrowing for college is now much more common than it was just a few decades ago. The shift has been particularly marked at community colleges, where traditionally students did not borrow for their education. This potentially has consequences for mobility because it creates the opportunity to invest in education but shifts onto the most disadvantaged students the cost (and risks) of postsecondary education (Conclusion 4-3). In the United States, moreover, students are funded by the same federal grant and loan programs whether they are pursuing career and technical training at a community college or a bachelor's degree at a university. In much of the world, by contrast, the funding models for the baccalaureate and sub-baccalaureate sectors are distinct: baccalaureate students are typically charged tuition and pay for tuition using loans, while this is rarely true for students in the sub-baccalaureate sector.

Against this backdrop, it is important to conduct comprehensive, distributive analyses of the economic costs, benefits, and risks of college and to explore the question of the extent to which U.S. postsecondary education is a replicator of inequality rather than an engine for economic mobility. In these analyses, attention should be paid to variations in returns across the heterogeneous postsecondary sector (Recommendation 4-2). Researchers should also explore whether postsecondary funding models in other countries—especially regarding sub-baccalaureate education—are more effective in generating economic mobility than the U.S. model (Recommendation 4-3).

There is a large body of rigorous evidence on how to stimulate student demand for postsecondary education, and research now needs to move to designing policies that stimulate demand within particular populations (defined, e.g., by level of academic preparation, race and ethnicity, income level, and age) and settings (e.g., rural; Recommendation 4-4). On the "supply side," the postsecondary sector in the United States has grown through the establishment and expansion of schools that receive relatively few resources but serve students with the most challenges, in contrast to the more redistributive K–12 education funding. Better understanding is needed of how to improve the quality of postsecondary education. Although a sizeable amount of literature has examined the effect of inputs, policies, and practices on K–12 education, the analogous literature addressing these questions in the postsecondary setting is astoundingly thin. More needs to be known about the effects of inputs, policies, and practices (e.g., curricula, pedagogical techniques, class size, connections to employment opportunities) on improving the quality of postsecondary education and the implications for economic and social mobility (Recommendation 4-5).

People transition into and out of school and work throughout their lives, including the growing "some college" group without bachelor's degrees, much more often than current policy recognizes. And, although transitions into the workforce and between careers are important to shaping economic mobility, they get far less attention than the transition into college. The technological landscape is changing rapidly, and many students end up working sooner than they expect (given low college completion rates) and will have longer working lives—but few existing policies account for these changes. It is important to recognize the need for multiple pathways to mobility, commensurate with many potential starting points and transitions in people's lives (Conclusion 4-4). More needs to be known about the effectiveness of job training programs, and a better understanding is also needed of the role of alternative credential programs, immersive training programs (e.g., educational bootcamps), and certifications for preparing for the transition into the workforce or changes in careers (Recommendation 4-6); although this latter sector has grown significantly, little is known about student experiences, quality of programs, or labor market returns.

WEALTH, CREDIT, AND DEBT

A growing body of research documents low levels of wealth mobility in the United States relative to other countries, coupled with a high degree of inequality in the concentration of wealth at the top of the distribution and stark racial/ethnic gaps in wealth that have grown over time. In comparison to its peer countries, the United States also stands out as the country with the highest level of wealth inequality and the top concentration in wealth.

Wealth is a primary factor in shaping intergenerational mobility in the United States. Perhaps the most distinctive feature of wealth is that—unlike education, occupation, or income—it can be transmitted directly to one's children and even grandchildren. However, the transmission of wealth can take place not only directly through transfers and bequests, but also indirectly through advantages that accrue to children in their early development, educational, and labor market experiences. In addition to monetary advantages, family wealth can provide a safety net or buffer that allows individuals with access to wealth the privilege of taking risks (Conclusion 5-1). The intergenerational behavioral implications of assets and debts are one frontier for future research on wealth and debt (Recommendation 5-1). Like most scholarship on social mobility, most existing studies on wealth are limited to a two-generation framework (i.e., the standard assessment of similarity in positions between parents and their children). However, both family assets and debts can exert influences far beyond immediate offspring. As a result, increased consideration needs to be given to the role of at least grandparental wealth and debt (Recommendation 5-2).

Housing is a key source of wealth and stability, including the value of the home itself, the resources homeownership provides (as compared with renting), and the home's neighborhood. Housing assets (home equity) are the primary source of wealth for the average U.S. household and for a majority of households. Wealth accumulation and intergenerational wealth transmission are shaped by multiple institutional and structural features of society that have not been and are still not race neutral—the segregated housing market and racialized lending practices are prime examples. The sources of disparities among racial/ethnic minority groups have changed shape over time, and they require ever more critical analysis, as direct forms of legal exclusion from asset accumulation have morphed into less explicit but potentially equally impactful ways of reproducing racial/ethnic wealth gaps, such as via weakened homeownership rights or predatory lending practices (Conclusion 5-2). Uncovering these institutions, policies, and practices remains an urgent task for future research. Moreover, although research has documented dramatic differences in wealth mobility between White and Black individuals, evidence on wealth mobility patterns among other groups is still very limited, and more needs to be known (Recommendation 5-3).

Credit and debt provide many individuals with opportunities to take risks that support wealth accumulation and upward mobility; yet, for some, credit and debt are insurmountable obstacles that hinder upward mobility, and in some cases, they are direct sources of downward inter- and/or intra-generational mobility. In other words, credit and debt are not monolithic, and they can carry both benefits and challenges to the individuals who borrow (Conclusion 5-3). It is therefore important to study situations in which credit and debt are productive and for whom (Recommendation 5-4). Student debt, which accounts for the largest share of nonmortgage debt of U.S. households, is one type of debt that represents this tension well: while generally considered a "productive" form of debt, as it can enable the pursuit of higher education and the earnings benefits that arise from a college degree, racial differences in the probability of carrying student debt and the amount of debt have contributed greatly to the maintenance of racial inequity in assets.

Many tax policies regulate gifts, capital income, trusts, and college savings accounts; however, few existing policies explicitly target the intergenerational persistence of wealth. However, a variety of interventions is possible. One approach is adopting policies that target different points of wealth distribution: inheritance and wealth taxation will impact only the very top, homeownership policies will help build middle-class wealth, and the regulation of credit and debt markets—as well as asset-building policies such as matched savings accounts—can lift the very bottom of the wealth distribution. A more universal approach would be to provide a wealth transfer to all families, young people, or the descendants of enslaved people through policies such as universal wealth grants, baby bonds, or reparations for slavery, respectively, thereby creating a more widely shared economic basis for families to invest in the success of their children (Conclusion 5-4). Although initial assessments of some of these policies are underway, far more needs to be known about their relative effectiveness and about the potential of existing and new tax policies that support such initiatives (Recommendation 5-5).

DATA INFRASTRUCTURE

The extensive agenda for research on economic and social mobility proposed in this report requires a complex data infrastructure. The United States is moving toward a modern integrated data system based on linked administrative data, a system that may ultimately rival the systems in European countries. Developing sustainable structures that ensure increased and equitable access to the new data resources remains the central challenge ahead. Achieving this goal requires cooperation among the many stakeholders in the data ecosystem, including executive and congressional branches of government, federal statistical agencies, state and local government officials, the research community, potential private funding organizations, and the public.

Linked administrative data form the backbone of data resources used to study intergenerational mobility; however, research still requires survey data for understanding factors that affect mobility that are not found in administrative data or are not available for research purposes. Surveys provide information regarding attitudes, behaviors, intentions, and contexts not contained in administrative data; hence, they are an important complement to administrative records. It is important that extensive surveys continue to be funded and that cost-effective ways be explored to alter survey methodology to leverage administrative data. It is critical to develop ways to combine administrative and survey data to enhance the value of both.

Research on mobility-relevant programs and policies requires blending survey and administrative data (e.g., tax and benefit data), along with a process for ensuring that qualified researchers can access these blended data within a secure environment that explicitly recognizes both the risk of using confidential administrative data in research and the benefits to society that can be produced from this research (Conclusion 6-1). Following the recommendations of the Foundations for Evidence-Based Policymaking Act of 2018 and the subsequent recommendations of the Advisory Committee on Data for Evidence Building, the chief statistician of the United States should work with federal agencies to advise legislators and policymakers on the need for revisions to regulations to improve data sharing across federal statistical agencies (Recommendation 6-1).

Beyond sharing across agencies, it is important to improve data access for researchers. Data access laws, such as Title 13 and Title 26, need to be modernized to facilitate research, as they have proven to be inadequate amid the recent growth of research using linked administrative data. It is critical that researchers be given tiered access to new blended data to evaluate the policies surrounding economic and social mobility. Federal agencies should review and revise policies concerning external data sharing with the broader research community (Recommendation 6-2).

The data infrastructure for studying economic and social mobility will be further strengthened if state agencies provide data on state transfer programs to the U.S. Census Bureau and data on vital statistics to the National Center for Health Statistics, and if the federal government is enabled to maintain a national database of student records (Conclusions 6-2 and 6-3). To create and provide access to these data, it is important to adequately fund agencies to allow them to provide data. Funding is required for streamlining the data application process, improving linking, supporting Federal Statistical Research Data Centers, enhancing the survey infrastructure, and expanding qualitative research (Conclusion 6-4). The National Secure Data Service (NSDS) should also work with federal agencies to ensure that improved data access, analysis, and linking mechanisms are implemented. To increase the value of data for studying economic and social mobility, federal agencies should collaborate with the NSDS to improve the data acquisition and linking process (Recommendations 6-2 and 6-3).

To build this data infrastructure and ensure continued research on mobility, the United States requires an institutional body charged with ensuring that the country's commitment to equal opportunity is considered properly when policy is developed and evaluated. Although many other federal executive departments are also relevant to the country's equal opportunity mission, none is focused on monitoring or equalizing opportunity. Because research on intergenerational mobility is central to assessing the well-being of the U.S. economy and society, the creation of a nongovernmental research center—a National Mobility Center—is appropriate (Conclusion 6-5).

NEW DIRECTIONS FOR REASEARCH AND POLICY

A forward-looking, policy-relevant research agenda on economic and social mobility is relevant to policymakers at every level of government—federal, state, county, and local. Policymakers can take a variety of approaches, and the findings in this report make clear that there is no single solution or even one pathway to enhancing mobility that is sufficient on its own. Indeed, policy levers will differ depending on the level of government of the policy actors and may have different effects on absolute and relative mobility. Many of the policies considered by the committee focus on improving the well-being of the disadvantaged, which as a result may improve both absolute and relative mobility. Alternatively, policies reducing benefits for higher-income households may improve relative mobility only because of the downward impacts for these households. While the committee acknowledges that channels for intergenerational economic persistence may be difficult to alter via social policy, we believe that there is great opportunity to promote mobility in the United States by dismantling economic and institutional barriers to economic prosperity and supporting mobility through policy intervention.

Policy approaches to enhancing mobility may be categorized into three broad strategies. The first is the most common—a safety net approach that generally seeks to puts a floor on the level of deprivation experienced by members of society. This sometimes involves setting up subsidiary institutions to serve low-income populations, operating in parallel to mainstream institutions; examples include Head Start, public housing or subsidized housing vouchers, workforce development centers, or financial instruments available only to lower-income families. The primary goal and stated purpose of these programs may be to reduce poverty rather than to enhance mobility, but in providing resources that support families such policies can have a positive effect on mobility outcomes. One of the side effects of the safety net approach is a one-sided focus on the mobility challenges faced by low-income populations, with little focus on the effects of disproportionate opportunities among those born at the top of the resource distribution.

Accordingly, a second strategy is to reform mainstream institutions to make them work better for all Americans. Such a strategy could make changes to the policy landscape to make institutions such as banks, schools, and housing development more inclusive. This might mean, for example, making bank accounts or lending at financial institutions more accessible to low-income families, or making a more concerted effort to integrate new housing developments by household income. The evidence base on this type of approach is limited, and compared with safety net approaches, less is known about how to reform mainstream institutions and what the outcomes of such changes would be.

Policies are often thought of as a means of enhancing economic and social mobility, but they have often been used for the opposite purpose. A third strategy would therefore look to roll back existing policies that constrict mobility or support the persistence of advantage across generations. This might include housing (e.g., zoning laws that reduce the availability of affordable housing), asset-related (e.g., tax policies that favor certain types of assets), educational (e.g., tax benefits that disproportionately help higher-income families save for college), or other policies that disproportionately favor high-income groups by providing subsidies or resources that further support the persistence of advantage across generations.

The conclusions and research recommendations presented in this report can be used to inform and advance all three policy strategies. A broad, multitiered approach to boosting economic and social mobility is critical, and it can be facilitated through the creation of a National Mobility Center that serves as a clearinghouse, resource center, and training hub. It would also be important for such a center to set standards and train researchers on best practices for rigorous qualitative inquiry and methods for deepening the understanding of how policies and interventions are perceived and valued by those for whom they are intended.

Economic and social mobility is a core measure of well-being, and it underlies a fundamental value held by many Americans: that anyone should be able to succeed economically based on their own merits, regardless of their circumstances such as their family life, home community, and the assets they start out with. This has been a fundamental tenet throughout U.S. history, even as many observers may rightly argue that it has been, at times and for many groups, severely constrained. This report provides a forward-looking framework for data, research, and policy initiatives to boost upward mobility and better fulfill promises of opportunity and advancement for all members of U.S. society.

1

Introduction

Intergenerational mobility is a central measure of the nation's economic well-being. While measures of economic growth capture average levels of material well-being, and measures of inequality capture the distribution of economic outcomes across the population, economic and social mobility measures the chances that people have to achieve economic prosperity regardless of their family backgrounds. Complementing measures of inequality of outcomes, intergenerational mobility provides information about equality of opportunity. A mobile society can foster economic efficiency by supporting human capital formation for all its members, regardless of family circumstances, and by providing labor market opportunities to people from diverse backgrounds. A mobile society could also support fairness by reducing barriers based on family income, offering opportunities that are not constrained by circumstances at birth. Mobility is not a desirable social goal in isolation. Rather, it makes sense as a policy goal only in combination with a sufficient level of economic growth that supports an adequate standard of living across generations.

Upward mobility and the egalitarian pursuit of prosperity are recurring motifs in American cultural narratives, ranging from Horatio Alger's 19th-century tales of "rags-to-riches" trajectories, to *The Jeffersons*' "moving on up" to overcome their working-class roots, and even to contemporary memes of the multi-billion-dollar business that started in a garage. The prospect of upward mobility, and the promise that individual effort, hard work, and talent will lead to economic well-being, have been a staple of the political discourse across the political spectrum since the founding of the republic (Sandel, 2020).

However, a sole focus on individual opportunity—driven by individual abilities and efforts—risks neglecting the social and institutional contexts that shape these opportunities. For instance, pervasive economic inequality hampers the development of human capital among children raised in poverty by limiting their access to resources. Economic segregation across neighborhoods exposes disadvantaged communities to underfunded schools; environmental hazards; pollution; and limited amenities such as parks, libraries, and health care facilities. Inadequate access to insurance against risks, such as illness or job loss, undermines disadvantaged families' ability to support their children's development. Financial and informational barriers to college thwart access to higher education among poor families. In sum, to understand the dynamics of intergenerational mobility in the United States, it is important to consider the social and institutional factors that support or hinder the development of individual abilities.

For all the value placed on equal opportunity in the American context, intergenerational mobility in the United States is relatively low compared with other affluent democracies. The degree to which adult children's earnings depend on family circumstances, known as relative mobility, is higher in the United States than in other wealthy countries (Corak, 2013b; Durlauf et al., 2022; Krueger, 2012). Additionally, the likelihood of adult children surpassing their parents' income level in the United States, known as absolute upward mobility, has declined over time, a trend similar to other wealthy countries (Berman, 2022; Chetty et al., 2017; Manduca et al., 2024). The decline in upward mobility has coincided with an increase in inequality, and some scholars suggest it might be driven, at least partially, by growing income disparities (Berman, 2022; Chetty et al., 2017).

Limited absolute and relative intergenerational mobility in the United States compared with peer countries invites a research agenda toward understanding this reality and developing evidence-based strategies for improving mobility. Developing such an agenda requires a clear understanding of the factors that influence mobility and their mechanisms, and how these factors can be affected by policy interventions. It also requires adequate data capable of tracing families across generations.

CHARGE TO THE STUDY COMMITTEE

In this context, the National Academies of Sciences, Engineering, and Medicine (National Academies) was asked by the Gates Foundation to carry out a consensus study on improving economic and social mobility in the United States. The specific charge to the National Academies was as follows:

An ad hoc committee of the National Academies of Sciences, Engineering, and Medicine will undertake a study that will review and assess what is known about the factors that influence economic and social mobility in the United States, the mechanisms through which these factors operate, how they are affected by policy interventions, and how these relationships and mechanisms vary across and within different population groups. The study will identify key, actionable knowledge gaps; discuss promising conceptual, methodological, and data approaches; and make recommendations for policy-relevant research and evaluation.

To conduct this study, the National Academies appointed the Committee on a Research Agenda for Improving Economic and Social Mobility in the United States. The study committee included 14 experts with backgrounds in areas such as economics, sociology, demography, statistics and methodology, public policy, and evaluation.

DEFINITIONS: WHAT IS MOBILITY AND HOW IS IT MEASURED?

The work of this committee focused on intergenerational mobility—namely, the association between parents' economic status and adult children's economic status. High intergenerational mobility suggests that individuals have a fair chance of achieving success regardless of their social origins. In contrast, limited mobility indicates that both poverty and privilege will persist from generation to generation, suggesting limited opportunity to achieve a standard of living independent of family (of origin) resources—and especially one that is better than the parents' generation (for in-depth reviews of theoretical, substantive, and methodological issues related to intergenerational mobility, see Black & Devereux, 2011; Fox et al., 2016; Jäntti & Jenkins, 2015; Torche, 2015a,b). As we discuss in the next two sections, intergenerational mobility has two dimensions: absolute and relative.

Ensuring equal opportunity does not mean eliminating all economic similarities between parents and children (Jencks & Tach, 2006; Swift, 2004). The key issue is the mechanisms that pass advantage or disadvantage across generations. When children are held back by their parents' limited financial, cultural, or social resources—or when adults face ethnic or racial discrimination that blocks fair rewards—the resulting intergenerational persistence reflects unequal opportunity (Chetty et al., 2014b, 2020, 2024; Darity, 2005; Oliver & Shapiro, 2006). It is true that some sources of intergenerational continuity are partially unavoidable and fall beyond the realm of public policy—for example, family priorities and values. As philosophers have acknowledged, "the family is an obstacle to equality of opportunity" (Rawls, 1971, as cited in Swift, 2004, p. 7). However, while this committee acknowledges that there are channels for intergenerational economic persistence that may be difficult or undesirable to alter via social policy, we believe that there is vast opportunity to promote mobility in the United States by dismantling economic and institutional barriers to economic prosperity.

Various measures of economic advantage can be used to measure intergenerational mobility, including earnings, income, occupational status, social class, wealth, and educational attainment. In the past, economists predominantly focused on pecuniary measures such as earnings and income, while sociologists focused on occupations, resources operationalized as social class, occupational status, and occupational prestige (Blau & Duncan, 1967; Hauser et al., 1975; Lipset & Bendix, 1952; Nam & Powers, 1968).

Research on occupational mobility has provided valuable insights about social mobility. Measures of social class distinguish groups based on the occupational resources they control—for example, employers, professional workers, managers, skilled manual workers, and unskilled manual workers. Measures of social class are relevant because they consider the specific kinds of labor market assets that people have access to and shape opportunity and inequality. Furthermore, given the different assets they control, social classes will be differently affected by economic and institutional factors such as technological innovation or labor market and welfare policies (Breen & Whelan, 1996). Sociological measures of occupational status and prestige rank occupations based on the average income and educational levels of people who hold those occupations. These rankings provide a one-dimensional hierarchy of socioeconomic advantage correlated with "permanent income" (i.e., income over the long run, purged from short-term fluctuations and changes over the life course; Torche, 2015a). Furthermore, in contrast to the challenges of collecting data on income across generations, which is prone to measurement error, occupational data are highly reliable and can be reported about parents and children with little error (Warren & Hauser, 1997).

Recent research has focused increasingly on economic measures such as earnings and income to measure mobility (Chetty et al., 2017; Deutscher & Mazumder, 2021; Sakamoto & Wang, 2020). The current emphasis in economic mobility is supported in part by (a) the growing availability of administrative data, which measures income of parents and children with limited error, and in part by (b) evidence that, in the United States, there is much economic inequality *within* social classes and occupational groups. Indeed, within-occupation earnings disparities account for a substantial portion of growing economic inequality since the 1980s (Mouw & Kalleberg 2010; Weeden et al., 2007).

Measures of economic and social or occupational mobility are both relevant and complementary. Labor market resources including occupational positions are central determinants of individual earnings and families' incomes. This report focuses on economic mobility because much empirical evidence on factors that shape one's chances of mobility—for example, family structure, education, and neighborhood of residence—use income and earnings rather than occupation as a measure of economic resources.

The concept of intergenerational mobility, measured by income, earnings, or occupations, encompasses two types: absolute and relative; each provides different measures of the persistence of advantages and disadvantages across generations.

Absolute Mobility

Absolute mobility focuses on upward or downward changes in income across generations. It captures the probability that adult children will reach an income threshold defined by parental income. The most common measure of absolute mobility is the likelihood that children will earn more than their parents in real dollars—in other words, that they will experience *upward mobility*.

Absolute mobility is especially salient in public debates because it provides a tangible benchmark against which individuals gauge their economic status. Typically, people assess their financial standing by comparing themselves with their parents, and parents often evaluate their children's success based on their ability to surpass their own earnings.

Measures of upward mobility were first reported in the United States by Isaacs et al. (2008). They found that about two-thirds of Americans exceeded their parents' income. More recent studies have shown a pronounced decline in the proportion of adult children who outearn their parents over time (Chetty et al., 2017; Davis & Mazumder, 2022). For example, the likelihood that adult children outearned their parents was 90 percent for those born in 1940 but 50 percent for children born in the 1980s (Chetty et al., 2017).

Estimates of declining upward income mobility in the United States are consistent with declining trends observed in other affluent countries (Berman, 2022), albeit not at levels observed in the United States (Manduca et al., 2024). The decline in upward mobility in the United States has occurred in the context of declining economic growth and growing economic inequality since the 1970s. Some research suggests that the rise in inequality is the central factor driving the declines in upward mobility. According to one estimate, reducing economic inequality to its 1940 level would reverse more than two-thirds of the decline in upward mobility between cohorts born in the 1940s and 1980s (Chetty et al., 2017). Figure 1-1 demonstrates the international comparisons of absolute upward mobility. As shown, the United States has low levels of absolute upward mobility compared to a selected set of wealthy democracies.

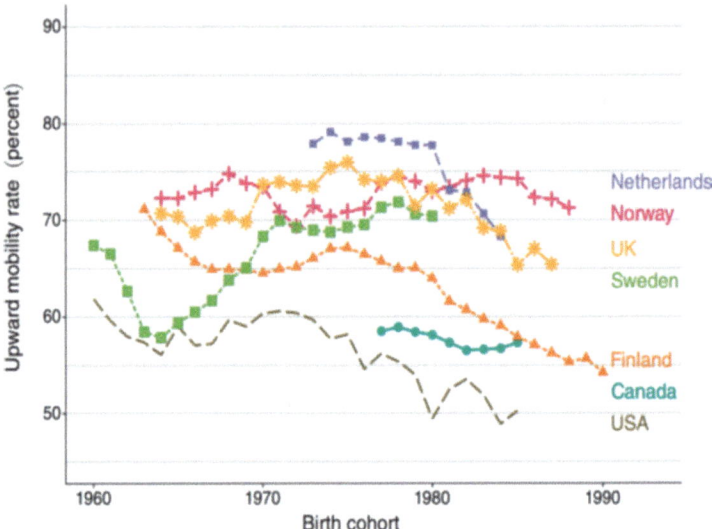

FIGURE 1-1 International comparisons of absolute upward mobility.
NOTES: The upward mobility rate is calculated as the percentage of children in each birth cohort whose family income at age 30, adjusted for inflation, was at least as high as their parents' family income at age 30. Incomes are measured using a combination of register and survey data in each country, as follows: Canada: Intergenerational Income Database; Finland: total-population register-based longitudinal data provided by Statistics Finland; Netherlands: Netherlands register data; Norway: full population data from Statistics Norway; Sweden: full population of Swedish nonimmigrants; United Kingdom (UK): analysis follows the "copula and marginals" method as described by Chetty et al. (2017) (the Family Expenditure Survey and the Family Resources Survey provide information on marginal earnings distributions, and the British Cohort Study provides data for the copula); United States (USA): analysis follows the "copula and marginals" approach introduced by Chetty et al. (2017) (copula constructed from Internal Revenue Service tax records; parent incomes are sourced from the 1940–2000 decennial censuses and the 2010 and 2015 American Community Survey; child incomes are sourced from the 1968–2021 Current Population Survey Annual Social and Economic Supplements). See Manduca et al. (2024) for further details.
SOURCE: Maduca et al. (2024). Copyright American Economic Association; reproduced with permission of the *American Economic Journal: Applied Economics*.

Relative Mobility

Relative mobility measures the strength of the association between parents' and adult children's incomes. A strong intergenerational association (or persistence) reflects low mobility, a situation in which having high-income parents predicts a high level of economic well-being and having low-income parents predicts poverty among adult children. A weak association, in turn, identifies a society in which the chances of achieving economic prosperity depend little on parental prosperity. Higher relative mobility suggests a more open society, where success is less influenced by family background. Like inequality, relative mobility is a concept that describes entire societies rather than specific individuals—"rags to riches" and "riches to rags" biographies exist in every society; relative mobility measures how prevalent these biographies are in a particular society. Unlike absolute mobility, measures of relative mobility require that for any upward move to happen, a downward move must "free up" a space in the socioeconomic hierarchy (Hout, 2004, 2015). It is important to highlight that relative mobility is conceptually distinct from inequality: inequality focuses on the dispersion of income across the population (i.e., on the income distances between the poor and the rich). Mobility, in turn, captures how likely it is for people to change income positions across generations.

The most common measure of relative persistence (and hence, lack of mobility) is the intergenerational income elasticity, which ranges approximately between zero and one. Lower values (closer to zero) of income elasticity indicate less persistence and greater mobility, while values closer to one signify strong replication of advantage or disadvantage across generations. Because measures of relative mobility are more abstract than those of absolute mobility, Box 1-1 defines intergenerational elasticity and other measures of relative mobility.

Abundant research exists on the intergenerational income elasticity in the United States. Estimates of earnings elasticity measuring the strength of the intergenerational association have proliferated over time as administrative data become available and methodological approaches become more sophisticated. Early measures of intergenerational elasticities yielded low values of 0.15–0.20 (Becker & Tomes, 1986; Behrman & Taubman, 1985), leading to the conclusion that earnings were not strongly transmitted across generations.

However, we now know that this finding was an artifact of using single-year measures of earnings and small, homogenous samples. The use of techniques that account for different sources of measurement bias has led to much higher elasticity estimates—between 0.40 and 0.60. Mobility scholars have offered 0.47 as a "preferred estimate" (Corak, 2006), and a range between 0.50 and 0.60 as plausible (Solon, 2008). A recent analysis

BOX 1-1
Measuring Relative Mobility

The most common measures of relative mobility are intergenerational elasticity, rank–rank slope, and intergenerational correlation.

Intergenerational elasticity captures, approximately, the average percent change in children's earnings associated with a 1 percent change in parents' earnings. It is the coefficient in a regression model predicting log-transformed adult children's earnings or income based on log-transformed parents' earnings. For example, an elasticity of 0.4 indicates that a 10 percent increase (decrease) in parents' earnings will lead, on average, to a 4 percent increase (decrease) in children's earnings.

Elasticities include information about both the association between parents and children and changes in the income distribution across generations. An increase in inequality across generations will increase the elasticity, and a decline in inequality will reduce it (and conversely, a decline in mobility will increase inequality). To control for changes in inequality across generations, researchers have used alternative measures such as the rank–rank slope and the intergenerational correlation.

The *rank–rank slope* is the coefficient in a regression predicting the percentile rank of children's earnings from the percentile rank of parents' earnings. A rank–rank slope of 0.4 indicates that a 10-percentile-point increase in parents' earnings rank results in a 4-percentile-point increase in children's rank. By using earning ranks rather than earning levels, this measure is unaffected—at least mechanically—by changes in inequality across generations.

The *intergenerational correlation* in log earnings adjusts the intergenerational elasticity by the standard deviation of parents' and children's income.

The choice of measure of relative mobility is consequential in contexts with different levels of economic inequality. For example, intergenerational persistence is stronger in the United States than in Sweden and the United Kingdom when using elasticity but similar using the rank–rank slope (or the correlation coefficient) (see Corak et al., 2014; Eberharter, 2013), suggesting that the low level of mobility in the United States is due to higher levels of inequality (see Figure 1-2).

These measures of relative mobility use a single estimate to capture intergenerational persistence. Naturally, reducing the mobility process to a single measure of linear persistence is a simplification. Recent work has used alternative strategies for capturing the pattern and not only the overall level of intergenerational association. These include matrices cross-classifying parents' and children's income quintiles, models allowing for nonlinearities in the intergenerational association, and quantile regression models examining income dispersion around the regression line (Corak & Heisz, 1999; Couch & Lillard, 2004; Eide & Showalter, 1999; Peters, 1992).

Based on these approaches, it is possible to examine whether average persistence is stronger for the rich or the poor, and whether the dispersion in children's income, intergenerational mobility, and equality of opportunity varies across the socioeconomic hierarchy. For example, Eide and Showalter (1999) found much more variance around predicted children's income for poor than for wealthy parents in the United States. Mitnik et al. (2023) found that intergenerational persistence is stronger among the upper-middle class than among the bottom half of the earnings distribution. Both findings signal stronger earnings persistence at the top than at the bottom.

SOURCES: Black & Devereux, 2011; Fox et al., 2016; Torche, 2015a.

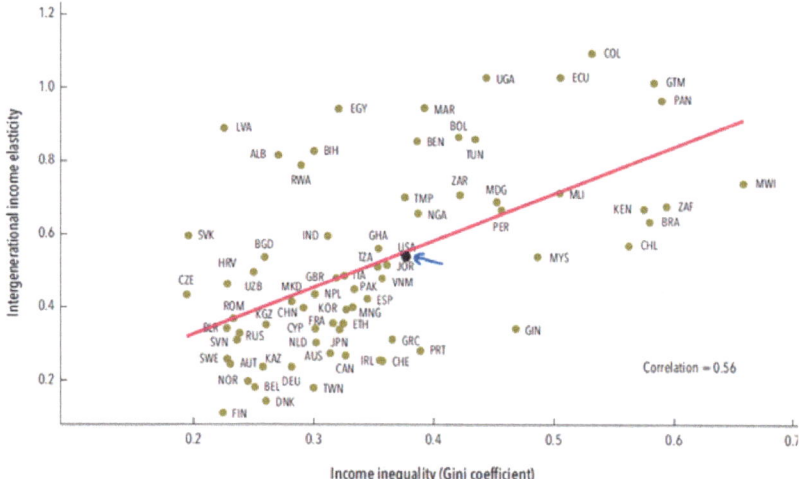

FIGURE 1-2 International comparisons of relative mobility (intergenerational income elasticity).
NOTES: Income inequality is measured as the Gini coefficient, using disposable household income as provided by the World Bank. Higher intergenerational income elasticity indicates lower relative intergenerational mobility.
SOURCE: Narayan et al. (2018). Licensed as a Creative Commons Attribution.

by Mitnik et al. (2023) estimates intergenerational earnings elasticity of 0.49–0.55.

Relative mobility is lower in the United States than in many other affluent democracies, suggesting that the United States is not a particularly open society where individuals have an equal chance to succeed regardless of their social origins. Indeed, the 0.47 value of the earnings elasticity in the United States at the turn of the 21st century compares with values between 0.15 and 0.41 in other wealthy nations (Corak, 2013b). Figure 1-2 shows the so-called Great Gatsby Curve, first described by Corak (2013b) to illustrate the correlation between levels of economic inequality when individuals were growing up and the extent of relative mobility they experience as adults (restricted to fathers and sons). This figure shows that the United States is both the more unequal and the least mobile country among wealthy democracies.

The question about whether relative mobility has declined in the United States over the last half-century amid growing inequality remains unsettled. Some evidence suggests a reduction in relative mobility starting with the cohorts coming of age since the 1980s (Aaronson & Mazumder, 2008; Bloome & Western, 2011). Other studies report stability in relative mobility from the mid-20th century onward (Bloome, 2015; Bloome et al., 2018; Hauser, 2010; Hertz, 2007; Lee & Solon, 2009).

Recent research using population-level tax data suggests that relative intergenerational mobility has changed little in the recent past. For example, the probability that a child reaches the top fifth of the income distribution as an adult given that their parents were in the bottom fifth of the income distribution is 8.4 percent for children born in 1971 and 9.0 percent for those born in 1986. Likewise, children born to the highest-income families in 1984 were 74.5 percentage points more likely to attend college than those from the lowest-income families, while the corresponding gap for children born in 1993 is 69.2 percentage points (Chetty et al., 2014b). The most recent analysis of mobility trends using population-level data based on tax records finds divergent change in mobility by race (Chetty et al., 2024). By evaluating change affecting cohorts born between 1978 and 1992, this study found that relative mobility—measured as the association between the income ranks of parents and adult children—declined for White individuals but increased among African American individuals, resulting in a smaller Black–White income gap for people growing up in low-income households. This study also shows that the intergenerational persistence of poverty has increased for White children, from 25 to 30 percent, and declined for Black children, from 40 to 34 percent, although a Black–White gap persists. Chetty et al. (2020) demonstrate that the Black–White gap exists mainly for Black men, while Black women experience similar mobility levels (both absolute and relative) as White women.

Evaluation of long-term relative mobility based on occupations since the 19th century provides a relevant context for understanding recent trends. Recent research suggests a long-term decline in the intergenerational occupational association (or persistence)—that is, an increase in mobility—since the 19th century (Jácome et al., 2025; Ward, 2023). These studies challenge the common notion that the United States was a "land of opportunity" characterized by high levels of occupational mobility in the late 19th and early 20th centuries (Feigenbaum, 2018; Ferrie, 2005; Long & Ferrie, 2013; Parman, 2011; Song et al., 2020). One reason for this discrepancy is that earlier studies focused narrowly on White men.

These studies of long-term occupational mobility further suggest that the increase in mobility has been driven by gains among African Americans during the 20th century. As concluded by Jácome et al. (2025), "the United States starts the 20th century much further from the 'American Dream' ideal of a mobile society but also improves more significantly when the full population is considered rather than only White men" (p. 348). Despite these recent gains for African Americans, Black men still earn considerably less on average than White men, and they experience less upward mobility than their White counterparts from similar socioeconomic backgrounds (Collins & Wanamaker, 2022). These recent studies highlight the importance of using nationally representative samples that include all racial/ethnic groups as well as women to obtain representative mobility estimates.

In sum, absolute and relative mobility capture two distinct dimensions of opportunity across generations in the United States. Absolute mobility focuses on both the chances that adult children will surpass their parents in terms of economic well-being (upward mobility) and the chances that children will achieve income levels lower than their parents (downward mobility). Relative mobility captures whether adult children have a similar chance to do well regardless of their parents' resources. A country can have high upward absolute mobility yet low relative mobility. For example, rapid economic growth may allow most adult children to earn more than their parents, but if growth disproportionately favors wealthy families, then the children of rich parents may still end up better off than children from poor families. Researchers have argued that relative and absolute mobility are only weakly correlated (Berman, 2022; Bloome & Opacic, 2024; Deutscher & Mazumder, 2023). However, at least one study (Chetty et al., 2014a) found a strong empirical correlation between relative and absolute upward mobility in the United States.

Both relative and absolute mobility are important, as they address different dimensions of equal opportunity and answer different policy questions. Limited absolute and relative mobility might be harmful for the United States. Low absolute mobility means there is limited opportunity for young cohorts to do better than their parents, which might reduce well-being and even induce frustration and social conflict. Meanwhile, a lack of relative mobility means that one's success is largely determined by one's parents rather than by one's effort or experience. The implications are wasted human potential and inefficient allocation of resources, which could be harmful for growth in the long term (Narayan et al., 2018).

INTERGENERATIONAL MOBILITY AND ECONOMIC INEQUALITY

Economic inequality has increased sharply since the 1970s in the United States. In 1967, 20 percent of households with the highest income received 42 percent of the total national income. By 2022, this share had increased to 51 percent. Similarly, the income share of the poorest 20 percent of households declined from 5.6 to 3.5 percent of the total national income over the last 50 years (Guzman & Kollar, 2023). High levels of inequality are a concern in part because they might hamper intergenerational mobility, especially relative mobility.

Several theoretical mechanisms suggest an association between high levels of inequality and reduced relative mobility (Durlauf et al., 2022). Wider inequality in the parental generation implies wider disparities in parental investments and less progressive human capital investments, which results in less mobility (Durlauf et al., 2022; Ermisch et al., 2012; Neckerman & Torche, 2007). Higher inequality is partly driven by higher returns to schooling in the labor and other markets, which is also correlated with intergenerational rigidity (Solon, 2004). Additionally, inequality may exacerbate residential segregation by income, resulting in a more skewed composition of peer groups and more segregated learning environments along socioeconomic lines (Durlauf, 1996; Reardon & Bischoff, 2011). An additional pathway of influence linking high inequality with reduced mobility might be the political process, if economic concentration strengthens the influence of the wealthy through political contributions and lobbying, thus reducing the scope for redistributive policies (Burtless & Jencks, 2003; Campante, 2011). These mechanisms are theoretically plausible but not necessary. While not yet observed empirically, it is possible that a highly unequal society, given sufficient political will, could invest in human and financial capital for children from low-income families and limit the intergenerational transmission of advantage among the wealthy. In this way, inequality in one generation would not necessarily determine opportunities in the next, and it will not necessarily lead to limited relative mobility. Additionally, a society that fosters robust and sustained economic growth could still promote meaningful absolute mobility, even if relative mobility remains modest.

To date, the evidence about an association between inequality and mobility is not conclusive, however. While empirical findings vary and are limited by data availability, there is no consistent evidence that mobility has declined as inequality has increased. Furthermore, it is exceedingly difficult to prove a causal link between growing inequality and declining mobility. Any impacts of growing inequality on mobility would likely take a long time to materialize and would be mediated by changes in institutions, policies, and investments favoring different socioeconomic groups (Nybom & Stuhler, 2024; Torche, 2015b). Indeed, it might take decades for persistently high inequality to permeate institutions and policies in a way that substantially alters intergenerational mobility. The mechanisms linking inequality and mobility are, however, plausible. While some level of inequality is inevitable and probably desirable to provide the right incentives to work hard, innovate, and invest in human capital (Krueger, 2012; Welch, 1999), the high levels of inequality that have characterized the United States over the last 50 years might result in diminished opportunities for children from low-income backgrounds to develop the skills necessary to share the fruits of economic growth.

MOBILITY IS NOT WITHOUT RISKS

Efforts to achieve upward mobility may carry risk. As with inequality, we presuppose that some degree of risk-taking is required for people to bolster their economic and social standing—for example, by taking out student loans to fund postsecondary education, obtaining credit to start a business, or seeking new employment or training to switch careers. Problems might arise when the level of risk individuals must assume carries the threat of downward mobility for a substantial proportion of the population.

The level of risk assumed by individuals depends on insurance systems, which after expanding in the 1960s and 1970s have been reduced since the 1980s. As a result, the last 40 years of American social policy have seen an increase in risk. They have also seen the responsibility for risk—in the financial, health care, educational, and retirement spheres—shift from governments, businesses, and other social institutions onto individuals and families (Hacker, 2019). Risk associated with investments and unexpected shocks has been partially privatized—that is, transformed from a collective into an individual responsibility (Grusky et al., 2019; Hacker & Pierson, 2002; Pierson, 1994, 1996; Starke, 2007). Weaker insurance mechanisms supporting family well-being and workplace security have led to greater financial instability for many families. This results in downward mobility related to painful experiences such as a plant closing, divorce, or skill obsolescence (Newman, 1999).

The committee emphasizes that not all sources of inequality and risk are harmful in themselves or pose a barrier to intergenerational mobility. We claim, however, that high inequality and excessive risk of economic downturn resulting from investments or unpredicted shocks prevent upward mobility and strengthen the association between parents' resources and adult children's well-being. Indeed, many policies designed to improve mobility are indistinguishable from policies designed to address inequality in resources or to strengthen the social safety net and reduce the exposure to risk, especially among vulnerable populations.

KINDS OF EVIDENCE ABOUT MOBILITY CONSIDERED IN THE REPORT

Mobility captures the relationship between adult children's outcomes and the conditions in which they were raised, a process observed over a span of at least two decades—from the child's birth to early adulthood. Because of this extended timeline, evaluating factors that *directly* affect mobility is much more challenging than assessing the determinants of specific outcomes, such as adult children's high school graduation or homeownership.

As a result, *direct* evidence on the correlates or determinants of mobility is scarce. One example of such evidence is cross-country comparisons, which show that higher inequality in the parental generation is associated with lower relative mobility among adult children (Corak, 2013a) and that strong redistributive policies via taxes and transfers are correlated with higher upward mobility from poverty (Parolin et al., 2024). Another example is research showing that higher government spending across U.S. states is linked to increased mobility (Mayer & Lopoo, 2005).

Most evidence on the factors shaping mobility is *indirect*, focusing on factors that are related to mobility rather than mobility itself. For example, research shows that providing information about college funding to youth from low-income backgrounds significantly increases college enrollment (Dynarski et al., 2021). Given the large economic payoff of a college education, a policy that provides information about college funding to low-income youth would likely increase their upward mobility. This is considered *indirect* evidence because the researchers do not directly measure intergenerational mobility; instead, they focus on a factor along the pathway connecting parental resources with adult children's outcomes.

The committee considered various types of direct and indirect evidence about intergenerational mobility, including descriptive, correlational, quasi-experimental, experimental, and qualitative evidence.

- *Descriptive evidence* provides information on the characteristics of mobility, its correlates, and contextual factors. For instance, the proportion of adult children earning more than their parents over time offers descriptive evidence about trends in upward mobility (Chetty et al., 2017), while data on racial/ethnic wealth gaps provides context for the analysis of disparities in wealth mobility (Aladangady et al., 2023).
- *Correlational evidence* examines the association between variables of interest. For example, research shows that growing up with a single parent is associated with lower educational attainment (McLanahan & Sandefur, 1994). This association varies by race and ethnicity and is weaker for Black children than for White children (Cross, 2020, 2023). Correlational evidence does not imply causality, as unmeasured factors may affect the relationship under analysis even when controlling for multiple factors such as parental education, age, or income.
- *Quasi-experimental evidence* involves exploiting quasi-random events or natural experiments to assess the impact of mobility determinants. For example, Johnson (2020) found that increases in

parental housing wealth raised the likelihood of children attending college, using neighborhood-level housing market booms and busts as a natural experiment and comparing homeowners with renters (Johnson, 2020). This is considered a natural experiment because fluctuations in the local housing market are plausibly driven by macroeconomic factors beyond families' control and therefore provide a quasi-random source of variation in parental wealth.
- *Experimental evidence* relies on the randomized assignment of a "treatment" to determine its effect, providing the strongest causal interpretations. For example, the Moving to Opportunity experiment, which provided housing vouchers to a random set of families in high-poverty neighborhoods, led to better health outcomes for parents and children in the treatment group than for those without vouchers (Ludwig et al., 2011, 2012; Pollack et al., 2019, 2023a).
- *Qualitative evidence* comes from in-depth interviews and ethnographic observations, capturing individuals' lived experiences, understandings of their circumstances, and decision-making processes. This type of nonquantitative evidence reveals rich insights into the opportunities and constraints people face and helps to interpret and make sense of quantitative findings. Qualitative research can be essential for developing hypotheses and understanding the mechanisms behind observed associations.

The committee viewed all these sources of evidence as valuable and complementary. The panel recognized that experimental evidence, which supports stronger causal claims, may not be available for many important (and sometimes broader) questions. However, other forms of evidence may offer critical insights. Throughout the report, we took care to specify the type of evidence we are considering and, where appropriate, to acknowledge the limitations of different evidence.

This report adds to other reviews of mobility evidence by incorporating qualitative research. The use of qualitative data in the social sciences has grown over time, as has its demonstrated value (Edin et al., 2024). Among other uses, qualitative research can interrogate important theoretical and policy assumptions; generate hypotheses for better-informed data collection or the refinement of econometric and structural models; identify potential causal mechanisms that explain the success of failure of different policies; and reveal the perceptions and beliefs held by those for whom policies are intended. The report considers qualitative evidence and offers some guidance on how to further develop it and integrate it into the infrastructure of mobility research in the future.

CONCEPTUAL FRAMEWORK FOR THE ANALYSIS OF MOBILITY

The committee developed a conceptual framework that relies on life course and ecosocial approaches to inform our analysis of research on intergenerational mobility. The life course perspective highlights how individuals' lives unfold over time and are shaped by time and place (Elder et al., 2003, 2015; Shanahan et al., 2016). Ecosocial perspectives emphasize the role of economic, institutional, and community contexts, which may have both direct and indirect influences on intergenerational mobility (Bronfenbrenner, 1979, 2005; Glass & McAtee, 2006; Krieger, 2011; Parolin et al., 2024; Sharkey, 2016).

Life Course Principles

Several life course principles are relevant to understanding the process of intergenerational mobility, including lifespan development, historical context, timing of life events, human agency, and linked lives.

Lifespan Development

The lifespan development principle illustrates how individual-level mobility unfolds across distinct life stages, acknowledging that individual trajectories are shaped by a series of transitions and turning points (Heinz & Marshal, 2003). Transitions such as achieving educational milestones, labor market entry, and marriage act as pivotal points in social and economic trajectories. Focusing on individual trajectories from birth to late adulthood, researchers can gain a nuanced understanding of the timing and cumulative impact of life events on the risks and opportunities for mobility.

Historical Context

Considering historical context is vital for understanding mobility dynamics and trends. Prior research has documented how historical conditions including macroeconomic cycles, demographic factors, institutional policies, and neighborhood contexts can impact risks and opportunities for mobility (Chetty et al., 2017; Elder, 1999).

Timing of Life Events and Exposures

The life course approach considers the specific timing of life events, such as completing education, entering the labor market, or having children, and exposure to macro-level events such as economic downturns or environmental hazards in influencing social and economic outcomes (Elder, 1999; Marshall & Mueller, 2003). The implications of these events for mobility depend on *when* they are experienced: the same event might have negative consequences at one stage of the life course and be neutral or even provide a positive turning point in other life course stages.

Human Agency

The principle of human agency acknowledges individuals' capacity to make choices and exert a degree of control over their lives that shape their life trajectories, even in the face of social and environmental constraints (Hitlin & Elder, 2007). Mechanisms such as personal decisions, educational choices, career transitions, and financial planning may elucidate how individuals experience levels of economic well-being that differ from those from their family of origin.

Linked Lives

The principle of linked lives emphasizes the interconnectedness of individual lives within social networks, including family networks in particular, but also networks of friends, colleagues, and members of local and interest-based communities. Based on linked lives, we expect the socioeconomic status of the family of origin to be the baseline against which the upward or downward mobility of adult children is evaluated. The principle of linked lives emphasizes families as the critical unit of analysis for the study of intergenerational mobility: the very concept of mobility focuses on the link between parents' resources when individuals were growing and children's trajectories from early life to adulthood.

Temporality

Temporality is an essential feature of mobility that describes changes in social and economic statuses across various dimensions of time. The concept of intergenerational mobility captures, by definition, change (or stability) across generations. In addition to intergenerational dynamics, the understanding of mobility needs to consider biographical change as individuals age (i.e., intragenerational mobility) and change across historical time periods, both changes in the historical context and across birth cohorts.

Status-Attainment Perspective

One variant of the life course approach specifically applied to the understanding of intergenerational mobility is the *status-attainment perspective*.

This perspective focuses on the socioeconomic association between parents and adult children, including critical milestones that mediate the intergenerational association (Blau & Duncan, 1967; Sewell et al., 1969). In its most parsimonious version, the status attainment model considers parents' education and occupational status as measures of parents' resources, adult children's educational attainment and entry to the labor market as mediating factors, and children's occupational status in adulthood as the outcome to be explained (see Figure 1-3).

This parsimonious model has been substantially updated and enhanced since the 1960s. Some important extensions include adding psychosocial determinants of children's educational and early occupational attainment, such as the influence of significant others and academic performance (Sewell et al., 1969) and expanding the model from a focus on men to incorporate women and family dynamics such as assortative mating (Beller, 2009; Chadwick & Solon, 2002; Mayer & Lopoo, 2005).

The status-attainment model has been appropriately criticized for being overly individualistic and not considering social and institutional determinants and barriers to mobility, including macroeconomic circumstances, institutional regulations, and structural discrimination, among others (Chetty et al., 2014a; Darity, 2005; Horan, 1978; National Research Council [NRC], 2004; Pager & Shepherd, 2008). However, it provides a valuable tool for conceptualizing mobility because it combines inter- and intragenerational components into a life course framework and because it formulates educational attainment as a key mediator linking parents' and adult children's socioeconomic status.

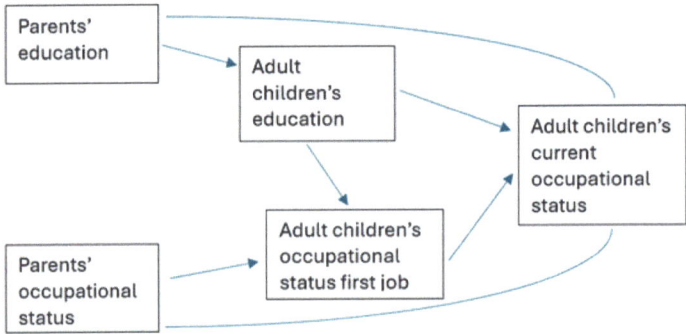

FIGURE 1-3 Status-attainment model of intergenerational mobility.

Life Course–Ecosocial Framework

Figure 1-4 presents a life course–ecosocial framework for understanding mobility processes. Intergenerational mobility is defined as the association between the socioeconomic resources of the parental generation and the adult children generation. As described in the introduction, socioeconomic resources can be measured by a variety of resources including earnings, income, occupational status, social class, wealth, and educational attainment.

Figure 1-4 highlights the role of the social context, represented across three dimensions: institutions, conditions, and space and place.

Institutions

Institutions represent societal systems with a structured set of rules, norms, and relationships that shape mobility processes in different domains, including family, education, labor market, legal or criminal justice, financial,

SOCIAL CONTEXT		
Institutions	**Conditions**	**Space and place**
Families	Macroeconomic conditions	Neighborhoods
Education	Demographic dynamics	Schools
Labor market	Structural discrimination	Community organizations
Legal/criminal system	Technology	Friendship networks
Financial	Culture	
Health care		

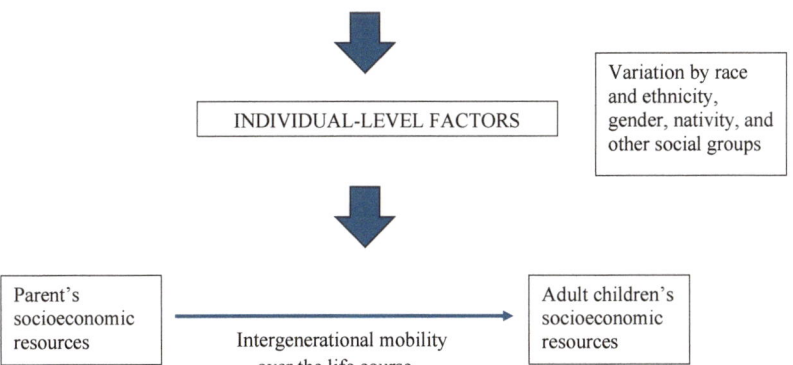

FIGURE 1-4 Life course–ecosocial framework to examine model of intergenerational mobility.

and health care, among others. In the case of formal institutions, policies (e.g., minimum wage, tax rates, affirmative action, penal codes) shape mobility opportunity by increasing or decreasing key factors mediating the mobility process, such as education, wages and income, housing, and access to health care.

The ways in which institutions affect individuals' risks and opportunities for mobility vary depending on other conditions such as macroeconomic factors, demographic dynamics, and technological development; these conditions in turn shape institutional contexts. For example, the educational system responds to population changes—specifically the size of different cohorts entering the educational system. In turn, the educational system shapes demographic dynamics if, for example, availability of high-quality education affects fertility or immigration decisions. Similarly, family arrangements and dynamics depend on economic conditions, legal incentives and constraints, and population dynamics. Institutions also depend on and shape spatially located dynamics.

Conditions

Conditions refer to contextual factors that shape and are shaped by institutional decisions over time. These include economic conditions, such as the decline of manufacturing jobs, rise of service sector, inflation, and unemployment trends that provide opportunities for upward mobility or increase the risk of downward mobility.

Structural discrimination refers to barriers restricting access to opportunities, resources, power, and well-being of individuals and social groups based on race and ethnicity; gender; nativity; and other statuses such as sexual orientation, disability, and national origin. Discrimination operates on multiple levels, including cultural orientations; institutions such as the criminal justice system, health care, and workplaces; and interpersonal interactions. We identify structural discrimination as a condition affecting mobility precisely because of its pervasiveness across multiple domains (Brown, 2016; Homan et al., 2024; NRC, 2004; O'Brien et al., 2020; Pager & Shepherd, 2008).

Inequalities manifested within institutions can reflect and reinforce discriminatory beliefs, values, and the unequal distribution of resources (Bonilla-Silva, 1997; Brown & Homan 2023; Hicken et al., 2021; Homan et al., 2021; Lee, 2024; Samari et al., 2021). The terms *structural racism* and *structural sexism* refer to the systematic exclusion based on race and gender, respectively, from access to resources, power, and opportunities across various societal domains (Brown & Homan, 2024; Homan, 2019; Mills, 1997; Pirtle & Wright, 2021). Similarly, *structural xenophobia* involves a climate of prejudice and political marginalization of foreign-born individuals or those in immigrant families (Samari et al., 2021).

Demographic dynamics capture changes in the demographic composition of contexts due to demographic behavior such as immigration, fertility, and mortality. For example, immigration patterns have dramatically changed the contexts of various cities, states, and regions of the country over the 20th and 21st centuries in ways that affect the risks and opportunities for mobility among both native- and foreign-born individuals (Abramitzky & Boustan, 2022; National Academies of Sciences, Engineering, and Medicine [National Academies], 2015; Sharkey, 2013). Other demographic changes, such as the decline in family size due to the postponement or abandonment of family formation (e.g., marriage and childbearing) have implications for mobility through intergenerational processes of child-rearing, educational attainment, and availability of resources (Zaidi & Morgan, 2017).

Technological change has further transformed institutional contexts in education, the labor market, and health care, requiring new knowledge for learning, working, and accessing care in an increasingly automated and digital world (Berger & Engzell, 2022; Galor & Tssidon, 1997; Goldin & Katz, 2008).

Finally, cultural forces shape mobility across social groups, including racial resentment, islamophobia, antisemitism, and anti-immigrant and anti-LGBTQ sentiment (Bonilla-Silva, 1997; Brown et al., 2025; Everett et al., 2022; Hatzenbuehler, 2016; Homan, 2019; NRC, 2004; Pager & Shepherd, 2008; Samari et al., 2021). For example, literature on immigration has identified "contexts of reception" to describe acceptance or tolerance of newcomers, which may promote or constrain their mobility (National Academies, 2015; Waters, 1990, 2009).

Space and Place

The spatial dimension of mobility includes the set of people (neighbors, extended family, romantic partners), institutions (schools, libraries, police departments, hospitals), processes (social interactions, community organization, political activity), resources (public spending, community wealth), and hazards (crime, pollutants, water quality) in the environment outside the home, spanning from the immediate residential neighborhood to cities, commuting zones, and regions of the country.

Social institutions and broad social conditions bear most directly on individuals' mobility opportunities according to where individuals live, work, and engage with others in everyday interactions. For example, children living in a low-resource, disadvantaged neighborhood and attending a low-quality school experience few opportunities for upward mobility as adults (Chetty et al., 2014a).

Mobility processes also depend on local resources within neighborhoods and schools in the form of job opportunities; highly educated neighbors; and high-quality teachers and advanced placement, and honors courses, among others. Sorting processes might reduce mobility by creating homogeneously wealthy or poor neighborhoods and schools (Grusky et al., 2019; Owens, 2017). Residential and educational segregation results in local social networks that are usually stratified by socioeconomic advantage and that can provide valuable mobility resources in the form of information, advice, mentorship, and connections to educational and work opportunities (Sharkey, 2016).

Individual-Level Factors

The impact of contextual factors on mobility is mediated by individual-level attributes and attainments, including individual health, educational attainment, cognitive skills, and noncognitive skills, among others. The committee recognizes the relevance of individual attributes and individual agency in understanding pathways to mobility, but we also recognize that individual outcomes are shaped by institutional and contextual factors over the life course.

When it comes to mobility processes, race, ethnicity, gender, and nativity matter. Unequal mobility trajectories along these attributes are well documented (Abramitzky & Boustan, 2022; Alba, 2023; Beck et al., 2012; Bhattacharya & Mazumder, 2011; Brown, 2016; Chetty et al., 2020, 2024; Choi & Tienda, 2021; Karlson, 2023; National Academies, 2015; O'Brien et al., 2020; Ward, 2023), even if research has faced limitations due to small sample sizes for some groups and limited information on mediators of mobility for these groups in administrative data (Mazumder, 2018).

Research has also demonstrated that human capital factors do not exhaust explanations about inequities across groups (Brown, 2016). Some researchers suggest that residual disparities that exist after accounting for resources and behaviors can be attributed to discrimination. However, such a conclusion operates under the untenable assumption that discrimination does not shape economic decisions and the acquisition of human capital in the first place, when research indicates that the opposite is true (Brown, 2012; Pager & Shepherd, 2008). With this evolution in understanding, it is becoming clear that focusing solely on individual factors leads to an incomplete understanding of differences in mobility patterns.

Research on mobility according to nativity status is another case in point. Immigrant mobility is often viewed through the lens of "immigrant integration," or the process by which foreign-born populations come to resemble the native-born population along social, economic, and cultural dimensions, driven by socioeconomic improvements among foreign-born individuals during their life (intragenerational) and across generations. Several large studies have identified the factors that matter most for understanding immigrant integration prospects and the risks and opportunities of mobility, including human capital and other attributes at entry—notably educational attainment, labor market skills, English fluency, mode of entry (visa/legal status), age at arrival, and race; country of origin and parental earning capacity for the children of immigrants; and the importance of settlement destination and subsequent geographic mobility (Abramitzky & Boustan, 2022; Alba, 2023; Beck et al., 2012; National Academies, 2015).

KEY DOMAINS

The conceptual framework outlined in Figure 1-4 is not intended to be exhaustive. Rather, it offers one way to organize the many multilevel factors that shape individuals' chances for mobility over time and the extent to which these factors are embedded and interact with each other. Informed by this conceptual framework, the committee decided to focus on a few key domains, including early life and family; the space and place where people live and work; postsecondary education; and wealth, credit, and debt.

Early life is a critical stage of the life course because it is highly sensitive to environmental exposures (Hertzman & Boyce, 2010) and highly consequential for individual long-term developmental, educational, and economic trajectories (Almond & Currie, 2011; Ben-Shlomo & Kuh, 2002; Heckman, 2006), shaping the transmission of inequality across generations (Torche & Nobles, 2024).

The phrase *space and place* is used for key features of local and regional contexts that embed mobility dynamics. The committee's understanding of spatial processes includes the immediate neighborhood contexts, as well as other relevant units such as cities, commuting zones, states, and regions of the country. Space considers people (neighbors, extended families), institutions (schools, police departments, hospitals), processes (social interactions, community organization), resources (educational spending, employment sources), and hazards (crime, pollutants) that are spatially located.

As discussed, multiple institutions shape mobility opportunity. Among these, the committee focused specifically on postsecondary education not because it is the most important point in the emergence of inequities in education and training, but rather because it has received significantly less attention from research and policy compared to elementary and secondary education (i.e., K–12). Additionally, a college degree is an increasingly important determinant of economic well-being (Autor, 2014) and of noneconomic outcomes such as health, crime, family formation, and engagement with the criminal justice system.

Finally, the committee's emphasis on wealth, credit, and debt is intended to supplement the historical focus of mobility research on labor market resources (mainly educational attainment) and rewards (mainly earnings) and consider an alternative avenue for the persistence of economic advantage across generations. Research on wealth stratification and mobility is rapidly expanding (e.g., Keister & Moller, 2000; Killewald et al., 2017). This research shows that wealth is different from earnings and other labor market rewards in that (a) it is a stock rather than a flow, (b) it can be used as a buffer in case of economic emergencies, (c) it can be directly transmitted from parents to children via inter vivos transfers and inheritances, and (d) it is more highly concentrated than income or earnings (Killewald et al., 2017; Spilerman, 2000). As such, wealth provides a strong mechanism for the intergenerational persistence of advantage. Similarly, credit and debt are critical determinants of mobility risks and opportunities that do not depend directly on the labor market. For example, access to credit may promote upward mobility by allowing individuals to finance higher education or start a business, while excessive debt might induce downward mobility by causing repayment difficulties and economic insecurity.

The factors reviewed in this report are limited by necessity. In particular, the committee did not devote a separate chapter to labor market institutions and dynamics. There is no doubt that labor markets are a key site for understanding determinants of intergenerational mobility. As seen in Figure 1-4, the labor market interacts with many of the other factors and domains in understanding mobility. Understanding how labor market dynamics shape mobility will be a critical piece of a policy-relevant agenda on social and economic mobility. However, based on the available evidence, the committee decided to focus on foundational "premarket" factors that feed into the labor market and offer policy-relevant conclusions that can guide the next generation of research. Thus this report offers chapters on a variety of these domains, all of which directly impact labor market resources and opportunities: early life and family and postsecondary education (and the human capital that they facilitate); space and place (and the labor market opportunities that are available to a person based on where they live); and wealth, credit, and debt (as an asset that can be used to support human capital accumulation and labor market success). In this report, discussion about the labor market is addressed in these substantive chapters when appropriate instead of in a stand-alone chapter.

An important consideration for this agenda is that much of the existing empirical research base concludes that a good deal of the differences in labor market outcomes seen today—by race, sex, educational attainment, or family income—reflect differences in human, social, and cultural capital that feed up into the labor market (e.g., Chetty et al., 2011, 2020; Deming, 2017; Hanushek & Woessmann, 2008; Heckman et al., 2006; Neal & Johnson, 1996). Where someone grew up and who is in their social networks; the characteristics of their household and family life; and whether they attained a higher education degree and in which institution all have impacts on labor market outcomes.

A case in point is discrimination. In Figure 1-4, discrimination is a contextual factor that can be present in the labor market—and all institutions. While considerable research indicates that discrimination persists in the labor market (Neumark, 2018), much discrimination appears to also operate prior to the market. For example, racial discrimination has large effects on parental human capital, housing and neighborhood, school quality, and access to credit (Pager & Shepherd, 2008). Unequal treatment within the labor market must be addressed and more research can help document this and potentially offer policy levers to address it. However, unequal outcomes will persist in the labor market until discrimination is addressed in all of these premarket domains.

In particular, the next generation of policy-relevant research on social and economic mobility needs to better understand the role played by labor market institutions in promoting or inhibiting mobility. Examples include trade unions (see DiNardo & Lee, 2004; Farber et al., 2021; Freeman & Medoff, 1985; LaLonde et al., 1996); labor market policies, such as minimum wages (see Bailey et al., 2021; Card & Krueger, 1995; Congressional Budget Office, 2019; Derenoncourt & Montialoux, 2021; Neumark et al., 2014); and related policy domains that impact labor market participation, such as the affordability of child care or availability of paid family leave (see Council of Economic Advisors, 2014; Morrissey, 2017). Understanding the implications for mobility of the decline of middle-income manufacturing jobs available to lower-educated men is clearly important (Autor & Dorn, 2013). Another factor that must be better understood is the monopsonistic power of firms to set wages below market rates and how such markets impact wage growth and, by extension, mobility (Barr & Roy, 2008).

ORGANIZATION OF THE REPORT

This chapter has provided basic definitions, contextual information, and motivation for understanding and addressing economic and social mobility in the United States. Chapters 2–5 explore key domains that shape mobility. Chapter 2 focuses on early life and family; Chapter 3 on space and place; Chapter 4 on postsecondary education; and Chapter 5 on wealth, credit, and debt. In each chapter, the committee assesses the evidence base critically, draws key conclusions regarding the state of knowledge, and makes recommendations for a policy-relevant research agenda. Chapter 6 includes discussion and recommendations regarding the data infrastructure required to support future research on economic and social mobility. Chapter 7 revisits the committee's key conclusions and recommendations regarding the domains that shape mobility, discussing how they fit together to inform broad policy approaches to increasing economic and social mobility in the United States.

2

Early Life and Family

The family is the first institution in which investments in children occur; it is the earliest "incubator" of human capital. As such, children's experiences in their family environments are central to their developmental trajectories and to their prospects for economic and social mobility.

Contemporary American families are characterized by a diversity of living arrangements, household structures and compositions, and kin and nonkin relationships, both within and between households, and these arrangements have become increasingly fluid over time (Berger & Carlson, 2020; Seltzer, 2019). Childhood environments also vary substantially by socioeconomic status, which both reflects and determines differential access to resources (Lareau, 2002, 2011; Roksa & Potter, 2011). This variation often stems from social, economic, and psychosocial factors that determine parental opportunities and constraints, thereby affecting parental behaviors and investments (Kalil & Ryan, 2020).

This chapter summarizes the evidence about the potential early life and family determinants of intergenerational economic and social mobility. Intergenerational mobility focuses on human capital or labor market outcomes (i.e., occupation or earnings) in adulthood. These outcomes are the result of the cumulation of life experience leading up to that point. As shown in Figure 2-1, the early life determinants of economic and social mobility begin even before conception (phase 1), include factors shaping pregnancy (phase 2), and span the more commonly studied early childhood period (phase 3). Moreover, strong theoretical reasons suggest that factors occurring earlier in the life course may causally shape mobility. For example, the circumstances shaping the period before conception—including

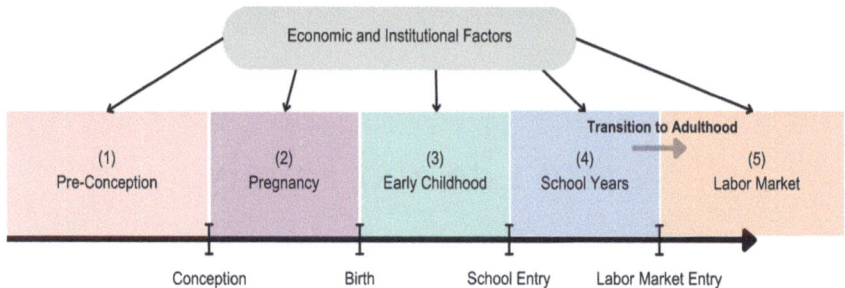

FIGURE 2-1 Lifetime determinants of economic and social mobility.

access to contraception and abortion—affect when a pregnancy occurs and with whom it occurs, and the economic and social circumstances into which a child is born and raised. Those circumstances interact with other social, economic, and institutional factors to shape early childhood, the school years (Figure 2-1, phase 4), and, eventually, transition to adulthood, including the child's own fertility and family formation patterns, with labor market outcomes (phase 5). In addition, each of these periods is itself influenced by laws and policies, institutions, social norms, and social and economic conditions, which shape intergenerational mobility differently by race and ethnicity, immigration status, socioeconomic status, geography or state of residence, and other characteristics.

The committee's review focuses primarily on absolute mobility—in particular, upward mobility from socioeconomic disadvantage (see Chapter 1 for detailed definitions). The reason is twofold: first, the persistence of disadvantage across generations is a relevant social problem in the United States; second, much research to date focuses on low-income and minority families. The committee expands this focus to also consider persistence of advantage (i.e., the mechanisms that high-income families use to provide advantages to their children, which support the persistence of privileged status). We also consider relative mobility, i.e., the association between parents' and adult children's economic circumstances at the societal level, when appropriate.

As explained in Chapter 1, relative mobility characterizes groups rather than specific individuals (much like inequality). Much of the evidence about relative mobility is indirect and focuses on known mediators of mobility rather than mobility itself. For example, if an economic support intervention targeted at families with children increases high school graduation among disadvantaged children, it is inferred that the intervention has the potential to increase occupational status or labor market earnings among these children (upward mobility), and, ultimately, decrease the persistence of disadvantage at the societal level (relative mobility). This is considered indirect evidence because the underlying research does not directly measure absolute mobility but a correlated pathway.

This chapter ends with a review of policy-relevant research for addressing these important issues. Early childhood education programs and reproductive health policies show promise for increasing upward intergenerational mobility, while pregnancy risk reduction programs and abstinence education programs are less promising. Economic support policies and programs show promise for increasing upward mobility across generations, while the evidence on parenting interventions shows limited impact. Understanding both the landscape of how early life and family circumstances shape children's life trajectories and the policies that may show impact in improving outcomes over the life course is essential for a policy-relevant research agenda on economic and social mobility.

Although there are strong theoretical reasons to believe that associations of early life and family contexts with intergenerational mobility reflect causal effects, it is difficult to randomize (or find quasi-experimental variation in) many factors that could play an important causal role in these relations (e.g., "parenting"). Additionally, examining mobility requires data following individuals over extended periods of time in order to include at least two generations. When available, this chapter notes evidence based on experimental and quasi-experimental approaches that support the assessment of causal relationships on early life outcomes that mediate the mobility process, such as school attendance, educational achievement, educational attachment, disciplinary issues, and others. We also present correlational evidence when evidence supporting causal interpretation is not available. Most of the empirical evidence focuses on relations of early life and family with key aspects of human capital, health, and well-being that are critical mediators in the intergenerational mobility process. The chapter also considers the largely quasi-experimental evidence regarding policies that promote healthy development in early life and family well-being and, by extension, suggest plausible pathways for mobility. On the whole, the available evidence suggests that policies that increase access to contraception and family planning, high-quality early education and care programs, and economic support are particularly promising for enhancing intergenerational mobility among those who grow up at the bottom of the economic ladder.

THE CIRCUMSTANCES OF PREGNANCY

Although largely absent from scholarly discussions about social and economic mobility, the circumstances of conception and childbirth—including social, economic, and institutional factors—are highly likely to influence parents' partnership decisions, mental health, schooling and career trajectories, economic status, and financial security. These circumstances in turn affect the intergenerational transmission of socioeconomic status and children's chances for upward or downward mobility. The committee believes that this report makes a unique contribution by examining the connections between the circumstances of childbirth and economic and social mobility.

One common characterization of the circumstances of conception relates to a definition adopted by the Centers for Disease Control and Prevention. *Unintended pregnancies* are defined as those that occur sooner than desired or when no child was planned at that time or at any point in the future. In recent years, however, research has moved away from using the term *intention* and has shifted toward language that more closely aligns with how this information is gathered on surveys or research instruments (Kost & Zolna, 2019; Maddow-Zimet & Kost, 2020; Potter et al., 2019). To represent the literature as precisely as possible, this chapter uses the terms *unintended*, *mistimed*, *unwanted*, and *desired* or *undesired* to reflect the terminology used in the specific research articles being summarized.

As recently as 2015, about 40 percent of all pregnancies in the United States occurred either sooner than desired or when no pregnancy was desired at any point in the future (Kost et al., 2023). Prior to the U.S. Supreme Court's decision in *Dobbs v. Jackson Women's Health Organization* in July 2022—which has allowed 20 states to restrict or eliminate abortion access (McCann et al., 2024)—about 40 percent of unintended pregnancies ended in abortion (Finer & Zolna, 2016; Kost & Lindberg, 2015).

Unintended pregnancies are strongly associated with mediators of intergenerational mobility, including adverse health, environmental, and economic circumstances in childhood. Children born from unintended pregnancies are disproportionately likely to have low birth weight and other birth complications (Kost & Lindberg, 2015; Mohllajee et al., 2007). Older children experience poorer-quality home environments after the unplanned birth of a younger sibling (Barber & East, 2009, 2011).

Unintended pregnancy and childbirth are also disproportionately followed by parental union dissolution, family complexity, instability in parents' romantic partnerships, and multiple-partner fertility (Guzzo & Hayford, 2020). Having an "unwanted" (as defined in the referenced article) child is correlated with higher levels of maternal depression and lower levels of happiness (Barber et al., 1999), as well as with a higher likelihood of harsh parenting styles (Gipson et al., 2008). Children whose births were unintended tend to have lower self-esteem and more frequent depression than their planned-birth peers (Axinn et al., 1998; David, 2006). Although the bulk of this literature is descriptive, theory suggests that at least some of the adverse relations between pregnancy intentions and outcomes are potentially causal.

FAMILY CIRCUMSTANCES AT BIRTH AND SUBSEQUENT FAMILY EXPERIENCES

The circumstances in which children are conceived, born, and raised vary considerably in the U.S. population. For example, more than two-thirds of births to married women result from intended pregnancies, compared with less than a quarter of births to cohabiting couples and less than a tenth of those to "single women," who are neither married to nor living with the child's father (Guzzo, 2021). These stark differences are shaped by social, economic, and institutional factors, including access to and knowledge of contraception. While roughly half of nonmarital births in the United States occur to cohabiting couples, the majority of such unions dissolve relatively early in children's lives (Sassler & Lichter, 2020).[1] Moreover, unintended pregnancies that result in childbirth are more likely to occur among women who are economically disadvantaged (Mosher et al., 2012), including younger and less educated women, and racial/ethnic minorities. Today, approximately 87 percent of first births to women over 30 occur within marriage, but the same is true for only 27 percent of first births to women younger than 24 (Brown, 2022).

There are also stark differences by maternal education and race and ethnicity in the circumstances in which births occur. Women with a high school degree or less education are half as likely as women with a college degree or more education to have their first birth within marriage, about three times more likely to have their first birth in the context of cohabitation, and nearly five times more likely to have their first birth while neither living with nor married to the child's father. White women are nearly three times more likely than Black women and about 30 percent more likely than Hispanic women to have their first birth while married. Black and Hispanic women are, respectively, 75 and 15 percent more likely than White women to have their first birth while cohabiting and 4.5 and 2.5 times more likely to have their first birth while neither married nor cohabiting (Brown, 2022).

---

[1] Demographic trends in the United States (and other wealthy countries) show a sharp rise in age at first marriage and age at first birth, as well as an increase in cohabitation prior to and in lieu of marriage (Bailey et al., 2014; Guzzo & Hayford, 2020). Yet, the delay in marriage has been greater than that in first births, such that a large proportion of births, particularly those to younger women (under age 30), occur outside of marriage, with roughly half to unmarried women and half to cohabiting couples.

Immigrants display higher fertility rates than U.S.-born women[2] and tend to give birth and raise children in very different family circumstances. Although immigrant families have disproportionately low socioeconomic status in terms of income, education, and employment, immigrant women tend to be older, on average, than U.S.-born women at the time of their first births and are much more likely to have marital than nonmarital births (Livingston, 2016). Yet, over time, immigrants, particularly second- and third-generation immigrants, become increasingly likely to marry and form families with native-born Americans (rather than other immigrants) and to see their divorce rates rise (National Academies of Sciences, Engineering, and Medicine [National Academies], 2015).

Differences in the circumstances in which pregnancies and births occur are associated with differences in the circumstances in which children are raised. Less socially and economically advantaged groups are not only disproportionately likely to have nonmarital births and births at younger ages, but they also exhibit lower rates of marriage and long-term parental partnerships; higher rates of parental union dissolution and divorce; and greater family complexity, instability, and multiple-partner fertility (Smock & Schwartz, 2020). Family instability (changes in household composition and parents' romantic partners and spouses), in turn, is thought to be a key mechanism linking nonmarital births to subsequent family dynamics and child development (Cherlin & Seltzer, 2014; McLanahan & Sawhill, 2015; Mitchell et al., 2015; Osborne & McLanahan, 2007; Seltzer, 2019). Notably, however, some evidence suggests that family instability plays a larger role in development for White children than for Black children (Fomby & Cherlin, 2007), and that the social and economic gains associated with marriage are larger for White than Black children and families (Fomby, 2024). Nonetheless, unintended pregnancy and nonmarital childbirth are, on average, associated with a host of factors that are thought to influence inter- and intragenerational economic and social mobility (Cooper & Pugh, 2020). As such, Fomby (2024) characterizes marriage as "both a product and a driver of social inequality" (p. 1285).

An extensive body of research documents that children who are raised in two–biological parent, married families exhibit advantages in numerous domains of development and success throughout the life course—potentially because such families are able to invest greater financial resources and time in children and to provide more consistent child-rearing environments

---

[2] The total (lifetime) fertility rate in 2019 for immigrants was 2.02 children, compared with 1.69 children for native-born individuals. Moreover, the 2019 birth rate (percent of women who gave birth) for immigrant women aged 15–44 was 5.7 percent, whereas it was 4.8 percent for native-born women (Camarota & Zeigler, 2021). On the whole, immigrants account for nearly a quarter of annual births, while representing less than 15 percent of the U.S. population.

throughout childhood (e.g., see Kearney, 2023, for a recent review). Despite an ongoing debate over whether relations of family structure with children's outcomes are causal in nature, it is well established that less-advantaged adults find themselves in fertility and family formation contexts that are associated with high levels of family instability (parental breakup and repartnering, multiple-partner fertility). In turn, children born to unmarried parents, on average, are at risk of poorer health, development, and well-being throughout the life course.

Research shows that the primary dividing factor in the family formation context is educational attainment; in particular, those with at least a college degree exhibit markedly different fertility and family formation patterns and, in turn, family contexts and child-rearing environments, from those of individuals with less educational attainment (Kearney, 2023; McLanahan, 2004; McLanahan & Jacobsen, 2014). McLanahan and Jacobsen (2014) argue that this divergence has been driven by changes over time in (a) ideational orientations toward gender roles, sexual behavior, and marriage; (b) diminished labor market prospects for low-skilled men relative to those for low-skilled women, which has implications for marriage markets; and (c) social welfare policies. Empirically, Edin and Kefalas (2005) draw on semistructured interviews and participant observation with 162 single mothers to shed light on the decline in marriage and rise of single parenthood in the past few decades. They find that, while mothers tend to think of marriage as a capstone institution that they aspire to—but only after they are financially secure—they tend to be less willing to wait for parenthood, which they view as central to a fulfilling life.

Notably, while the general pattern that children raised in two–biological parent, married families exhibit advantages and experience better outcomes relative to peers raised in other family circumstances holds across racial/ethnic groups, research suggests that the relationship may not be similarly causal across groups. Cross et al. (2022), for example, highlight that factors such as racism and male-centric social structures jointly influence family formation patterns, access to resources, family stress, parenting behaviors, and child development in ways that make identification of the "effects" of family structure on child development for racial minorities (in particular, Black families) problematic. Relatedly, Torche and Abufhele (2021) find that the negative effect of nonmarital fertility on infant health declines as marital fertility becomes less prevalent, suggesting that part of the marriage premium for children might be contextual, depending on how normative marriage is in a given society.

Cross (2020) shows that socioeconomic characteristics meaningfully explain (in an accounting sense) the differential relationship between family structure and on-time high school completion for Black children, implying that father absence may be less independently salient for Black families. In addition, Cross (2023) found a relatively small overall association between family structure and educational achievement among Black adolescents, albeit with some variation by family economic resources, suggesting that any impact of family structure might be relatively muted for Black Americans. Other studies suggest that Black families experience smaller disadvantages associated with single motherhood than White families, whereas Hispanic families experience larger disadvantages. In addition, some evidence suggests that other social and economic risk factors are more strongly associated with economic disadvantage for Black and Hispanic families than for White families, regardless of family structure (Baker, 2022; Williams & Baker, 2021).

In sum, an extremely large body of research, albeit predominantly correlational in nature, demonstrates associations of nonmarital births and family instability with poorer outcomes in childhood and early adulthood, which vary in size from modest to large, suggesting that nonmarital fertility and family stability are associated with opportunities for upward mobility (or lack thereof) for low-income children. Similarly, greater family stability may provide an avenue for high-income families to pass their advantages to their children. Family context might also influence the level of relative mobility. In aggregate-level analyses, Chetty et al. (2014a) found that the factor most strongly correlated with upward economic mobility across U.S. communities was growing up in a neighborhood characterized by a lower fraction of single-parent families. Interestingly, this association was observed for children growing up in single-parent and two-parent households, suggesting pathways beyond the nuclear family, plausibly related to families as role models and sources of social capital at the community level, as anticipated by Wilson (1996) and Coleman (1988), among others. While this correlational evidence does not support the claim that family structure drives upward mobility, it suggests that family environments and their potential implications for mobility may be important at both the individual and community levels.

Some studies—for example, those employing fixed effects and leveraging natural experiments as identification strategies—point to potential causal links between family structure during childhood and adult outcomes (McLanahan et al., 2013). At the same time, it is important to recognize that there is considerable variation in outcomes for children born outside of marriage by subsequent family experiences, including transitions in family composition and involvement by nonresident fathers, coresident step/social fathers, and other kin (grandparents) and nonkin caregivers (Adamsons & Johnson, 2013; Berger & McLanahan, 2015; Dunifon, 2013; Gold & Edin, 2021; Mollborn et al., 2011). Intergenerational linkages in socioeconomic status are weaker in families with stepkin, as households with stepkin engage in lesser intergenerational transfers than those without stepkin

(Schoeni et al., 2022). It is also important to recognize that the majority of studies have focused on children's outcomes during childhood and, to a lesser extent, young adulthood, with few studies focusing on outcomes well into adulthood (McLanahan & Jacobsen, 2014). Moreover, the committee is not aware of studies to directly identify causal links between family structure and intergenerational mobility at the individual level, although Bloome (2017) shows, descriptively, that adults who did not grow up in a stable two-parent home are disproportionately likely to experience downward mobility and low incomes.

PARENTING, THE CAREGIVING ENVIRONMENT, AND CHILD DEVELOPMENT

Parents influence children's development and well-being through the child-rearing environment and parenting behaviors they provide. Genetic attributes and predispositions, in isolation, appear to explain only a minority of the variation in individual differences in human development (Duncan et al., 2023), whereas environments and life experiences of parents and children are thought to be considerably more important. These include the preconception and pregnancy periods, as well as contextual social and economic factors (see Figure 2-1). Such environments and life experiences shape how genes are expressed in the context of individuals' opportunities and challenges, with potential implications for economic and social mobility. That is, intergenerational correlations in well-being are highly influenced by shared environmental exposures and experiences for parents and children, including access to material resources, stress, exposure to toxins, family stability and functioning, health behaviors, and parenting behaviors (Almond & Currie, 2011; Ellis & Boyce, 2008; Reichman & Teitler, 2013; Torche & Nobles, 2024). In particular, high-quality parenting behaviors may buffer against (and low-quality parenting behaviors may exacerbate) unfavorable epigenetic effects of exposure to adversity on children's development (Provenzi et al., 2020). Yet, because providing high-quality care is both time and emotionally intensive, in addition to being expensive, more-advantaged parents are, on average, able to make greater investments in their children and offer them higher-quality caregiving environments than their less-advantaged counterparts. As such, Wadsworth and Ahlkvist (2015) argue that economic inequality may be a primary cause of disparities in parental behaviors and investments in children and, thereby, in children's development and human capital formation.

A growing body of evidence suggests that even mild shocks during the prenatal and early childhood periods—which are disproportionately experienced by families of lower socioeconomic status—can have lifelong, potentially causal consequences, although these consequences may vary by genetic and (subsequent) environmental factors, including family resources and associated exposures that further influence social and biophysiological development (Aizer & Currie, 2014; Almond & Currie, 2011; Almond et al., 2012, 2018; Torche & Nobles, 2024). Early life is a critical period for brain development and the formation of structures and mechanisms that shape cognitive, physical, social, and emotional well-being throughout the life course (National Academies, 2000). Indeed, early childhood experiences are crucial for the development of socioemotional skills and executive function that set the stage for future development (Duncan et al., 2023). Moreover, child development occurs in cascading fashion, such that early investments provide the scaffolding and skills to support and respond to later investments (and challenges), and development of skills in one domain facilitates development of skills in other domains (Cunha et al., 2006; Heckman, 2006, 2008). As such, socioeconomic gaps in development in early childhood typically do not narrow, and may even compound, over time (Bradbury et al., 2015).

The relationship between parent (or primary caregiver) and child is, generally, the most important factor for early childhood development. High-quality parenting is characterized by three key dimensions: warmth and responsiveness, support for child autonomy, and well-defined behavioral expectations coupled with consistent age-appropriate feedback (Kiernan & Mensah, 2011; Moullin et al., 2018). It is composed of high levels of affection, patience, and nurturing; support for child exploration and interests; provision of enriching activities, materials, and educational support; promotion of skill development through positive reinforcement; and setting of clear and consistent rules that reflect children's abilities and are explained and (re)enforced through reasoning, persuasion, and nonphysical discipline (Baumrind, 1971; Bornstein, 2019; Kalil & Ryan, 2020; Ulferts, 2020). Children experiencing such parenting exhibit better cognitive, educational, and socioemotional outcomes, including greater self-esteem and less anxiety, depression, and engagement in antisocial behaviors; they are also more successful as adults (Bornstein, 2019; Clayborne et al., 2021; Madigan et al., 2019; Masud et al., 2019; Spera, 2005).

Parental warmth and responsiveness, particularly in the early years of life, help children attain a sense of security, regulate their emotions, and develop frameworks for exploring their environments (Morris et al., 2017; Moullin et al., 2018; Sroufe et al., 2010). As such, parental emotional support has been linked to greater educational achievement and attainment (Drake et al., 2014; Ogg & Anthony, 2020). Parental emotional support is also associated with children's development of self-confidence and self-esteem (Zakeri & Karimpour, 2011) and, thereby, their ability to cope with adversity (Moran et al., 2018). Parenting behaviors that include language-rich communications, use of decontextualized language, turn-taking, age-appropriate help with emotion regulation, and opportunities for child autonomy have also been strongly linked to positive developmental outcomes (see, e.g., Bornstein, 2019).

In short, extant research indicates that, across childhood, parental warmth, responsiveness, supportiveness, appropriate monitoring and supervision, flexibility, and autonomy-granting are associated with better socioemotional health, cognitive skills and academic achievement, and educational attainment. In contrast, harsh parenting and behavioral control are associated with poorer outcomes in these domains (Gorostiaga et al., 2019; Majumder, 2016; Masud et al., 2015). Yet, as will be discussed further because high-quality parenting behaviors are time and labor intensive, wealthier and more highly educated parents are considerably more likely to engage in such behaviors than their less-advantaged counterparts. Wealthy parents are also more likely to engage in a range of activities to secure advantages for their children. As shown by qualitative research based on interviews and participant observations, advantaged parents enroll children in enrichment activities, coach them, and negotiate with educational and other institutions to secure benefits for their children (Calarco, 2018; Lareau, 2011). Moreover, their children tend to imitate these behaviors, beginning as early as the preschool years (Calarco, 2018; Streib, 2011).

Racial/ethnic differences in maternal parenting behaviors have also been well documented, with the most pronounced differences reflecting cognitive support and stimulation (language use, conversation, reading; Brooks-Gunn & Markman, 2005). Notably, however, observed differences in parenting behaviors by race and ethnicity and immigrant status are likely confounded by differences in parental socioeconomic status and associated differential selection into fertility, family formation, and subsequent child-rearing contexts, as well as by experiences with racism and discrimination (which are typically unobserved in existing quantitative studies). Moreover, there is considerable variation in parenting behaviors by socioeconomic status within racial/ethnic groups, and research on between-group differences in parenting behaviors for parents of similar socioeconomic status has produced inconsistent results (Brooks-Gunn & Markman, 2005; Gibbs & Downey, 2020; Lareau, 2011). Nonetheless, racial/ethnic differences in parenting behaviors appear to explain a nontrivial portion—half to two-thirds—of racial/ethnic differences in school readiness, which have lifelong implications for success. For the most part, associations between parenting behaviors and school readiness are relatively similar across racial/ethnic groups, albeit with some exceptions (Brooks-Gunn & Markman, 2005; Gibbs & Downey, 2020). Moreover, differences in parenting behaviors by both socioeconomic status and race and ethnicity are thought to reflect substantial differences in parental opportunities (the extent to which parents' choice sets are constrained) and stress, each of which influences parenting behaviors. That is, parenting behaviors reflect the contexts in which families live, such that lower-income and non-White families disproportionately experience lower-quality and more stressful environments (housing, neighborhoods) and institutional supports (childcare, schools), which affect parental well-being (stress, mental health, cognitive load) and behaviors, as well as the home environment. Such differences in family context, in concert with historical and contemporary public policies, enable more advantaged parents to access, acquire, and leverage goods and services, social networks, and economic and social opportunities to promote their children's upward mobility that are unavailable to less-advantaged parents (Reeves, 2018). In turn, socioeconomic status and parenting behaviors function both independently and interactively to shape child development and life chances (Brooks-Gunn & Markman, 2005; Gibbs & Downey, 2020).

When considering the evidence linking parenting behaviors with children's subsequent development, and its potential implications for economic and social mobility, it is crucial to recognize that the vast majority of research on parenting behaviors has focused on mothers; considerably less attention had been paid to the behaviors of resident and nonresident fathers (Cabrera et al., 2018), or to other resident or nonresident kin (grandmothers) or nonkin caregivers (Dunifon, 2013; Mollborn et al., 2011; Tach et al., 2014). Given the high levels of family diversity, complexity, and fluidity that characterize contemporary American families (Berger & Carlson, 2020), including considerable growth in the proportion of children who spend time in a household that includes one or more grandparents (Harvey et al., 2021; Pilkauskas, 2012, 2014; Pilkauskas & Cross, 2018), future research would be well served by examining the caregiving behaviors of a wider range of individuals, with a focus on their potential contributions to child development and, in turn, mobility. Considering the role of extended family may be especially salient with respect to non-White populations (Cross, 2018; Cross et al., 2018).

IMPLICATIONS OF SOCIOECONOMIC DIFFERENCES IN PARENTING

Parental investments of financial resources and time matter for children's development and life chances. Parental financial resources shape the goods and services parents purchase to promote their children's development. Yet, disparities by socioeconomic status in parental expenditures in the United States are substantial and have widened significantly over time. The average difference in expenditures on enrichment activities for children between families in the highest and lowest income quintiles more than tripled between the early 1970s and mid-2000s, from an annual gap of approximately $2,700 per child to an annual gap of roughly $7,500 per child (Duncan & Murnane, 2011).

Differences in expenditures reflect the fact that parents of higher socioeconomic status have greater resources with which to acquire more and better goods and services, including neighborhoods, housing, food, medical care, childcare, and schooling, among others. However, differences in choices made by parents of higher and lower socioeconomic status may also reflect differences in knowledge of age-specific developmental needs, as well as in parental health, mental health, and stress, and family functioning and stability (Berger & Font, 2015), and access to social networks and related opportunities (Reeves, 2018). That is, in addition to facing more stringent budget constraints, parents of lower socioeconomic status may have less information, knowledge, skills, social connections, and opportunities for selecting high-quality options to promote child development than those of higher socioeconomic status (Case & Paxson, 2002; Kalil & Ryan, 2020; Reeves, 2018). This may be particularly salient for immigrant families (Cabrera et al., 2021).

Parents also provide physical care and cognitive and emotional stimulation, play with children, and arrange and accompany children in activities. On average, parents of higher socioeconomic status devote substantially more time to these activities than their counterparts of lower socioeconomic status (Dotti Sani & Treas, 2016; Guryan et al., 2008). Through the course of these activities, higher socioeconomic status parents provide greater cognitive and emotional stimulation, warmth, responsiveness, and consistency, and engage in less harsh parenting and physical discipline (Kalil & Ryan, 2020; Organisation for Economic Co-operation and Development, 2021; Reeves & Howard, 2013; Yoshikawa et al., 2012). Differences in these behaviors are thought to predominantly reflect differences in economic context. Economic scarcity is associated with psychological distress that undermines the quality of parental support and parent–child interactions, including by inducing cognitive biases such that, in the context of economic scarcity, parents are more likely to make decisions based on short- rather than long-term objectives and less likely to engage in purposeful, goal-directed parenting (Crnic & Coburn, 2019; Kalil & Ryan, 2020). Also, in the context of low-quality or unsafe neighborhoods, parents are more likely to exhibit what is conventionally considered poorer-quality (Furstenberg et al., 1999; Ludwig et al., 2012) and authoritarian parenting behaviors, perhaps in part to protect their children (Doepke & Zilibotti, 2019). Parenting behaviors can also change in response to living in safer neighborhoods (Darrah & DeLuca, 2014; DeLuca et al., 2016).

Exposure to economic precarity and low-quality environments and institutions, in turn, is thought to both directly and indirectly (via stress experienced by both parents and children) adversely influence children's neurological and biological development, with long-term implications for cognitive and socioemotional development (Atkinson et al., 2015; Duran et al., 2020; Thompson, 2014). Notably, whereas causal evidence of the effects of income on parenting behaviors, on average, is lacking, a growing body of research indicates that income is causally linked to both child maltreatment–related behaviors and to child protective services involvement (Berger et al., 2017; Bullinger et al., 2023; Cancian et al., 2013; Rittenhouse, 2023; Wildeman & Fallesen, 2017).

In short, parents of higher socioeconomic status spend more time engaged in child-focused activities, provide more cognitive simulation and emotional support to children, and use less harsh discipline than their counterparts of lower socioeconomic status. They are also able to access greater social and educational opportunities for their children. These differences reflect greater financial constraints and higher levels of stress, which are associated with poorer functioning (greater cognitive load, impaired executive function), and may result in greater parental anxiety and depression, as well as cognitive biases and impulsive decision making (Kalil & Ryan, 2020), which are thought to be core mechanisms linking family resources with child development (Kiernan & Mensah, 2011). Specifically, evidence suggests that parenting practices (cognitive stimulation, control, harsh discipline) mediate associations of socioeconomic status with socioemotional and cognitive development, including executive function (Baker & Brooks-Gunn, 2020), and that parental emotion dysregulation is associated with lower-quality parenting and, in turn, with emotion dysregulation among children (Shaw & Starr, 2019).

Given substantial differences in the contexts to which families of higher and lower socioeconomic status are exposed, socioeconomic status–related disparities in development and well-being emerge in the prenatal period and persist throughout life, spanning physical and mental health, cognitive and socioemotional functioning, educational achievement and attainment, employment and earnings, and a host of other domains (Berger et al., 2009; Bradbury et al., 2019; Case et al., 2002; Fletcher & Wolfe, 2016; Washbrook et al., 2014). Notably, whereas most research on associations between parenting behaviors and child development has been correlational in nature, strong theoretical underpinnings and some, albeit limited, evidence (e.g., Björklund et al., 2010; Fiorini & Keane, 2014) suggest plausible causal effects. The large literature linking exposure to adverse social and economic environments (and shocks therein), from the prenatal period onward, to poor outcomes throughout the life course is also suggestive of causal relations (Aizer & Currie, 2014).

In sum, diverse factors connect socioeconomic disadvantage to less than optimal parenting practices, which, in turn, predict children's socioemotional and cognitive development. These intermediate outcomes then predict long-term educational and economic outcomes in adulthood, including high school graduation and labor market earnings. While no studies to date examine all of these pathways jointly, the literature reviewed on each specific pathway strongly suggests that parenting practices are implicated in the persistence of both advantage and disadvantage across generations.

EFFICACY OF EARLY LIFE AND FAMILY POLICIES AND PROGRAMS IN SHAPING THE DETERMINANTS OF ECONOMIC AND SOCIAL MOBILITY

A range of policies and programs has the potential to influence the circumstances in which pregnancy occurs and children are born, as well as children's subsequent family and early life experiences, with potential implications for their health, development, and well-being and, thereby, life chances. The two major approaches to reducing unplanned (and, in particular, teen) pregnancy are (a) promoting sexual abstinence or pregnancy risk reduction through education and (b) increasing access to effective contraception and abortion.

A pressing policy question relates to how *Dobbs v. Jackson Women's Health Organization* (2022) will affect the multitude of factors in the first three life phases depicted in Figure 2-1. There has been little evidence on this question given the short amount of time between the *Dobbs* decision in 2022 and the publication of this report in 2025. Although the historical record may not apply directly to the post-*Dobbs* era, evaluations of previous policy changes restricting or increasing access to abortion or contraception provide the best available evidence and guidance on this question. We provide a high-level summary of this evidence here.

Despite a substantial decline in teen births in the United States in recent decades (Hamilton et al., 2023), the evidence on (teen) pregnancy prevention education programs on the whole indicates that they have largely been ineffective at reducing pregnancy, particularly programs that promote abstinence only (Chin et al., 2012; Juras et al., 2019; Marseille et al., 2018).

In contrast, the evidence on policies and programs to increase access to effective contraception has been quite promising (Bailey, 2013; Flynn, 2023; Kelly et al., 2020; Lindo & Packham, 2017; Sawhill, 2014), suggesting that granting greater legal and financial access to contraception and legal access to abortion has direct causal effects on unintended pregnancy and childbirth (Ananat & Hungerman, 2012; Bailey, 2013; Guldi, 2008). Moreover, programs and policies that increase access to contraception and abortion directly raise parents' education, employment, and economic and financial security, and reduce dependence on public assistance (Ananat & Hungerman, 2012; Bailey, 2006, 2013; Bailey et al., 2012, 2018; Miller et al., 2020). They also appear to causally affect partnership and marriage decisions by altering the timing of marriage, choice of parenting partner, and marital stress, thereby influencing the stability of those partnerships, including their likelihood of union dissolution and divorce (Bailey et al., 2018; Christensen, 2011; Goldin & Katz, 2002; Rotz, 2016).

Increased access to family planning programs in the 1970s appears to have causally raised the economic resources available to children and reduced child poverty (Bailey et al., 2018). Because parents' individual education and employment decisions, as well as their partnership decisions, affect the resources and environments available to children across the life course (Brooks-Gunn & Duncan, 1997; Duncan & Brooks-Gunn, 1997; Duncan et al., 2011), there are strong theoretical reasons to suggest that access to contraception and abortion have implications for upward mobility of disadvantaged children. While this body of research has not directly examined intergenerational mobility as an outcome, it has found that greater access to contraception affected determinants of intergenerational mobility. That is, the culmination of the effects of mothers' greater contraceptive access resulted in their children going on to attain higher rates of college completion, labor-force participation, wages, and family incomes as adults (Bailey, 2013).

Even today, differential fertility patterns across groups are thought to, at least in part, reflect differential access to the full range of existing contraceptive options. A recent randomized controlled trial found that eliminating out-of-pocket costs for contraception for uninsured women—making all contraceptive options free—raised the use of any birth control by 40 percent, doubled the value of the birth control purchased, increased days covered by purchased birth control, and had a significant effect on the efficacy of the contraceptive methods used (Bailey et al., 2023). The study also found that making contraceptives free had large and similar effects on contraceptive efficacy across a broad set of subgroups, including stratifications by Hispanic ethnicity, education, relationship/marital status, motherhood, and religiosity. In short, causal evidence suggests that changes in access to contraception in today's policy context may have important effects on a number of mediators of intergenerational mobility, especially upward mobility from disadvantaged backgrounds (see Figure 2-1).

Of course, not all unplanned pregnancies result in a birth. Prior to the *Dobbs* decision, about 40 percent of unintended pregnancies ended in abortion (Finer & Zolna, 2016; Kost & Lindberg, 2015). It will be important for future research to examine whether changes to state-level abortion policies in the aftermath of the 2022 *Dobbs* decision affect fertility and family formation patterns, particularly for teens and disadvantaged populations.

Evidence on the causal effects of abortion policy stems from legalization of abortion in the 1960s and early 1970s. Abortion was first legalized in a subset of states and then in the remaining states in January 1973 with *Roe v. Wade*. According to the Guttmacher Institute, nearly 20 percent of pregnancies ended in abortion during the first year following *Roe v. Wade*, and this share rose to 30 percent over the next decade, before decreasing through today (Henshaw & Kost, 2008). Research finds that abortion legalization led to a 5–8 percent reduction in the birth rate of women of childbearing age (Angrist & Evans, 1996; Levine et al., 1999). Some evidence also suggests that increased abortion access translated into changes in women's socioeconomic outcomes, with potential implications for economic and social mobility. Angrist and Evans (1996), for example, show that abortion reform appears to have improved schooling and labor market outcomes among Black women, although the statistical strength of these results tempers their conclusions.

Beyond access to contraception and abortion, policies and programs that promote marriage and healthy relationships have sought to increase the proportion of children born within marriage, to encourage marriage once pregnancy or childbirth has occurred, and to assist couples in engaging in high-quality relationships and maintaining their marriages. These programs have largely been targeted to populations of lower socioeconomic status, which are disproportionately at risk of nonmarital birth, parental union dissolution, and family complexity, including multiple-partner fertility. A substantial body of research over the past two or more decades has documented that these initiatives have not, in general, produced promising results with respect to increasing marriage, family stability, parenting quality, or parental relationship quality. This likely reflects, at least in part, low take-up rates in most programs, although results across programs and program sites have been heterogeneous (Avellar et al., 2018; Halpern-Meekin, 2019; Lundquist et al., 2014; Moore et al., 2018; Randles, 2016; Wood et al., 2012, 2014). Evaluations of recent federal and state initiatives in this arena are ongoing, and additional evidence of their impacts, when available, will further inform the efficacy of such programs.

Once children are born, policies and programs addressing parenting, economic support, and early childhood education and care have the potential to promote high-quality parenting and early life experiences, both by increasing family economic resources and by providing direct services to parents and children (see Figure 2-1, phase 3). Such interventions aim to improve parental education; employment; earnings; time and financial investments in children; and other aspects of parenting quality such as cognitive support, warmth, and responsiveness, as well as child cognitive and socioemotional skills. Parenting interventions take a wide range of forms and vary considerably in terms of intended target populations (defined by child age, parent and child characteristics, "risk" factors, etc.); intended duration and intensity of delivery; mode of delivery (in-home, classroom based, virtual; whether they are provided independently or in concert with another early education and care or school-based program); program quality; curricula, behaviors, skills, and outcomes targeted (parent–child relationships and interactions; child cognitive skills, socioemotional development, health); staff qualifications; cost; and scalability. This heterogeneity makes it difficult to evaluate the efficacy of parenting programs writ large.

With these caveats in mind, evidence suggests that, on the whole, parenting interventions, including most home visiting programs, have shown inconsistent and limited impacts on child development and well-being, likely at least in part due to low take-up and engagement rates, although direct effects on parents have been somewhat more promising (Berger & Font, 2015; Duncan et al., 2023; Kalil & Ryan, 2024; Ryan & Padilla, 2019). As such, there is little reason to suspect such programs, in their current forms, have substantial impacts on economic and social mobility, although the committee is aware of no studies to assess such effects directly. Future research in this area is warranted given the importance of parental stress and mental health for understanding parental investments and parenting quality (Kalil, 2014a,b; Kalil & Ryan, 2024).

Research on the role of economic support programs has produced much more promising findings. Such programs transfer income or in-kind resources that may either assist parents in purchasing goods and services that promote child health and development or provide such goods and services directly. Core economic support programs in the United States include the Child Tax Credit (CTC); Earned Income Tax Credit (EITC); Unemployment Insurance; Supplemental Nutrition Assistance Program (SNAP, formerly the Food Stamp Program [FSP]); Special Supplemental Nutrition Program for Women, Infants, and Children (WIC); Temporary Assistance for Needy Families (TANF); Child Support Services; Supplemental Security Income; and health care programs, such as Medicaid and the Children's Health Insurance Program. In addition to (or as a result of) increasing recipient families' resources, some such programs (including CTC, EITC, SNAP, WIC, and Medicaid) have been shown to reduce stress and improve emotional well-being, parental investments of time and money in children, parenting quality (including reducing child maltreatment), and child health and development (see summaries in Duncan et al., 2023; National Academies, 2023a,b), all of which are plausible mechanisms for supporting upward mobility. Evidence that such programs appear to affect these core mechanisms (family resources, stress, parenting quality, early childhood health and development) suggests that they may have positive impacts on intra- and intergenerational mobility. Although child support is a leading antipoverty program, evidence regarding its impact on mobility is currently limited (see Box 2-1).

A growing body of recent research leveraging exogenous variation in program rollout, expansion, and eligibility and access provides direct evidence that economic support programs—most notably tax transfers (CTC, EITC), SNAP/FSP, and Medicaid—have plausibly causal effects on

> **BOX 2-1**
> **Child Support and Mobility**
>
> The Title IV-D child support program, which facilitates child support transfers, serves nearly 13 million children annually, making it the "third-largest human services program affecting children" in the United States (McDonald et al., 2024, p. 2). Moreover, although more than half of families with child support orders do not receive the full amount they are due, and that about a third receive none of the support they are due (Grall, 2020), child support receipt and, by extension, the child support program, has been shown to substantially reduce poverty among recipient families (Cancian & Meyer, 2018; McDonald et al., 2024). Child support receipt has also been found to be positively and reciprocally (bidirectionally) correlated with nonresident parent (typically father) involvement with children (Nepomnyaschy, 2007), as well as to be positively associated with recipient children's well-being (Nepomnyaschy et al., 2022). However, data limitations and barriers to identifying suitable counterfactual conditions against which to isolate causal effects of child support receipt on children's developmental and, in particular, on their adult outcomes have precluded causal estimates of the long-term effects of child support receipt. The committee is aware of only one study to examine such effects. Kong et al. (2024) found child support receipt among welfare-participating families to be associated with greater adult earnings for recipient children. Given the scarcity of compelling evidence regarding both causal and long-term effects of child support receipt on adult outcomes, the committee finds that the existing evidence base is inadequate to support conclusions regarding whether child support may impact economic and social mobility or the core mechanisms to which it is related.

mechanisms related to upward mobility. Research indicates that increased parental income from child-related tax benefits during a child's first year of life results in increased achievement test scores, fewer school suspensions, a higher probability of high school graduation, and greater earnings in adulthood (Barr et al., 2022). Research also shows that EITC receipt during childhood leads to greater educational attainment, employment, earnings, and income, and lower rates of poverty and social welfare program participation in adulthood (Bastian & Michelmore, 2018; Guerrero, 2023; McInnis et al., 2023). Additionally, focusing on the precursor to the Aid to Families with Dependent Children and subsequent TANF programs, Aizer et al. (2016) leverage exogenous variation in access to cash benefits via the Mothers' Pension program, finding that benefit receipt during childhood resulted in greater education and adult income.

Expanded in utero and early childhood access to and participation in SNAP/FSP has been shown to result in better adult health and greater human capital (educational attainment and occupational status), earnings and income, economic self-sufficiency (greater employment and less social welfare program participation), and better neighborhood quality, as well as less criminal conviction and incarceration, social welfare program participation, and mortality (Bailey et al., 2020; Barr & Smith, 2023; Hoynes et al., 2016). Access to Medicaid in utero and during childhood has been shown to improve children's adult health and increase educational attainment, employment, and earnings, as well as to decrease teen births, disability, mortality, and social welfare program participation (Brown et al., 2020; Cohodes et al., 2016; Goodman-Bacon, 2021; Miller & Wherry, 2019). Moreover, recent research has identified intergenerational effects of health care access: a mother's access to Medicaid while she was in utero or during her childhood improves the birth and infant health of her daughters' children (East et al., 2023; Noghanibehambari, 2022). Research also shows that access to Medicaid in utero increases second-generation income mobility relative to one's parents' position in the income distribution (O'Brien & Robertson, 2018).

Beyond family economic resources and the home environment, high-quality early childhood education and care programs may benefit child development and thereby have implications for subsequent economic and social mobility. Access to childcare has also been shown to increase maternal labor supply (Berlinski et al., 2024; Wikle & Wilson, 2023); to the extent that it increases family income, increased maternal labor supply provides more opportunities to children and thus may also promote mobility. Such programs include center-based childcare for children from birth to age 3 and early education (preschool/prekindergarten) for children aged 3–5 years. Programs may be universal or targeted (means tested), public or private (though potentially publicly subsidized), full or part time, and may vary considerably in terms of teacher qualifications, curriculum, and support for cognitive and socioemotional development.

There is strong evidence from early experimental studies of small-scale, high-quality, and high-intensity programs targeting low-income families that were implemented between the 1960s and 1980s (Abecedarian, High Scope/Perry Preschool, Infant Health and Development Program). These studies show substantial positive effects spanning childhood through adulthood in a wide range of domains, including cognitive and socioemotional skills, educational achievement and attainment, family formation and stability, health, employment and earnings, criminal justice involvement, and participation in social welfare programs (Elango et al., 2015). These studies indicate that children who participated in high-quality early childhood education and care programs had better outcomes in these domains throughout the life course relative to otherwise similar children who did not participate in such programs; however, the studies did not directly assess whether participating children had better outcomes (e.g., education, earnings, income) than their parents and, thus, whether the programs resulted in upward intergenerational mobility.

Quasi-experimental evidence leveraging county variation in rollout of the Head Start program, which began in the 1960s and targeted children from low-income backgrounds, also suggests substantial long-term effects on human capital development, educational attainment, and economic self-sufficiency, including greater employment and reduced poverty and participation in social welfare programs (Bailey et al., 2021). Moreover, Barr and Gibbs (2022) show that Head Start in the 1960s and 1970s had effects on intergenerational mobility, in that the children of original program participants saw increased educational attainment, lower rates of teen pregnancy, and reduced criminal engagement; the authors estimated that these factors increased these children's wages in adulthood by 6–11 percent.

Evidence suggests that contemporary early childhood education and care programs, on the whole, help prepare children for entry into kindergarten and primary school, but that program quality and associated effect sizes vary considerably. Moreover, short- and long-term effects, when found, tend to be largest for the least advantaged children, children of immigrants, and dual-language/English-learning children, as well as for programs using domain-specific rather than generalist ("whole child") curricula. Large-scale randomized evaluations of the Head Start (for 3- to 5-year-olds from low-income backgrounds) and Early Head Start (for children under age 3 years from low-income backgrounds) programs—the largest public early childhood education and care programs in the United States—have demonstrated short-term benefits in cognitive skills, socioemotional skills, and health that are largest (and most likely to persist) for the least advantaged children (Love et al., 2013; Puma et al., 2010).

While some studies report that these effects tend to fade during the school age years, this simplistic interpretation belies the methodological challenges associated with the fact that children in the comparison group went on to attend alternative preschools/high-quality care at very high rates (Bitler et al., 2014; Feller et al., 2016; Kline & Walters, 2016; Zhai et al., 2014). That is, a large portion of comparison group children received a fairly comparable (although slightly later) treatment, leading them to catch up to the Head Start group. This has different implications than the conclusion that the benefits for the Head Start group fade over time. Although evidence from these evaluations does not yet extend past primary school, the strongest evidence from quasi-experimental studies suggests that there may be long-term positive effects of Head Start (Bailey et al., 2021; Barr & Gibbs, 2022). In short, while research on the effects of contemporary early childhood education and care programs has shown mixed results, it suggests that high-quality, intensive programs can have positive developmental impacts for disadvantaged children, children of immigrants, and dual-language learners (Duncan et al., 2023).

DATA LIMITATIONS AND OPPORTUNITIES

Recent advances in linking longitudinal administrative data systems have greatly expanded the ability to assess economic and social mobility patterns across generations and to consider the multigenerational roles of factors such as education, income, employment, neighborhood conditions, and access to and participation in social welfare programs (see, e.g., National Academies, 2023b).

While these efforts have facilitated—and will continue to facilitate—innovative research on economic and social mobility, they are limited with respect to assessing the roles of pregnancy and childbearing circumstances, as well as family context, parenting, and early life experiences. As this chapter highlights, whether pregnancies and childbearing are intended, parental resources, such as time and money, and parenting behaviors are likely important determinants of child development and well-being; adult health; social and economic well-being; and intergenerational mobility, especially upward mobility for children from disadvantaged households. Yet, examining how policies and programs affect (potentially causal) relations between parental well-being and intergenerational mobility has been stymied by a paucity of longitudinal survey data supporting the study of intergenerational relationships from the prenatal period onward, across multiple generations. These data limitations constrain researchers' abilities to identify policies and programs that reduce the intergenerational transmission of inequality. In addition, despite calls for more than a decade for multigenerational research that includes three or more generations (Mare, 2011, 2014; Pfeffer, 2014), the vast majority of evidence continues to be grounded in two-generation models. Further, existing population-based studies of three or more generations typically leverage either administrative data or survey data (most commonly from the Panel Study of Income Dynamics [PSID]), which vary in the extent to which they include high-quality measures of pregnancy or birth intentions or desires, family functioning, parenting behaviors, and child development spanning generations.

Two ongoing longitudinal panel studies in the United States currently follow multiple generations from birth onward: the PSID and the Future of Families and Child Wellbeing Study (FFCWS).[3] Both the PSID and the FFCWS include economic, demographic, social (including information on pregnancy intendedness), contextual, and biological data on at least two generations; however, to date, comprehensive parenting and child development data are available for only one generation. The PSID has followed a nationally representative sample of individuals and their household members and offspring since 1968 and collected survey data on parenting and

---

[3] The FFCWS was originally called the Fragile Families and Child Wellbeing Study.

child development for a subsample of children from 1997 to 2008.[4] Since 2014, the study has been periodically collecting such data on all children born in sample households in 1997 or later, including those born to children (now adults) comprising the initial (1997–2008) cohort. The FFCWS is a birth cohort study of children born in 20 large U.S. cities between 1998 and 2000.[5] These children and their parents have been followed since their births, and survey and biological data are currently being collected on the third generation (children of the initial birth cohort) as soon as possible after their births. Because the FFCWS oversampled nonmarital births (although, when weighted, the data are representative of all births in large cities during the sampling period), the sample is extremely diverse (48% Black, 27% Hispanic, 25% White or other race or ethnicity; 17% non-U.S. born). Both the PSID and the FFCWS are being expanded to include detailed parenting and child development data on children now being born to female sample members. Ongoing data collection on all children born to cohort members—who could be followed from the in utero period onward and assessed at relatively frequent intervals representing key developmental stages of childhood, adolescence, and young adulthood—would greatly enhance research on intergenerational economic and social mobility.

SUMMARY, KEY CONCLUSIONS, AND RECOMMENDATIONS

The family plays a critical role in the mobility process, serving as the primary institution through which investments are made in children, thus shaping human capital development from the prenatal period onward. Parents are central to this process, investing resources in their children's upbringing to directly affect their future economic and social prospects. Family environments are highly variable in the United States, largely based on social and institutional factors, family socioeconomic status, and the resources and opportunities they afford.

The circumstances of pregnancy and childbirth are closely linked to the prenatal and childhood environment and parental investments in children. Populations of lower socioeconomic status are disproportionately likely to have unintended and nonmarital births. Unintended pregnancy and childbirth are adversely associated with infant and maternal health, cognitive and human capital development, and social and economic well-being for parents and children. Children resulting from unintended pregnancy and those experiencing single-parent households are disproportionately likely to experience a variety of worse health, family, and economic circumstances.

---

[4] https://psidonline.isr.umich.edu/
[5] https://ffcws.princeton.edu/

Conclusion 2-1: Unintended pregnancies and childbirth are adversely associated with multiple determinants of upward mobility from poverty and persistence of advantage, in domains such as infant and maternal health, cognitive and socioemotional development, human capital formation, and economic well-being.

Parents play a crucial role in shaping children's development and well-being in early life. Parental behaviors—including physical care, cognitive and emotional stimulation, opportunities for child autonomy and age-appropriate play, and activity engagement and arrangement—can require substantial investments of time and resources. Associations of family context and parental investments with child development are well documented, as are associations of child development with social and economic well-being throughout the life course, yet most of this research is correlational rather than causal. Socially and economically disadvantaged parents make fewer investments in their children than their more advantaged counterparts, reflecting differential access to resources and differences in their life experiences, as well as contextual social and economic factors. Inequalities emerge before children are born, as disparities in socioeconomic status affect children's prenatal environments and have lifelong consequences for social and biophysiological development. Although racial/ethnic differences in parenting behaviors have been well documented, these differences may be confounded by disparities in parental socioeconomic status and associated differential selection into parenthood, family formation, and subsequent child-rearing contexts, as well as by experiences with racism and discrimination (which are typically unobserved in existing quantitative studies).

Conclusion 2-2: Socioeconomic disparities in parenting behaviors and resources are associated with disparities in the social and economic well-being of children throughout the life course, thus providing a mechanism for the persistence of advantage and disadvantage across generations.

Reproductive health policies and programs that increase access to contraception and abortion are the most promising means of reducing undesired pregnancy and childbirth. Indeed, rigorous evidence suggests that such programs and policies have a variety of causal effects on promoting parents' and children's health and social and economic well-being, suggesting their potential to increase upward intergenerational mobility of both parents and their children. In contrast, the evidence on the effectiveness of pregnancy risk reduction programs—and abstinence education programs in particular—has not been encouraging.

Economic support programs—particularly the EITC, SNAP, and Medicaid—are particularly promising for promoting upward mobility for disadvantaged children. Rigorous evidence indicates that such programs have positive effects on the key determinants—including family resources, stress, parenting quality, and early childhood health and development—that link childhood experiences with adult health and social and economic well-being; these programs also have direct positive impacts on adult health and social and economic well-being. In contrast, parenting interventions have shown inconsistent and limited impacts on child development and well-being, suggesting that such programs, even if scaled, are unlikely to have large population-level effects.

Historical evidence on the benefits of early childhood education, such as Head Start, for upward social mobility is promising, showing positive effects from childhood through adulthood across a wide range of developmental, educational, social, and economic domains. However, evidence on the long-run effects of more recent programs has generally been mixed, in part because of limitations in research designs and the short time horizon during which participating children can be followed.

Conclusion 2-3: Early childhood education programs and reproductive health policies and programs that increase access to contraception and abortion show promise for increasing upward intergenerational mobility. Economic support policies and programs that increase access to financial resources, food, and health care also show promise for increasing upward mobility. In contrast, the evidence on other pregnancy risk reduction, abstinence education, and parenting intervention programs is less encouraging.

Research to date offers limited evidence on whether associations among family context (pregnancy intendedness, family formation, family structure and stability), parenting behaviors and the caregiving environment, child development, and economic and social mobility are causal. Research on the mechanisms through which these factors may operate, such as children's cognitive and socioemotional development and educational attainment, is also limited, although a growing body of work suggests causal effects on these intermediate factors. Future research needs to expand the use of longitudinal administrative and survey data, and to further employ quasi-experimental approaches and (when possible) randomized controlled trials, with the following goals:

- Further examine the effects of access to contraception and abortion, particularly in the wake of the *Dobbs* decision and subsequent

state policies, on the circumstances of pregnancy and childbirth, family dynamics, and parent and child outcomes.
- Leverage exogenous factors that may influence family context and specific parenting behaviors and investments (e.g., by evaluating innovative programs) to identify causal effects of family context and parenting behaviors on child development and economic and social mobility.
- More fully investigate the family context, parenting behavior, and child development mechanisms through which economic support policies may influence economic and social mobility.
- Develop and test the causal assumptions implied by comprehensive models of economic and social mobility that incorporate biological, social, economic, and contextual factors related to early life and family.

Recommendation 2-1: The vast majority of research linking early life and family experiences to intergenerational mobility is descriptive in nature. Researchers should expand the use of existing longitudinal, administrative, and survey data and, when possible, further employ quasi-experimental and experimental approaches to obtain a better understanding of the causal mechanisms through which family context (pregnancy intendedness, family formation, family structure and stability), parenting behaviors and the caregiving environment, and child development affect economic and social mobility, as well as potential heterogeneity in such relationships for demographic subpopulations.

Existing survey and administrative data are not fully adequate for facilitating comprehensive research on malleable pathways through which social and economic (dis)advantages are transmitted within and across generations. The PSID and the FFCWS, which are currently the only ongoing long-term U.S. panel studies to follow multiple generations of family members, are the two primary longitudinal studies currently used to study early life and family. Both studies include economic, demographic, social (including information on pregnancy intendedness), contextual, and biological data on at least two generations; to date, however, comprehensive parenting and child development data are available for only one generation. Both the PSID and the FFCWS need to be maintained and further expanded to include detailed parenting and child development data on subsequent generations of all children born to respondents. Children of respondents need to be followed from the in utero period onward and assessed regularly at intervals representing key developmental stages of childhood, adolescence, and young adulthood. Such data would provide an efficient means of facilitating studies of multigenerational patterns of economic and social mobility and the range of mechanisms through which they may occur.

> Recommendation 2-2: Existing survey and administrative data are not fully adequate to support comprehensive research on intergenerational economic and social mobility and the range of mechanisms through which mobility may occur. Existing longitudinal surveys, such as the Panel Study of Income Dynamics and the Future of Families and Child Wellbeing Study—currently the only long-term ongoing U.S. panel studies to follow multiple generations of family members—should be maintained and expanded to include detailed information on pregnancy intention and the circumstances of pregnancies, parenting, and child development for all children born to current sample members. In addition, the samples that support these surveys should be refreshed with respondents that represent the contemporary population, especially Latino/Hispanic and immigrant subgroups. The children should be followed in utero and onward and assessed regularly at intervals representing key developmental stages of childhood, adolescence, and young adulthood. In addition, these surveys should be linked to administrative data from the U.S. Census Bureau, the Internal Revenue Service, and state and federal agencies that administer core social welfare programs.

3

Space and Place

Decades of research on intergenerational income mobility in the United States have focused on the challenge of estimating the degree to which economic status in one generation is passed on to the next. But newly available data suggest that any research efforts to understand economic mobility must consider the extent to which it varies by geography—a single, national estimate of economic mobility obscures the substantial heterogeneity across neighborhoods, cities, and regions of the country.

Using data from the Internal Revenue Service, a series of studies conducted by Raj Chetty along with several collaborators (Chetty & Hendren, 2018; Chetty et al., 2014a) has demonstrated that in some sections of the United States, such as the North Central states, spanning from Utah to Minnesota, children from low-income families have a reasonable chance of rising upward in the income distribution when they reach adulthood, while in other sections, including much of the Southeast, children from similar families are much more likely to remain poor as adults (Chetty et al., 2014a; Graham & Sharkey, 2013; The Pew Charitable Trusts, 2012). Even within the same commuting zones and counties, there is wide variation across Census tracts in children's chances of upward mobility (Chetty et al., 2018). This research demonstrates that upward mobility varies substantially across America's metropolitan areas and among neighborhoods within U.S. towns and cities.

This chapter examines the spatial dimension of intergenerational mobility in the United States. *Space* means the set of people (neighbors, extended family, romantic partners), institutions (schools, libraries, police departments, hospitals), processes (social interactions, community organization, political activity), resources (public spending, community wealth), and hazards (crime, pollutants, water quality) in the environment outside the home. Although most of the relevant evidence is currently at the Census tract level, research is increasingly being produced at broader levels, such as counties, cities, commuting zones, states, and regions.

The focus on the link between space and intergenerational mobility is motivated by two basic claims. First, inequality across multiple domains is organized, to varying degrees, along spatial lines. Some of these lines were formed historically and demographically by forces such as immigrants from similar countries choosing to live in similar places in the United States or groups of people with similar interests, such as jobs, choosing to live together. But some lines were drawn intentionally to exclude people from housing markets on the basis of race or to maximize local resources in school districts. Some lines, such as zoning codes, are drawn to regulate what is built, which in turn affects who can live in a given community (Dreier et al., 2014; Jargowsky, 2015; Lens, 2022). Second, research across disciplines converges to conclude that the spatial organization of inequality has causal influences on the probability of upward or downward economic and social mobility. However, as discussed below, the exact underlying mechanisms remain unclear. Space may affect economic mobility through multiple pathways: (a) directly, through exposure to resources, opportunities, risks, and hazards in the individual's environment (quality schools, social networks, labor market opportunities, violence), and (b) indirectly, through social interactions, preferences, norms, and perceptions that are conditioned by the residential environment (Galster & Sharkey, 2017). To date, most scholarship linking spatial factors with economic and social mobility outcomes considers absolute mobility (i.e., increase or decrease in economic well-being across generations). For that reason, the chapter will use the terms *mobility* and *absolute mobility* interchangeably and will clarify when the analysis refers to relative mobility.

The chapter begins with a review of the ways social scientists have studied the spatial dimension of economic and social mobility over time, before considering mechanisms that underlie the geography of mobility. It concludes by considering the implications of this evidence for public policy and for future directions for social science.

SPACE AND MOBILITY

The resurgence of interest in the role of residential environments in influencing economic and social mobility is often traced back to *The Truly Disadvantaged*, in which William Julius Wilson (1987) described how a set of economic, demographic, and social forces had led to a new form of concentrated poverty that was most pronounced in Black neighborhoods across U.S. cities. Wilson argued that the concentration of poverty and the decline of employment opportunities in central city neighborhoods contributed to deteriorating social institutions and shifts in cultural norms, which amplified the effects of family poverty. In other words, it was difficult to grow up poor but worse to grow up in a neighborhood where most other families were also poor (see also Wilson, 1996).

The scientific turn toward understanding the role of urban neighborhoods in influencing the life chances of residents was also catalyzed by Massey and Denton (1993) on the persistence and consequences of racial and economic segregation for racial inequality, and later, research on the precarity of middle-class status for Black Americans (Pattillo, 1999), urban violence (Anderson, 1999), the spatial location of jobs (Kain, 1992), and the role of public policy in addressing the challenges of concentrated poverty (Goering & Feins, 2003).

While much of the early quantitative research on the impact of residential environments struggled to overcome the methodological challenges associated with nonrandom selection into neighborhoods and cities, recent evidence has led to something close to a consensus in support of the claim that residential environments can have a causal impact on economic mobility and on other intermediate outcomes related to mobility—most notably academic achievement, cognitive skill development, and health (Sharkey & Faber, 2014). Increased access to geocoded data, improved tools for spatial analysis, and the rise of quasi-experimental and experimental research designs undergird this view.

One prominent example of experimental research designs that demonstrates that neighborhoods matter comes from the Moving to Opportunity (MTO) program, a large-scale social experiment implemented by the U.S. Department of Housing and Urban Development (HUD), which randomly assigned housing vouchers with different restrictions to families in public housing in five cities (Goering & Feins, 2003). Results from the experiment were complex: take-up of the offer of a voucher was low in several sites; some families who used the voucher moved back into higher-poverty neighborhoods over time; and there was substantial heterogeneity in the program's impact depending on origin neighborhood conditions, the outcome being studied, the gender of children in the family, and the age of children when the family moved (Burdick-Will et al., 2011; Chetty et al., 2016; Ludwig et al., 2012; Rosenblatt & DeLuca, 2012; Sampson, 2008; Sanbonmatsu et al., 2011). An influential reanalysis of the program's impact on children's long-term economic outcomes showed that children who moved to a low-poverty neighborhood at a young age (younger than 13) experienced meaningful increases in adult earnings (i.e., upward economic mobility), along with a host of other positive outcomes (Chetty et al., 2016). For this subgroup of families with young children, successfully using a voucher to move to a low-poverty neighborhood leads to $3,477 higher earnings per year in early adulthood.

Other studies using quasi-experimental research designs have produced strong evidence that moving to a relatively low-poverty neighborhood has a causal effect on economic outcomes or intermediate outcomes, such as high school dropout rates. Chyn (2018), for instance, compared outcomes of children in Chicago public housing developments that were demolished to nearby children in developments that were not demolished and found positive impacts on high school dropout rates, employment, and labor market earnings. Similarly, a 40-year follow-up of the Chicago Gautreaux program—a desegregation remedy that helped Black families in public housing move to predominantly White neighborhoods across the Chicago metropolitan area—builds on and confirms earlier evidence (e.g., DeLuca et al., 2010) that the program increased children's lifetime earnings, employment, and wealth, supporting upward mobility (Chyn et al., 2023).

A few studies demonstrate that exogenous changes in individuals' environments can lead to shifts in their prospects for economic and social mobility. However, other research using experimental or quasi-experimental designs leads to somewhat different conclusions. Initial analyses from the full sample of MTO families found no effects on children's test scores and later earnings (Sanbonmatsu et al., 2011); however, a subsequent analysis showed that the impact on cognitive skills varied widely across the five sites (Burdick-Will et al., 2011). Chyn (2018) found positive effects of moving out of highly disadvantaged public housing developments among both younger children and older children, while Chetty et al. (2016) found positive effects of moving out of high-poverty neighborhoods only for children who moved at a young age.

One of the limitations to the research on place-based factors affecting economic mobility is that most of the evidence comes from urban areas. There is much less evidence on the factors affecting economic mobility within or between suburban or rural areas. Evidence generated shortly after the initial work by Chetty et al. (2016) suggests that there may be different mechanisms at work in rural areas that affect economic mobility. For example, the racial makeup of a county, the quality of the schooling, and *social capital*—that is, the resources that come as a result of one's social relationships in the community, particularly those from different backgrounds and income levels—appear to be even more important in rural areas than in urban areas (Weber et al., 2017). County-level labor market conditions and the outmigration of young adults between decennial censuses is also associated with positive upward mobility in rural areas (Krause & Reeves, 2017). Using measures such as the percent of the population with a high school degree and other factors of production, such as the per capita value of capital in an area, Islam et al. (2015) showed that lower levels of human capital account for almost 80 percent of the income differential between persistently poor counties and the rest of the country, providing more evidence for the importance of quality schooling in these areas. Finally, a historical analysis by Edin et al. (2023) of extreme disadvantage in rural communities shows that a common set of factors tends to be found in places characterized by persistent poverty and limited upward mobility: segregated schools, violence, poor social capital, corruption, structural racism, and poor economic opportunities.

These heterogeneous findings suggest the need to go beyond the basic question of whether the neighborhood influences economic and social mobility and instead consider how residential environments and larger urban and rural settings provide opportunities for upward mobility, how mechanisms differ by environment, and who is most affected. The impact of the residential environment on individual life trajectories is a product of conditions in the immediate neighborhood and the larger area and region of the country, the timing and duration of individuals' exposure to these environments, and individuals' characteristics and unique vulnerabilities (Harding et al., 2011). In short, it is time to move toward questions of when, where, why, how, and for whom residential contexts matter (Sharkey & Faber, 2014).

MECHANISMS LINKING SPACE AND ECONOMIC AND SOCIAL MOBILITY

While scholarship on the "effects" of place has grown considerably over time, less attention has been paid to the mechanisms that undergird these effects and their heterogeneity—vital considerations for using research to improve policy. In this section we review evidence at the neighborhood level that points to schools, community violence, and local social networks as examples of central mechanisms linking the local residential environment with economic and social mobility. This review is not designed to be exhaustive, as there is evidence for numerous additional pathways by which the residential environment may affect upward mobility through, for instance, children's exposure to environmental toxins (Mohai et al., 2009; Muller et al., 2018) or through exposure to institutions such as the jail and prison system (Western & Pettit, 2010). While we focus on key factors through which scholars believe place has effects on economic and social outcomes, we emphasize that more research is needed, specifically research that directly identifies how these mechanisms work to produce outcomes that foster upward mobility by improving human and social capital.

Schools

Because school quality and neighborhood advantage tend to be highly correlated (largely a function of public school catchment areas being zoned by residence), studies exploring schools as a key causal mechanism for economic and social mobility require designs that employ exogenous variation in school quality. H. Schwartz (2010) analyzed data on test performance among students from low-income backgrounds in Montgomery County, Maryland, one of the wealthiest urban school districts in the nation. Montgomery County is unique not only because of the quality of its public schools and the funds directed toward students from low-income backgrounds, but also because it features the nation's oldest and most extensive inclusionary zoning program. As part of its zoning policy, the county's housing authority is able to purchase up to one-third of the units set aside by developers to be rented or sold at below-market rates. The housing authority randomly assigns families selected for housing assistance to these units, which are scattered across all neighborhoods and school attendance zones throughout the county, affording some children from low-income backgrounds a chance to attend higher-performing and more diverse schools than those in their previous neighborhoods.

Exploiting this random assignment, Schwartz (2010) estimated the effect of attending elementary schools with relatively low levels of student poverty versus moderate or high levels of poverty. The study tracked academic performance among 850 students from low-income backgrounds over 5–7 years and found that students in low-poverty elementary schools performed 0.4 standard deviations higher in math and 0.2 standard deviations higher in reading than similar students assigned to schools with 20 percent or higher poverty rates. By the end of elementary school, the gap between students from low-income backgrounds assigned to low-poverty schools and their peers in the larger student body had been cut by half in math and by a third in English. Importantly, because of the unique ability to compare the outcomes of low-income students in relocated students' original schools (which receive significantly more targeted resources than more affluent schools) to those that attended schools with more socioeconomic diversity (by virtue of the assignment to subsidized units through the program), the study suggests that one's peers seem to matter more than high levels of school funding. Given the association between test scores, educational attainment, and later earnings, this study provides strong evidence that the socioeconomic composition of school peers contributes to upward mobility among children from low-income backgrounds.

Dobbie and Fryer (2011) analyzed the effect on academic performance of attending a charter school run by the Harlem Children's Zone (HCZ). The HCZ is a community organization targeting a roughly 100-block area of Harlem with high-quality social services, schools, and programs for youth and families. In order to identify the causal effect of attending an HCZ school, the authors exploited the fact that attendance at the HCZ Promise Academy Schools was based on a lottery among all applicants. As a second identification strategy, the researchers used variation in the probability of attending HCZ schools derived from the interaction of the student's address and birth cohort. The study found that both older and younger students who attended a Promise Academy experienced substantial improvement in English and math performance and were less likely to be absent from school. Effect sizes ranged from one-quarter to four-fifths of a standard deviation, with larger gains in math.

Johnson and Nazaryan (2019) found that exposure to desegregated schooling—leveraging quasi-random variation in the timing of desegregation court orders—increased Black children's long-term economic prospects, without reducing the prospects of White children. Through increases in school quality and the funding ushered in by desegregation, Black children had higher educational attainment, lower rates of incarceration, reduced risk of poverty, and higher lifetime earnings, signaling substantial upward mobility.

This literature provides support for the idea that schools are a central mechanism through which the residential environment affects children's academic and developmental trajectories. It is also clear that the neighborhood and school settings likely have independent effects on children's prospects for upward mobility (e.g., Rich & Owens, 2023; Wodtke et al., 2023).

Community Violence

A growing literature suggests that children's exposure to community violence affects outcomes related to cognitive functioning and academic performance (Harding, 2009; Sharkey et al., 2014). The central challenge in estimating the impact of community violence on children's outcomes is overcoming the problem of nonrandom selection into violent neighborhoods. To address this problem, Sharkey (2010) exploited exogenous variation in the timing of children's interview assessments and local homicides to identify the effect of extreme local violence on children's performance on cognitive skills assessments. He found that children perform substantially worse on cognitive skills assessments if they are given the assessments in the immediate period of 4–7 days following a local homicide.

Other studies have exploited exposure to specific incidents or episodes of violence, such as a school shooting or a series of random sniper shootings, and found that children in closer proximity to violence exhibit more extensive symptoms of posttraumatic stress and worse performance in school (Gershenson & Tekin, 2018; Sharkey, 2010; Sharkey et al., 2012, 2014). International research from Mexico and Brazil shows that school failure rises and student test scores decline during periods of intense violence driven by gang warfare (Caudillo & Torche, 2014; Monteiro & Rocha, 2017).

While most of this research focuses on proximate outcomes, such as cognitive development and academic achievement, that are mediators of economic and social mobility, Sharkey and Torrats-Espinosa (2017) use shocks in the timing of federal law enforcement grants to localities to estimate the direct effect of changes in exposure to violence during young adulthood on upward mobility. They find that living in counties where violence was falling during the 1990s led to a meaningful increase in adult income for young people raised in low-income families.

Social Networks

Connections to nearby peers, friends, and neighbors is one of the fundamental mechanisms through which neighborhoods influence culture, norms, aspirations, information, and resources that may ultimately translate into upward or downward mobility. Much of the research focusing on networks and economic and social mobility is correlational, however, and identifying the causal impact of close connections has proven challenging (Anelli & Peri, 2019; Black et al., 2013; Carrell & Hoekstra, 2010; Lavy & Schlosser, 2011).

A recent set of papers (Chetty et al., 2022a,b) leveraged billions of Facebook friendships and found that children growing up in places with greater "economic connectedness"—that is, where more low-income people are friends with high-income people—tend to have greater economic mobility. Economic connectedness requires people with low income to be exposed to people with high income, as well as for people of both groups to be willing to forge those friendships. This finding affirms a century of social science in which social capital has been theorized as a key resource supporting economic advancement (Coleman, 1988; Du Bois, 1898; Granovetter, 1973).

Chetty et al. (2024) report that for children born between 1978 and 1992, earnings gaps decreased between Black and White people with low income, while earnings gaps increased between White people with high or low income. A proposed mechanism is the employment of same-race parents nearby, so that places with increases in parental employment also saw increases in children's income ranks and vice versa. The paper shows that these diverging trends result from changes in childhood environments proxied by parental employment rates within communities defined by county, race, and class. Importantly, the study by Chetty et al. (2024) suggests that while one's own parents matter, so do the other parents one grows up around, a finding consistent with an earlier paper pointing to the significance of two-parent families in neighborhoods as a key factor predicting upward mobility for Black children—even for those who themselves have been raised by a single parent (Chetty et al., 2020).

Mechanisms at the Level of Cities, Urban Areas, and Commuting Zones

In their initial analysis exploring the features of commuting zones linked with economic mobility, Chetty et al. (2014a) found that rates of single parenthood and high school dropout, prevalence of violent crime, measures of social capital, overall economic inequality within commuting zones, and the degree of racial and economic segregation were linked with economic mobility. Although this study was not designed to establish causal relationships, it provides a starting point for considering likely mechanisms operating at levels wider than the immediate residential environment. The present report next focuses on two dimensions of the larger geographic environment: labor market conditions and racial and economic segregation.

Job loss is among the important "mechanisms that affect mobility and define opportunity structures" (Brand, 2015, p. 1). One strand of research exploits shocks in local economic conditions to examine the impact of employment on outcomes that are mediators of upward mobility, such as youths' academic achievement and educational attainment. To identify the effect of local job losses on children's academic performance, Ananat et al. (2011) exploited factory plant closings in North Carolina counties and found that changes in local economic conditions arising from plant closings have large effects on children's reading and math scores throughout the area. Other research has found that large-scale transformation of the local economy, such as the opening of casinos on Native American reservation lands or the regional development investments made as part of the federal Tennessee Valley Authority, can have substantial positive effects on educational attainment, income, and employment (Akee et al., 2010; Kline & Moretti, 2014; Wolfe et al., 2012).

Local labor markets have been shaped in significant part by decades of macroeconomic transformation due to globalization and trade policies (see, e.g., Autor et al., 2021; Green & Sanchez, 2007). Seltzer (2024) finds that "declines in manufacturing have contributed to growing disparities in upward intergenerational income mobility" (p. 1223), with children living in counties that experienced large contractions in manufacturing throughout their adolescence facing larger economic penalties in adulthood. Similarly, Berger and Engzell (2022) use "data on local labor markets in the United States to document that automation significantly has reduced the chances for upward mobility among children born in low-income families in the early 1980s" (p. 11). The authors posit that automation affects children's economic attainment by eroding the ability of families to invest in their human capital.

Turning to racial and economic segregation, Graham and Sharkey (2013) used data from three U.S. surveys that include at least two generations of family members and found a robust and consistent association between economic segregation and relative economic mobility (measured by the intergenerational income elasticity [see Chapter 1]) across all three samples. While this result is correlational, a small number of studies have made meaningful progress in generating causal evidence on the historical processes and policies leading to segregation and migration and their impact on economic mobility. For example, Aaronson et al. (2021a) analyzed the long-term effects of boundaries used by the federal Home Owners Loan Corporation to develop an appraisal process that used neighborhood-level characteristics to assess the risk of making home loans in cities across the country, a process that came to be known as "redlining." Using multiple identification strategies, Aaronson et al. (2021b) found that the grades representing the riskiness of different neighborhoods had substantial causal effects on economic mobility for cohorts born many decades later (in the late 1970s and early 1980s).

These findings reflect the large body of evidence showing how active efforts to maintain and reinforce racial segregation have had long-term consequences on the trajectories of neighborhoods and the long-term educational and economic outcomes of different segments of the population, particularly Black Americans (Faber, 2020; Massey & Denton, 1993; Rothstein, 2017; Sharkey, 2013). Several studies using quasi-experimental designs support this conclusion. Chyn et al. (2022) leveraged variation in the historical placement of railroad lines in northern cities to instrument for (and identify the impacts of) racial segregation, showing a strong negative impact of segregation on upward mobility for all children and pronounced negative effects for Black children across the income distribution. Derenoncourt (2022) focused on the long-term effects of the Great Migration on economic mobility among Black Americans. Using a shift-share instrument for the scale of Black migration into non-Southern commuting zones,[1] Derenoncourt (2022) found that Black Americans born in the 1980s had lower rates of upward mobility in commuting zones that absorbed a larger share of Black Americans decades earlier. She points to spending on police, rates of incarceration, and rising violence as potential explanations for the findings.

---

[1] The author uses a shift-share approach to "[c]ombine information on pre-1940 Black southern migrants' location choices with supply-side variation in county out-migration from 1940 to 1970, predicted from southern economic variables" (Derenencourt, 2022, p. 370).

The Role of Qualitative Research in Understanding How Space and Place Affect Economic and Social Mobility

Qualitative research has deepened the understanding of mechanisms that connect place to economic and social mobility. For example, recent work has focused on why the residential moves of low-income households often do not translate into gains in neighborhood quality. Ethnographic and interview-based fieldwork has revealed that, rather than select specific neighborhoods for moves, poor households are often pushed out of where they live, forced to combine decisions of whether to and where to move in one rushed step, frequently under duress (Carillo et al., 2016; DeLuca & Jang-Trettien, 2020; DeLuca et al., 2019; Harvey et al., 2020; Rosen, 2017). Housing instability—spurred by factors such as poor housing quality or violence—has profound consequences for the sorting of households and children into neighborhoods and schools (Cuddy et al., 2020; DeLuca et al., 2024). Understanding these processes and constraints informs effective policies aimed at reducing spatial inequality.

Another, longer-standing qualitative literature in cultural and urban sociology has focused on how people living in high-poverty, high-violence neighborhoods adapt to the threats and constrained resources. Bourgois (2003), for example, documents how drug dealers in East Harlem often have worked in the formal economy, but as a result of experiences of disrespect and discrimination, feel driven to the drug economy and adopt street culture as a "badge of pride." MacLeod (1987) and Anderson (1999) similarly explore the adaptive behaviors adopted by some men with low incomes when opportunity to achieve their aspirations is blocked.

Other qualitative scholars have explored the challenges that young people growing up in high-poverty, high-violence communities face in coping with adverse events and in navigating their social networks, families, and communities (see Small et al., 2010). For example, social isolation and avoidance of risky peers may protect youth from violence in the near term but may also limit the building of human and social capital, which can in turn limit their upward mobility and risk locking them in disadvantaged communities over the long term (Chan Tack & Small, 2017; DeLuca et al., 2024; Edin et al., 2015).

A less-often explored but important additional mechanism through which place may affect children's long-run prospects is through neighborhood effects on parent well-being and mental health. Earlier qualitative literature found that parents responded to living in low-income, high-crime communities through vigilance to protect their children, which can be additionally taxing to parents (Anderson, 1999; Furstenberg et al., 1999). Mixed methods combining qualitative and quantitative research on the MTO experiment found that moving to safer neighborhoods can lead to substantial improvements in parent mental health (Ludwig et al., 2012; see also DeLuca et al., 2016; Turney et al., 2013). Such mechanisms can also help explain a puzzle that remains from Chetty et al. (2016): how is it that long-term economic mobility improved for young MTO children, despite small to no improvements in their schools after moving? Neighborhoods may have direct effects on children through safety and exposure to more advantaged peers, and they may also have indirect effects through improved parental mental health, which is particularly relevant for young children.

While much of this qualitative research focuses on urban areas, some recent work has shifted the focus to rural communities. For example, in their analysis of communities with persistent high poverty, poor health outcomes, and low economic mobility, Edin et al. (2023) highlight the history of state-sanctioned violence that pervades many of these places. They posit that community-level violence impedes upward mobility, and limited mobility can in turn spur violence (see also Mann et al., 2024).

IMPLICATIONS FOR SOCIAL POLICY

Evidence on the importance of neighborhoods and larger urban areas for economic and social mobility raises the question: how can neighborhood quality be improved for more households? Two common policy approaches include housing mobility policies that help move families to higher-opportunity areas and "place-conscious" policies (Pastor & Turner, 2010) aimed at bringing opportunity and investment into less-resourced communities. This section reviews selected evidence for each of these approaches. It is critical to acknowledge that many policies, including historical policies such as redlining and current policies such as residential zoning, have created or maintained spatial inequality and, likely, limited upward mobility. The section concludes by discussing a third approach to social policy, which involves curtailing or abolishing existing programs and policies that may be amplifying spatial inequality.

Evidence from Housing Mobility Programs

Policies for assisting low-income households in relocating to less-segregated, lower-poverty neighborhoods with housing voucher subsidies—known as housing mobility programs—have been implemented for nearly 50 years. Several of these interventions have included quasi-experimental or experimental changes in families' neighborhoods and schools, increasing the validity of causal claims about neighborhood effects (DeLuca & Dayton, 2009; DeLuca et al., 2010; de Souza Briggs, 1997). James Rosenbaum's pioneering research on Chicago's Gautreaux desegregation program first provided evidence that housing policy that assisted low-income families in relocating to communities with more resources, lower crime, and better schools could serve as a tool for economic and social mobility (Rubinowitz & Rosenbaum, 2000). The Gautreaux remedy required HUD and the Chicago Housing Authority to provide housing opportunities to Black families in public housing, allowing more than 7,000 Black households a chance to move to a wide range of neighborhoods, including the affluent and predominantly White Chicago suburbs.

Early evidence on Gautreaux showed that moving to Chicago's mostly White and affluent suburban communities improved academic outcomes for children (Kaufman & Rosenbaum, 1992; Rosenbaum et al., 1991; Rubinowitz & Rosenbaum, 2000). The program had small to moderate effects on parental employment and earnings (Mendenhall et al., 2006). Strikingly, a recent 40-year follow-up of Gautreaux households with a more rigorous research design found that children who moved to mostly White, economically advantaged neighborhoods in the Chicago metro area earned more as adults, worked more years, were more likely to own a home, and were more likely to live in low-poverty and diverse neighborhoods decades later as adults compared with similar counterparts who moved to mostly Black segregated areas (Chyn et al., 2023). Thus, such moves led to durable and multigenerational benefits for families (see also Keels et al., 2005). A housing mobility program developed in Baltimore as a result of a different desegregation program also showed benefits to low-income Black families, including long-term moves to higher-opportunity, less-segregated communities and moderate gains in children's test scores (DeLuca & Rosenblatt, 2017; DeLuca et al., 2016).

Motivated in part by the strong initial findings from Gautreaux, the MTO experiment was designed to test whether moving into low-poverty neighborhoods affected the social and economic outcomes of families living in areas of concentrated poverty (de Souza Briggs et al., 2010; Goering & Feins, 2003; Sanbonmatsu et al., 2011). As previously described, early MTO findings were complex: adults in treatment group households were no more likely to be employed nor less likely to be using public assistance than the control group; there were no improvements in children's test scores and even an increase in delinquency among boys (Clampet-Lundquist et al., 2011; Sanbonmatsu et al., 2006, 2011). Yet, there were improvements in mothers' mental health on par with those achieved through best practices in antidepressant medication (Ludwig et al., 2012). These outcomes are complemented by Chetty et al.'s (2016) influential reanalysis of the program's positive long-run impact focused on children younger than age 13. Recent research also shows that children who received housing vouchers through MTO had lower hospitalization rates for asthma and psychiatric disorders, lower inpatient medical spending, and lower utilization of outpatient and clinic services (Pollack et al., 2019, 2023a). Findings on the reduction of asthma attacks were replicated for children in the Baltimore mobility program (Pollack et al., 2023b). Yet the MTO findings discussed previously also suggest significant heterogeneity in the effects of residential mobility programs across subgroups of families.

In addition to Gautreaux and MTO, many other housing mobility programs have generated evidence suggesting that moving out of highly disadvantaged communities can lead to positive effects on children's academic trajectories and economic outcomes. Evidence from the "Mt. Laurel" program in New Jersey, which followed families as they moved into a new mixed-income housing development (compared with those on a wait list), showed improvements in study habits but no change in grades (Massey et al., 2013). Evidence from families in public housing in Denver showed strong effects of various neighborhood characteristics, most notably violent crime rates, on high school academic success for low-income Latino and African American adolescents (Galster et al., 2016). Ludwig et al. (2010, as cited in Burdick-Will et al., 2011) analyzed data from housing assistance recipients in Chicago who had been randomly assigned a position on a wait list before the local housing authority opened this wait list for the first time in years. Exploiting variation in the timing of when families were offered housing in lower-poverty neighborhoods, the researchers found that children offered housing vouchers experienced improvements in both reading and math scores relative to children in the control group.

Such a convergence of powerful and rigorous evidence across cities and time has already led to an expansion of federal funding to scale housing mobility efforts, not only based on the quality of the evidence on impacts (Lubell et al., 2023), but also on the quality of the evidence on implementation and policy design (Bergman et al., 2024; DeLuca et al., 2023).

Evidence on Place-Conscious Investments

Place-conscious investments include policies and programs that direct resources to disadvantaged communities or urban areas, or to the families and individuals within disadvantaged places. A wide range of investments could fit under the umbrella of place-conscious investments, making it difficult to summarize the literature. However, some policies have been studied in great depth and provide insights into this approach.

One set of programs focuses on providing job experiences and training along with supplemental supports to residents of disadvantaged communities. The New Hope program, implemented in Milwaukee during the mid-1990s, stands out as a unique experiment in addressing low-wage labor market challenges and promoting economic mobility (Duncan et al., 2009). Unlike many contemporaneous welfare-to-work programs, New Hope adopted a place-conscious approach, specifically targeting individuals from low-income backgrounds residing in disadvantaged neighborhoods within the city.

The program randomly assigned applicants to take part, showing significantly higher employment and earnings while the program was operational (Huston et al., 2003). These positive employment outcomes can be partially attributed to the program's guarantee of community service jobs for participants who were unable to secure private-sector employment. Beyond employment gains, the program demonstrated success in reducing poverty. By the fifth year, the poverty rate in the treatment group fell to 52 percent, compared with 60 percent in the control group. Furthermore, children of the adults in the treatment group experienced improvements in academic performance and behavior, indicating that the benefits were cross-generational (Duncan et al., 2009; Huston et al., 2001, 2003). Specifically, children in the treatment group scored significantly higher on reading and language assessments than their counterparts in the control group (Huston et al., 2003). The findings are notable because most previous studies of active labor market policies found that guaranteed or subsidized public-sector employment has no long-term impact on participants' employment or earnings (Card et al., 2018).

The Jobs Plus program, implemented by HUD in the 1990s, stands as another noteworthy example of a place-conscious intervention designed to bolster employment prospects within specific communities. Unlike conventional welfare-to-work initiatives, Jobs Plus adopted a targeted approach, focusing on residents living in public housing developments across five diverse cities: Baltimore, Chattanooga, Dayton, Los Angeles, and St. Paul (Bloom & Riccio, 2005).

The program aimed to saturate these public housing developments with comprehensive employment-related services that were intended to equip residents with the necessary skills and support to secure and maintain employment over time. Additionally, Jobs Plus incorporated rent incentives as a means to financially encourage work participation among residents. Evaluations of the program revealed promising outcomes in three of the five sites that implemented the full spectrum of services and incentives offered (Bloom & Riccio, 2005). In these locations, residents experienced meaningful increases in both employment rates and annual earnings. Specifically, the program generated an estimated 10 percent rise in employment and an 8–19 percent increase in annual earnings (Bloom & Riccio, 2005).

Whereas New Hope and Jobs Plus targeted individuals within high-poverty areas, the Empowerment Zones/Enterprise Communities program in the mid-1990s offered tax breaks designed to encourage firms to expand, invest in, and improve local employment outcomes by hiring local residents (Tach & Wimer, 2017). The evidence base behind this program and others designed to stimulate demand in areas of disadvantage is mixed.

Busso et al. (2013) presented the most compelling evidence of positive impacts, estimating a 15 percent increase in jobs and an 8 percent wage increase for residents within designated zones (compared with nonselected sites) between 1990 and 2000. These findings contrast with other studies that have reported minimal program effects in specific locations (Elvery, 2009; Oakley & Tsao, 2006). Additionally, concerns have been raised regarding the cost-effectiveness of such spatially targeted initiatives, particularly in the absence of additional investments (Glaeser & Gottlieb, 2008; Ladd, 1994). However, Austin et al. (2018) argued that place-based policies can be relatively cost-effective in improving economic outcomes, considering the high costs associated with moving to a new geographic area.

While the interventions discussed thus far focus primarily on poverty reduction, labor market prospects, and job creation in disadvantaged neighborhoods, it is crucial to acknowledge that economic opportunity is just one factor influencing economic mobility. A broader range of place-based interventions has been implemented to address various challenges within communities, including school quality, crime reduction, and community health (Braga, 2005; Dobbie & Fryer, 2011; Heller, 2014; Heller et al., 2013; H. Schwartz, 2010). These interventions, while not focused on labor market outcomes directly, may impact upward economic mobility indirectly by addressing factors such as exposure to violence, access to quality education, and overall community well-being, all of which are intricately linked to economic prospects.

The recognition that economic disadvantage tends to be concentrated in areas that face a range of associated challenges is the motivation for a set of interventions that have come to be identified as community change initiatives (CCIs). These interventions aim to "flood" such areas with resources in multiple domains, encompassing economic development, institutional support, physical infrastructure improvements, and social services (Kubisch et al., 2010). However, translating this vision into reality presents significant challenges. As Kubisch et al. (2010) highlighted, many CCIs have not received the sustained funding needed for transformative change. Coordinating services, building institutional capacity, and engaging residents are additional hurdles (Chaskin, 1997; Kubisch et al., 2010).

Evaluating the impact of CCIs is equally challenging. Programs often lack clear designs for assessment, and their reduced scale rarely allows for generating and sustaining tangible change (O'Connor, 1995, 1999; Sharkey, 2013). Those who live in communities targeted by such investments often move out, further complicating evaluation efforts (Theodos et al., 2015). One descriptive study of a high-profile CCI—the Sandtown Neighborhood Transformation Initiative in Baltimore—found that while relatively large investments in brick-and-mortar improvements led to higher rates of home ownership 20 years later (comparing Sandtown with other similarly situated neighborhoods in the city that did not receive such funds), it also likely led to higher rates of foreclosures during the 2008–2010 Recession

(Rosenblatt & DeLuca, 2017). Compared with similar neighborhoods, Sandtown saw no improvements in children's test scores, violent crime, or life expectancy rates.

Infrastructure and development decisions by various levels of government also influence the availability of affordable housing, restricting or expanding opportunities for low-income families to live in different kinds of neighborhoods. Policies such as the low-income housing tax credit and the decisions of developers can significantly alter the supply of affordable housing (Owens & Smith, 2023). Furthermore, current practices of school assignment by residence can perpetuate spatial inequality by confining students to schools in their local, often low-income, neighborhoods. Other notable policy measures include inclusionary zoning, acquisition of housing in high-opportunity areas by public housing authorities, and efforts to eliminate vacant lots and abandoned homes in neighborhoods.

Although targeted interventions aimed at neighborhood revitalization have yielded mixed results, research on large-scale economic transformations suggest that substantial investments capable of altering the local economic landscape can have lasting positive effects on residents. For example, studies estimating the long-term impact of the Tennessee Valley Authority (TVA), a federal initiative established in the 1930s to revitalize the economically depressed Tennessee Valley region, demonstrate long-term economic benefits for residents (Kline & Moretti, 2014). Similarly, research on the introduction of casino gaming on American Indian reservations reveals positive economic impacts for these communities, including job creation and increased income levels (Akee et al., 2010; Wolfe et al., 2012); however, the benefits of casinos may be due in part to the fact that they are restricted to very specific areas. An evaluation of the Delta Regional Authority, which funds rural development projects in the Mississippi River Delta region, found positive earnings impacts in the health care and social services sectors but not on overall employment rates (Pender & Reeder, 2011). These examples suggest that although large-scale economic transformations have the potential to benefit residents in disadvantaged areas and support upward mobility, much more research is needed before concluding that large-scale infrastructure investments similar to the TVA would result in similar outcomes in other areas and historical contexts.

Interventions Amplifying Spatial Inequality

Programs that invest in disadvantaged areas and those that support moving out of poor neighborhoods remain the most prominent approaches to addressing the link between place and upward mobility. However, some policies and programs active in the United States have the opposite effect: they constrain economic mobility and amplify spatial inequality. Therefore, a third approach to addressing concentrated disadvantage and supporting upward mobility involves scaling back or ending these interventions.

An extensive literature has documented the historical policies that exacerbated racial inequality in America's neighborhoods and urban areas through the civil rights era, including racial zoning in such cities as Louisville, St. Louis, and Baltimore; explicit discrimination in new suburban housing developments; racially restrictive covenants that limited who could buy or lease homes; blockbusting and contract lending in cities absorbing growing Black populations leaving the South; the razing of Black neighborhoods during the period of interstate highway construction and urban renewal; and the federal provision of explicitly segregated public housing (Coates, 2014; Hirsch, 2009; Massey & Denton, 1993; Rothstein, 2013). New evidence has documented the long-term consequences of such policies, demonstrating their impact on segregation and, decades later, on economic mobility (Aaronson et al., 2021b; Faber, 2020).

Less attention has been given to policies and interventions that continue to generate or reinforce spatial inequality in the present by constraining residential mobility, subsidizing home ownership among the most affluent, and limiting the development of affordable housing. For example, the largest federal housing programs are tax subsidies such as the mortgage interest deduction, the property tax deduction, and the exclusion of capital gains on the sales of homes—all of these are highly regressive federal policies that provide strong incentives for the most affluent families to take on deep debt and purchase more expensive homes in exclusive areas (Fischer & Huang, 2013; Turner et al., 2013). In 2017, high-income households received four times the benefits of low-income households, half of which were due to the mortgage interest deduction (Fischer & Sard, 2017; see also Chapter 5). However, the reduction of the mortgage interest deduction through the 2017 Tax Cut and Jobs Act led to a more equitable distribution of taxes (Ambrose et al., 2022), as well as a more equitable geographic distribution (Blouri et al., 2023). Turning over the power to determine local land use regulations to policymakers in individual towns and cities limits the production of new housing and contributes to economic segregation (Glaeser & Gyourko, 2002; Gyourko et al., 2013; Rothwell & Massey, 2010). These are only a few examples of the active interventions in housing that continue to benefit high-income families and further divide American space and contribute to residential segregation by race and ethnicity and by income. Altering or ending existing housing and land use policies that exacerbate inequality, and instead implementing programs that confront inequality, would represent an initial step in an urban policy agenda designed to reduce neighborhood inequality.

A FORWARD-LOOKING SCIENCE OF SPACE AND MOBILITY

For a long period of time, quantitative academic research on the link between space and upward mobility centered on the question of whether neighborhoods matter (Sharkey & Faber, 2014). With improved data and methods, there now exists compelling evidence that the environments in which people spend their lives influence and constrain their decision-making, the opportunities available to them, and the hazards and risks that surround them. In building a forward-looking research agenda, the committee argues for a focus on a more complex set of questions that requires new forms of data and evidence.

The committee identified seven areas of research to help fill gaps in the existing research on space and economic and social mobility and to strengthen the connection between research and policy. Those seven areas focus on (a) improved evidence on mechanisms linking space and mobility; (b) evidence on heterogeneity in the relationship between space and mobility; (c) a greater reliance on qualitative methods to inform social policy; (d) rigorous research on the causal impact of various types of investments in places; (e) an expansion of policy discussions that consider the consequences of existing interventions that impact places; (f) consideration of the general equilibrium effects of social policies, as well as the feasibility and costs of different approaches; and (g) an expansion of research to disadvantaged places outside of metropolitan areas that dominate the literature.

First, more convincing evidence is needed on the mechanisms underlying the link between space and upward mobility. Existing research has demonstrated that schooling, public funding, community violence, social capital, and racial and economic segregation are all strongly associated with economic mobility. However, causal evidence on the importance of these and other factors is limited. More evidence is needed to understand the processes by which these factors lead to upward mobility. Identifying the central mechanisms underlying the link between space and mobility is crucial to moving the literature beyond the common focus on the poverty rate or other basic measures of disadvantage in places and instead considering the specific institutions, processes, or phenomena that impede or facilitate economic and social mobility. Such evidence could be qualitative research to identify hypotheses for why it is that violence affects children's school performance or what specifically it is about mentors or local role models that helps promote educational or employment success; or it could be more archival or historical research focusing on how specific programs or policies have changed within places over time in ways that would directly impact economic and social mobility through institutional resources, labor market expansion, school redistricting, etc. A more refined focus on mechanisms is also essential to inform policy responses and to target investments more effectively.

Second, a more complete understanding of heterogeneity in the relationship between space and upward mobility is closely related to the goal of generating better evidence on mechanisms. As an example, early results from quantitative and qualitative analyses of MTO families revealed substantial heterogeneity in every aspect of the experiment, including take-up of the voucher, mental health improvements for mothers (Turney et al., 2013), destinations into which families moved (Rosenblatt & DeLuca, 2012), and the divergent impact on boys versus girls (Clampet-Lundquist et al., 2011; Sampson, 2008). Years later, reanalysis of the data from MTO showed that the characteristics, such as the level of violence, of communities in which families started and ended up made a substantial difference in whether the move led to improved outcomes for children (Burdick-Will et al., 2011). Reanalysis also showed that children who moved at young ages tended to see better outcomes than those who moved at older ages (Chetty et al., 2016). All of these examples are from MTO, but the focus on heterogeneity also needs to consider variation in findings across studies. For instance, while findings based in urban areas have shown that the benefits of MTO may decline as children age (Chetty et al., 2016), suggestive evidence for rural areas indicates that migration when older is still beneficial (Krause & Reeves, 2017). Foregrounding heterogeneity enables an understanding of which groups are most likely to take advantage of and benefit from social policies designed to reduce spatial inequality or increase economic and social mobility (Heckman & Landersø, 2022).

Third, more qualitative research is needed to strengthen the link between evidence and policy. Researchers can use survey and administrative data to powerfully illustrate national patterns in economic mobility with a scope that extends across geographies and generations, and identify factors associated with social mobility. These sources of data can often show where to look but cannot necessarily show how to make sense of what is seen there nor how to apply it to make more efficient policy investments. For this, a research approach is needed that combines these sources of data with rigorous qualitative methods. Social science has historically operated in methodological silos, with quantitative, statistical research on one side and qualitative, ethnographic research on the other. Yet both approaches are necessary to understand social opportunity and design effective policies for promoting upward mobility.

Qualitative research has already been enormously valuable for illuminating the mechanisms by which individuals' environments influence their decision-making about where to live, how to stay safe, and how to get ahead (DeLuca et al., 2019; Edin et al., 2023; Harding, 2010; Harvey et al., 2020; Jones, 2009). Qualitative research also exposes the ways that local institutions become salient in the lives of families (Small, 2004) and the strategies residents deploy as they interact with peers; neighbors; employers;

and representatives of the state, such as case workers, teachers, or police officers.

While it is often difficult to peer inside the black box to understand how a large-scale social experiment such as MTO is experienced by the people targeted by the program, qualitative research can shed light on why a program is or is not working (Clampet-Lundquist et al., 2011; DeLuca & Rosenblatt, 2010; Kling et al., 2005). As an example, qualitative studies of housing programs in Baltimore and Seattle showed the challenges that families face as they attempt to find housing with poor credit and family instability, and revealed how intensive counseling and support gave families expanded choices and a greater chance to successfully transition into new, racially diverse communities with low rates of poverty and more abundant economic opportunities (Bergman et al., 2024; Darrah & DeLuca, 2014; DeLuca et al., 2023). This kind of research can then inform subsequent policy, such as the Seattle Creating Moves to Opportunity housing voucher experiment, which leveraged not only financial resources but also housing "navigators" to support families, resulting in significantly higher rates of opportunity moves for treatment families (Bergman et al., 2024). All of this work has led to substantial investments devoted toward expanded housing mobility programs in eight more sites.

Some of the most important questions that can be explored with qualitative data include the following:

- What are the mechanisms through which violence shapes academic outcomes?
- How do social ties (e.g., churches, local employment-based connections, nonprofit or socially minded community organizations) among Black families help explain recent gains in income mobility?
- Why do some places foster more social capital or economic connectedness than others?
- Why is the evidence inconclusive as to whether schools account for the effects of neighborhoods?

In particular, the committee believes there is great value in funding qualitative research—which was particularly fruitful in MTO—not only on its own, but also to accompany randomized controlled trials and quasi-experimental studies and studies relying on administrative data. The insights generated by qualitative data can also inform the collection of survey data and the hypotheses that are evaluated using survey data.

Fourth, while much of the research discussed is based on programs estimating the impact of residential moves, the literature on the impact of investing in places is much less developed. Comprehensive data on where public and private investment flows is a starting point for establishing the relationship between funding and economic and social mobility. Looking beyond streams of funding, data on community-level social processes, institutions, political power, social networks, and other forms of social capital are crucial to developing a more complete accounting of the explanations for spatial inequality and economic and social mobility. A large literature points to dimensions of community life, such as *collective efficacy*—defined as neighborhood social cohesion and the willingness to act on behalf of the common good—as central to the capacity for residents to provide informal oversight of public spaces and achieve common goals such as the reduction of violence (Sampson et al., 1997), or to the array of institutions in a larger urban area that facilitates civic engagement and upward mobility (Chetty et al., 2022a,b; Putnam, 2000). While this research provides suggestive evidence that social capital is strongly linked with economic and social mobility, data limitations and a lack of convincing causal evidence have not allowed for strong causal claims on how social capital promotes mobility.

More broadly, the vast literature on investments in places—such as comprehensive community development initiatives—has not provided clear, causal evidence on the most effective ways to invest in communities or entire cities and regions, or how policymakers can or even whether they should intervene in places to improve economic and social mobility.

Fifth, while policy discussions on reducing spatial inequality typically focus on two approaches—moving people out of or investing in disadvantaged places—the committee argues for an expansion of this debate to include approaches to end or scale back existing interventions that amplify spatial inequality, as described above. For example, federal housing policies such as the mortgage interest deduction incentivize families to take on more debt to purchase more expensive homes in more exclusive areas; state occupational licensing requirements generate a constraint on geographic mobility that makes it more difficult for households to make moves across state lines in order to take advantage of economic opportunities; and land use policies implemented by local towns and cities can limit the development of affordable housing, creating extreme inequality across the localities within a given metropolitan area (and additional inequality in access to amenities such as high-performing schools and safety). In addition to developing and advocating for new interventions, it is important to draw attention to the ways that these and other existing policies exacerbate spatial inequality in ways that are often taken for granted.

Sixth, moving from theory and research into policy expands the type of knowledge needed. This is particularly true when considering the relative value of people- versus placed-based investments. As an example, improving educational opportunities for young people in highly disadvantaged areas may improve long-term prospects for economic mobility, and yet it also may raise the probability that they leave their communities for sections of the country offering greater economic opportunity.

The more general challenge of understanding the equilibrium effects of social policy is often neglected (Galster, 2012). Voucher programs designed to give children the chance to attend a high-quality school or to give families the chance to move to a community with lower poverty may, in fact, benefit those who receive the voucher—but if such efforts are scaled up, they may alter system-level dynamics in the sending and receiving schools or neighborhoods. Failing to consider the equilibrium impacts of social policy (i.e., the full range of effects on all potentially affected domains of society, including program participants and nonparticipants and focal and nonfocal communities) can lead to unanticipated challenges.

Additional research is needed to go beyond the consideration of what types of policies affect economic and social mobility to consider the system-level impacts of social policy as well as the magnitude, feasibility, and costs of different policy approaches. To move toward this goal, the committee argues for greater investment in research tools such as agent-based models designed to model the general equilibrium consequences of social policy.

Seventh, greater focus is needed on areas that have received relatively little attention in the literature on neighborhood effects and upward mobility, including "deeply disadvantaged" rural areas (Islam et al., 2015) and rural-adjacent small towns and suburbs. Examples include wide swaths of the Southern states that have extremely low rates of economic mobility, rural communities of the South and Appalachian regions, and Native American tribal lands that have been disconnected from sustained public investment and economic growth (Edin et al., 2023). Because much of the literature on neighborhood effects has focused on concentrated poverty in central cities, the study of space and economic and social mobility is heavily biased toward urban poverty. The most severe areas of disadvantage in the United States are not found in central cities, however, and the same attention and policy focus must expand beyond the nation's urban areas. Similarly, the literature often misses rural-adjacent suburban towns and smaller cities.

SUMMARY, KEY CONCLUSIONS, AND RECOMMENDATIONS

While much of the early quantitative research on the impact of residential environments struggled to overcome the methodological challenges associated with nonrandom selection into neighborhoods and cities, recent evidence has led to something close to a consensus in support of the claim that residential environments can have a causal impact on economic and social mobility and intermediate outcomes related to mobility—most notably academic achievement, cognitive skill development, and physical and mental health. Increasing access to geocoded data, improved tools for spatial analysis, and the growth of convincing quasi-experimental and experimental research designs has undergirded this view. The findings also suggest that there is considerable heterogeneity in the effects of space and place. The impact of the residential environment on individual life trajectories is a product of conditions in the immediate neighborhood and the larger area and region of the country, the timing and duration of individuals' exposure to these environments outside the home, and individuals' characteristics and unique vulnerability to the effects of the residential context. This perspective on the link between place and individual outcomes moves beyond the question of whether neighborhoods matter and toward the questions of when, where, why, and for whom residential contexts matter.

Conclusion 3-1: Recent evidence suggests that residential environments have a causal impact on economic and social mobility (measured by income, earnings, or occupation) and on intermediate outcomes related to mobility, such as cognitive development and educational attainment. The link between place and individual outcomes has now moved beyond the question of whether neighborhoods matter and toward questions of when, where, why, and for whom residential contexts matter.

While scholarship on the effects of place has grown considerably over time, less attention has been paid to the mechanisms that undergird these effects and the heterogeneity of these effects—vital considerations for using research to improve policy and understanding the potential scalability of existing interventions. Evidence at the neighborhood level points to schools, community violence, environmental exposures, and local social networks as examples of mechanisms linking the local residential environment with economic and social mobility. Evidence at larger levels of analysis—such as cities, counties, and commuting zones—points to segregation and local labor market conditions as examples of forces that influence economic and social mobility.

Research on *school quality* shows that attending schools in low-poverty areas leads to better academic outcomes for students from low-income backgrounds, with peer socioeconomic diversity potentially being more important than school funding. While the effects of exposure to phenomena such as *community violence* are difficult to identify, available causal evidence indicates significant negative effects vis-à-vis indirect outcomes such as cognitive functioning and academic performance. Evidence points to long-term positive impacts on income mobility in communities where violence decreased. *Connections to peers, friends, and neighbors* are hypothesized to influence local culture, norms, and resources, and thus economic mobility—although most evidence is correlational. Researchers have only recently employed quasi-experimental designs, concluding that economic mobility is positively influenced by low-income populations' "exposure to" and friendships with high-income people in their communities. Similarly, parental employment rates in the neighborhood are an important determinant of upward mobility, especially among Black boys from low-income backgrounds.

At larger levels of analysis, such as cities, counties, and commuting zones, available evidence highlights segregation and local economic and labor market conditions as key determinants of economic and social mobility. Research on variation in mobility across commuting zones specifically highlights negative associations with greater economic inequality and racial *segregation*. Work leveraging historical processes related to segregation provides causal evidence on long-term mobility impacts as well. Studies examining redlining and other segregationist spatial policies document lasting negative effects on intergenerational mobility in the most affected neighborhoods. While research exploiting shocks to *local labor market conditions* and their mobility consequences is limited, negative shocks such as localized job losses are associated with worse academic performance among children, while positive changes, such as casino openings in disadvantaged areas, show positive effects on education, income, and employment.

Conclusion 3-2: At the neighborhood level, the mechanisms linking the local residential environment with economic and social mobility include schools, community violence, and local social networks. At larger levels of analysis—such as cities, counties, and commuting zones—the forces that influence economic and social mobility include segregation and local labor market conditions.

This large and growing body of evidence on the importance of different geographic areas for economic and social mobility is consistent with research asking how to best employ spatial policy in a way that benefits the most households and facilitates upward intergenerational mobility. Broadly speaking, most spatial policy strategies are either housing mobility policies, which help relocate disadvantaged families to higher-opportunity areas, or place-conscious investments, which aim to bring opportunity and investment into disadvantaged communities. Housing mobility programs—such as the Gautreaux desegregation program and the MTO experiment—have shown positive impacts on academic outcomes, employment, and earnings, particularly for children moving to low-poverty neighborhoods. Place-conscious investment initiatives—such as the New Hope, Harlem Children's Zone, and Jobs Plus programs—that target residents of disadvantaged communities with employment opportunities, training, and support services and/or provide resources to foster job creation and economic development have also shown success in improving employment, earnings, and academic outcomes for participants. However, the impacts of place-based programs that have not targeted people in disadvantaged communities and provided a range of supports have been mixed.

A third approach emphasizes the importance of ending existing programs and policies that have historically amplified spatial and racial inequality and continue to do so. Zoning, discriminatory housing practices, and some regressive federal housing programs (e.g., mortgage interest deduction, property tax deduction, exclusion of capital gains on the sales of homes) reinforce residential segregation and constrain residential mobility. While federal homeowner policies exist that assist low-income families (e.g., affordable mortgage programs and credit programs), many homeownership policies disproportionately benefit the most affluent communities and households, further entrenching economic segregation and the concentration of economic mobility-relevant resources in higher-income areas.

Conclusion 3-3: Most spatial policy strategies are either housing mobility policies, which relocate families to higher-opportunity areas, or place-conscious investments, which aim to bring opportunity and investment into disadvantaged communities. Although both have the potential to boost economic and social mobility, evidence on the effectiveness of place-based programs that do not target people in disadvantaged communities and do not provide a range of supports is mixed.

Conclusion 3-4: In addition to new housing mobility initiatives and place-based investments, it is important to consider approaches that focus on ending existing programs and policies that have historically amplified spatial and racial inequality and continue to do so.

For a long period of time, quantitative academic research on the link between space and mobility centered on the question of whether neighborhoods matter. With improved data and methods, there now exists compelling evidence that the environments in which individuals spend their lives influence and constrain their decision-making, the opportunities available to them, and the hazards and risks that surround them. The committee identified seven areas of research to help fill gaps in the existing research on space and economic and social mobility and strengthen the connection between research and policy.

First, more convincing evidence is needed on the central mechanisms underlying the link between place and economic and social mobility. This is crucial to moving the literature beyond the common focus on the poverty rate or other basic measures of disadvantage in places and instead considering the specific institutions, processes, or phenomena that impede or facilitate upward mobility.

Second, moving toward a more complete understanding of heterogeneity in the relationship between space and mobility is closely related to the goal of generating better evidence on mechanisms. By foregrounding heterogeneity, one is in a better position to understand which groups are most likely to take advantage of and benefit from social policies designed to reduce spatial inequality or increase economic and social mobility.

Third, there needs to be a larger role for qualitative research in strengthening the link between evidence and policy. Qualitative research can help illuminate the mechanisms by which individuals' environments influence their decision-making about where to live, how to stay safe, and how to get ahead and the ways that local institutions become salient in the lives of families, as well as the strategies residents deploy as they interact with peers; neighbors; employers; and representatives of the state, such as case workers, teachers, or police officers.

Fourth, while much of the research discussed by the committee is based on programs estimating the impact of residential moves, the literature on the impact of investing in places is much less developed and has not provided clear, causal evidence on the most effective ways to invest in communities or entire cities and regions. This is another area where qualitative research can make a valuable contribution.

Fifth, policy discussions focused on how to reduce spatial inequality typically focus on two approaches: moving people out versus investing in places. However, this discussion should be expanded to include existing policies (e.g., federal housing policies, local land use policies) that exacerbate spatial inequality.

Sixth, consideration should be given to the general equilibrium effects of social policies, as well as the feasibility and costs of different approaches. For example, improving educational opportunities for young people in highly disadvantaged areas may lead to improvements in long-term prospects for economic mobility, and yet it also may raise the probability that they leave their communities for sections of the country offering greater economic opportunity.

Seventh, there needs to be a greater focus on regions and areas that have received relatively little attention in the literature on neighborhood effects and upward mobility, including deeply disadvantaged rural areas, rural-adjacent small towns, and suburbs. Although much of the literature on neighborhood effects has focused on concentrated poverty in central cities, the most severe areas of disadvantage in the United States are not found in central cities.

Recommendation 3-1: Researchers should strengthen the evidence base on space and place in the following areas: (1) causal impacts of the key mechanisms that link place with economic and social mobility; (2) heterogeneity in the relationship between place and economic and social mobility; (3) qualitative approaches to understanding the mechanisms that undergird the causal effects of place, as well as the mechanisms that explain evidence on effective policy; (4) causal impacts of various types of place-based investments; (5) existing policies and interventions that amplify spatial inequality; (6) general equilibrium effects of social policies and the feasibility and costs of different approaches; and (7) neighborhood contexts of disadvantaged rural, small town, and suburban areas.

4

Postsecondary Education

Postsecondary education, and in particular the attainment of a 4-year bachelor's degree, is a key predictor of individual economic well-being. A college degree carries a large premium in terms of wage, earnings, and income, and this premium grows over a lifetime (Autor et al., 2008; Katz & Autor, 1999). A college degree is increasingly important given the growing proportion of jobs characterized by "knowledge" work, which usually require a bachelor's degree (Autor, 2019; Goldin & Katz, 2008; Kalleberg, 2011) and, increasingly, an advanced degree (Posselt & Grodsky, 2017).[1]

Attainment of a bachelor's degree is also associated with noneconomic outcomes such as health, longevity, marriage, parenting, crime, and political participation (Case & Deaton, 2020; Cutler & Lleras-Muney, 2008; Lochner, 2011; Oreopoulos & Salvanes, 2011). Furthermore, the marked propensity of highly educated people to marry each other means that the college premium is increasingly concentrated among high-income, dual-earner households, where both partners have degrees (Hirschl et al., 2022; C. R. Schwartz, 2010).

Postsecondary educational attainment—and, especially, the attainment of a 4-year bachelor's degree—is also central to the understanding of economic and social mobility in the United States (National Academies of Sciences, Engineering, and Medicine [National Academies], 2023b) because education plays a critical role in the intergenerational transmission of economic well-being. On one hand, education is an avenue for intergenerational

---

[1] Autor (2014, Figure 6A) shows that the growth in the "college premium" is largely driven by people with an advanced degree.

persistence, if advantaged families are able to afford more and better education for their children. In other words, educational attainment is a key mediator between parents' and adult children's socioeconomic resources. On the other hand, postsecondary education can be a vehicle for mobility—both absolute and relative—if attaining a degree detaches individuals from their social origins and provides a pathway for upward mobility. A college degree is particularly central not only because of the high economic returns attached to the credential but also because research suggests that the opportunity of economic success (or failure) does not depend from parental resources among bachelor's degree holders, in contrast to those with lower levels of attainment (Bloome et al., 2018; Chetty et al., 2017; Hout, 1988; Pfeffer & Hertel, 2015; Torche, 2011, 2018).[2]

Postsecondary education policy can affect the cost of postsecondary education as well as its potential benefits. For example, financial aid and tuition policies affect the cost of college and how it differs across socioeconomic groups. Need-based grants and free tuition policies can increase postsecondary opportunities among low-income families (for a review of this large literature, see Dynarski et al., 2023a). And public (dis)investments in colleges can affect the benefits of a college education; for example, differences in instructional spending across colleges and college sectors have been linked to wide differences in graduation rates and economic benefits of postsecondary attainment (Lovenheim & Smith, 2023).

Yet, as this chapter discusses, many students who enroll in a 4-year program will not finish. Thus, other postsecondary pathways through which individuals may increase their earnings and career prospects must also be considered. These may include career and technical education, community college degrees and certificates, and job training programs. While research showing that a bachelor's degree confers more economic benefits than other postsecondary education and training is relatively clear, the evidence on the returns to other sub-baccalaureate education is significantly more mixed. Although there are some returns to students who enroll in associate's degree and certificate programs—especially in the applied health fields—such benefits have to be considered alongside the evidence that these programs may also divert students away from more lucrative 4-year degrees (see Lovenheim & Smith, 2023, for a review).

This chapter discusses trends in postsecondary attainment since the early 20th century and disparities based on family income, race and ethnicity, and gender. It then moves to the institutional organization of the postsecondary educational system and its funding structure and supply-side factors related to the quality of educational institutions. Finally, the

---

[2] This sentence was added after release of the report, correcting for its erroneous deletion during the editing process.

chapter covers alterative pathways to accumulating human capital and transitioning to the labor market. All these topics are central in the role that postsecondary education plays in the mobility process because they shape the two components of the mediating role of education in the process of mobility—namely, the association between parents' resources and their children's educational attainment, and the socioeconomic returns of educational attainment for adult children.

The committee's focus on postsecondary education should not be taken as an indication that prekindergarten (preK), elementary, and secondary education (i.e., preK–12) is unimportant for economic and social mobility. In fact, this is a critical building block period of cognitive and socioemotional development that is essential for future academic and labor market success, both through and independent of postsecondary education. It is also one of the most well-studied periods when it comes to understanding how education shapes mobility; also well studied are interventions intended to identify core investments that improve and equalize mobility-relevant outcomes. Box 4-1 describes what is known about earlier periods of education from prekindergarten to high school, drawing from the recent National Academies report *Reducing Intergenerational Poverty* (2023b). Postsecondary education, in contrast, has received significantly less attention from research and policy, and it is therefore the focus of the report.

POSTSECONDARY ATTAINMENT IN THE UNITED STATES: TRENDS AND DISPARITIES IN ACCESS AND RETURNS

Given the large economic payoff of a bachelor's degree, graduating from college could offer a pathway for mobility to young people from low-income households or racial minorities. Conversely, if the chance to enroll in and graduate from college is strongly determined by family income, then postsecondary education will serve as a vehicle for the intergenerational persistence of inequality.

The economic payoff of a college degree is greater in the United States than in any other rich democracy (Autor, 2014). The earnings gap between people with a bachelor's degree and those with lower levels of schooling grew sharply starting in the late 1970s, driven by a growing demand for highly educated workers that was not met by comparable supply (Goldin & Katz, 2008). Since the early 1980s, the economic payoff to advanced degrees—including master's, professional, and doctoral degrees—has increased even faster than that of terminal bachelor's degrees (Autor, 2014). Even if wages of low-skill workers appear to have recovered some lost ground in the last decade (Aeppli & Wilmers, 2022), the college and advanced degree earnings premium remains substantial.

> **BOX 4-1**
> **PreK–12 Education and Economic and Social Mobility**
>
> *Reducing Intergenerational Poverty* (National Academies, 2023b) reviewed evidence on interventions targeting the elementary and secondary stages of schooling. It emphasized the importance of **educational quality**, drawing attention to the challenges faced by schools in poor and racially/ethnically segregated communities. Aside from non-schooling-related barriers to education and learning in these communities (e.g., unstable housing, violence), these schools often have worse facilities, underqualified teachers, overcrowded classrooms, and insufficient textbooks and materials. Consequently, reforms that **increase school funding**—particularly in low-income areas—have positive impacts on educational outcomes, although their long-term effects in adulthood remain unclear. The report cautioned that such funding reforms are no panacea, as **persistent school segregation** remains a cause of income and racial/ethnic disparities in student success. The report also highlighted the effectiveness of **efforts to intervene on educational quality directly**, including reducing class sizes, recruiting STEM (science, technology, engineering, and mathematics)–trained teachers, and using personalized tutoring. Charter schools, particularly "no excuses" schools using a stricter educational model, have shown promise in improving outcomes such as test scores and 4-year college enrollment for the low-income urban students they predominantly serve. The importance of the **"match" between students and teachers** is a promising area as well, with recent research indicating higher rates of high school completion and college enrollment among Black boys who have Black teachers or enroll in ethnic studies–centered curricula, possibly because of higher educational expectations and less harsh disciplining. Finally, Reducing Intergenerational Poverty underscored the importance of **well-implemented career and technical education programs** that provide an alternative path to better jobs for some students—especially those who return to schooling after starting full-time work.

Figure 4-1 shows trends in educational earnings gaps across levels of schooling from 1963 to 2017 in the United States. In these plots, the vertical axis measures the cumulative change in earnings since 1963. For example, the graph on the left shows that in 1999 male high school dropouts were earning about the same as their counterparts in 1963; by contrast, males with graduate degrees were earning about 55 percent more in 1999 than their counterparts in 1963. The real earnings of workers with a terminal bachelor's degree have grown by approximately 40 percent for men and more than 50 percent for women during this period. The increase in real earnings reaches 70 percent for those with an advanced degree. In contrast, real earnings have grown little for workers with low levels of schooling and particularly for men with a high school diploma or less. Since the 2010s, workers with the lowest levels of schooling have benefited from some increase in real earnings. Still, low-education workers, particularly men, have

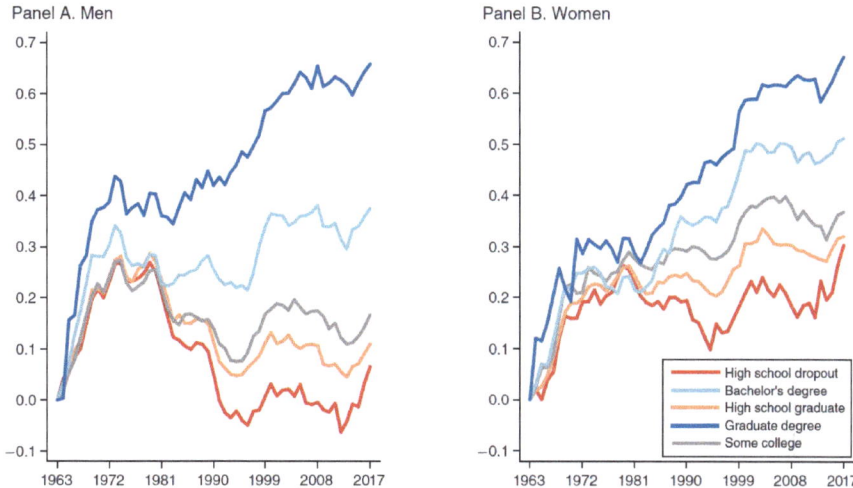

FIGURE 4-1 Cumulative change in real weekly wage of adults aged 16–64, United States, 1963–2017.
NOTES: Figure uses March Current Population Survey Annual Social and Economic Supplement data for earnings years 1963 to 2017. Series correspond to (composition-adjusted) mean log wage for each group, using data on full-time, full-year workers aged 16–64. The data are sorted into sex-education-experience groups of two sexes, five education categories (high school dropout, high school graduate, some college, college graduate, and postcollege degree), and four potential experience categories (0–9, 10–19, 20–29, and 30–39 years). Educational categories are harmonized following the procedures in Autor et al. (2008). Log weekly wages of full-time, full-year workers are regressed in each year separately by sex on dummy variables for four education categories, a quartic in experience, three region dummies, Black and other race dummies, and interactions of the experience quartic with three broad education categories (high school graduate, some college, and college plus). The (composition-adjusted) mean log wage for each of the 40 groups in a given year is the predicted log wage from these regressions evaluated for White individuals, living in the mean geographic region, at the relevant experience level (5, 15, 25, or 35 years depending on the experience group). Mean log wages for broader groups in each year represent weighted averages of the relevant (composition-adjusted) cell means using a fixed set of weights, equal to the mean share of total hours worked by each group between 1963 and 2005. All earnings numbers are deflated by the chain-weighted (implicit) price deflator for personal consumption expenditures. Earnings of less than $67 per week in 1982 dollars ($112/week in 2000 dollars) are dropped. Allocated earnings observations are excluded in earnings years 1967 and on, using either family earnings allocation flags (1967–1974) or individual earnings allocation flags (1975 earnings year and on). Earnings are in 2022 constant dollars and include wage and salary workers who are employed full time, 25 years and over, excluding incorporated self-employed weekly usual earnings multiplied by 52 to obtain annual estimate.
SOURCE: Autor (2019). Copyright American Economic Association; reproduced with permission of the AEA Papers and Proceedings.

lost substantial economic ground over the last six decades. The earnings of workers with some postsecondary education (including an associate's degree) have grown somewhat more than those with a high school diploma but far less than those of workers with a bachelor's degree or more. Educational disparities in earnings have been less pronounced for women than men. Yet women with a high school diploma have experienced no earnings gains between the 1970s and 2017.

Wide earnings gaps by education are directly relevant for intergenerational mobility because there are enormous disparities in degree attainment in the United States by income, race, and other measures of socioeconomic status. It is important to understand that these differences in degree attainment arise not just from postsecondary policies, programs, and institutions but from individual exposure to unequal resources, opportunities, and investments, from birth through adolescence.

Quantitative data and qualitative research reveal some of the mechanisms through which family background shapes postsecondary access and success, perpetuating educational inequality. For example, numerous qualitative studies have found that students from more affluent backgrounds with more educated parents have, even from a young age, much better preparation for college because they know the "hidden rules of the game," and take honors and advanced placement courses in high school, supplement their coursework with SAT preparation tutoring, and approach teachers for recommendation letters and help (Calarco, 2018; Hamilton et al., 2018; Lareau, 2011; Persell & Cookson, 1985). These same students are also more equipped when applying to colleges and attending them—they understand which colleges are selective, which majors are most lucrative, and how to get the most out of their college experiences through relationships with faculty and advisors (Binder et al., 2016; Hamilton, 2016; Stuber, 2011). Intensive mentoring programs have been shown to increase postsecondary attainment for low-income high school students; an example is Carrell and Sacerdote (2017). Dynarski et al. (2023b) review the broader evidence on this type of intervention.

Many nontraditional students—and even their parents—are less likely to ask for help or leverage institutional settings to their advantage (Hamilton et al., 2018; Jack, 2016, 2019; Lehmann, 2014). Lower-income students at broad-access institutions such as community colleges are very likely to drop out without a degree. Qualitative research suggests they have difficulty covering the cost of basic needs such as food, housing, and transportation while attending college (Hart, 2019; see also Goldrick-Rab et al., 2018). Evidence further suggests that administrative burdens and academic barriers also play a role (Deil-Amen & Rosenbaum, 2002, 2003).

Postsecondary attainment rose steadily over the 20th century (Goldin & Katz, 2008). Among cohorts born around the turn of the 20th century, a majority of young people had at least some postsecondary experience (Figure 4-2). By contrast, the share of the young people graduating from college—that is, those who attained a bachelor's degree—has grown much more slowly and fitfully.

Based on the most current data available, about two-thirds of young people born in the late 1990s have attained some postsecondary education. However, only about half of those college entrants have completed a bachelor's degree and only about a sixth also hold a graduate degree (a master's, Ph.D., or professional degree). Substantial differences between men and women have emerged since the 1970s birth cohort, when the gender gap in postsecondary attainment favoring men reversed and women started to surpass men. Among the youngest cohorts born in the late 1990s, about a quarter of men but almost a third of women have attained a bachelor's degree by age 25.

The growing female advantage in college attainment is poorly understood. Factors that have been explored include girls' superior overall academic performance and motivation, and the narrowing of the gender gap favoring men in math and science scores. Researchers also point to growing educational and professional expectations among women, a rising age of marriage, and faster growth in the economic returns from college for women than men (Buchmann & DiPrete, 2006; DiPrete & Buchmann, 2006, 2013; Goldin et al., 2006; Lundberg, 2020). Buchmann and Di Prete (2006) show that the growing educational advantage of women is larger among low-income, single-parent families (see also Autor et al., 2019).

Researchers are beginning to examine the consequences of the reversal of the educational gender gap for the next generation of children. Recent research highlights that highly educated women are increasingly likely to marry men with lower levels of education (rather than remain single), and their marriages are increasingly stable compared with the past (Van Bavel et al., 2018). Women's growing educational advantage will likely have broader consequences for intergenerational processes involving fertility, children's and educational opportunities, and growing gaps between families in which both parents have high or low levels of schooling. Interestingly, a recent study from Sweden suggests that growing gender equality in the labor market reduces intergenerational mobility by increasing intergenerational persistence in women's earnings and the household income of both men and women (Engzell & Mood, 2023). While no similar studies have been conducted in the United States, the educational and economic gains experienced by women might result in a similar outcome. This finding shows that gender-specific mobility is a complex phenomenon, and in this case, declining mobility can be the result of something that many would see as desirable.

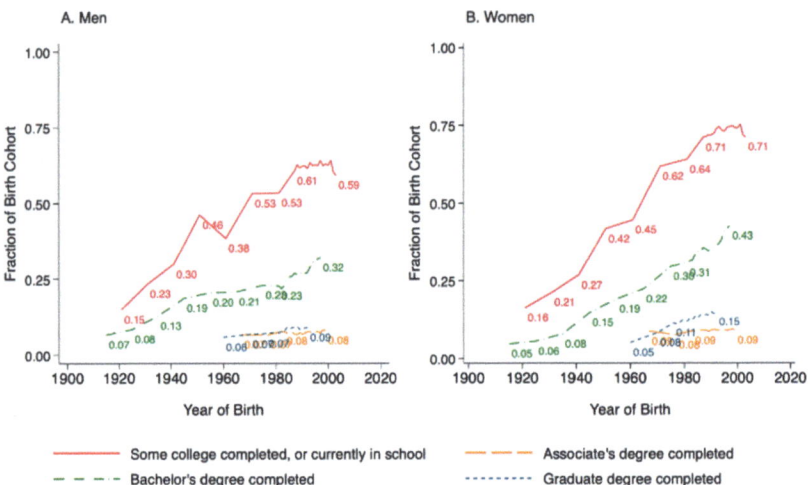

FIGURE 4-2 Trends in postsecondary educational attainment in the United States; cohorts born 1915–2001.

NOTES: Variables measuring educational attainment are operationalized somewhat differently across years because of changes in the U.S. Census and American Community Survey (ACS) questionnaire. *Some college completed* is defined as a person having attended at least some college at age 19. For 1940–1950 samples, the committee used a person's highest grade of school attended (*higraded*) and whether they were in school (*school*). A person is coded as having attended some college if their highest grade was greater than or equal to "didn't finish 1st year of college," or their highest grade was equal to 12th grade and they were in school at the time of the interview. For 1960–1980 samples, we used a person's highest grade of school attended (*higraded*) and their current grade (*gradeatt*). A person is coded as having some college if their highest grade was greater than or equal to "didn't finish 1st year of college" or if they were "attending college" at the time of interview. For 1990–2022 samples, we used a person's educational attainment (*educd*), whether they are currently in school (*school*), and their current grade (*gradeattd*). A person is coded as having attended some college if their educational attainment was greater than or equal to some college (including less than 1 year), if their educational attainment was at least 12th grade and they were in school at the time of the interview, or if their recent grade level was at least "college undergraduate."

Associate's degree completed is defined as having an associate's degree, but no higher degree, at age 23. For 1990–2022, we use a person's educational attainment (*educd*). A person is coded as having an associate's degree if they have completed an associate's degree (which may be occupational or academic). A person is coded as *not* having an associate's degree if they have any other higher or lower level of educational attainment. This information is not available prior to 1990. *Bachelor's degree completed* is defined as a person having a college degree (i.e., a bachelor's degree) at age 25. For 1940–1980, we used a person's highest grade (*higraded*). A person is coded as having a college degree if their highest grade is greater than or

FIGURE 4-2 Continued

equal to their fourth year of college. For 1990–2022, we use a person's educational attainment (*educd*). A person is coded as having a college degree if they have completed a bachelor's degree or more. *Graduate degree completed* is defined as a person having a graduate or professional degree at age 30. This is only measured as part of their educational attainment in 1990–2022 (*educd*), as 1940–1980 questions about graduate-level educational attainment were substantively distinct. A person is coded as having a graduate degree if their educational attainment was a master's, professional, or doctoral degree. Estimates of the proportion of each birth cohort with some college, college, or graduate degrees use Census weights. Person weights were used for all years except 1950, in which we used sample-line weights.
SOURCES: U.S. Census and ACS samples downloaded from IPUMS USA. U.S. Census samples include 1940–1970 (1%) and 1980–2000 (5%). ACS samples include 2006–2022 (1-year samples). ACS samples 2001–2005 are excluded because they did not include persons living in group quarters.

The overall trends presented mask substantial inequality in college enrollment and college completion by family income. Figure 4-3a shows the probabilities of entering college by household income quartile among people born between 1961 and 1964 (dotted line) and among those born between 1979 and 1982 (solid line). Figure 4-3b shows the same probabilities for college graduation.

The figures reveal two clear patterns. First, the probability of attending and graduating from college strongly depends on household income. Second, the income gap has widened across cohorts. The college graduation rate was 5 percent for youth from the poorest households in the older cohort (born in the early 1960s) and rose to 9 percent for the younger cohort (born around 1980)—an increase of 4 percentage points. In contrast, the highest-income group experienced an increase of 18 percentage points (from 36% to 54%) in college graduation across cohorts. As a result, the income gap in college graduation grew from 4 to 18 percentage points.

A body of literature has examined the relationship between family income and educational attainment, and some have examined changes over time (Belley & Lochner, 2007; Duncan et al., 2017; Jackson & Holzman, 2020). These studies typically rely on small samples, combine different data sources, consider specific historical periods, or lack information about degree attainment. In fact, it is impossible, with the data sources currently available in the United States, to evaluate changes in the association between parents' income and bachelor's degree attainment over time—a critical factor of intergenerational mobility. Box 4-2 discusses this issue and outlines avenues for addressing it.

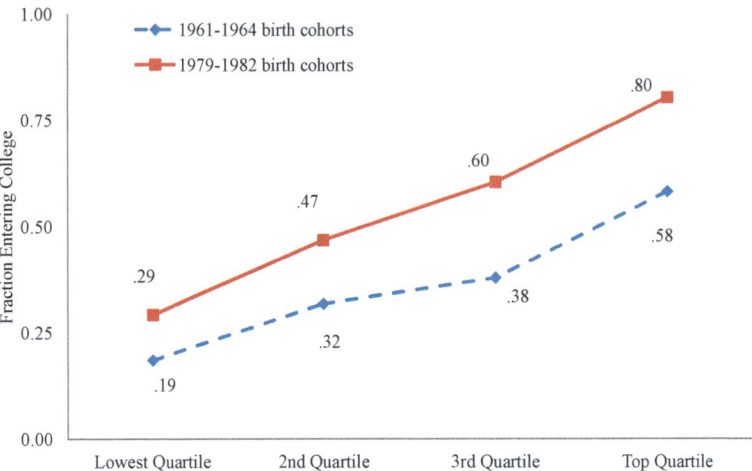

FIGURE 4-3a Proportion of students entering college by household income quartile and birth year.

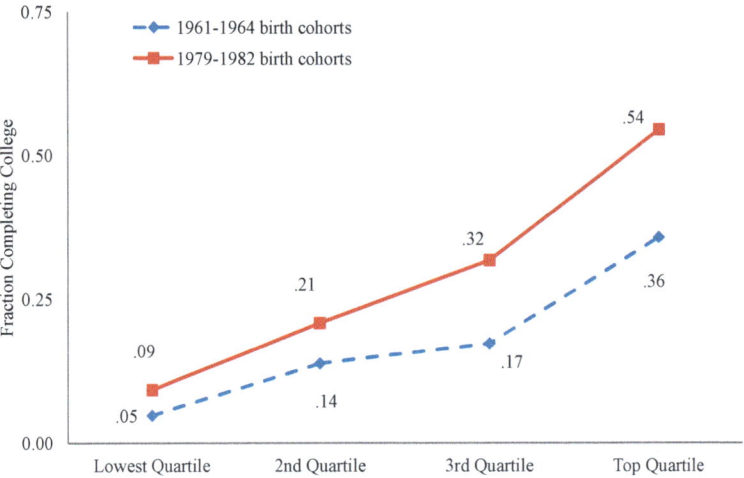

FIGURE 4-3b Proportion of students graduating from college by household income quartile and birth year.
NOTES: Household income measured at the time of each baseline survey, when cohort members were 15–18 years old. pp = percentage points.
SOURCE: Bailey and Dynarski (2011), based on the National Longitudinal Survey of Youth 1979 and 1997, U.S. Bureau of Labor Statistics. © 2011 by Martha J. Bailey and Susan M. Dynarski. All rights reserved.

BOX 4-2
Linking Administrative and Survey Data to Track Educational Mobility in the United States

Understanding whether postsecondary education is an engine for intergenerational mobility or a replicator of inequality requires information linking parental income with children's postsecondary attainment. Currently available data, however, are limited. For instance, while the National Longitudinal Survey of Youth provides data that allow for high-quality estimates, it is limited to cohorts that are nearly two decades apart (1979 and 1997 cohort). The Panel Study of Income Dynamics includes more cohorts, allowing for estimates of year-by-year changes, but these estimates are noisy, given small sample sizes. The Current Population Survey annual data cannot be used because samples are restricted to coresidential parents and children, creating a selected sample, given that many children leave the parental home to attend postsecondary education. Data from tax records, such as used by Chetty et al. (2014b), can link parental income with college attendance based on the presence of a 1098-T (tuition statement) filed by a college on behalf of the student to the Internal Revenue Service (IRS), but does not provide information on college graduation.

One strategy for addressing these data limitations is to use administrative data to supplement currently available surveys, as suggested by Dynarski (2014). Several sources of administrative data would allow for a robust examination of the link between parental income and degree attainment and its change over time. For instance, because of various federal policies that require reporting of student-level data, states track all students from kindergarten through at least high school. Data from administrative sources cover the entire population of elementary and secondary students in public schools. Data from the National Student Clearinghouse cover as many as 93 percent of students at colleges nationwide. These administrative sources can be linked to survey data on a broader range of variables collected by the National Center for Education Statistics, as well as to administrative data from sources such as the IRS, which contain detailed information on household characteristics, including income. This strategy would conserve resources that could be used to collect survey data that are not available through administrative sources. Because these data sources are available annually, they would support continuous evaluation of the parental income–college attainment link. (The strategy of a national database of student records is also supported by Conclusion 6-3 in Chapter 6.)

SOURCE: Based on Dynarski, 2014.

Gaps in college attendance, and especially college graduation, by race and ethnicity are also pronounced. Figure 4-4 shows trends in college attainment across ethnoracial groups among young people aged 25–29 from 1972 to 2022. About two-thirds of Asian young adults and about 45 percent of White young adults have attained a bachelor's degree in 2022. In contrast, only 28 percent of Black young adults and 25 percent of Hispanic young adults have earned a degree. While all ethnoracial groups have made progress in bachelor's degree attainment since the 1970s, the gaps based on race and ethnicity have persisted. Furthermore, disparities in access to selective colleges are more pronounced and have increased over time. Black and Hispanic youth have become increasingly less likely than their White peers to attend selective 4-year colleges (Oh et al., 2024). A recent study shows striking racial differences in the association between parents' and children's educational attainment (i.e., educational mobility). While the Black–White gap in upward educational mobility has closed substantially, Black people continue to be much more likely than White people to experience downward mobility from the top of the educational distribution (Karlson, 2023). This suggests that the socioeconomic status achieved by the Black population in the United States continues to be much more precarious than that of the White population.

A clear conclusion from Figures 4-3 and 4-4 is that the college dropout rate is much higher among low-income and minority populations, precluding a critical avenue for upward mobility. The wide socioeconomic gaps in college completion matter because, as shown in Figure 4-1, the attainment of a bachelor's degree, and not just college attendance, is a dividing line in the U.S. income distribution. Those with some college education, or with a sub-baccalaureate credential (associate's degree or a certificate) have earnings closer to high school graduates' than to those with a bachelor's degree (Autor, 2019). Many interventions supporting 4-year college enrollment and graduation among disadvantaged and minority populations have been tested (Avery et al., 2019; Dawson et al., 2020; Dynarski et al., 2023a,b; Holzer & Baum, 2017; Ibsen & Rosholm, 2024; Scrivener et al., 2015). Given the multiple reasons why young people drop out of college or enroll in less lucrative postsecondary programs—including financial barriers, information, familiarity with the college experience, and academic preparation—no single intervention is likely to be sufficient or to serve all low-income or minority youth.

A key question for mobility researchers is which combination of interventions might most effectively support college persistence and graduation among disadvantaged populations. In order to better understand which interventions might work, one needs to understand not only how one's family background matters for college success, but also how postsecondary decisions are made. Qualitative research is illuminating on this point, and

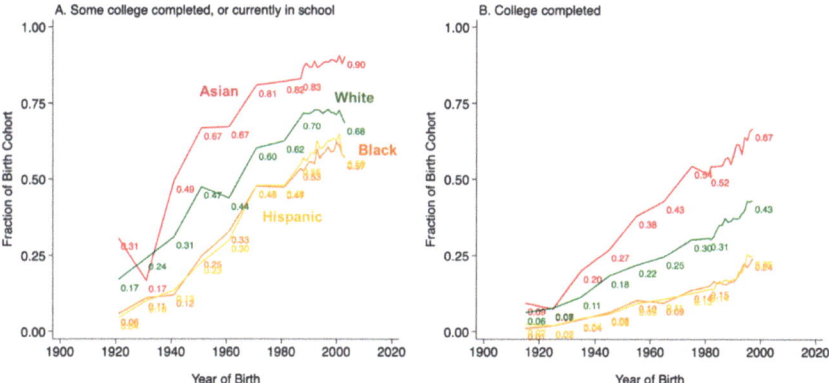

FIGURE 4-4 Percentage of 25- to 29-year-olds, by ethnoracial category, with some college completed or a bachelor's degree, 1972–2022.

NOTES: Variables measuring educational attainment are operationalized somewhat differently across years because of changes in the U.S. Census and American Community Survey (ACS) questionnaire. *Some college* is defined as a person having attended at least some college at age 19. Samples from 1940–1950 used a person's highest grade of school attended (*higraded*) and whether they were in school (*school*). A person is coded as having attended some college if their highest grade was greater than or equal to "didn't finish 1st year of college," or their highest grade was equal to 12th grade and they were in school at the time of the interview. Samples from 1960–1980 used a person's highest grade of school attended (*higraded*) and their current grade (*gradeatt*). A person is coded as having some college if their highest grade was greater than or equal to "didn't finish 1st year of college" or if they were "attending college" at the time of interview. Samples from 1990–2022 used a person's educational attainment (*educd*), whether they are currently in school (*school*), and their current grade (*gradeattd*). A person is coded as having attended some college if their educational attainment was greater than or equal to some college (including less than 1 year), if their educational attainment was at least 12th grade and they were in school at the time of the interview, or if their recent grade level was at least "college undergraduate." *College* is defined as a person having a college degree (i.e., a bachelor's degree) at age 25. For 1940–1980, the committee used a person's highest grade (*higraded*). A person is coded as having a college degree if their highest grade is greater than or equal to their 4th year of college. Samples from 1990–2022 use a person's educational attainment (*educd*). A person is coded as having a college degree if they have completed a bachelor's degree or more. Estimates of the proportion of each racial group and birth cohort with some college and college were generated using Census weights. Person weights were used for all years except 1950, in which we used sample-line weights. Four racial groups are shown, created based on IPUMS simplified race and Hispanic ethnicity variables (*race* and *hispan*). *Asian* includes persons whose race is categorized as Chinese, Japanese, or Other Asian or Pacific Islander and not categorized as Hispanic. *Black* includes persons whose race is categorized as Black or African American, and not

continued

FIGURE 4-4 Continued

categorized as Hispanic. *Hispanic* includes persons of any race who are categorized as Hispanic, including Mexican, Puerto Rican, Cuban, or Other Hispanic ethnicities. *White* includes persons whose race is categorized as White and who are not Hispanic. Excluded from this graph, given small sample sizes, are persons whose race is categorized as American Indian or Alaska Native, a race other than those included in the prior categories, or two or more races and who are not Hispanic.
SOURCES: Figure created using U.S. Census and ACS samples. U.S. Census samples include 1940–1970 (1%) and 1980–2000 (5%). ACS samples include 2006–2022 (1-year samples). ACS samples 2001–2005 are excluded because they did not include persons living in group quarters.

an emerging body of work has begun to focus on postsecondary choices, revealing some of the mechanisms that underlie inequality in the selectivity of postsecondary institutions students attend by race and income, and why more non-White first-generation college students from low-income backgrounds seem to underinvest in their postsecondary education by starting at community colleges and for-profit sub-baccalaureate programs (with relatively lower returns), while their advantaged counterparts start at selective 4-year institutions. It can be easy to conclude that low-income students are unaware of optimal strategies—which is certainly true for many—but students might also be rationally choosing nontraditional and seemingly suboptimal postsecondary pathways, and policies need to be informed as to how and why.

Some qualitative research finds that traditional college choice models fail to capture the decisions of non-White first-generation college students from low-income backgrounds (Bloom, 2007; Cox, 2016). For example, in interviews, Black students say they choose for-profit occupational programs because they offer transparent connection to work (through these schools' aggressive targeted advertising) and flexibility (e.g., rolling enrollments, online options, the ability to switch between full- and part-time student status depending on work schedules, the ability to stay near home to care for siblings; DeLuca et al., 2016; Holland & DeLuca 2016; Iloh, 2018; Iloh & Tierney, 2014). They also share that sub-baccalaureate postsecondary credentials are attractive because they are short term, and even high-performing high school graduates from low-income backgrounds and unstable home lives seek credentials they can finish quickly, possibly because they (perhaps accurately) predict a high likelihood of adverse events that could interrupt or derail a longer postsecondary program, such as a 4-year degree (DeLuca et al., 2016; Holland & DeLuca, 2016).

Other students from low-income backgrounds worry about failure to complete a degree and career payoff, and some decide to put off 4-year college or any college until they have settled on a major/career, gained occupational experience, and attained residential or economic independence in an effort to hedge against what they reasonably believe might derail their degree: distractions, inexperience, and financial shocks (Cilesiz & Drotos, 2014; DeLuca & Burland, 2023; DeLuca et al., 2021; Young & DeLuca, 2020).

THE STRUCTURE OF POSTSECONDARY EDUCATION AND INTERGENERATIONAL MOBILITY

The U.S. postsecondary system is heterogeneous and stratified (Labaree, 2017). Colleges vary dramatically in their inputs (spending per student, student preparation, governance) and their outcomes (graduation rates, economic payoff for graduates). Furthermore, the most disadvantaged students attend the institutions with the fewest resources and the worst outcomes (Lovenheim & Smith, 2023). A key question for research, therefore, is whether U.S. postsecondary education serves as an engine for upward economic mobility by disentangling low-income people from their social origins, or if it functions as an intergenerational replicator of inequality by providing privileged access to wealthy families. The answer to this question requires considering variation across the vast and heterogeneous postsecondary sector, with broad-access universities playing a different role from that of selective institutions (see Box 4-3).

The U.S. postsecondary system is highly decentralized. It comprises thousands of institutions that vary by institutional control, mission, and degrees or credentials offered. While in many developed countries, the postsecondary sector is in the federal domain, in the United States, it is the states that have the greatest responsibility in provision, with cities and counties also playing a relevant role in some states. States heavily subsidize and oversee public postsecondary institutions.

In addition to public colleges, there are thousands of private nonprofit colleges and universities (there is also a considerably smaller sector of for-profit colleges and universities). Private-sector universities educate roughly 25 percent of students. They are enormously diverse; this group includes both highly selective Ivy League institutions and very small trade schools.

In the public sector, colleges and universities are primarily funded, controlled, and operated by state governments. In the private sector, colleges and universities are controlled by nongovernmental agencies and funded primarily through private funds. Private institutions may be either nonprofit, including those affiliated with religious organizations, or for profit. Postsecondary institutions are generally structured to offer either 4- or 2-year programs. Four-year institutions offer bachelor's degrees and may additionally grant graduate degrees, including master's, professional,

> **BOX 4-3**
> **What About Elite Colleges?**
>
> Elite colleges, such as those in the Ivy League, draw significant attention from the media and politicians. In the United States, these colleges are an extremely narrow gateway to political, cultural, economic, and intellectual power—to the elite 1 percent or even 0.1 percent. Research shows that students from families in the top 1 percent of the income distribution are much more likely than middle-class students to be admitted to these institutions, even when they have similar test scores. Additionally, attending an elite school increases the chances of reaching the top 1 percent of the earning distribution by 60 percent (Chetty et al., 2023). A critical determinant of the high-income admissions advantage at elite colleges is *legacy admissions*—the preferential treatment of applicants who are children or other relatives of alumni. This policy, often framed as a way to strengthen alumni loyalty and boost fundraising, disproportionately benefits wealthy, predominantly White families who have historically been overrepresented at these institutions, giving them an advantage over capable candidates from underrepresented or lower-income backgrounds (Golden, 2007; Kahlenberg, 2010).
>
> Who goes to these schools has a substantial impact on the makeup of the country's elite leadership. These schools train the politicians, journalists, jurors, owners, and investors who wield enormous power. If these schools do not admit and graduate students who mirror society, they help to perpetuate a rigid social, economic, and political structure that limits mobility. The discussions around affirmative action policies for disadvantaged groups are especially salient in this sector.
>
> While elite colleges shape who is in the very top echelons of power and prestige, the mobility of the other 99 percent is driven by the education programs, policies, and institutions that are the focus of this chapter. These include job training programs, career and technical education, community colleges, and thousands of 4-year colleges across the country.

and doctoral degrees. Two-year institutions offer credentials or degrees up to the level of associate's degrees and potentially provide students credits that they can transfer to 4-year institutions.

In 2021–2022, there were 3,899 postsecondary institutions serving more than 18.6 million students in the United States. About half of students were enrolled in 4-year public universities, about one-fifth were enrolled each at 4-year private nonprofit (21.9%) and 2-year public (24.0%) institutions, while a small minority attended 4- and 2-year private for-profit institutions (5.3%; Figure 4-5). Public colleges educated almost three-quarters of students in the United States in 2022, particularly those with lower incomes (Reber & Smith, 2023). As such, public institutions have the greatest potential to provide opportunity for upward intergenerational mobility.

The postsecondary educational landscape has changed substantially in the last few decades. Many 2-year institutions have begun to offer 4-year

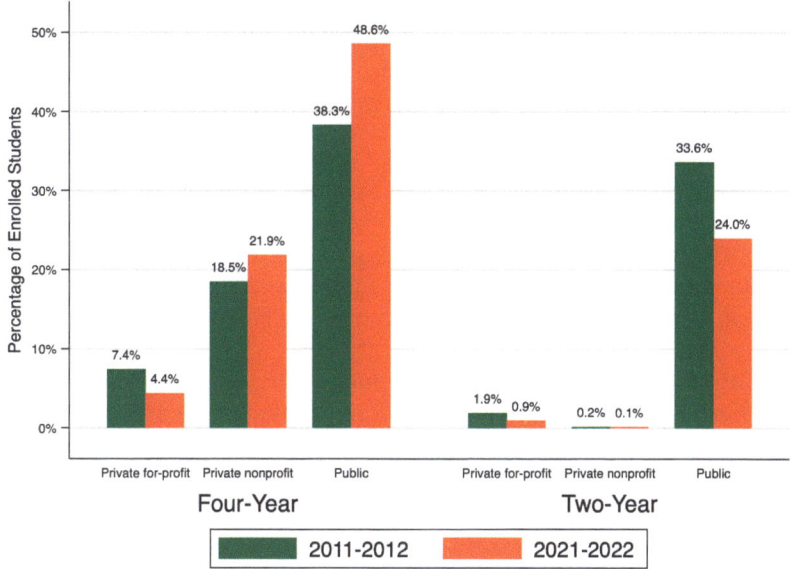

FIGURE 4-5 Proportion of enrolled students by type of postsecondary institution, 2011–2012 and 2021–2022.
NOTES: Figure generated using data from 2022 *Digest of Education Statistics* from the National Center for Educational Statistics. See Table 303.25 (enrolled students). Enrolled students documented as of Fall 2011 and Fall 2021.
SOURCE: U.S. Department of Education, National Center for Education Statistics, 2011–2012 and 2021–2022.

bachelor's programs, leading to a reclassification of some 2-year institutions as 4-year institutions (Lederman, 2011). More dramatically, the past two decades have seen the rise and fall of private, for-profit institutions (Beaver, 2017). In the early 2000s, for-profit institutions grew in number and size, facilitated by new infrastructure for online education. Under the Obama administration, the Department of Education increased scrutiny of these institutions—which often left students with high levels of debt—leading to new regulations and enforcement of rules that limited students' ability to use federal student aid to attend. Since then, regulatory development and enforcement has shifted depending on partisan control of federal executive offices, with the Trump administration removing some regulations and the Biden administration reinstating them (Nadworny, 2023). Nonetheless, the cumulative result of these regulatory efforts is that many private for-profit institutions have closed. Between 2011–2012 and 2021–2022, the proportion of students served by private for-profit institutions dropped from 7.4 percent to 4.4 percent.

VARIATION ACROSS POSTSECONDARY INSTITUTIONS: RESOURCES, GOVERNANCE, AND GRADUATION RATES

The amount of economic resources colleges use to educate their student bodies varies substantially across institutions, resulting in considerable heterogeneity in cost and quality. For example, among 4-year institutions, total expenses per full-time-equivalent student in year 2020–2021 were $69,145 in private nonprofit colleges, $52,897 in public colleges, and only $17,660 in private for-profit institutions (National Center for Education Statistics [NCES], 2023). Even within the public sector, there is considerable variation, with 2-year colleges expending about half as many resources as 4-year colleges.

Institutional resources have consequences for mobility, but more information is needed. These disparities have consequences for mobility because low-income and minority students are more likely to be served by institutions with reduced investments (Hamilton et al., 2024; Lovenheim & Smith, 2023). In elementary and secondary education, research has shown that spending matters for student outcomes, both in the near and long terms (National Academies, 2023b). There is far less evidence on this link in postsecondary education, but the existing research strongly supports the hypothesis that fewer resources translate into worse outcomes in college (Lovenheim & Smith, 2023). This is therefore an important research priority.

The degree of government oversight, governance, and coordination of public colleges also varies, especially across states. California has the most coordinated system of community colleges, state universities, and flagships, with clear standards for who can be admitted to each of these schools and how students can transfer between them. Michigan is at the opposite extreme, with a constitutional ban on a statewide higher education coordinating board.

Governance can have relevant implications for students. In California, students can transfer from community colleges to state universities with relative ease, carrying with them their credits earned. In Michigan, the ability of a student to transfer credits depends on whether the two colleges have agreed on which credits can transfer.

Governance can have consequences for mobility. Community colleges have traditionally been the entryway to postsecondary education for disadvantaged populations. When students can easily transfer from community colleges to schools that grant bachelor's degrees, the former serve as a gateway to the economic mobility associated with a bachelor's degree. When students cannot easily transfer, community colleges can serve as a barrier to mobility.

Graduation rates also have consequences for mobility and vary substantially across institutions. Among students entering 4-year colleges in 2015, graduation rates within 4 years reached 58 percent at private nonprofit colleges, but only 44 percent at public colleges, and a very low 23 percent at private for-profit colleges (NCES, 2022). College dropout is, then, a critical barrier to upward economic mobility for youth from disadvantaged backgrounds. Among college dropouts, students who take student loans are particularly vulnerable, as their debt burden compounds the limited returns to their educational investments, hampering their financial well-being. As discussed in the next section, a growing number of students rely on loans to fund their educational investments, and student loan debt is stratified by family income and race and ethnicity.

THE FUNDING OF POSTSECONDARY EDUCATION IN THE UNITED STATES AND THE GROWING IMPORTANCE OF LOANS

While private postsecondary institutions have always charged tuition, historically, public colleges had tuition prices near zero, enabled by the large subsidies provided by state governments. This began to change in the 1980s as a series of tax revolts swept the states. In the past 40 years, states have disinvested from their public institutions, and those schools have turned to tuition to prop up their revenues. As a result, the cost of a public college education has shifted from taxpayers to individual students (The Pew Charitable Trusts, 2019).

As tuition prices have risen, the federal government has stepped in to assist students and families with grants and, particularly, loans. Borrowing for college is now much more common than it was just a few decades ago (Lochner & Monge-Naranjo, 2016). The shift to loans has been particularly marked at public 2-year colleges. In 2000, just 5 percent of students at community colleges took out loans; in 2012, that figure had tripled, to 17 percent (Looney & Yannelis, 2024). These students, who are disproportionately disadvantaged, are among the most likely to default on their loans, leading to substantial financial distress.

Borrowing has always been very high at for-profit schools, which enroll a population similar to community colleges and where default rates are also very high (Looney & Yannelis, 2024). A key question for future research is whether for students at these schools, which have low graduation rates, the downside risks of borrowing outweigh the benefits of attending college. As this chapter has documented, there is extensive research estimating how college costs, borrowing, graduation, or labor market returns differ across sectors and socioeconomic status (see Lovenheim & Smith, 2023, for a comprehensive review). To the committee's knowledge, however, no research has integrated these estimates into a comprehensive, distributive analysis of the net costs, benefits, and risks of college.

A relevant source of public support for higher education expenses is tax benefits such as the American Opportunity Tax Credit; the Lifetime Learning Credit; deductions for student loan interest; and tax-advantaged savings plans, such as 529 accounts. These policies aim to reduce the cost of education by lowering tax liability or encouraging savings. However, the benefits disproportionately accrue to middle- and upper-income families who are more likely to have the financial literacy and resources to take advantage of them. Furthermore, research indicates that these tax-based subsidies have no impact on increasing educational attainment, as the delayed nature of the benefits fails to incentivize enrollment decisions for financially constrained families (Bulman & Hoxby, 2015; Dynarski & Scott-Clayton, 2016). Instead, these programs often function as a post hoc subsidy for families who are already able to afford higher education, thereby reinforcing existing disparities.

The United States is unusual in having students pay tuition and borrow for vocational training, which is typically provided by community colleges and for-profit schools. In much of the world, by contrast, students seeking vocational training do not pay tuition or borrow to fund their training. There is also a closer link between this training and the labor market (e.g., Germany's apprenticeship system). A key question for mobility research is whether funding models in other countries are more effective in generating economic mobility through vocational training than the U.S. model.

There is also room for historical research because the responsibility for career and technical training has shifted over time in the United States. Career and technical training, including that for displaced workers, was once funded primarily by the U.S. Department of Labor in the form of free training programs. Now it is largely the responsibility of the postsecondary sector.[3] Unemployed workers seeking job retraining are steered toward community colleges or for-profit training schools, where they may borrow for college costs. What was considered a societal obligation to train workers is now framed as the private responsibility of individual students investing in their education. It is important to understand how this has affected individual welfare, incentives to invest in education, and economic mobility. (The effectiveness of job training programs is discussed below, in the section "Alternative Transitions and Pathways to the Labor Market.")

---

[3] Overall funding for federal training programs peaked in the 1970s, both in real dollars and as a share of gross domestic product (GDP), and it has declined precipitously since then (Mueser et al., 2023). By fiscal year 2021, funding for training programs relative to GDP had fallen by 90 percent since the 1970s and, compared with funding in 2014, had fallen by 21 percent.

POSTSECONDARY EDUCATION: BALANCING RISKS AND RETURNS

A college degree, on average, more than pays for itself, even after accounting for tuition costs and wages forgone while in school (Daly & Bengali, 2014). Beyond earnings, a college degree yields benefits in terms of health, family stability, and social connections (Hout, 2012). Research using quasi-experimental data to identify causal effects suggests a substantial effect of 2-year and 4-year colleges on students' probability of college graduation and later earnings (Chetty et al., 2023; Goodman et al., 2017; Mountjoy, 2022, 2024). This effect is usually measured for "marginal students" (i.e., those who are on the threshold of enrolling in college, rather than for students that would enroll with certainty). Critical for upward mobility, the economic benefits of both associate's and bachelor's degrees is larger for disadvantaged students (Goodman et al., 2017; Mountjoy, 2022) and for students who are the least likely to enroll, who usually come from families with low levels of schooling and earnings (Brand, 2023). There is also substantial variation in the return to college across school and college characteristics. The U.S. Department of Education's College Scorecard website[4] reports the earnings of former students by school and shows substantial variation even restricted to 4-year bachelor degrees. While some of this variation can be attributed to the characteristics of the student body, a growing literature shows that at least some of the variation across schools and sectors is causal (e.g., Chetty et al., 2023; Conzelmann et al., 2023; Goodman et al., 2017; Mountjoy, 2022, 2024).

Like any investment, education is not without risk. This risk includes variation in the payoff of a credential from a given school and major, as well as substantial uncertainty in whether a student will graduate. The growing literature on heterogeneous returns to college shows that returns vary by student race and family income. The field of study selected by students has emerged as a key stratifying mechanism, which suggests that the payoff to postsecondary attainment can vary not only across institutions but also within them (Bleemer & Quincy, 2024; Kim & Tamborini, 2019; see review in Lovenheim & Smith, 2023). On the one hand, the United States has a very flexible postsecondary system with expansive options across sectors and degree programs, and many "on- and off-ramps." On the other hand, this flexibility can exacerbate inequality and hamper mobility, as students from less advantaged backgrounds must navigate this complex institutional landscape with fewer resources.

A key question for policy is who bears these risks. And for mobility researchers, a key question is whether the benefits of a college education

---

[4] https://collegescorecard.ed.gov/compare/?togglepercent3Dinstitutions

outweigh its risks, particularly for students from low-income backgrounds, first-generation college students, immigrants, and racial minorities. These students often have much to gain from a postsecondary education (Brand, 2023; Goodman et al., 2017; Mountjoy, 2022). But they are more likely to attend institutions with fewer resources needed to support degree completion (Fry & Cilluffo, 2019, p. 3; Reber & Smith, 2023, Figure 2). These students also have little in the way of a safety net if the investment does not pay off. In particular, the for-profit sector disproportionately enrolls students of lower socioeconomic status while generating limited educational benefits (Gelbgiser, 2018) and no observable economic benefits (in some cases even negative returns; Cellini & Turner, 2019). Enrollment in this sector is counterclyclical, booming during recessions when stressed community colleges and job training programs cannot serve the surge in people seeking to build their job market skills (Looney & Yannelis, 2024).

The growth of alternative and industry-provided credentials, bootcamps, and certifications means that the postsecondary landscape has also become even more complex and uncertain for students most at risk (Stevens & Kirst, 2015). While alternative credential providers have grown exponentially over the last decade, and such programs may serve an important need for those not pursuing college or transitioning between jobs, very little is known about the experiences students have in these programs and what the returns are on these investments. Given that many students choosing these programs may come from relatively disadvantaged families, these programs might have implications for upward mobility. More research in this area would be relevant.

Public policy can play a role in mediating risk. If tuition is low and grants support living expenses, then the risk to the individual student is minimized. If tuition is high and students borrow to pay for tuition and living expenses, then the risk to the individual is very high. Policies such as need-based aid and income-based loan repayment lie between these two extremes.

FROM DEMAND SIDE TO SUPPLY SIDE: RESEARCH ON IMPROVING COLLEGE QUALITY

There is now a large body of rigorous evidence on stimulating student demand for postsecondary education (Dynarski et al., 2023a,b). Research now needs to move to designing policies that stimulate demand for particular populations and settings. Evidence about specific populations defined by level of academic preparation, race and ethnicity, income levels, and age is needed, as is evidence for settings defined by proximity to nearby colleges (including higher education "deserts") and for type of institutions, including community colleges, nonselective 4-year, and selective 4-year.

Research is also needed on how to improve the quality of postsecondary education at all levels (Arum & Roksa, 2011; Holzer & Baum, 2017; Lovenheim & Smith, 2023). In the United States, as in many other countries, the postsecondary sector has grown through the establishment and expansion of schools that receive relatively few resources, as described in the previous section. Community colleges, less-selective 4-year colleges, and for-profit colleges spend far less per student than do selective, elite colleges. Yet the former service the students with the most challenges.

This is the opposite of the pattern in funding in elementary and secondary education, where additional federal money flows to schools that serve more students who live in poverty, are English learners, or have disabilities (Jackson et al., 2016; Johnson, 2015; Wong, 1999). This priority in funding reflects the understanding that it is more expensive to educate students who come to school with more disadvantages.

A recent literature has shown convincingly that spending matters in elementary and secondary education (Jackson et al., 2016). Districts and schools that receive more funding per student produce better outcomes for those students, both in the short and long terms. Analogous research is now needed on how spending affects outcomes in the postsecondary sector.

Furthermore, research needs to explore how to use that funding to achieve the desired outcomes. An enormous amount of literature has examined the effect of inputs, policies, and practices on children's education from preschool through high school, answering basic questions, such as

- How does class size affect learning?
- How does teacher training affect student outcomes?
- What curricula are most effective in teaching math and reading?
- Which pedagogical techniques and curricula boost learning and improve graduation rates?
- How does school size affect student learning?
- How does the composition of classrooms affect learning?
- When and where does ability grouping improve student learning?

By contrast, analogous literature addressing these questions in the postsecondary setting is astoundingly thin. Instead, research on postsecondary education has focused overwhelmingly on who goes to college, whether they finish, who pays for it, and how much they pay. Although these are important questions, they have overshadowed the equally important question of how to improve the quality of education in the postsecondary sector. Given the heterogeneity in returns to college (observed at all levels), more information is needed about what kinds of programs and inputs work for which students, not only in terms of graduation rates but also in terms of job placement, career growth, and earnings.

ALTERNATIVE TRANSITIONS AND PATHWAYS TO THE LABOR MARKET

This chapter, as does most research on postsecondary education, refers largely to educational experiences that happen shortly after high school graduation and that precede a transition to paid employment. Yet the distinction between periods of education and work in the life course has never been this clear. Table 4-1 shows that students have long worked while attending both high school and college, although research is mixed on the benefits of such employment while attending school (Bozick, 2007; Davis, 2023; Lee & Staff, 2007; Mortimer, 2010; Scott-Clayton, 2012). Nearly one out of six students—especially non-White students from low-income backgrounds—delay college in order to get work experience, figure out what they want to study in college, or save money for college (Bozick & DeLuca, 2005, 2011; Holland & DeLuca, 2016; Roksa & Velez, 2010).

Over time there has also been an increase in the share of people earning a college degree at age 30 and older (Figure 4-6), reflecting delayed enrollments, longer times to degree completion, and periods of "stopping out" during one's college trajectory, during which time individuals are working or looking for work (see also Hart, 2019; Turner, 2004). The growing "some college but no degree" group (Figure 4-6) also means that many young adults are entering work sooner and perhaps with less training or preparation than hoped for. Such trends mean that the transitions from school to work (and back again) are relevant when considering policies for economic mobility. In other words, people are dipping into and out of school and work throughout their lives, much more than current policy recognizes. However, not enough is known about how work experiences in high school and college shape career transitions and choices, and thus how these experiences hinder or facilitate economic mobility.

There is therefore a critical need to support transition-to-work pathways for large segments of the population throughout the life course (see Bailey et al., 2015; Holzer & Baum, 2017; Rosenbaum et al., 2006). This includes younger adults who do not plan to go to college (or pursue a bachelor's degree), those completing or dropping out of any postsecondary education, and any adults who want to change jobs or need to transition into different fields because of changing labor demands. Given longer lifespans, growing numbers of current U.S. workers are likely to pursue further education and training throughout their lives (Stevens et al., 2022). Yet no coherent policy approach is in place to best support the economic mobility of students and workers during these transitions, both for those with a bachelor's degree and for those without one or who hold a sub-baccalaureate credential (Gardyan et al., 2024).

TABLE 4-1 Proportion of College Students Who Worked, by Birth Cohort, 1940–2002

	Birth Cohort							
	1940	1950	1960	1970	1980	1990	2000	2002
Proportion employed (not self-employed)	0.41	0.42	0.48	0.55	0.58	0.51	0.51	0.54
Proportion worked at least 1 week last year	0.82	0.86	0.86	0.88	0.85	0.74	0.73	0.74
Proportion worked at least 14 or more weeks last year	0.46	0.52	0.59	0.66	0.68	0.56	0.51	0.54

NOTES: The sample includes students in college, measured at age 20. Person weights were used for all waves. College students are defined as persons who were in college. For U.S. Census waves 1960–1980, this is defined as persons who were attending college (identified using *gradeatt*). For U.S. Census and American Community Survey (ACS) waves greater than 1990, this includes persons whose educational attainment is greater than or equal to grade 12 and less than or equal to 3 years of college and who were in school (identified using *educ*). U.S. Census and ACS waves after 2000 additionally include persons who report their grade as college undergraduate or 1st to 4th year of college (identified using *gradeattd*). The first row of the table shows whether students were employed or not. Students are coded as 0 if they were unemployed, not in the labor force, or self-employed, and 1 if they were employed (but not self-employed) (identified using *empstat* and *classwkr*). The second row of the table shows the proportion of students who worked at least 1 week in the prior year. Students are coded as 0 if they did not work at least 1 week in the prior year and 1 if they worked 1 or more weeks in the prior year (identified using *wkswork2*). The third row of the table shows the proportion of students who worked at least 14 weeks in the prior year, included to avoid confusing changes in the proportion of students who work seasonally (e.g., summer internships) with changes in the proportion of students who work more than a single season. Students are coded as 0 if they did not work at least 14 weeks, and 1 if they worked 14 weeks or more.
SOURCES: Estimates based on data from the U.S. Census (1960, 1970, 1980, 1990, and 2000) and the ACS (2010, 2020, and 2022), downloaded from IPUMS USA.

Other efforts help support labor market transitions for individuals outside of the education sector, including enlistment in the military (see Box 4-4) and job training programs. These are especially important for those who may not be interested in or perform well in educational institutions, those with some college who earned no degree, workers displaced because of labor market shocks, and others who want to move from low- to higher-wage employment. The existing evidence on job training programs, especially those targeted to youth or dislocated workers, shows mixed results (e.g., Stanley et al., 1998). However, more recent research indicates that these programs do provide positive benefits to participants. The multisite Career Academies randomized controlled trial, which used a random research design in a diverse group of high schools across the United States, showed that the programs (which combined academic and technical

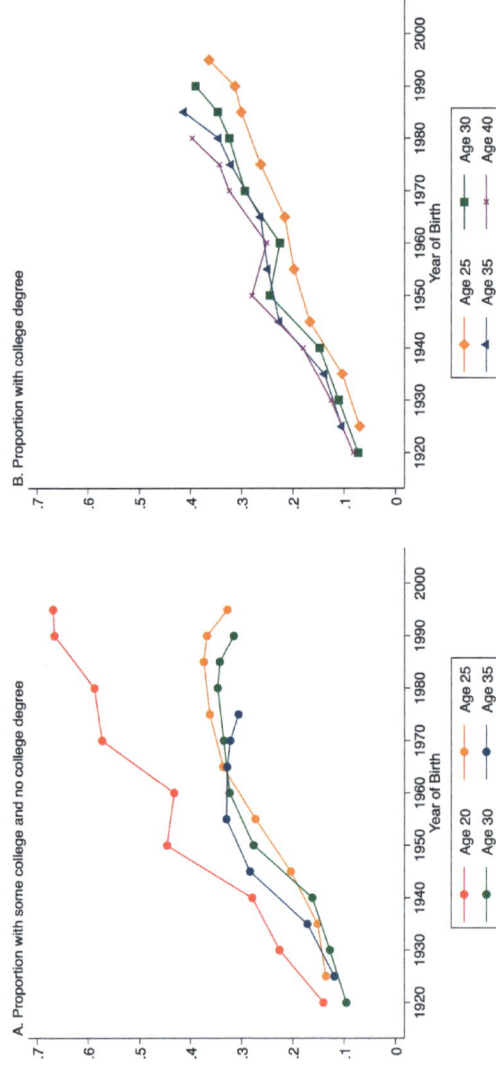

FIGURE 4-6 College attainment by cohort, by age.
SOURCES: Estimates based on data from the U.S. Census (1960, 1970, 1980, 1990, and 2000) and the American Community Survey (2010, 2020, and 2022), downloaded from IPUMS USA.

BOX 4-4
Enlistment in the U.S. Military as a Pathway to Upward Mobility

The postsecondary landscape in the United States is vast, such that the educational and training tracks highlighted in this chapter are not the only postsecondary pathways available to Americans completing high school. The military has historically been, and remains, a key social institution promising "individual opportunity" to millions of Americans (Bailey, 2009), especially in working-class and minority communities, for whom it provides valuable educational, training, and skill-development opportunities that can engender labor market success (Bailey & Sykes, 2018; Greenberg et al., 2022; Kleykamp, 2013; National Academies, 2019). Indeed, it is quite distinct from either education or training, separately, as a flexible postsecondary option. It often represents a transitionary stage in young people's career trajectories, serving as a critical springboard to continued education and/or postservice employment (Kelty et al., 2010). However, it also can provide a stable and well-paying career path in its own right (Asch et al., 2010; Hosek et al., 2018), with defined criteria for advancement rooted in a meritocratic orientation toward skill-based promotion (Kelty et al., 2010).

Military service provides adults with access to educational benefits, such as tuition assistance, scholarships, and training programs, that can provide avenues for career advancement and social mobility upon leaving the military (Barr, 2019; National Academies, 2019; Skocpol, 1995). Likewise, military service provides training in a range of technical, leadership, and interpersonal skills that are valued in civilian employment sectors (Kleykamp, 2009), in addition to the positive "signaling" value of military service in the labor market (Bailey & Sykes, 2018). Beyond the direct mobility-relevant resources that the military provides vis-à-vis career advancement, it also provides adults with a degree of baseline economic and/or social stability that is necessary to pursue upward mobility within or across generations, as might be the case for the various health care, housing assistance, and retirement benefits that servicemembers and families receive both during and after military service (Chevan, 1989; Skocpol, 1995; Wilson & Kizer, 1997).

Extant research further suggests that these economic and social benefits can prove particularly valuable for upward mobility among socially disadvantaged men, who are historically overrepresented in the military (National Academies, 2019), although research shows that at least some of these benefits have been limited to White men (Greenberg et al., 2022; Sampson & Laub, 1996; Teachman & Tedrow, 2004; Turner & Bound, 2003). Greenberg et al.'s (2022) analysis of army applicants from 1990 to 2011—linked to tax records and other administrative data—is an example of recent empirical work suggesting that the military is a key institution for reducing the Black–White earnings gap.

curricula around a career theme and established partnerships with local employers) led to earnings gains of 11 percent (about $27,000 in 2024 dollars) on average, sustained through the 8-year follow-up, and primarily for young men (Kemple & Willner, 2008). Both experimental and quasi-experimental evaluations (Andersson et al., 2024; Fortson et al., 2017; Heinrich et al., 2008, 2013) find significant impacts on earnings of the Workforce Innovation and Opportunity Act Adult worker program, while training services had a minimal impact on earnings for participants in the Dislocated Worker program. In a meta-analysis of job training programs from a wide range of countries, Card et al. (2018) found increased rates of employment of 5–10 percent within 2–3 years after participation. The best indication of the impact of providing training to young people comes from the Schochet (2021) experimental evaluation of Job Corps; the study found that older participants (those who enrolled at ages 20–24) were more successful than individuals in the control sample, but that differences to the younger participants faded after the initial 3-year evaluation window.

The most promising evidence to date shows large earning benefits for participants in targeted training programs that provide participants the skills necessary to obtain a high-quality job with career advancement opportunities in health care, informational technology, or advanced manufacturing (Hendra et al., 2016). Katz et al. (2022) summarized the results from four experimental evaluations of sectoral training programs, showing they produce annual earnings gains of as much as 35 percent. Baird et al. (2019) find that a training program in New Orleans funded through the Department of Labor's Workforce Innovation Fund (WIF) produced similar results for recently unemployed workers, while Bollinger and Troske (2023) found smaller returns at lower cost from an online training program in Louisville that was also funded through WIF.

SUMMARY, KEY CONCLUSIONS, AND RECOMMENDATIONS

Elementary and secondary education (i.e., K–12) is a critical building block period of cognitive and socioemotional development that is essential for future academic and labor market success, both through and independent of postsecondary education. Indeed, it is one of the most well-studied periods when it comes to understanding how education shapes mobility, as are interventions intended to identify core investments that improve and equalize mobility-relevant outcomes. The committee's focus in this chapter is on the postsecondary stage, not because it is the most important point in the emergence of inequities in education and training, but because it requires significantly more attention from research and policy.

Postsecondary educational attainment—and, especially, the attainment of a 4-year bachelor's degree—is central to the understanding of the economic and social mobility in the United States. In effect, college has become something of a prerequisite to the subsequent maintenance of economic well-being and security within and across generations. The economic payoff of a college degree is also greater in the United States than in any other rich democracy. The earnings gap between people with a bachelor's degree and those with lower levels of schooling has grown since the late 1970s, partly driven by a growing demand for highly educated workers that was not met by comparable supply. It is important to note that a bachelor's degree, and not just college attendance, is a dividing line in the U.S. income distribution; those with some college education or with a sub-baccalaureate credential (associate's degree or a certificate) have earnings closer to high school graduates' than to those with a bachelor's degree.

Trends in postsecondary attainment mask substantial inequality in college enrollment and college completion by family income. The probability of attending and graduating from college strongly depends on household income, and this income gap has remained large across cohorts. Disparities in college attendance, and especially college graduation, by race and ethnicity are also pronounced. There is a growing female advantage in college attainment, which will likely have broader consequences for intergenerational processes involving fertility, children's educational opportunities, and growing gaps between families in which both parents have high or low levels of schooling.

Conclusion 4-1: Postsecondary education in the United States is a very strong predictor of economic well-being and is a critical determinant of intergenerational mobility. However, there are considerable disparities in college enrollment and completion by family income, location of residence, and race and ethnicity. There are also growing disparities by gender, favoring women, the consequences of which are poorly understood.

Recommendation 4-1: Researchers should examine the implications for economic and social mobility of growing gender differences in college completion.

It is not possible with existing data sources to annually measure the association between parents' income and bachelor's degree attainment—a critical fact of intergenerational mobility. One strategy for addressing these data limitations is using existing sets of large, high-quality administrative data to supplement currently administered surveys.

Conclusion 4-2: Existing data sources cannot be used to properly evaluate current changes in the association between parent's income and bachelor's degree attainment. This data limitation can be addressed by linking survey data with administrative data.

The U.S. postsecondary system is heterogeneous, decentralized, and stratified. It comprises thousands of institutions that vary by institutional control, mission, and degrees or credentials offered. Colleges vary dramatically in their inputs (spending per student, student preparation) and outcomes (graduation rates, economic payoff for graduates). Furthermore, the most disadvantaged students attend the institutions with the fewest resources and the worst outcomes. Although a college education can result in a large economic payoff, there is enormous variation around the averages. Like any investment, education is not without risk. Risk is particularly salient in the sub-baccalaureate sector, which includes both public community colleges and private for-profit schools; the students in this sector are also the most disadvantaged. A key question for research and policy, therefore, is whether U.S. postsecondary education serves as an engine for upward economic mobility by disentangling students from low-income backgrounds from their social origins, or if it functions as an intergenerational replicator of inequality by providing privileged access to wealthy families (including, among other things, through legacy admissions at elite colleges and tax benefits to reduce the costs of higher education). The answer to this question requires considering variation across the vast and heterogeneous postsecondary sector, with broad-access universities playing a different role from that of selective institutions.

As tuition prices have risen, the federal government has stepped in to assist students and families. Some of this aid has taken the form of grants, but much has been in the form of student loans. Borrowing for college is now much more common than it was just a few decades ago. The shift has been particularly marked at community colleges, where traditionally, students did not borrow for their educations. This may have consequences for mobility because it shifts onto the most disadvantaged students the cost (and risks) of postsecondary education. There is extensive research estimating how college costs, borrowing, default, graduation, or labor market returns differ across sectors and socioeconomic status. To the committee's knowledge, however, no research has integrated these estimates into a comprehensive, distributive analysis of the net costs, benefits, and risks of college.

Conclusion 4-3: Although the attainment of a 4-year bachelor's degree is a very strong predictor of economic well-being and security, postsecondary education has become an increasingly risky proposition for many adults and families, especially those who have low incomes and are racial minorities. Broad-access institutions, certificate programs, and the growth of for-profit schools and other educational providers has increased the menu of options but has not necessarily increased completion rates or returns.

Recommendation 4-2: Researchers should conduct comprehensive, distributive analyses of the economic costs, benefits, and risks of college and explore the question of the extent to which U.S. postsecondary education is a replicator of intergenerational inequality rather than an engine for intergenerational mobility. Attention should be paid to variations in returns across the heterogeneous postsecondary sector, with broad-access institutions playing a central role for the vast majority of the population, different from that of more elite and selective universities.

In the United States, students are funded by the same federal grant and loan programs whether they are pursuing career and technical training at a community college or a bachelor's degree at a university. In much of the world, by contrast, the funding models for the baccalaureate and sub-baccalaureate sectors are distinct. Baccalaureate students are typically charged tuition and take out loans, while this is rarely true for students in the sub-baccalaureate sector. Organizational and funding models in other parts of the world may provide useful insights for the United States.

Recommendation 4-3: Researchers should explore whether postsecondary funding models in other countries—especially with regard to sub-baccalaureate education—are more effective in generating economic mobility than the U.S. model.

There is a large body of rigorous evidence on how to stimulate student demand for postsecondary education, and research now needs to move to designing policies that stimulate demand within particular populations (defined, e.g., by level of academic preparation, race and ethnicity, income level, and age) and settings (e.g., rural). On the "supply side," the postsecondary sector in the United States has grown through the establishment and expansion of schools that receive relatively few resources but serve students with the most challenges, in contrast to the more redistributive K–12 education funding.

Better understanding is needed on how to improve the quality of postsecondary education. A vast literature has examined the effect of inputs, policies, and practices on K–12 education. However, the analogous literature addressing these questions in the postsecondary setting is astoundingly thin. Research on postsecondary education has focused overwhelmingly on who goes to college, whether they finish, who pays, how much they pay, and what happens at the entry and exit points—but it rarely looks at what is happening in college and what kinds of programs and inputs work for which students. Given the heterogeneity in returns to college, the committee calls for a comparative body of work that will address questions about the quality of higher education, including the ways in which curricula, pedagogical techniques, and class size improve learning and graduation rates as well as job placement, career growth, and earnings.

> Recommendation 4-4: Researchers should study ways to stimulate demand for postsecondary education for particular populations and settings. Evidence is needed about specific populations defined by level of academic preparation, race and ethnicity, income levels, residential location, and age.

> Recommendation 4-5: Researchers should study the effects of inputs, policies, and practices (e.g., curricula, pedagogical techniques, class size, connections to employment opportunities) on the quality of postsecondary education and the implications for economic and social mobility.

People transition into and out of school and work throughout their lives, including the growing "some college" group without bachelor's degrees, much more than currently policy recognizes. And, although transitions to work and transitions between careers are important to shaping economic mobility, they receive far less attention than the transition into college. This is despite the rapidly changing technological landscape and the fact that many students end up working sooner than they expect (given low college completion rates) and will have longer working lives. It is important to recognize the need for multiple pathways to mobility, commensurate with people's many starting points.

There is considerable evidence that job training programs, especially sectoral employment approaches, can increase earnings. Career and technical training, including that for dislocated workers, was once funded by the U.S. Department of Labor in the form of free training programs; now, however, such training is largely the responsibility of the postsecondary sector. It is important to understand how this has affected individual welfare, incentives to invest in education, and economic mobility. A better data infrastructure is also needed to track participants nationally and to incorporate job training data into other longitudinal record data efforts. There is also a need to understand the role of alternative credential programs, immersive training programs (e.g., educational bootcamps), and certifications for preparing for the transition to work or changes in careers; this sector has grown significantly, and little is known about student experiences, quality of programs, or labor market returns.

Conclusion 4-4: People transition between school and work and between careers throughout their lives and in different ways. Economic and social mobility can be enhanced by recognizing the need for multiple pathways to mobility beyond a college degree, commensurate with people's many starting points and transitions.

Recommendation 4-6: Researchers should study the effectiveness of programs and policies to support the trajectories of those without bachelor's degrees, as well as multiple transitions and pathways between schooling, training, and work.

5

Wealth, Credit, and Debt

This chapter focuses on the role of wealth, credit, and debt in the attainment, maintenance, and—in many instances—loss of economic and social status both within and across generations (i.e., intra- and intergenerational mobility). Wealth is itself a central dimension of social mobility in the United States but also a driver of other socioeconomic and racial/ethnic inequalities (e.g., Shapiro, 2017; Zucman, 2019). Over the last decades, research on inequality and mobility in wealth has expanded rapidly (Keister & Moller, 2000; Killewald et al., 2017). This research typically measures wealth as a household's net worth: the total sum of all real assets (e.g., house, vehicle) and financial assets (e.g., savings accounts, stocks), minus any debts (e.g., credit card debt, student debt). Household net worth and household income are of course positively associated, but this association is far from perfect, with a correlation of approximately 0.60 between net worth and income (Killewald et al., 2017). Even when income is averaged across multiple observation years, wealth constitutes a partly distinct dimension of socioeconomic well-being and inequality. Therefore, when assessing mobility, wealth deserves attention alongside and in addition to differences in income or consumption (see also National Academies of Sciences, Engineering, and Medicine [National Academies], 2024a).

Recent work also shows that wealth mobility in the United States is lower than income and consumption mobility (Fisher & Johnson, 2023). This lower level of wealth mobility is coupled with a high degree of inequality in the concentration of wealth (at the top of the distribution; Pfeffer & Waitkus, 2021) and stark racial/ethnic gaps in wealth that have persisted for many decades and have grown again recently (Addo et al.,

2024; Derenoncourt et al., 2023). Indeed, distinctive features of wealth include its very high degree of inequality and its concentration at the top. The Gini coefficient of U.S. household wealth in 2022 was around 0.83 (the Gini coefficient of U.S. household income was around 0.61) and the top 1 percent of the wealth distribution owned about 35 percent of all U.S. wealth. In comparison with its peers, the United States stands out as the country with the highest levels of wealth inequality and top concentration in wealth (Pfeffer & Waitkus, 2021). Furthermore, racial/ethnic gaps in wealth are very large: The median net worth of Black families in 2022 was just 16 percent of the median net worth of White families, while the ratio of the means is 15 percent; the median net worth of Hispanic families was 22 percent of the median net worth of White families (Aladangady et al., 2023). Others have noted that "the 400 richest Americans [...] have more total wealth than all 10 million Black American households combined" (Williamson, 2020, p. 1).

Amid the rapid expansion of research on wealth and mobility, the distinct role of credit and debt—and inequality therein—has often been neglected, especially in the understanding of differences in mobility-relevant risks and rewards associated with specific assets and debts. Even the composition of assets and liabilities can have disparate impacts on well-being (see Boen et al., 2021). The existing literature on wealth and economic mobility typically draws a conceptual distinction between wealth and credit and debt, but the use of measures of net worth, which subtracts debts from assets, tends to conceal or at least de-emphasize the distinct and separate role of credit and debt. This is problematic, as debt and credit play a major role in the economic well-being and mobility of U.S. families: as of the first quarter of 2023, American households held more than $17 trillion in debt, including approximately $12 trillion in mortgage debt, $340 billion in home equity–based debt, $1.6 trillion in student loan debt, $1.6 trillion in auto debt, $1 trillion in credit card debt, and $500 billion in "other" debt (Federal Reserve Bank of New York, 2023a). These figures suggest a ratio of total household debt to U.S. gross domestic product ($25.5 trillion in 2022) of 0.67, such that the total debt held by U.S. households amounts to about two-thirds the size of the entire yearly economic output of the country (U.S. Bureau of Economic Analysis, 2023). Moreover, despite variation with macroeconomic conditions and policy responses to the Great Recession and COVID-19 pandemic, both aggregate and per capita debt in each of these categories has generally trended upward over the past four decades (Federal Reserve Bank of New York, 2023b). Indeed, the aggregate household debt-to-income ratio in the United States is estimated to have grown from 0.63 in 1980 to 0.96 in 2017, reaching a high of 1.24 in 2007 (Ahn et al., 2018). These figures suggest that debt is, increasingly, a substantial and common element of household finances (Morduch & Schneider, 2017).

Notably, however, the figures exclude obligations such as civil and criminal legal debt, medical debt, unpaid bills, loans from nonfinancial institutions (employers, family, friends), and child support debt. Such debts are particularly salient for disadvantaged and minoritized households (Finnigan & Meagher, 2019; Fourcade & Healy, 2013; Ghaffary, 2019; Halpern-Meekin et al., 2015; Harris, 2016; Wherry et al., 2019).

Growth in household debt over the past few decades is thought to be driven, at least in part, by financial market deregulation, expanded access to credit, and the emergence of new credit products that have substantially increased options for borrowing, especially for population groups that have traditionally been excluded from mainstream financial markets. However, household debt is also thought to have led to repayment difficulties and associated economic insecurity for many households, particularly those experiencing adverse shocks to income or asset values and those with low or unstable incomes (Board of Governors of the Federal Reserve System, 2017; Campbell et al., 2011; Federal Reserve Bank of New York, 2017; Fourcade & Healy, 2013; Hyman, 2011; Wherry et al., 2019). These factors are relevant to both secured debt (e.g., mortgage, auto, and home equity loans) and unsecured, or uncollateralized, debt (e.g., education, credit card, personal finance, subprime [payday and title] loans; Ryan et al., 2011; Xiao & Yao, 2011a,b).

In light of these ongoing and, to some extent, parallel trends in both wealth and credit and debt, this chapter seeks to give full attention to each on its own, rather than only in their joint distribution. It starts by acknowledging net worth as important for mobility, calling attention to the many mechanisms by which it maintains the high economic and social status for those at the top end of the distribution, while limiting opportunities for those in the middle and bottom. Delving into the stratification of different classes of assets within the U.S. population, the chapter highlights the centrality of housing as a source of wealth for most adults and families; it is also a key structural factor in equalizing intergenerational mobility between racial/ethnic groups. In turn, credit, lending, and debt are the primary means by which individuals enter (or are excluded from) the housing market. Critically, the committee emphasizes that credit and debt are not monolithically "good" or "bad," but instead context-specific mechanisms of mobility. Beyond housing, credit and debt provide many individuals with opportunities to take risks that engender wealth accumulation and upward mobility; yet, for others, they are insurmountable obstacles that hinder mobility, if not direct sources of downward inter- and/or intragenerational mobility. Finally, we acknowledge that wealth is unique in its importance as both a mechanism of mobility and an outcome (or measure) of mobility.

WEALTH

Wealth is a key force of mobility and driver of socioeconomic and racial/ethnic disparities. Over the last decades, research on inequality and mobility in wealth, especially focused on household net worth, has expanded rapidly; it demonstrates relatively low levels of wealth mobility in the United States, a high degree of inequality, and stark racial/ethnic gaps in wealth that have grown over time.

Intergenerational Wealth Transmission

Perhaps the most distinctive feature of wealth is that it can be passed on directly to one's children and grandchildren. Unlike education, occupation, or income—the measures of socioeconomic status central to decades of research on social mobility—wealth can be transmitted quite simply by handing it over to one's offspring, either in the form of gifts during one's lifetime or as an inheritance (see National Academies, 2024a, for discussion on interhousehold transfers for measuring income and wealth). Accordingly, much scholarly attention has been paid to the role of gifts and inheritances in contributing to the intergenerational transmission of wealth; however, as pointed out later, direct monetary transfers are just one channel of wealth transmission. This section reviews the current evidence (mainly descriptive and correlational) on the level and shape of intergenerational correlations in wealth and on the main mechanisms of intergenerational wealth transfers (see National Academies, 2024a), and broader channels that contribute to the intergenerational persistence of wealth (for other recent reviews, see Hällsten, 2024; Lersch et al., 2024).

Most existing evidence on intergenerational wealth correlations in the United States is based on the Panel Study of Income Dynamics, as it is the only nationally representative household panel study that has collected measures of family wealth early enough—starting in the 1980s—and has continued to do so long enough to allow the comparison of the wealth holdings of parents and their adult children. The earliest contributions that estimated intergenerational wealth correlations were limited to measuring the wealth outcomes of adult children in their 30s—relatively early in their life course (Charles & Hurst, 2003; Conley & Glauber, 2008; Mulligan, 1997). One method for measuring the level of mobility is to use the magnitude of the relation between parental wealth and children's wealth. These wealth relationships (or elasticities) were estimated (based on the association of the logged wealth of parents and their children) to lie between 0.28 and 0.37. Later, Pfeffer and Killewald (2018) drew on an older sample of adult children, estimating considerably higher elasticities—up to 0.54 for those aged 55–64—and correlations in relative wealth ranks of up to 0.44.

These updated estimates put the level of intergenerational persistence of wealth at a similar level to that of income. Measuring wealth during offsprings' later adulthood is crucial as the intergenerational correlation of wealth (measured by the magnitude of relation between parental rank in the wealth distribution and children's rank in the wealth distribution, called the *rank–rank slope*) rises substantially with age (Fisher & Johnson, 2023; Pfeffer & Killewald, 2018). Therefore, restricting the view to earlier life course stages would suggest that the intergenerational persistence in wealth was lower than that of income or consumption (see Brady et al., 2020; Fisher & Johnson, 2023). Also, since inequality in wealth is higher than inequality in income or consumption, estimates of wealth mobility are suppressed more than those of income and consumption mobility for mobility measures that depend on the level of inequality (e.g., elasticities, Gini index of mobility; see Fisher & Johnson, 2023).

Fisher and Johnson (2023) provided a comparative assessment of absolute upward mobility, finding that upward wealth mobility (i.e., the probability of children to exceed their parents' wealth at similar ages) is considerably lower than upward mobility in income and consumption. Furthermore, the extent of upward mobility in wealth has decreased precipitously over time, from about half of all children born in the 1950s and 1960s being upwardly mobile in terms of wealth to just 28 percent for children born in the 1980s. Intergenerational wealth correlations have also been estimated for additional countries in just the last few years (see Hällsten, 2024, for a review). The international evidence suggests that the U.S. intergenerational correlation in wealth is higher than in other countries, meaning that levels of wealth mobility are lower in the United States. For instance, the estimated wealth rank correlation is 0.17 in Norway (Fagereng et al., 2021), 0.20–0.40 in Denmark (Boserup et al., 2017; Daysal et al., 2022), 0.30 in the United Kingdom (Gregg & Kanabar, 2022), and 0.30–0.40 in Sweden (Adermon et al., 2018; Black et al., 2020).

Intergenerational correlations in wealth have been shown to be largely linear across most of the wealth distribution, with the exception of the upper tail, where wealth is particularly stable (Black et al., 2020; Boserup et al., 2017; Pfeffer & Killewald, 2018). Intergenerational correlations below the very top can also be approximated well with indicators of housing wealth or even home values, reflecting the centrality of housing in not just the distribution of wealth but also its intergenerational transmission (Blanden et al., 2023; Daysal et al., 2022; Pfeffer & Killewald, 2018), which this chapter will discuss in greater detail.

Like most work on social mobility, scholarship on wealth mobility has been largely restricted to a two-generation paradigm (i.e., the standard assessment of similarity in positions between parents and their children). However, particularly for wealth, it is likely that family socioeconomic status can also be transmitted across more than two generations, including through direct transfers from grandparents to their grandchildren (Mare, 2011; Pfeffer, 2014). A few contributions have assessed the persistence of wealth across three generations. For the United States, Pfeffer and Killewald (2018) found that three-generational wealth correlations were about two-thirds the size of the parent–child wealth correlation. They also show that only half of the grandparent–grandchild association flows through parental wealth, meaning that grandparental wealth is associated with grandchild wealth net of parental wealth. The relative importance of multigenerational wealth transmission appears to be even more pronounced in Denmark, where the size of the grandparent–grandchild wealth correlation is about three-quarters that of the parent–child correlation and most of the grandparent–grandchild association persists when parental wealth is controlled (Boserup et al., 2014). Conversely, multigenerational wealth transmission appears less pronounced in Sweden, where three-generational wealth correlations are about 40 percent the size of two-generational correlations but most of the grandparent–grandchild association flows through parental wealth (Adermon et al., 2018). Nonetheless, Hällsten and Pfeffer (2017) documented the substantial and independent influence of grandparental wealth and grandchildren's educational achievement, even in Sweden.

Finally, and importantly, research has documented drastic differences in wealth mobility between White and Black individuals in the United States. Pfeffer and Killewald (2019) showed that Black children, in addition to being severely disadvantaged in terms of their wealth background, are also far more likely to be downwardly mobile in terms of their own wealth attainment compared with White children. For instance, among children who grow up in the middle quintile of the parental wealth distribution, 39 percent of Black children fall to the bottom wealth quintile as adults, compared with 16 percent of White children. The authors concluded that today's Black–White wealth gaps arise from both historical disadvantages reflected in the unequal starting position of Black and White children, as well as contemporary processes—including continued structural discrimination—that make Black children more likely to be relegated to the bottom of the wealth distribution (see further discussion below). Fisher and Johnson (2023) also showed that the Black–White differences in wealth mobility are driven by the particularly disadvantageous mobility outcomes of Black women: Black women have especially high rates of downward mobility from the top of the wealth distribution and especially low rates of upward mobility out of the bottom.

Evidence on wealth mobility patterns among other racial/ethnic groups is still very limited. Keister et al. (2015) found that despite considerable disadvantages in childhood conditions and early young adulthood, Mexican Americans have gained greater access to wealth than Black Americans.

Much future work is needed to document the wealth mobility patterns of other racial/ethnic groups. Immigrant wealth mobility patterns are also likely to diverge from those of White families, based on the lower wealth starting positions, the potential need for reverse transfers from children to their parents, and remittances—all of which may limit immigrants' wealth accumulation and mobility.

Trajectories of Wealth Accumulation

Intragenerational wealth trajectories—stability and change in wealth over the life course—are also key components of economic mobility. Economic studies of wealth accumulation processes often focus on the roles of income, consumption, capital gains, and financial transfers (Feiveson & Sabelhaus, 2019), with a paucity of evidence on the role of taxation, which will be discussed below. Few studies jointly consider wealth alongside other dimensions of socioeconomic well-being. Fisher et al. (2016) showed that the level of short-term intragenerational mobility in wealth is similar to the level of mobility in income and consumption, although the persistence at the top of the distribution is more pronounced for wealth than for income and consumption. Importantly, empirical research on intraindividual (and intrahousehold) wealth trajectories spanning many years (and waves of data) remains relatively rare because high-quality panel data on wealth accumulation are limited. Nonetheless, literature on key economic and social determinants of wealth mobility is growing (see further discussion below). Improved wealth data are greatly needed (see National Academies, 2024a), and efforts are currently underway to create measures of wealth and intergenerational wealth transmission in the United States (see "Wealth and Mobility Study" in Chapter 6).

A recent working paper by Goda and Streeter (2021) took a broad approach to examining wealth trajectories across life milestones, including marriage, homeownership, childbirth, divorce, disability, health shocks, retirement, and widowhood.[1] The authors found significant long-run increases in wealth associated with homeownership and retirement, and significant long-run reductions in wealth associated with divorce, health shocks, and disability. Relatedly, a longitudinal study by Kapelle (2022) showed how and why there are wealth differences between divorcees and continuously married individuals. Using data from the German Socio-Economic Panel Study and matching techniques in tandem with random-effects growth curve models, Kapelle (2022) found that divorce leads to declines in net worth primarily because of loss in housing wealth around the time of

---

[1] Goda and Streeter (2021) used panel data from the NLSY79 sample of the National Longitudinal Survey and from the Health and Retirement Study.

divorce, although divorcees' rates of postdivorce wealth accumulation are comparable to those of married individuals. Prior research has also shown that acute health events lead to changes in household wealth, with differential effects across racial groups: while health shocks affect both White and Black families, they have a disproportionately deleterious impact on the financial well-being of Black families as the family heads approach retirement (Thompson & Conley, 2016). Indeed, research suggests heterogeneity across demographics, socioeconomic status, and risk protection, and identifies populations and life stages most vulnerable to large wealth reductions (Goda & Streeter, 2021).

A novel study by Chen et al. (2019) used panel data from the Health and Retirement Study to examine longitudinal wealth trajectory patterns (after age 50) and the impact of socioeconomic status on these trajectories. Results identified four distinct latent classes of wealth trajectories: stable high (reference), low and increasing, stable low, and high but declining. Moreover, three key life course mechanisms shaped wealth trajectories: (a) disadvantaged socioeconomic status in adulthood, (b) accumulated exposure to risks, and (c) downward socioeconomic disadvantage were respectively associated with increased odds of stable low, low and increasing, and high but declining (relative to stable high wealth).

While research on racial inequality in trajectories of wealth is relatively rare, growing evidence calls into question the utility of the dominant life cycle model of wealth accumulation (see Modigliani, 1988) for understanding the wealth patterns among low-wealth racial groups, where people accumulate wealth by saving throughout their working years in anticipation of retirement, and then begin dissaving. For example, a study by Brown (2016) used ten waves of panel data from the Health and Retirement Study and random coefficient growth curve models, revealing stark racial/ethnic inequality in wealth trajectories among White, Black, and Mexican Americans. Brown (2016) noted substantial racial inequality in wealth by midlife: White households had accumulated an average net worth of $105,000, compared with less than $5,000 and $39,000, respectively, for Black and Mexican American families. In addition, White individuals experience much faster rates of wealth accumulation in their 50s and 60s than their minority counterparts, resulting in wealth inequalities that increase with age, consistent with a process of cumulative disadvantage. At the apex of their wealth trajectory (age 66), White individuals had roughly $245,000 more than Black individuals and $219,000 more than Mexican Americans (Brown, 2016).

Similarly, Killewald and Bryan (2018) showed that the advantage of White individuals compared with Black and Hispanic individuals in accumulating wealth increases over the life course. Half of this advantage can be accounted for by intergenerational advantage, arising from the higher-wealth starting position of White individuals. However, by middle adulthood, intragenerational processes (i.e., disparities in wealth-enhancing traits, such as income, marriage, and homeownership) explain a greater share of racial/ethnic gaps in wealth accumulation (family size and structure could also be added to this list, as shown by Keister, 2004). Killewald and Bryan (2018) concluded that both past and present racialized processes explain today's racial/ethnic gaps. More broadly, scholars who study racial inequities in wealth emphasize that factors related to historical racism (e.g., slavery, Jim Crow laws, unequal access to GI Bill and Social Security benefits, lending discrimination, racial covenants) and contemporary structural racism (e.g., segregation in housing, schooling, and jobs; discrimination in lending, health care, and the criminal legal system) likely play a role in the production and maintenance of wealth inequality (Brown, 2016; Darity & Mullen, 2020; Killewald et al., 2017; Oliver & Shapiro, 1995; Pfeffer & Killewald, 2019).

Avenues for Wealth Mobility

The bulk of empirical work has been dedicated to estimating the contribution of inheritances and bequests and inter vivos transfers to the maintenance of wealth across generations. This work generally finds that a large share (often half) of the intergenerational wealth correlation can be explained by these direct monetary transfers (see, e.g., Adermon et al., 2018). Empirical work has shown that wealth transmission does not arise from the genetic inheritance of traits, as intergenerational correlations in wealth are also high in adoptive families (Black et al., 2020; Fagereng et al., 2021).

While much of the literature is focused on inter vivos gifts and inheritances, wealth transmission also occurs through more indirect channels. For instance, more than half of the intergenerational transmission of wealth in the United States arises through channels earlier in life, including offspring's educational attainment, acquisition of homes and businesses, and marriage (Pfeffer & Killewald, 2018). Studies of wealth reproduction therefore need to pay at least as much attention to early life, indirect investments by parents, as well as grandparents, in their offspring. Toney and Robertson (2021) show that the younger adult generation's income level is significantly affected by its parents' and grandparents' wealth. Zang et al. (2024) show the impact of both parental and grandparental wealth on mediating factors between previous generations' wealth and income, including an increased likelihood of college attendance and steady employment and decreased likelihood of nonmarital births and joblessness.

Beyond the inherent importance of wealth in direct, intergenerational investments, parental (and grandparental) wealth can also fulfill an important insurance or safety net function (Hällsten & Pfeffer, 2017; Shapiro, 2004). The precautionary savings motive that neoclassical economics assumes as one of the main drivers of wealth accumulation within a generation may thus also extend intergenerationally: wealth serves to reduce risks intergenerationally, and it needs to be better appreciated as a mechanism by which some individuals have the opportunity to take risks—and potentially fail—while others do not.

Wealth as a Mechanism of Mobility

As noted above, wealth transmission also occurs through indirect channels, such as when family wealth supports children's development, educational achievement, and degree attainment, as well as their early careers and labor market experiences. Accumulation of earnings can lead to higher income and wealth. A nascent but growing literature has established independent links between parental wealth and child development (see Gibson-Davis & Hill, 2021), such as positive behavioral (Ream & Gottfried, 2019; Shanks, 2007) and health outcomes (Boen et al., 2021). The strong relationship between parental wealth and children's educational outcomes has been documented repeatedly (e.g., Conley, 1999; Doren & Grodsky, 2016; Jez, 2024; see also summaries in Gibson-Davis & Hill, 2021; Killewald et al., 2017). The relationship especially between parental wealth and children's college attainment has also strengthened over time (Pfeffer, 2018). Beyond educational attainment, parental wealth also appears to shape the occupational attainment of the next generations (Conley, 1999; Pfeffer, 2011). While these earlier-life intergenerational influences of family wealth can be thought of as indirect channels of intergenerational wealth mobility, they are also the foundation for an even broader role of family wealth in processes of intergenerational mobility: family wealth fosters early life advantages that eventually support social mobility in other dimensions, such as educational, income, and occupational mobility. In this sense, wealth can both support and inhibit a variety of forms of economic and social mobility. For instance, Fisher and Johnson (2023) showed that children from higher-wealth backgrounds have a higher probability of intergenerational movement out of the bottom of the income distribution, as well as remaining at the top of the income distribution. Rodems and Pfeffer (2021) showed that high wealth can serve as a buffer against negative life events, as the probability to experience material hardship in the wake of an unemployment spell, earnings loss, and other demographic events is lower among those with high wealth. Understanding the indirect mechanisms through which wealth shapes other social mobility dimensions may also help elucidate racial/ethnic mobility differences. For instance, Fox (2016) found that parental wealth facilitates upward income mobility for White children growing up in low-income families but does not have the same benefits for Black children growing up in low-income families.

Housing as a Primary Source of Wealth and Inequality

The composition of wealth portfolios differs greatly across the wealth distribution (Wolff, 2017). The wealth of the top 1 percent is dominated by financial assets. By contrast, the (lack of) wealth in the bottom 10 percent is dominated by debt. The debt held by the very bottom of the wealth distribution tends to be "productive debt" (e.g., business loans), reflecting their ability to borrow rather than a destitute overall economic position. For the average U.S. household and for a majority of households, housing assets (home equity) make up the largest wealth component (McCabe, 2016). However, home equity makes up a greater portion of total wealth for Black households than for White households (LaBriola, 2024).

Housing—including the value of the home, the resources and use value the home provides (compared with renting), and the housing and other amenities around the home (i.e., neighborhoods, neighbors, schools)—is a source of wealth and stability. As a mechanism of intergenerational transmission, the effects of housing are likely multifold (Choi et al., 2018; Pfeffer, 2018), including the transmission of home equity (Benetton et al., 2024), and the reduction of credit constraints, such as the ability to pay for college (Johnson, 2020; Lovenheim, 2011). In particular, in the United States, one's relative ability to invest in housing typically translates into investments in the schools nearby, which benefit the household (in terms of equity) and also benefit one's children (in terms of better school quality that produces mobility dividends; Goldstein & Hastings, 2019; Lareau & Goyette, 2014).

American housing policy has long promoted homeownership, codified in postwar lending practices, as a vehicle for increasing economic and social mobility and wealth-building specifically (Fischel, 2005; McCabe, 2016). However, as noted in Chapter 3 (Space and Place), housing sits atop an unequal geography of opportunity that systematically disadvantages certain groups and can hamper the wealth-generating effects of home-buying. Residential racial and economic segregation results in lower-value homes in places with fewer White people and fewer wealthy people.

Some housing policies and institutions have also created racially disparate impacts in the returns to homeownership for Hispanic and Black Americans relative to White Americans (Baradaran, 2017; Flippen, 2004; Killewald & Bryan, 2016; Rothstein, 2017; Taylor, 2019). Housing policy from the New Deal forward helped create a racially stratified housing market in the United States, through the support of federally backed mortgages and subsidization built on racially discriminatory lending practices (Quillian et al., 2020), resulting in significant gaps in the rates of homeownership by race and the large racial wealth gap noted above.

New rigorous research on *redlining*—the practice of categorizing the investment risk of residential areas based on race, ethnicity, and other non-housing characteristics—has been associated with long-term consequences for communities. Through federally sponsored redlining, many Black communities were considered too risky for investment and were cut off from access to credit through mortgages; they then subsequently became vulnerable to subprime markets and practices that extract more fees (Satter, 2009; Taylor, 2019). Communities that were designated as low-grade (C or D) on the original Home Owner's Loan Corporation (HOLC) maps, over time, experienced lower rates of Black homeownership, property values, and rent, and higher rates of racial and economic segregation and vacancy in the decades following (Aaronson et al., 2021a). Specifically, across all neighborhoods, the HOLC map boundaries can account for between 15 and 30 percent of the difference in proportion of residents who were Black between the lowest (D) and next lowest (C) areas of risk (Aaronson et al., 2021b).

While Black households had restricted access to mortgages in the first half of the 20th century, still other Black individuals became homeowners through predatory inclusion in the decades after, through the practices of subprime lending and other risky financing (Rugh & Massey, 2010; Seamster & Charron-Chénier, 2017). Subsequently, the consequences of the foreclosure crisis of the 2000s were stratified by race and by neighborhood (Rugh & Massey, 2010). Conversely, housing market appreciation during this same period largely benefited White homeowners, and recent research has found that such housing market dynamics can account for nearly three-quarters of the increase in the median White–Black wealth gap between 1984 and 2019 (LaBriola, 2024).

While most of the research on racial disparities in homeownership has focused on the impacts of lending practices and institutions, recent work also points to the risks of acquiring properties without the protection of institutionally regulated mortgages. While not an entirely new practice (see Pietila, 2010; Satter, 2009), informal and unregulated housing markets still exist, especially in low-income, mostly Black communities in places such as Detroit and Baltimore (Jang-Trettien, 2022). Some practices in these communities—such as land contracts, contracts for deeds, or informally gifting properties within families—can lead homeowners to purchase properties without clear titles or with significant liens and structural problems with the homes (Jang-Trettien, 2022).

While racial inequality in homeownership is essential to understanding economic mobility and wealth, more than one-third of families—and most low-income households—rent their homes (e.g., the National Low Income Housing Commission). However, by prioritizing homeownership, housing policy has fallen short of the needs of renters to obtain housing security, let alone wealth (DeLuca & Rosen, 2022). Low-income renter households pay more of their income toward housing than their more affluent counterparts but do not realize the benefits of policies such as the mortgage interest tax deduction; its reduction through the Tax Cuts and Jobs Act of 2017 led to more equitable distribution of taxes (see Ambrose et al., 2022). Most of the government spending for homeowners goes to the top fifth of households by income (Fischer & Sard, 2017). The affordable housing crisis has hit renters especially hard, and federal policy has not responded adequately: unlike the Supplemental Nutrition Assistance Program and other entitlement programs, housing assistance in the United States is not guaranteed by income; only about one of four income-eligible households receives rental assistance. In part, this is because of the stagnant supply of housing choice vouchers and the shift in federal housing policy since the 1970s toward market-based rental subsidies (relying on private-market landlords) rather than the construction of public housing units (Hackworth, 2007; Rosen, 2020; Schwartz, 2015). As such, renters—especially those who are racial minorities—are more vulnerable to housing insecurity than homeowners.

CREDIT AND DEBT

As clearly demonstrated in the case of housing and homeownership, access to credit and the ability to borrow are key resources that enable income and consumption smoothing, facilitate investments in human capital, and allow the cost of goods and services to be allocated over time. As such, borrowing provides opportunities to improve economic and social well-being, particularly over the long term. At the same time, debt repayment may strain current household resources, resulting in reduced consumption and, potentially, economic stress, distress, and hardship, with negative implications for health and well-being, particularly among disadvantaged households (Drentea, 2000; Drentea & Lavrakas, 2000).

Credit and Debt Are Not a Monolith

Households borrow in heterogeneous contexts and via heterogeneous credit mechanisms, reflecting differences in financial resources as well as in the timing of and reasons for borrowing, with implications for amounts borrowed, types of debt accrued, loan terms, and ability to meet the terms of the loan. Berger and Houle (2019) provide a framework for considering the role of household debt vis-à-vis individual agency in borrowing (i.e., the degree to which decisions to borrow reflect deliberate, future-directed intent versus constrained resources for meeting immediate economic needs), magnitude borrowed (amount of debt in absolute terms and relative to income or assets), and cost of borrowing (interest rates and fees, which are closely tied to loan type). Dwyer (2018) further categorizes debts by the extent to which they are accrued via prospective credit offer versus retrospective obligation, as well as whether they are owed to market or state actors. Prospective offers from state institutions include federal mortgage and student loans; prospective offers from market institutions include private-sector mortgages, and home equity–based, education, auto, and unsecured (credit card, personal finance, payday, title, pawnshop) loans. Retrospective obligations to state institutions include criminal and legal fines and fees, other monies owed to government (tax penalties; fines, fees, and interest, including that owed for unpaid taxes and child support arrears; reimbursement for social welfare benefit overpayments) and past-due public utility/amenity bills. Retrospective obligations to market institutions include medical debt, past-due rent and other bills, and child support arrears owed to custodial parents.

Just as with wealth and asset portfolios, specific types of credit and debt are unevenly accessed by different population groups. Most notably, economically disadvantaged and racial/ethnic minority families are disproportionately likely to take on high-cost unsecured debt in order to meet basic expenses (Shah et al., 2012) and in response to adverse economic (Barr, 2012; Sullivan, 2008) and health shocks (Babiarz et al., 2013), reflecting lower levels of income and assets, and connoting lesser agency in borrowing and lesser access to low-cost (prime) credit mechanisms. They are also disproportionately likely to face retrospective debt obligations to both state and market institutions. In contrast, more advantaged and White populations are disproportionately likely to accrue debt for prospective investment in human capital and asset acquisition, and to do so via lower-cost mechanisms (Dwyer, 2018).

Indeed, whereas access to credit has expanded for all segments of the population, economically disadvantaged and racial/ethnic minority populations are disproportionately more likely than their higher-income counterparts to borrow for consumption rather than investment and to hold retrospective debt obligations to both government and market actors, and to be unbanked (Boel & Zimmerman, 2022; Houle & Addo, 2022; Servon, 2017; Tach & Greene, 2014; Wherry & Chakrabarti, 2022). They also tend to receive higher-cost (including subprime) loan terms and experience higher rates of delinquency and default in each major loan category—home, education, auto, and unsecured—although disparities in unsecured debt burden are particularly large (Avtar et al., 2021; Houle, 2014a; Houle & Addo, 2022; Mills et al., 2022; Seamster & Charron-Chénier, 2017; Wherry & Perry, 2021; Williams et al., 2005). Notably, whereas less-advantaged and racial/ethnic minority households tend to hold less total debt, on average, than more advantaged households, they also tend to face higher relative debt burdens as a result of both lesser income and assets and less-beneficial loan terms (Avtar et al., 2021; Houle, 2014a; Mills et al., 2022; Sullivan

& Kaufman, 2012). These factors raise important questions regarding the extent to which credit and debt—and particular types thereof—may promote or impede upward (or downward) economic and social mobility, both overall and for population groups with greater and lesser degrees of social and economic (dis)advantage.

Indirect Pathways to Mobility

Whereas a substantial body of research has established that wealth is linked to inter- and intragenerational patterns of economic and social (dis)advantage and mobility, comparatively little is known about whether and how access to credit and (particular types of) debt may be linked to intra- and intergenerational mobility. Indeed, the committee is aware of no study to explicitly examine such links; however, as discussed below, a small group of studies have examined links between access to credit and key mechanisms for economic and social mobility, such as investments in children's human capital, college attendance and completion, and young adult earnings (Braxton et al., 2024; Lochner & Monge-Naranjo, 2012; Mayer, 2021; Ringo, 2019; Sun & Yannelis, 2016). Yet, a growing body of research examining relations among credit and debt, inequality, and adult and child well-being implies, albeit indirectly, that debt patterns have the potential to influence economic and social mobility (Dwyer, 2018). As noted above, the ability to borrow at reasonable terms vis-à-vis one's financial situation may enable investments in human capital (e.g., education) for oneself or family members. This has the potential to lead to greater income and assets (e.g., a home, the primary source of wealth for Americans), which in turn can increase in value over time and thereby provide wealth gains and associated opportunities for transferring wealth, as well as opportunities for borrowing at reasonable cost to make subsequent investments or respond to adverse economic shocks. Conversely, borrowing under economic duress, potentially with limited agency and at high cost, may adversely affect subsequent consumption, savings, and investment. Each of these possibilities may have implications for intra- and intergenerational well-being and, thereby, economic and social mobility.

Research to date points to several overarching patterns. First, household debt is relatively common across the U.S. income distribution, but it is disproportionately associated with investment at higher income levels and with immediate consumption at lower income levels (Dwyer, 2018). Second, lower-income households are increasingly experiencing high debt burdens, which grow over the life course (Dwyer, 2018). Third, although middle-income American households appear to have particularly high levels of debt relative to lower-income (and also higher-income) households (Fitzgerald & Leicht, 2014; Hodson et al., 2014; Houle, 2014b; McCloud

& Dwyer, 2011; Sullivan et al., 2001), this may, at least in part, reflect inadequate measurement and omission, in both the surveys and administrative (credit report) data used to measure debt. Indeed, many forms of debt that are common among low-income households—including alternative financial services loans (payday loans, title loans), civil and criminal legal debt, medical debt, unpaid bills, loans from nonfinancial institutions (employers, family, friends, pawn shops), child support debt, and other debts owed to government—are frequently missing from these data sources (Finnigan & Meagher, 2019; Fourcade & Healy, 2013; Ghaffary, 2019; Halpern-Meekin et al., 2015; Harris, 2016; Wherry et al., 2019). Fourth, common adverse experiences such as chronic health conditions, adverse health shocks, family disruptions, criminal and civil legal judgments, and unstable employment and income are associated with high levels of unsecured debt among low-income households, many of which struggle to repay these debts (Berger & Houle, 2016; Houle & Keene, 2015; McCloud & Dwyer, 2011). Fifth, unsecured debt is associated with economic hardship, financial strain and distress, and poorer health and well-being, particularly among disadvantaged populations (Berger & Houle, 2016, 2019; Berger et al., 2016; Dwyer et al., 2011, 2016; Keese & Schmitz, 2014; Loibl et al., 2022; Sun & Houle, 2020).

Despite a large and long-standing research literature linking economic resources, such as income and wealth, to the health and well-being of both adults and children, only recently have scholars begun to examine the potential effects of (particular types of) debt on well-being. On the whole, research to date has produced inconsistent findings with respect to the magnitude and direction of relation between debt, generally defined, and adult well-being. However, studies investigating links between particular types of debt and adult well-being predominantly suggest that higher-cost unsecured debt, which is primarily used for consumption, is adversely associated with adult well-being, particularly among disadvantaged populations and those with greater debt burden. These findings span financial stress and anxiety (Drentea, 2000; Norvilitis et al., 2006; Worthington, 2006), decision-making (Lea et al., 2012; Shah et al., 2012), health and mental health (Berger et al., 2016; Bridges & Disney, 2010, Brown et al., 2005; Drentea, 2000; Drentea & Lavrakas, 2000; Drentea & Reynolds, 2012; Jenkins et al., 2008; Keese & Schmitz, 2014; Reading & Reynolds, 2001; Turunen & Hiilamo, 2014; Walsemann et al., 2015), and marital quality and relationship strain (Dew, 2007, 2008). Notably, however, there is no consistent evidence that lower-cost secured (particularly mortgage) debt, which is primarily used for investment, is similarly associated with adverse outcomes, and some evidence (Moulton et al., 2022) suggests that ability to borrow against one's home may facilitate disease management. Moreover, research suggests substantial heterogeneity in associations between student loan debt and well-being across population groups and by factors such as loan amounts and terms, types of educational institutions attended, and subsequent educational attainment (see Dwyer, 2018, for a summary).

It is also possible that parental debt may influence child well-being either directly via consumption or indirectly via parental stress and accompanying characteristics of parenting behaviors and the quality of children's caregiving environments. The committee is aware of only three studies that examine relations between debt and child well-being directly. Berger and Houle (2016), using child fixed-effects regressions, found associations of mortgage and educational debt with better child socioemotional development, potentially reflecting greater parental educational attainment, wealth, and neighborhood quality, and between greater unsecured debt and poorer child socioemotional well-being, potentially reflecting greater parental stress and/or constrained consumption. Berger and Houle (2019), using a hierarchical linear modeling strategy, found unsecured debt to be associated with growth in child behavior problems over time, with effects being particularly concentrated among younger children and children from less-advantaged families. They found no associations of home, education, or auto debt with children's socioemotional developmental trajectories. Finally, Nepomnyaschy et al. (2021), using cross-sectional regressions to assess associations of resident mothers' unsecured debt, nonresident fathers' unsecured debt, and nonresident fathers' child support debt for children at age 9 and 15, find associations between nonresident fathers' child support debt and greater child behavior problems, with larger effect sizes at age 15 than 9, but no associations of resident mothers' or nonresident fathers' unsecured debt with behavior problems at either age (controlling for nonresident fathers' child support debt).

Finally, several studies point to plausibly causal relations of parental access to credit with investments in their children's human capital, their children's college attendance and completion, and their earnings in young adulthood, each of which is thought to be a key mechanism through which economic and social mobility may occur. Lochner and Monge-Naranjo's (2012) review of the literature linking credit constraints with children's educational attainment, for example, indicates that access to credit has played an increasingly important role in college enrollment decisions in recent decades, but also that constrained credit during early childhood may adversely affect investments in children's human capital to an even greater degree than access to credit during later childhood and adolescence affects college-going. Mayer (2021) demonstrates that constrained access to (prime) credit limits parents' investments in their children's human capital vis-à-vis homeownership and access to high-quality schools. Sun and Yannelis (2016) and Ringo (2019) further provide evidence that greater parental credit constraints result in lesser college attendance and completion for their children. And, most recently, Braxton et al. (2024) show that greater parental access to credit during children's adolescence is associated with greater earnings for their children during young adulthood. At the same time, however, they also found that expanded access to credit for disadvantaged families can suppress intergenerational economic mobility because, whereas expanded access to credit (increased credit limits and decreased cost of bankruptcy) offers increased opportunities for human capital investment, it also reduces incentives for saving among disadvantaged families, which are more likely than advantaged families to reach their credit limits and struggle with repayment and, in response, may decrease human capital investments in children. Together, this evidence suggests that access to credit may both promote and suppress opportunities for economic and social mobility. Moreover, research shows a strong intergenerational correlation between parents' credit scores during their children's childhoods and their children's credit scores as adults (Hartley et al., 2019).

Credit "Worthiness"

While much of the above discussion focuses on the potential mobility-related consequences of debt as burden, or as a *negative* asset, credit is an increasingly important social and economic "attribute" that determines individuals' access to valuable social and economic opportunities and resources across multiple domains (Dwyer, 2018). Specifically, individuals' credit worthiness—as largely determined by their credit score—is a de facto measure of social and economic worthiness when it comes to access to fundamental drivers of mobility, such as employment and housing (see also Goodman et al., 2020; Hartley et al., 2019). Individual and household debt may affect employment and, particularly, housing opportunities in a context in which employers and landlords perform credit checks to inform hiring and rental decisions. The existing literature on employment suggests that credit checks are not typically the deciding factor in hiring decisions but are often taken into consideration, which may constrain employment options for those with poor credit scores. At the same time, research evaluating legal bans on employer credit checks has produced mixed results on whether such policies increase or decrease employment among disadvantaged populations (see, e.g., Ballance et al., 2020; Friedberg et al., 2021).

Returning to the issue of housing, landlords' increasing reliance on credit scores as a screening criterion for access to rental properties presents an understudied but potentially important dimension for understanding the role of debt and credit in shaping economic mobility. Evidence of income-to-rent ratios above 2 or 3 and proof of steady employment have long been common tenancy requirements; however, landlords increasingly use credit scores to decide whether applicants for rental housing are acceptable tenants (DeLuca et al., 2023; Desmond, 2016; Galvez, 2010; Reosti, 2021; Rosen et al., 2021). Moreover, credit checks may serve as a proxy for other stigmatized traits, such as race or housing subsidy status, allowing landlords to discriminate by these traits legally (Rosen et al., 2021). As in other domains, such as criminal justice processing and hiring practices, the use of credit scores in housing decisions may reinforce racial and class-based hierarchies (Brayne & Christin, 2021; Doleac & Stevenson, 2020; Dressel & Farid, 2018; Fourcade & Healy, 2013; Kiviat, 2019; Starr, 2014). As scholars have long noted, credit scores have stratified access to homeownership, exacerbating inequality by race (Avery et al., 2009; Baradaran, 2019; Wherry et al., 2019). In the aftermath of the 2008 housing market crash, credit histories of renters have become increasingly available to landlords (Frazier, 2021). Frazier (2021) reported, "In 2011, Experian introduced RentBureau, a service that offers rent-payment history to landlords. [...] TransUnion debuted SmartMove. [...] Equifax also offered screening reports. Next came the rent-payment platforms [... that] track who has paid on time and funnels that data back to the credit bureaus, which aggregate it and sell it back to landlords" (p. 20). Landlords also use eviction history as a screening criterion, and some research suggests that eviction itself reduces access to credit, creating a negative feedback effect (Humphries et al., 2019).

Having one's rental applications rejected—sometimes repeatedly—is a demoralizing and sometimes expensive experience. Worry about rejection may affect the housing searches of low-income families and increase the chances that they rent lower-quality housing units in neighborhoods with lesser economic opportunity (Bergman et al., 2024; DeLuca et al., 2013, 2023; Reosti, 2021; Rosen, 2020), given that landlords of low-end rental units, which are disproportionately likely to have housing code violations, may less frequently require credit checks (Rosen et al., 2021). In addition, whereas having a poor credit history is problematic, so is not having a credit history at all; almost 20 percent of the American population is considered credit invisible or unscorable (Consumer Financial Protection Bureau [CFPB] Office of Research, 2015). Brevoort et al. (2018) discusses the differences in credit invisibility. Rates of "no credit history" are higher among residents of low-income neighborhoods, where 30 percent of residents are credit unscorable, on average (compared with 4 percent of residents in high-income neighborhoods). Moreover, Black and Hispanic populations face credit reporting barriers at nearly double the rate of White and Asian populations (CFPB Office of Research, 2015). Nonetheless, far too little is known about how widespread is the use of credit checks in the private rental market and whether credit checks are a primary cause or mechanism through which to understand restricted housing and neighborhood opportunities—and thus economic mobility—of low-income and racial minority households.

POLICY IMPLICATIONS

Besides established tax policies that provide income supplements (e.g., Earned Income Tax Credit, Child Tax Credit), existing tax instruments support asset-building (e.g., home mortgage interest deduction, preferential treatment of trusts and college savings accounts, lower tax rates on capital income). However, few existing policies seek to target the intergenerational persistence of wealth explicitly.

One important exception is the taxation of inheritances (i.e., estate tax). The main normative argument in favor of inheritance taxation is, indeed, to prevent the creation of a wealthy elite that inherits its status across many generations (Beckert, 2008). So far, empirical studies of the potential effects of inheritance taxation have focused on the question of whether and to what degree it may impact the level of wealth inequality; these studies have found that, in the long run, inheritance taxation helps reduce overall wealth inequality (Nekoei & Seim, 2023). It remains an open empirical question whether inheritance taxation can also limit the extent to which the top-most wealth positions in the country remain in the same families for generations. If there are indeed any direct effects of today's system of inheritance taxation on wealth mobility, they should be expected to be quite limited in scope, as only a miniscule fraction of wealthy households is impacted by the estate tax: the expected number of 2023 estate tax returns that will be subject to the U.S. estate tax is estimated at just 4,000 estates. That means, just about 0.14 percent of decedents will be subject to an estate tax (Tax Policy Center, 2024). At the beginning of the 21st century, before the implementation of the Economic Growth and Tax Relief Reconciliation Act of 2001, this number was more than ten times higher, with 50,000 estates taxed (Tax Policy Center, 2024) and much higher in many prior periods that were marked by lower estate tax thresholds and higher estate tax rates (Joint Committee on Taxation, 2015). With that, the United States is one of several nations in which the estate tax has first risen and then fallen in importance (Genschel et al., 2023). Generally, though, estate taxation may play a crucial role in financing other interventions geared at enabling wealth mobility that will be discussed further below. In addition to impacting only a very small fraction of the population, the potential direct impact of estate taxes on wealth mobility may also be limited by their timing. The average age of receiving an inheritance is around age 50 (Piketty, 2014)—that is, an age at which much of offspring wealth has already been accumulated and, at least, in part shaped by the advantages arising from their parents' wealth (see also Pfeffer & Killewald, 2018).

A potential policy response to the limited impacts of inheritance taxation is taxing wealth earlier than at the point of death—namely, through direct wealth taxation. Unlike other nations (e.g., see Limberg & Seelkopf, 2022), the United States has never implemented a comprehensive system of wealth tax, and its constitutionality is debated by law scholars (Ackerman, 1999). Nonetheless, the potential revenue flowing from progressive wealth taxation would be large (Saez & Zucman, 2019) and, similar to the revenue raised through estate taxation, could fund other policies geared at building wealth and supporting wealth mobility.

Some of these wealth-building policies can be classified by the point of the wealth distribution they target: homeownership policies help build middle-class wealth, asset-building policies (such as matched savings account) can lift off the bottom of the wealth distribution, and increased regulation of credit and debt markets can rule out exploitative credit products that keep households indebted. Beginning with housing policy, as stated above, the federal tax and policy environment has been quite beneficial for many middle-class families in allowing them to gain access to homeownership and to accumulate home equity.

Many policies attempt to increase affordable housing. Examples include the Federal Housing Administration (and low–down payment mortgages), government-sponsored affordable housing goals, and affordable mortgage programs through state housing finance agencies that target households with weak credit profiles (see Hayes, 2020; Mehrota et al., 2024; Moulton, 2022). However, both the access to homeownership and families' ability to use it for wealth accumulation have been deeply stratified, particularly along racial lines. For instance, the GI Bill's housing provisions (in the form of the home loan guarantee program) have been shown to benefit White individuals to a much greater degree than Black individuals (Agbai, 2022). This policy-induced racial inequity in access to housing wealth continued and even magnified among the descendants of the GI Bill generation (Meschede et al., 2022). Racially biased housing policy or racial bias in its implementation continued throughout the century in myriad ways, restricting access to homeownership for Black families and other racial minorities (Satter, 2009; Taylor, 2019). The resulting Black–White homeownership gap also meant that Black households were less likely to profit from the long upswing in home prices. As a consequence, the long-term housing market appreciation of the last half-century alone can explain nearly three-quarters of the overall growth in Black–White wealth inequality (LaBriola, 2024). Conversely, the loss of housing wealth during the Great Recession starting in 2008 impacted non-White families disproportionally (Pfeffer, 2018). Insufficient regulation of the mortgage credit market facilitated the emergence of predatory lending through the use of subprime mortgages and, importantly, allowed financial providers to target neighborhoods with a higher representation of Black and Hispanic households (Hwang et al., 2015; Rugh & Massey, 2010). Finally, U.S. tax policy has supported homeownership through the mortgage interest deduction, a tax expenditure that is highly regressive because it benefits higher-income households. And although initial analyses suggest no direct racial bias in the home mortgage interest deduction, through their underrepresentation at higher income levels, racial minority households also benefit less from this tax provision (Cronin et al., 2024).

Asset-building policies typically offer financial instruments that are designed to induce poor households to save, such as through matched savings accounts (Sherraden, 1991). Randomized controlled trials have shown that these instruments may indeed help poor households build up a small amounts of savings, such as $500 (Schreiner & Sherraden, 2007). However, given the vast inequality in wealth, it appears unlikely that these assets could transform the opportunities of the next generation in such a way that asset-building policies could alter patterns of intergenerational wealth mobility meaningfully.

Credit and debt policy is tasked with achieving a delicate balance between promoting access to credit while also protecting consumers (particularly those of subprime credit products) from exorbitant and, in some cases predatory, costs of borrowing. Thus, designing equitable and efficient credit regulation policies is challenging. Such policies can generally be described as falling into four broad domains: (a) information regulation, such as "truth in lending" laws that govern lender disclosure of precise loan terms; (b) price regulation, such as usury (interest rate) and small-dollar loan laws that constrain total costs and fees that can be charged on particular types of loans (payday loans, auto-title loans)—in some cases, policies ban these types of loans; (c) risk regulation, such as debt restructuring (e.g., bankruptcy) and, more recently, debt forgiveness policies; and (d) access regulation, which aims to prevent discriminatory lending policies via "fair lending" laws (Campbell et al., 2011; Fleming, 2018; Horn, 2017; Johnson & Leary, 2017). Whereas research has examined some of the short-term impacts of such policies on factors such as loan-taking, loan amounts, and repayment patterns (Agarwal et al., 2015; Rigbi, 2013; Seira et al., 2017), the committee is aware of no rigorous studies to examine these policies' long-term effects on financial stability or human capital development. Thus, there is no existing evidence base on which we can assess the potential influence of such policies on economic and social well-being and, in turn, mobility. These areas are ripe for future research (Horn, 2017; Johnson & Leary, 2017). Likewise, future research is warranted to better inform how the use of credit histories, scores, and other data can improve underwriting and targeted access to (prime) credit for disadvantaged and underserved groups (Blattner & Nelson, 2021; Meursault et al., 2022), as well as the efficacy of alternative approaches to credit-building, such as lending circles (Wherry et al., 2019).

Besides the targeted wealth policies described above, universal policies that provide a wealth transfer to all or most families or young people have recently gained interest. Zewde (2020) discusses how public and private pension policies, educational financing, progressiveness of taxation, and health care financing can help and hinder the impact on inequality over the life course. External events such as recessions can create disparities across the life cycle cohorts as people experience events at different ages, especially if participants experience differential rates of return. For instance, capital endowment programs would provide a universal wealth transfer to all young adults (e.g., $125,000 paid out at age 21 or age 25; Ackerman & Alstott, 1999; Piketty, 2020).

Baby bond programs (Hamilton & Darity, 2010), another universal wealth transfer policy, would provide children up to $50,000 at birth, depending on their parents' wealth, and would guarantee them a 2 percent annual rate of return until they turn 18. In 2023, Connecticut was the first U.S. state to implement a statewide baby bond program. Washington, DC, and California have also passed baby bond legislation, and such legislation has been proposed in 14 more U.S. states recently. Of course, it will take time to assess the impacts of these programs.

Although baby bond policies are race neutral, recent simulations suggest that they could be very effective in reducing or even eliminating the Black–White wealth gap (Dvir-Djerassi, 2024; Zewde, 2020). As such, policies that involve direct wealth transfers (such as baby bonds) to all or part of the population have been successful in terms of reducing racial wealth gaps (see also Darity et al., 2024, for the importance of reparations, and National Academies, 2024a, for other wealth transfers). Reparatory policies have been used in the United States and in other countries—for example, for Holocaust victims (U.S. Department of State, 2020), American Indians (Trosper, 1994), Japanese internment victims (Bilmes & Brooks, 2024), and victims of armed conflict in Colombia (Bogliacino et al., 2025)—and they have been proposed for Black American descendants of enslaved people (see, e.g., Darity et al., 2024). However, continued processes of structural discrimination that continue to push the next generation into lower wealth positions also need to be addressed (see, e.g., Killewald & Bryan, 2018; Pfeffer & Killewald, 2019).

Finally, acknowledging that wealth advantage is transmitted to the next generation throughout their life course and through multiple channels, broader policies and reforms could consider reforming the institutions that currently require families to rely on wealth to facilitate their offspring's success. For instance, educational reforms that expand low-tuition, public higher education would reduce the reliance of families to draw on their own wealth and/or to take on debt in support of the advancement of their children and the nation (see Chapter 4). That is, an alternative policy approach to increasing intergenerational wealth mobility is making accessible resources that support individuals' mobility, such as higher education, that currently rely on private wealth. Inheritance, gift, and wealth taxation are potential avenues for meeting the associated revenue needs. Future research should study the potential of the existing taxation system and new tax policies for these purposes.

SUMMARY, KEY CONCLUSIONS, AND RECOMMENDATIONS

A growing body of research consistently documents relatively low levels of wealth mobility in the United States, coupled with a high degree of inequality in the concentration of wealth (at the top of the distribution) and stark racial/ethnic gaps in wealth that have grown over time. Compared with its peer countries, the United States also stands out as the country with the highest level of wealth inequality and top concentration in wealth.

Wealth is an important component of intergenerational mobility in the United States. Perhaps the most distinctive feature of wealth is that—unlike education, occupation, or income—it can be transmitted directly to one's children and grandchildren. However, the transmission of wealth can take place not only directly through transfers and bequests, but also indirectly through advantages that accrue to children in their early development, educational, and labor market experiences. These indirect channels of wealth transmission also undergird wealth's role in sustaining other forms of social mobility. Family wealth has broad intergenerational impacts that accrue through multiple mechanisms. In addition to monetary advantages, family wealth can provide a safety net or buffer that allows individuals with access to wealth the privilege of taking risks. The intergenerational behavioral implications of assets and debts are one frontier for future research on wealth and debt.

Like most other scholarship on social mobility, most existing studies on wealth are limited to a two-generation framework (i.e., the standard assessment of similarity in positions between parents and their children). However, both family assets and debts can exert influences beyond immediate offspring. As a result, increased consideration of the role of at least grandparental wealth and debt is crucial.

Housing is a key source of wealth and stability, including the value of the home itself, the resources a home provides (as compared with renting), and the homes around the home (i.e., neighborhoods). Housing assets (home equity) are the primary source of wealth component for the average U.S. household and for a majority of households. As a mechanism of intergenerational transmission, the effects of housing are likely multifold. One such mechanism is the ability of homeowners to take on additional debt (through home equity–based lending) that they can use to support their children's postsecondary educational attainment in a context of high and rising college costs.

> *Conclusion 5-1: Wealth is transmitted across generations. This transmission occurs partly directly, through transfers and bequests, but also indirectly, through advantages that accrue to children in their early development, neighborhood, educational, and labor market experiences; these indirect channels of wealth transmission undergird wealth's role in sustaining other forms of economic and social mobility. In addition to monetary advantages, family wealth can provide a safety net or buffer that allows individuals to take risks.*

Recommendation 5-1: Researchers should examine the intergenerational behavioral implications of assets and debt to better understand the indirect channels through which wealth is transmitted.

Recommendation 5-2: Researchers should expand the traditional two-generation mobility framework by considering the role of grandparental wealth and debt.

Wealth accumulation and intergenerational wealth transmission are shaped by multiple institutional and structural features of U.S. society that have not been and are still not race neutral, with the segregated housing market and racialized lending practices being just one prime example. The sources of disparities among racial/ethnic minority groups have shifted in scope over time but require ever more critical analysis, as direct forms of legal exclusion from asset accumulation have morphed into less explicit but potentially equally impactful ways of reproducing racial/ethnic wealth gaps, such as via weakened homeownership rights or predatory lending practices (see Dyer et al., 2008 for a discussion of the issues surrounding heirs' property). Uncovering these institutions, policies, and practices remains an urgent task for future research. Moreover, although research has documented dramatic differences in wealth mobility between White and Black individuals, evidence on wealth mobility patterns among other groups is still very limited.

> *Conclusion 5-2: Wealth accumulation and intergenerational wealth transmission are shaped by multiple institutional and structural features of U.S. society that have not been and are still not race neutral.*

Recommendation 5-3: Researchers should further examine the ongoing role of institutions, policies, and practices in reproducing racial/ethnic wealth gaps and expand beyond White and Black populations to generate evidence on wealth mobility patterns for other racial/ethnic groups.

Credit and debt provide many individuals with opportunities to make investments in human capital and core assets, such as a home, as well as opportunities to take risks that engender wealth accumulation and upward mobility. However, for others, credit and debt are insurmountable obstacles that hinder upward mobility; they may even be direct sources of downward inter- and/or intragenerational mobility. In other words, credit and debt are not monolithic; their particular types can carry both important benefits and challenges to the individuals that access them. It is therefore important to study the circumstances in which credit and debt are productive and for whom. Student debt, which accounts for a sizeable share of the debt burden of U.S. households, is one type of debt that represents this tension well: while generally considered a "productive" form of debt, as it can enable the pursuit of higher education and the earnings benefits that arise from a college degree, student debt has contributed greatly to the maintenance of racial inequity in wealth and indebtedness.

Conclusion 5-3: Credit and debt are not monolithic. For many individuals, they provide opportunities to make core long-term investments and take risks that engender wealth accumulation and upward mobility. For others, they are hindrances to upward mobility, if not direct sources of downward mobility.

Recommendation 5-4: Researchers should study in what circumstances, how, and for whom different forms of credit and debt are helpful or harmful for economic and social mobility.

Few existing policies explicitly target the intergenerational persistence of wealth. However, a variety of different interventions is possible. One approach is to adopt policies that target different points of the wealth distribution: inheritance and wealth taxation will impact only the very top of the wealth distribution; homeownership policies will help build middle-class wealth; and the regulation of credit and debt markets, as well as asset-building policies such as matched savings accounts, can lift the very bottom of the wealth distribution. A more universal approach would be to provide a wealth transfer to all families, young people, or the descendants of enslaved people through policies such as universal wealth grants, baby bonds, or reparations for slavery, respectively. These policies can create a more widely shared economic basis for families to invest in the success of their children. Although initial assessments of some of these policies are underway, far more needs to be known about their relative effectiveness.

Finally, acknowledging that wealth advantage is transmitted to the next generation throughout the life course and through multiple channels, broader policies and reforms could consider reforming the institutions that currently make families rely on wealth to facilitate their offspring's success. For instance, as discussed in Chapter 4, educational reforms that expand low-tuition, public higher education would reduce families' reliance on their wealth or debt in support of the advancement of their children.

Conclusion 5-4: Targeted policies can address the intergenerational transmission of wealth at different points of the wealth distribution, from the top (through inheritance and wealth taxation), to the middle (chiefly through housing policies), to the bottom (through credit market regulation and asset-building policies). More universal policies (e.g., universal stakeholder grants, baby bonds, reparations) can build a common stock of wealth for all. However, more needs to be known about the relative promise of each of these approaches and of the mechanisms for funding them.

Recommendation 5-5: Researchers should study the relative costs, benefits, and long-term effects of (1) policies that target the intergenerational transmission of wealth at different points in the wealth distribution (top, middle, and bottom); (2) universal policies that seek to provide wealth transfers to all families or young people or provide reparations for slavery; and (3) broader institutional changes that would reduce the necessity of families to rely on their private wealth to support the success of the next generation. Researchers should also study the potential of the existing taxation system and new tax policies to support these initiatives.

6

Data Infrastructure

Intergenerational mobility is challenging to measure for at least six reasons: (a) Mobility is a multidimensional process that plays out across a wide range of interrelated outcomes (e.g., earnings, income, wealth, occupation, class, prestige). Although this challenge is typically skirted by focusing on just one type of mobility, doing so ignores trade-offs and other ways in which different types of mobility are related to one another. If one sought to instead analyze mobility holistically, the data demands quickly become complex. (b) Mobility is affected by continuous changes across the life course, but measures occur at moments in the life course (e.g., mobility between "parent's occupation at age 45" and the child's "first occupation after they complete schooling"). If one wants to examine multigenerational mobility (e.g., mobility between grandparents, parents, and grandchildren), these continuous changes become yet more complicated to characterize. (c) Familial resource-sharing dynamics complicate measurement; such dynamics include rapid changes in nonmarital cohabitation and childbearing, new patterns of divorce, and evolving norms of resource-sharing across multiple partnerships and extended families. Because these changes imply fluidity in resource-sharing arrangements, they complicate the measurement of socioeconomic status. (d) Mobility is highly variable and differs across neighborhoods, gender, race and ethnicity, nativity, and other subpopulations. Because the effects of these different dimensions on the mobility process may interact, a very large sample is often needed to properly examine cross-group differences in mobility. (e) Mobility has a wide range of effects on many dimensions of human well-being (e.g., health, happiness, family formation) that are themselves challenging to measure. (f) Mobility has varied causes—both individual-level and institutional causes—that interact with one another in complicated ways. For all of these reasons, large samples that cover long periods are typically needed to measure mobility and the wide range of mechanisms that potentially affect mobility.

This chapter begins by summarizing how the current data infrastructure meets these many challenges. It first discusses some of the most frequently used survey data as well as new administrative datasets that will make it increasingly possible to meet these challenges. Next, it reviews some of the ongoing data infrastructure initiatives that will soon bear fruit. Although these initiatives open new opportunities for research, much additional data collection and data-sharing are still required, including the ability to combine ongoing survey data with administrative data. The concluding section provides recommendations for improving accessibility and dissemination. The chapter text is followed by tables outlining surveys and datasets pertinent to economic and social mobility, as well as a glossary of relevant terms.

CURRENTLY AVAILABLE DATA RESOURCES

Survey Data

Annex Table 6-1 lists some of the survey data that have been used to study intergenerational mobility in the United States. This section offers brief comments on their relevance to mobility research.

The Panel Study of Income Dynamics (PSID) and the National Longitudinal Surveys of Youth (NLSY) have long been relied upon because they have evolved to include long panels on the adult children of the original survey respondents. In addition, the PSID and NLSY contain child and youth supplements that can be used to further assess mobility, and the NLSY is currently undergoing planning for a new cohort in 2027. The Wisconsin Longitudinal Study (WLS) also offers a very long panel, with rich and extensive follow-ups as the cohort moved through early adulthood, middle age, and old age. Whereas the WLS follows a birth cohort that is now very old, the Future of Families and Child Wellbeing Study (FFCWS) and National Longitudinal Study of Adolescent to Adult Health (Add Health) follow more recent birth cohorts and have thus become increasingly attractive for contemporary mobility analysis (see James et al., 2021, for FFCWS, and Harris et al., 2019, for Add Health). Although the FFCWS was fielded to study the effects of family structure and Add Health to monitor health outcomes, both provide exhaustive coverage of life experiences. The Survey of Income and Program Participation does not have an explicitly intergenerational design in recent waves but matches to administrative earnings records facilitate its use for intergenerational analyses. The Health and Retirement Study (HRS) covers an extensive range of birth cohorts, includes retrospective data on childhood family life, and can be linked to earnings records and other administrative data. Because respondents do not age into the HRS until they are approximately 50 years old, recent trends in mobility are not immediately detectable in the HRS.

Whereas most of the preceding longitudinal household surveys lack adequate samples of immigrants (e.g., PSID, Add Health, FFCWS, NLSY97), two influential longitudinal studies—the New Immigrant Survey (NIS)[1] (whose sample consists of new permanent residents) and the Children of Immigrants Longitudinal Study (CILS)[2]—are designed to study the intragenerational mobility (NIS) and intergenerational mobility (CILS) of immigrants. These surveys have generated much important research on immigrant mobility; unfortunately, the last wave of NIS data was collected in 2007–2009 and the last wave of CILS data was collected in 2001–2003. The available samples sizes in these surveys are also quite small (see Annex Table 6-1).

The decennial censuses and large population surveys, by contrast, have sizeable samples of immigrants (e.g., Current Population Survey [CPS], American Community Survey [ACS]), but lack the longitudinal information required to assess inter- or intrageneration mobility (but see the discussion on opportunities for linking Census and administrative data). Both the CPS and ACS contain birthplace, citizenship, and year of entry to the United States; however, only the CPS (March supplement) includes information about birthplace of parents, which most studies use to derive estimates of intergenerational mobility (see National Academies of Sciences, Engineering, and Medicine [National Academies], 2015). The ACS, which provides timely information about inter-Census changes in population characteristics, lacks this information. The committee concurs with Recommendation 10-1 in a report by the National Academies (2015) to include new question on parental birthplace in the ACS.

The next set of panel studies in Annex Table 6-1, all of which are fielded by the National Center for Education Statistics (NCES), provide samples of successive cohorts of middle- or secondary-school students (see Annex Table 6-1). The High School and Beyond study represents high school sophomores and seniors in 1980; the National Educational Longitudinal Study of 1988 represents eighth graders in the 1988 academic school year; the Educational Longitudinal Study of 2002 represents high school sophomores in 2002; and the High School Longitudinal Study of 2009 represents ninth graders in 2009. Because the parents of these students were interviewed in all four of these NCES studies, and because extensive follow-up data on student employment outcomes were also collected in all four studies, these

---

[1] https://nis.princeton.edu/project.html
[2] https://www.icpsr.umich.edu//web/DSDR/studies/20520

data provide valuable descriptive evidence on early life course mobility (and thus usefully complement the HRS's late life course design).

The remaining surveys in Annex Table 6-1 are cross-sectional and rely on retrospective questions about parental education, occupation, and income to allow for intergenerational studies. The Occupational Changes in Generation Surveys cover relatively old birth cohorts, while the General Social Survey covers over a century of birth cohorts. The latter has been especially useful in monitoring trends despite the small per-year sample sizes. The American Voices Project (AVP) is a probability sample of qualitative interviews that has not yet been extensively used but may prove helpful in understanding the long arc of intergenerational mobility.

Linked Administrative Data

The surveys described above will no doubt continue to be important resources for research addressing many of the mechanisms that lie behind intergenerational mobility. At the same time, other important research questions cannot readily be answered with surveys, as the available sample sizes are too small to disaggregate by neighborhood, detailed occupation, detailed racial/ethnic groups, and other important sources of variability in mobility processes. For this reason, it is likely that future research will increasingly rely either on (a) linked administrative datasets and (b) survey data linked to administrative data (Grusky et al., 2015; Johnson et al., 2015).[3] Several new linked datasets deserve mention because they offer important opportunities for mobility research.

Multigenerational Longitudinal Panel

The recently released IPUMS Multigenerational Longitudinal Panel (MLP), which spans 9 Census years (from 1850 to 1940), contains more than 700 million individual records and 200 million links (Helgertz et al., 2022). The full-count historical data with names have been digitized by Ancestry and FamilySearch.org and have been assigned a historical identification key by IPUMS. This panel will continue to expand as newly identified data are released. In 2022, the 1950 full-count Census with names was released. IPUMS worked with Ancestry to digitize most of these names, and recently the 1950 Census was linked to the MLP.[4] The resulting dataset will be an important asset for mobility analysis because it covers a long time

---

[3] Two recent reports by the National Academies (2023a, 2024a) emphasize the need for better data to measure intergenerational mobility.

[4] Individual- and household-level Decennial Census data are released only after 72 years. For information on the MLP, see https://usa.ipums.org/usa/mlp/mlp_versions.shtml.

period, allows for multigenerational analysis, and offers very large sample sizes. In addition, MLP was constructed using highly reliable linking methods, resulting in very low error rates.

While MLP pioneered methods of linking women across censuses within their birth family or within their marriage family by using coresidence with other individuals, these data have known limitations. The most obvious problem is that, because women typically change their name at marriage, it is difficult to track them from their birth to marriage families. This means that the MLP only represents a selected set of women who remained in the same household across Census years. Another problem is that, prior to 1940, Census data contained information about occupation, industry, and literacy, but no information on wage earnings or educational attainment. The 1940 Decennial Census was the first to include information about wages and education. A third issue with linking historical Census records is that new immigrants appear only in the recent Census data and cannot be linked to censuses before they resided in the United States. In addition to naturalized citizens and legal permanent residents (i.e., green card holders) who are immigrants, the foreign-born population includes a broad range of temporary visa holders, such as students, diplomats, and visitors, as well as undocumented residents who either entered without inspection or overstayed visas. Visa status information is essential to exclude nonimmigrants from assessments of immigrant mobility. To do so, administrative data on visa type collected by U.S. Citizenship and Immigration Services needs to be made available for researchers to link with Census and administrative data. The committee concurs with Recommendation 10-6 in a report by the National Academies (2015) to allow administrative data on visa status information to be available to researchers in secure data enclaves.[5]

The MLP is nonetheless valuable because it includes rich sociodemographic information—such as age and birth cohort, race and ethnicity, country of birth, and region—that facilitates subgroup analyses. While still preliminary, one potential avenue for improving the cross-Census matching of women from their birth family to marriage family is to use vital statistics data, as in the Longitudinal, Intergenerational Family Electronic Micro-database (LIFE-M; Bailey et al., 2022) or Census Tree projects (Price et al., 2021).

---

[5] The committee's focus on immigrants who may be identified by visa status will exclude undocumented immigrants unless they are linked to data sources that include place of birth. Even then, the data would need information about the place of birth for parents of U.S.-born children to describe intergenerational mobility. Taking account of the full population of immigrants—documented and undocumented—is a challenge.

The LIFE-M Project

The LIFE-M project links all birth certificates for the states of Ohio and North Carolina to forbears and children and grandchildren (Bailey et al., 2022). The project's 2022 public release[6] contains 15 million individuals born from 1841 to 1968 belonging to more than 4 million families and spanning four generations (Bailey et al., 2022). Because birth certificates contain women's birth ("maiden") names, LIFE-M follows women at roughly the same rates as men. In addition to the variables available in MLP (LIFE-M links to these files through an identification code), LIFE-M contains information on health (date and place of death, cause of death), birth family characteristics (parity, sibling sex composition, age differences, twinning, number of siblings), marriage family characteristics (age and place of marriage, married name, spouse name and spouse background characteristics from the Census), own births (number of children, mortality of own infants and children, timing of births, sex composition, and twinning), and lifetime mobility (geographic location—town or county—at birth, marriage, Census enumeration through 1940, and death). Efforts to link more state records and the 1930 and 1950 censuses are ongoing. However, as noted, projects like LIFE-M also have limitations related to the Census data to which they link.

The Census Tree Project

The Census Tree project combines Census information with a diverse set of records on FamilySearch.org, one of the largest user-created genealogical platforms (Price et al., 2021). FamilySearch.org information is largely generated by its users, who search the website's trove of information (e.g., vital records, newspapers, cemetery documents, Census records) to link their family's ancestral records. The Census Tree combines these user links (which its creators estimate to be correct 95% of the time) with machine links (which its creators estimate to be correct 86%–89% of the time) to produce a large intergenerational database containing both men and women. The project's public release boasts an overall match rate of 62–65 percent for almost 89 million matches and a false positive match rate of around 6–7 percent (Price et al., 2023). This dataset is still growing and developing, and ongoing efforts will continue to add more information and continue to improve the data. In addition to those related to the Census data (as noted above), a limitation of user-generated data is that the family trees will represent the set of users on the FamilySearch.org site.

---

[6] www.OpenICPSR.org

Linked Census Bureau Data

For Census Bureau products that do not meet the 72-year rule, the Census Bureau allows researchers to apply for access to linked administrative datasets that are then analyzed in Federal Statistical Research Data Centers (FSRDCs) by researchers with Special Sworn Status (with disclosure avoidance review undertaken to ensure that publicly released statistics do not allow for reidentification). There are, for example, ongoing research projects entailing the analysis of the 2000 Decennial Census linked to the 2005–2023 ACS. The household roster in the 2000 Decennial Census can be used to identify parent–child pairs (among young children who are living with their parents), and the adult occupations and income of those children can then be identified for the subset of such children who show up in subsequent versions of the ACS.

Longitudinal Employer–Employee Household Data

One existing rich source of individual-level data is the Census Bureau's Longitudinal Employer–Employee Household Data (LEHD; Graham et al., 2022). The LEHD are administrative data consisting of individual-level records on quarterly earnings and employment based on the information that employers report to state unemployment insurance agencies. The Census Bureau links individuals to their employers and assigns a protected identification key (PIK), a unique identifying code, which allows these data to be linked to other Census data sources, including characteristics such as race, sex, years of education, and occupation. For records that cannot be linked, the LEHD imputes this information. These data can also be linked to Census residence files so that residence-level employment and earnings records can be formed. The availability of the data varies by state (with most states making data available starting in the early to mid-1990s). These data can be linked to Decennial Census data (as described below) to produce a more complete picture of households at a point in time, which allows researchers to follow individuals in the future when they enter the labor market.

Linked Federal Tax Data

Another source of data for studying intergenerational mobility is individual federal tax data. These data have provided the foundation for very important recent studies of economic mobility (e.g., Chetty et al., 2018). Currently, the Census Bureau has some information on tax filers' 1040 forms from 1969, 1974, 1979, 1984, 1989, 1994, and 1995 onwards, but only the data for years prior to 1995 are available to researchers outside the

Census Bureau (Alexander et al., 2024). Although only limited tax information is available currently, the expectation is that more tax information (as well as other data) will be made available soon. Another limitation is that only the 1994 data include identifiable information for dependents. For all other years, dependents in the household cannot be followed over time. Even with these data limitations, there is potential for more in-depth intergenerational research using these data. For example, of the more than 212 million individuals in the 1994 filers' data, 179 million can be linked to the 2020 Decennial Census data. Furthermore, of the 53.4 million individuals in the 1940 Census that have PIKs, 23.7 million can be linked to the 1994 tax data.

Aggregate and Contextual Data Products

The datasets described above allow for analyses of individual- or household-level records. Although these are critical for many types of mobility analyses, it is also important to provide aggregated mobility statistics that, like other aggregate labor market statistics (e.g., measures of employment and unemployment), can assist with research and inform the public and policymakers. Annex Table 6-2 lists some of the most important sources of such aggregated mobility data. The table also lists datasets that provide other types of contextual data pertaining to spatial units (e.g., neighborhoods, counties, states), educational institutions (e.g., primary, secondary, and postsecondary schools), labor market institutions (e.g., firms, industries, occupations), and policy (e.g., local government finances, laws pertaining to structural racism, other state laws). The latter types of data are not "mobility data" in and of themselves but may be useful in understanding institutional sources of mobility.

The first set of data sources in Annex Table 6-2 pertain to intergenerational mobility and other data (e.g., poverty, employment) aggregated up to different types of spatial units (e.g., neighborhoods, states). The Opportunity Atlas is a leading source of mobility data at the Census tract level, which is developed from links between federal tax data, 2000 and 2010 Decennial Census microdata, and microdata from the 2005–2015 ACS. Social Explorer is a leading source of demographic data aggregated up to block groups, zip codes, congressional districts, and states. The remaining spatially aggregated data sources in Annex Table 6-2 pertain to measurements of residential segregation (i.e., the Segregation Explorer), population flows (Safegraph Places Dataset), and justice outcomes (i.e., Justice Outcomes Explorer).

The next set of data sources in Annex Table 6-2 pertains to data aggregated at the school level (i.e., primary, secondary, and postsecondary schools). These datasets provide information on the characteristics of schools (e.g., tuition, admission rates, racial and gender composition), their educational output (e.g., test scores, degrees conferred), and their labor market correlates (e.g., earnings). The main sources of these data are the Stanford Education Data Archive, the Integrated Postsecondary Education Data System, the Common Core of Data, the National Student Clearinghouse, and the LEHD.

The third set of data sources in Annex Table 6-2 are aggregated up to key labor market institutions (e.g., occupations, firms, industries). The Occupation Information Network provides measures of occupational activities and skills; the LEHD provides measures of hires and jobs at the firm level; and the Bureau of Labor Statistics (BLS) provides a host of labor market measures (e.g., employment, compensation, productivity) at the industry, occupation, state, and national levels. The final set of data sources in Annex Table 6-2 provides measurements of policy, government finances, structural racism, and state laws.

The Census Bureau's Mobility, Opportunity, and Volatility (MOVS) project is not listed in Annex Table 6-2 because only the initial year of data has been released.[7] Once completed, MOVS will provide an especially important source of aggregated mobility indices that could be conceived as the analogue to, say, the U1–U6 measures of unemployment. This project involves integrating 1040 tax data from the Internal Revenue Service (IRS), Social Security Administration data from the Census Bureau Numident file (containing individual birth date and place, sex, citizenship, and date of death information), and demographic data collected in Census Bureau censuses and surveys. The goal is to produce public-use, aggregated statistics for individuals and households measuring income growth, income volatility, and economic mobility. These statistics, many of which will be disaggregated by race, ethnicity, and other demographic characteristics, will allow researchers to explore income mobility patterns in richer detail. By providing a full suite of regularly released measures of mobility at varying levels of geography, the MOVS project is an important step toward regularizing the reporting of real-time mobility data.[8]

A related project to MOVS is the Income Distributions and Dynamics in America project, which uses the same data as the MOVS project to create publicly available measures of income inequality and mobility for detailed racial/ethnic groups by geographic location.[9]

---

[7] https://www.census.gov/library/stories/2024/05/movs.html

[8] There is the possibility that the linked individual- and household-level data will be made available to researchers in the future.

[9] https://www.minneapolisfed.org/institute/income-distributions-and-dynamics-in-america

DATA RESOURCES UNDER DEVELOPMENT

Important individual- and household-level data projects on mobility are underway. Although the MLP, LIFE-M, and Census Tree projects described above make it possible to characterize the mobility processes of early U.S. birth cohorts, no administrative datasets are available to scholars seeking to characterize the mobility processes of cohorts born after 1940 and before 1970.[10] Two new projects develop intergenerational linkages for more recent cohorts. The American Opportunity Study (AOS) will allow for multigenerational analyses after 1950 (whereas 1950 is the latest Census year available for MLP, LIFE-M, and the Census Tree), while the State Longitudinal Data Systems (SLDS) initiative provides linkages between educational and earnings data for recent cohorts.

The American Opportunity Study

The AOS[11] builds from the Decennial Census Digitization and Linkage Project (DCDL) at the Census Bureau (Genadek & Alexander, 2019).[12] The purpose of DCDL is to connect the 2000, 2010, and 2020 censuses to the ACS using PIKs, while the purpose of the AOS is to extend the DCDL initiative by allowing for such linkages to earlier decennial censuses. Because names in the 1960–1990 censuses are handwritten and saved in microfiche, the Census Bureau—in collaboration with Opportunity Insights, Brown University, the Institute for Social Research at the University of Michigan, and the Stanford Center on Poverty and Inequality—has developed new methods for digitizing these data.[13] After digitization, the Census Bureau will add a PIK to each individual record in the 1960–1990 censuses, IRS tax data, and data from the Social Security system, which will transform these records from large cross-sections into large longitudinal datasets of individuals. When the linking is completed (expected in 2026), Decennial Census data from 1850 through 2020 will be longitudinally linked, to the extent possible.

Of course, not all individuals will be linked. Although PIK rates are extremely high and well validated, linked data tend to be unrepresentative (Bailey et al., 2022; Ruggles, 2006). This means that—as well as adding a richer set of questions—surveys will play an important role in validating the quality and representativeness of administrative data. To protect the confidentiality of individuals in the Census, these linked longitudinal data will again be available only to a select set of researchers who can obtain

---

[10] There have, however, been internal Census Bureau analyses of these birth cohorts.
[11] https://www.census.gov/about/adrm/linkage/projects/aos.html
[12] https://www.census.gov/about/adrm/linkage/projects/aos.html
[13] https://censusdigitization.org

Special Sworn Status and conduct their research in FSRDCs. While these restrictions limit who can access the data, the Census Bureau and other agencies are working to lower the cost of access while still protecting respondent confidentiality.

The AOS can be used to evaluate the short- and long-run effects of thousands of social programs implemented in the last 70 years and can enable a host of related sociodemographic analyses. Because it is, in effect, a massive individual-level longitudinal panel dataset, other datasets (e.g., program data, education data, past experiments) may be combined with this population-level infrastructure to learn about intergenerational mobility.

The State Longitudinal Data Systems Initiative

The SLDS initiative, which is sponsored by the U.S. Department of Education, provides funding for states to construct datasets linking individual students from preschool through secondary and postsecondary school and then to quarterly earnings records obtained from the unemployment insurance system in the state (which captures all formal employment). These data also include information about schools, including certification and licensure of teachers, the percent of students receiving free or reduced-price meals, and scores on standardized tests for all students in a building (Bloom-Weltman et al., 2021). Several states are also supplementing this information with vital records data, data on participation in transfer programs, corrections data, and driver's license data. While these data typically have information only back to the early 2000s, their longitudinal and generational coverage will grow with time. In addition, with state approval they can be linked to administrative data on intergenerational mobility to construct more granular measures of school quality and provide better information on participation in transfer programs, compared with data available from other federal agencies.

The SLDS initiative also has a cross-state component. To track migration of students and to address the lack of a national student-level data system, states have begun to connect their data systems across states with interstate data sharing agreements. Two important examples of cross-state initiatives are (a) the Western Interstate Commission for Higher Education's Multistate Longitudinal Data Exchange, and (b) Coleridge Initiative members who are enabling interstate data sharing via the Administrative Data Research Facility.

Other Data Linkage Initiatives

The sources of longitudinal data described above form the core of the data available to study intergenerational mobility, but they can be supplemented with outcomes from different sources. Annex Table 6-2 provides, for example, a description of some contextual datasets that could be linked to the ACS.

A range of "newer" data sources also provides new data linkage opportunities. For example, efforts to add PIKs to criminal justice data, data about veterans from the Department of Defense, geolocational data from cell phones, and credit reports and other data from private companies are expanding research opportunities to study intergenerational and intragenerational mobility. Prominent examples of such "linkable data" include commercial data on housing (e.g., Zillow, Black Knight/Core Logic), spending information (e.g., Affinity data in OI), and combined credit and spending information (e.g., JPMorgan Chase Institute). Also, JPMorgan Chase data have been used to examine income and spending volatility and mobility over a short time period, and Vanguard data have been used to evaluate retirement choices over time. Because researchers have only recently begun to use these data, their strengths and weaknesses are still being discovered.

Another notable linkage effort is the Census Bureau's 2020 administrative record Census simulation (Brown et al., 2023). In this project, records from the Census Bureau with PIKs and linked administrative records from 31 federal and state agencies, including information from the Centers for Medicare & Medicaid Services, the Department of Housing and Urban Development (HUD), the Federal Housing Administration, Immigration and Customs Enforcement, Indian Health Services, IRS, U.S. Postal Service, U.S. Citizenship and Immigration Services, and U.S. Customs and Border Protection. The Census Bureau has proposed an annual administrative record census. These administrative data from nonstatistical federal agencies are important because they contain information on issues such as immigration, health, and support programs (which are often unavailable or poorly reported in common survey data), and because they are large enough to allow one to identify small populations (e.g., recent immigrants, homeless population). Combining administrative records with other longitudinal data using PIKs will allow research on many new outcomes, mechanisms, and contextual factors shaping the transmission of intergenerational mobility.

In summary, substantial headway is being made to address data challenges that have limited the study of intergenerational mobility in the United States. The AOS, in combination with historical data, will allow an examination of mobility over the long sweep of history across multiple generations, within the context of complicated family structures, at the granular neighborhood level, and across many different subgroups and types of mobility (e.g., occupation, income). When combined with the LEHD, the AOS will have individual and household earnings records for many individuals and households starting in the mid-1990s, while the tax data available prior to 1995 will provide a more complete description of the household. The SLDS initiative does not cover as long a sweep of history, but it includes additional data on program participation, educational outcomes, and much more. Although the transition to administrative data analysis has been underway for many decades, the initiatives described above will likely accelerate this transition.

REMAINING DATA SHORTFALLS

Even with the substantial data infrastructure projects mentioned above, data for studying intergenerational mobility remain incomplete. Some important challenges include the comprehensiveness of available data, the quality of available data, and the infrastructure for accessing data in the United States. This section addresses each in turn.

Continuing Problems With Data Comprehensiveness

Mobility research hinges on measuring a variety of resources (e.g., income, occupation, wealth) across two or more generations, making comparisons within and across subpopulations, examining the mechanisms for transmitting advantage and disadvantage (e.g., families, educational systems, labor markets, neighborhoods), and understanding the effects of programs and policies on opportunities. In attempting to meet these objectives, existing datasets fall short in seven ways.

Wealth

One prominent data gap is around measures of wealth. The Federal Reserve's Survey of Consumer Finances is an important source of wealth data, but its sample of families is too small (6,500 families were interviewed in the most recent survey) to conduct in-depth analysis across key subgroups (e.g., race, ethnicity) and across the wealth distribution. The new Wealth and Mobility (WAM) study, which is being conducted at the Stone Center for Income Dynamics at the University of Michigan (in partnership with the IRS), has the potential to produce more detailed data on wealth, but only aggregate data will be released (and hence linkages to existing household- or individual-level administrative data will not be possible). It is important that efforts such as WAM continue to receive support and that opportunities to undertake analyses with the individual or household data (in FSRDCs or equally secure facilities) are opened more broadly to qualified scholars. The committee agrees with the conclusions in a report by the National Academies (2024a) stating that agencies need to collaborate to produce a data infrastructure that (a) includes both income and wealth (and consumption) data that are consistent with each other, and (b) includes demographic and geographic variables for the analysis of both inequality and mobility.

Although it is no easy task to infer wealth from tax data, the most fundamental problem is that of data access. To date, only a small number of research teams have access to the data needed to build unit-record wealth data, a limitation that undermines basic science, policy evaluation, and the development of new policy. In addition, researchers need to develop ways to better measure wealth among the hardest-to-measure groups—those at the top and bottom of the wealth distribution—and ensure that these data are available to other researchers. Most of the new data infrastructure initiatives that are discussed above focus on making individual-, household-, or tax reporter–level data available to qualified scholars in a secure environment, an approach that would also be appropriate for wealth data (especially as it accesses tax records).

Occupation

The U.S. Census Bureau and Statistics of Income are currently collaborating to develop new occupational coding algorithms for the occupational write-ins on Form 1040 that will be comparable to the occupation codes available in the ACS and decennial censuses. These data should improve accuracy of occupational information available in more standard data, such as the ACS or CPS, as well as with the tax data. This will make it possible to carry out data-intensive analyses of neighborhood effects, the extent to which detailed occupational transmission is a key mechanism of mobility, and to incorporate more complicated familial processes (e.g., occupational assortative matching). These new linked data will also support studies of occupational mobility within a person's lifetime and across generations. It remains unclear whether these new occupational data will be made widely available to all qualified scholars working within secure computing facilities.

Education

It has been difficult to examine the role that education plays in promoting intergenerational mobility in U.S. history, because education was not asked as part of the Decennial Census until 1940. However, the 1940 Census contains information on educational attainment for all individuals alive in 1940, thus making it possible to construct statistics on educational attainment back to cohorts born in the 1880s (recognizing that the trends may be impacted because educational requirements increased over time and differential mortality occurred for less-educated groups). In addition, as of 2010, measures of educational attainment are available only in the ACS and CPS—not the Decennial Census. However, approximately 20 percent of the population has been part of the ACS since 2005, and the ACS and CPS Annual Social Economic Supplement data have been assigned PIKs, allowing completed education to be linked to decennial censuses.[14] Other ways to capture educational information for individuals include linking student records obtained as part of the Post-Secondary Employment Opportunity project (Annex Table 6-2) in the 28 states currently participating in the project. The availability of education data could also be improved if the BLS worked with the Census Bureau to assign PIKs to all CPS monthly files (as far back as is feasible). Encouraging the Census Bureau and the Department of Education to work together to link (using PIKs) FASFA[15] filers and students that receive federal financial aid to the state's SLDS records would enable these data to be linked to the AOS, ACS, LEHD, and other administrative data.

Additionally, information on the quality of schooling, standardized test scores (ACT, SAT, or other achievement test scores), and vocational certifications are largely absent from the administrative data infrastructure, although they are available in many surveys. Allowing these surveys to be linked would allow deeper understanding of the joint processes of educational and economic mobility by assessing, for example, how education "mediates" economic mobility (e.g., parents' income is correlated with adult children's education, which in turn shapes children's earnings and income). Finally, the ability to link the longitudinal SLDS data to both federal records and longitudinal data on the parents of these students would further enhance research on the educational pathways for mobility.

Race and Ethnicity

Obtaining consistent measures of race and ethnicity is critical in examining social and economic mobility. Surveys contain a variety of questions to obtain race and ethnicity from respondents, and the recent changes in *Statistical Policy Directive No. 15* (see U.S. Office of Management and Budget [OMB], 2024) to include multiple responses for race and ethnicity may complicate the ability to create consistent estimates over time (Marks et al., 2024). In addition, most administrative data (e.g., tax data) do not have measures of race and ethnicity. To overcome this problem, the Census Bureau has created a Title 13 Race and Ethnicity File, denoted the "Best race and ethnicity file" in Deaver (2021), using multiple decennial censuses to obtain consistent measures. This file can be linked to tax records, as recommended in a report by the National Academies (2024a), to evaluate

---

[14] Approximately 1 percent of the population is included in the ACS each year.
[15] *FAFSA* stands for Free Application for Federal Student Aid.

disparities in income, consumption, and wealth. Alternatively, researchers at the U.S. Department of the Treasury have developed a method for imputing race to the tax data (see Cronin et al., 2024). To facilitate research, these linked data need to be included in the expanded set of restricted data available to researchers (as discussed in the recommendations). Data equity also requires that these linked and imputed data need to be evaluated for errors and misrepresentation (as discussed in National Academies, 2023d).

Nonmonetary Transfers

Many income measures only capture labor market earnings, and even those that capture income from sources other than jobs ignore government transfers (e.g., via Supplemental Nutritional Assistance Program [SNAP], formerly known as the Food Stamp Program), housing subsidies, health insurance from Medicare and Medicaid, or the earned income tax credit. Given that existing research highlights the important role monetary income plays in intergenerational mobility, it would be useful to know the impact nonmonetary sources have on mobility, especially for low-income groups.

Qualitative Measurements of Mobility

The main government funding agencies (e.g., National Science Foundation, National Institutes of Health) support the development and maintenance of a bevy of quantitative datasets, whereas very little funding goes to support the development of qualitative datasets. The vast majority of mobility analysis is, therefore, undertaken with quantitative measurements of the underlying resources (e.g., earnings, income, wealth, occupation) and observed mediating variables (e.g., networks, education, incarceration). Although field experiments and quasi-experiments have improved our capacity to make causal inferences with such quantitative data, our understanding of underlying mechanisms could be further enhanced by coupling such research with a more robust program of qualitative research (DeLuca, 2023). This is because, even when a field experiment or quasi-experiment identifies a likely causal effect, it often remains unclear why that effect is generated. When a quasi-experiment reveals, for example, that a particular program (e.g., a childcare program, housing voucher program, affordable housing program) increases mobility, our understanding of the sources of such effects is often complicated by the large bundle of social processes that a given program typically entails. Without knowing which part of this bundle is delivering the desired effect, commitment to programs must be somewhat blind (e.g., a "sociology of programs" rather than processes) and cannot be adjusted easily as circumstances change. This problem can be overcome, in part, by combining field experiments and quasi-experiments with the targeted qualitative research that can help us to ferret out the mechanisms lying behind black box program effects.

AVP—the country's first nationally representative, large participation, public-use qualitative dataset—is a trial initiative that can also assist in this buildout of qualitative research (Edin et al., 2023). The AVP asks people to "tell the story of their life" through a series of semistructured prompts about their work life, family life, friends, religion, and much more. The resulting narratives about individual life arcs can assist in (a) discovering possible pathways through which mobility trajectories unfold, and (b) identifying the many critical junctures that might be targeted by new interventions. These life arc narratives reveal, for example, the prominent role of family traumas (e.g., sexual assaults), a "helping hand" (e.g., the help of a friend), personal struggles and problems (e.g., a drug addiction), and all manner of other pathways and junctures. Because this type of qualitative data can help researchers identify emerging problems, develop hypotheses about important mediators (which can be subsequently evaluated using both survey and administrative data), and otherwise engage in "discovery work," a strong case can be made for building a permanent platform for collecting nationally representative qualitive data and linking these data to administrative data when possible.

Institutional and Policy Effects

The introductory chapter to this report stresses the many pathways through which various institutions, policies, and programs affect mobility. Given the important role of these institutional forces, more comprehensive data on policies and institutional practices need to be assembled and combined with microdata on individuals and families. As indicated in Annex Table 6-2, several sources for policy data exist (e.g., Agénor et al., 2021; Bailey & Duquette, 2014; Hendren & Sprung-Keyser, 2020; Torche & Rauf, 2021), but more support is needed for developing these sources.

Ongoing Problems With Data Quality

Issues with data quality also limit studies of intergenerational mobility.

Hidden, Difficult-to-Link, or Small Populations

The administrative datasets currently being built would ideally represent populations that are often hidden from view. However, some administrative datasets exclude or underrepresent individuals who are undocumented or unhoused; who recently immigrated; or who work in informal sectors of the economy (e.g., childcare). In addition, some individuals cannot be linked for a variety of reasons (e.g., premature death, do not include the proper name in the Census, name changes across censuses). These problems can be addressed in part by building more comprehensive population indices that combine "conventional" sources of administrative data (e.g., tax data, Census data, ACS, birth records) with the point-in-time counts, social program data, administrative data on education, and other sources. The Census Bureau's initial effort to conduct an administrative records census demonstrates the potential value of administrative data and the ability to identify difficult-to-reach or small populations, such as noncitizens. At present, however, these populations are not sampled with sufficient frequency or at high-enough rates or are excluded from administrative data altogether, making them difficult or impossible to study. Because these populations may be highly upwardly mobile (e.g., they migrated from difficult circumstances to the United States) or downwardly mobile (e.g., being unhoused), their omission from data resources limits the study of important and often vulnerable populations.

Reporting Problems

Because of the problems with administrative data discussed above, surveys remain crucial to studying mobility and its mechanisms. Surveys must therefore continue to be supported, and new solutions need to be developed for emerging problems with nonresponse and attrition. In many commonly used surveys, declining willingness to report income or respond at all is a growing concern, particularly since the COVID-19 pandemic (Rothbaum & Hokayem, 2021). The National Experimental Wellbeing Statistics project is one effort being conducted by the U.S. Census Bureau to address these problems, but such efforts need to be expanded to other agencies and data sources. At the same time, increasing reliance on administrative sources of data generates other types of reporting problems, such as "autofill" algorithms, upon which respondents may sometimes rely. It is increasingly common for statistical agencies to fill in missing data by borrowing from other administrative sources, another practice that tends to lead to overstated persistence (because those sources inevitably draw on past—rather than present—circumstances). These types of errors are likely to be systematic and need to be addressed through improvements in statistical inference, in algorithmic borrowing practices, and through new data collection.

Sample Coverage

Sample coverage is an important aspect of data quality and can have important implications for studying the mechanisms that affect mobility. In the FFCWS, for example, some two-thirds of hospitals did not allow mothers or fathers younger than age 18 to be included in the study (Reichman et al., 2001). The FFCWS sample therefore partially excludes a policy-relevant portion of the birth cohort, those with teenage parents. Moreover, fathers, especially noncustodial fathers, have lower response and retention rates than mothers; fathers' response rates become even lower after the early interviews, so that the fathers who remain in the sample are a select group that are more involved with their children and the children's mothers. More generally, survey attrition is a problem that needs to be considered when using longitudinal data to study intergenerational mobility (see, e.g., Schoeni & Wiemers, 2015).

Legal Obstacles to Data Access

It will be difficult to solve many of the foregoing problems without addressing legal obstacles restricting data access. Although the 2018 Evidence Act mandated that federal agencies increase data sharing and researcher access to these data, only a few agencies other than the U.S. Census Bureau are providing access. For example, the BLS only makes a small subset of their data available to researchers in the FSRDC, while the Department of Education and the Centers for Disease Control and Prevention have refused to put most restricted-access data in the FSRDC system.[16] In addition, IRS data are largely available only to researchers within FSRDCs when working on a project with Census Bureau or IRS employees. Finally, many of the agencies that provided records for the 2020 administrative records census are unwilling to provide these data on an ongoing basis. This reluctance or resistance to sharing data raises the burden on other administrative agencies and limits research on intergenerational mobility.

In other cases, the law itself is outdated and needs to be changed. Several laws place significant limits on building or sharing data infrastructure. U.S. Code Title 13, which governs access to U.S. Census Data, and U.S. Code Title 26, which governs access to IRS data, have been interpreted as requiring that any research done with administrative data must improve the operation of the agency, regardless of the wider social benefits of this research (National Academies, 2023b). In addition, only one part of the

---

[16] The BLS does have its own process for accessing confidential administrative data (https://www.bls.gov/rda/), but because it operates separately from the more widely used FSRDC system, it is more difficult for researchers to link administrative data from other agencies, and it adds unnecessary costs to the federal system for accessing administrative data.

originally proposed Confidential Information Protection and Statistical Efficiency Act (CIPSEA), which governs access to administrative records at other federal statistical agencies, was enacted. The remaining portion, which would have formalized the requirements for sharing data across federal agencies and with nongovernmental researchers, has never been enacted by Congress. Consequently, this type of sharing currently requires formal memoranda of understanding every time agencies share data with other agencies or with outside researchers, significantly raising the cost of using the data. In addition, part of the reauthorization of the Higher Education Opportunity Act (2008) prohibits the federal government from maintaining a national database of student records. Many of these laws were written more than 20 years ago and prior to the growth of new computing capabilities, the development of new technology to protect data, and the growth in the use of administrative data in research. Conducting large-scale studies of economic and social mobility requires that Titles 13 and 26, and CIPSEA be modernized, and that the federal student record ban be repealed.

DISSEMINATION AND ACCESS

Much headway has been made over the last quarter-century in building powerful new datasets, principally via cross-sectional and longitudinal linkages of administrative resources. These new datasets promise to revolutionize the study of mobility. Although, as discussed above, these data construction efforts might be supplemented and expanded in many ways, a larger challenge is ensuring that these new blended data continue to protect privacy while being securely available for a wide variety of researchers. It is fitting, therefore, to conclude this chapter with a discussion of the many dissemination and access challenges that remain.

Building Secure Facilities for Analysis

Combining multiple data sources (including Census data, administrative and tax data, birth records, educational data, and family and wealth information) that may be linked both within a period and longitudinally raises the risks from disclosure. It is essential that these data be protected and accessed in a secure research environment, which is feasible using existing protocols and safeguards. For example, protections could follow the Five Safes discussed in National Academies (2024a,b): safe data, projects, people, settings, and output. The protections criteria could be guided by a risk-utility framework using both traditional disclosure and privacy-enhancing techniques (see National Academies, 2024b). Additional methods are in development at the federal statistical agencies (IRS, Census Bureau FSRDCs). Research from the National Secure Data Service demonstration project (NSDS-D) may inform the development of a mobility data infrastructure. The committee agrees with the National Academies (2024b) report stating that the "framework for making decisions about acceptable disclosure risks given expected usefulness of data depends on whether that framework is dynamic," and also with that report's Conclusion 3.2, in that tiered access is a "key component of a dynamic disclosure risk/usefulness framework, to reflect differences in acceptable risks given policy priorities" (p. 43). In short, this report argues that increased data are required to conduct research on intergenerational mobility. Given this priority, multiple methods exist for managing the risks of disclosure when accessing data.

Because linked administrative data are typically analyzed in secure facilities, FSRDCs are a crucial component of the data access infrastructure. FSRDCs provide researchers secure access to restricted federal data outside of the Census Bureau. Currently, there are 33 FSRDCs located around the country, and the Census Bureau plans to add three more in 2024 and possibly another four in the near future. Nagaraj and Tranchero (2023) show that economic researchers closer to FSRDCs are more productive, underscoring the value of the FSRDC network. Efforts to include more data from federal statistical agencies in the FSRDC network would further enhance access and productivity. This would likely require additional funding to defray the costs of including data in the FSRDC network. Efforts to expand and simplify access to blended data are especially important for democratizing data access to junior and underresourced scholars.

One cost-effective alternative to building more FSRDCs is increasing virtual FSRDCs. This method of access was popularized during the COVID-19 pandemic out of necessity, and its success demonstrated the feasibility of doing so on a larger scale. With the end of the pandemic, virtual access to tax data has been rolled back. Increasing virtual FSRDC access gives many more researchers access, enhancing the benefits to the statistical agencies that share the data and to the research community (see National Academies, 2023b).

At the same time, many of the new nonfederal data sources (e.g., credit data, cell phone data, qualitative data) require the same level of protection, and increasing access to them requires FSRDC-like protections. This requires building facilities but also new procedures for reducing the costs of time-intensive disclosure avoidance review. Financial support for these activities—both for researchers submitting these disclosure requests and federal agencies reviewing the requests—is desperately needed. Enhanced technology, by improving access while protecting the confidentiality of the data, could reduce the time costs for researchers and reviewers alike (see National Academies, 2024b).

Simplifying Application Processes

Before the data can be analyzed, researchers need to apply for Special Sworn Status—a time-consuming process. The Standard Application Process (SAP) allows researchers to request access to confidential data from federal statistical agencies using a single application portal. An oversight board is needed to monitor the introduction of the SAP to ensure that it is well supported, that information about it is well disseminated, and that it is otherwise institutionalized successfully. It is important to incorporate administrative data from nonstatistical federal agencies into the SAP system. In many cases, key nonfederal mobility datasets (e.g., the AVP) likewise are accessed via application, but the application procedures are not standardized and are often difficult to navigate.

Simplifying Data Sharing

Recent improvements in data access reduce the need for individual researchers to negotiate their own data use agreements. Although researchers interested in carrying out research with these new datasets (e.g., AOS) still have to apply to use the data via SAP, they will not have to negotiate one-off interagency agreements themselves. There will, however, inevitably still be boutique cases in which these new datasets are inadequate to the task and researchers thus need to negotiate new one-off agreements. The NSDS, which is designed to help facilitate access, linkages, and data sharing across federal agencies, has received pilot funding for this purpose (see National Academies, 2024b). The main goal of NSDS is to make it easier to secure access and carry out analyses and thus reduce time and cost for delivery. To ensure that these goals are met, it is important that the NSDS continue to report measures of time to delivery.[17]

An additional benefit of having a centralized data access system is the ability to archive data for use in replication. Archiving data in the FSRDCs is encouraged, and researcher requests for access are feasible, but they require a separate application and justification.

A related development at the subfederal level is the Coleridge Initiative, which facilitates data sharing across states and local agencies. To date, Coleridge's efforts have focused exclusively on state data, so it is important to develop procedures that will allow the linking of federal and state data. The processes for combining privately owned data (e.g., cell phone data, credit reports) with state and federal datasets (see National Academies, 2023a,b, 2024b) need to be simplified. For example, a recent report on protecting privacy in the Survey of Income and Program Participation

---

[17] https://www.researchdatagov.org/agencyInfoMetrics

recommended creating a secure online data access mechanism (see National Academies, 2023b).

SUMMARY, KEY CONCLUSIONS, AND RECOMMENDATIONS

As the discussion in this chapter makes clear, the United States is moving toward a modern integrated data system based on linked administrative data, a system that may ultimately rival the systems in European countries. Developing sustainable structures that ensure increased and equitable access to the new data resources remains the central challenge ahead. This will require cooperation among the many stakeholders in the data ecosystem, including the executive and congressional branches of government, federal statistical agencies, state and local government officials, the research community, potential private funding organizations, and the general public.

This chapter also makes clear that, while linked administrative data form the backbone of data resources used to study intergenerational mobility, research still requires survey data to understand factors affecting mobility that are not found in administrative data or are not made available for research purposes. Surveys provide information regarding attitudes, behaviors, and contexts not contained in administrative data. Other key factors (e.g., parenting practices) are not contained in administrative sources at all, and surveys will remain critical for ascertaining them. It is important that extensive surveys continue to be funded and that cost-effective ways be explored to alter survey methodology to leverage administrative data. Although the committee's recommendations focus on the importance of increasing access to administrative data for research purposes, continuing to support survey work is just as important. It is critical to develop ways to combine administrative and survey data to enhance the value of both sources.

Conclusion 6-1: Research on mobility-relevant programs and policies requires the use of blended, multigenerational data for multiple domains—especially family, place, education, and wealth—including both surveys and administrative data (e.g., tax and benefit data). Also needed is a process for ensuring that qualified researchers can access these blended data within a secure environment; this process needs to explicitly recognize both the risk of using confidential administrative data in research and the benefits to society that can be produced from this research.

Mechanisms to allow agencies to share data and allow researcher access to the blended data may be restricted because the laws governing the access are outdated and need to be changed. Several laws place significant limits on building or sharing data infrastructure. U.S. Code Title 13, which governs access to U.S. Census data, and U.S. Code Title 26, which governs access to IRS data, have been interpreted as specifying that research done with administrative data must improve the operation of the agency, regardless of the wider social benefits of this research. In addition, only one part of the originally proposed CIPSEA, which governs access to administrative records at other federal statistical agencies, was enacted. The remaining portion, which would have formalized the requirements for sharing data across federal agencies and with nongovernmental researchers, has never been enacted by Congress. Consequently, this type of sharing currently requires formal memoranda of understanding every time agencies share data with other agencies or with outside researchers, significantly raising the cost of using the data. In addition, part of the 2008 reauthorization of the Higher Education Act prohibits the federal government from maintaining a national database of student records. As discussed in Chapter 5, however, education through the postsecondary level is a key domain for economic and social mobility research. These laws were written prior to the growth of new computing capabilities, the development of new technology to protect data, and the growth in the use of administrative data in research. Large-scale studies of economic and social mobility would benefit from modernizing Title 13, Title 26, and CIPSEA and repealing the federal student record ban. In revising these statutes, the committee agrees with the recommendations in the Year 2 report of the Advisory Committee on Data for Evidence Building (2022) and the National Academies (2024a) report, which state that Congress should adopt standards that recognize the trade-offs between the risk of disclosure of administrative data and the usefulness of research using these data.

Given the importance of using income to measure economic mobility, well-measured income for individuals and households is needed. As discussed in recent National Academies (2023c, 2024a,b) reports, improving income measurement requires both administrative and survey data. For example, comprehensive measures of household income and wealth will need information on Schedule C income; all income reported on 1099 forms; other business income, transfer payments, alimony, and child support; tax credits; and long- and short-term capital gains. For a complete income measure, it would be helpful for state agencies to provide benefit data to the U.S. Census Bureau, including state data from SNAP, the Temporary Assistance for Needy Families program, the HUD Section 8 housing voucher programs, the unemployment insurance system (including both recipient information and quarterly wage record data), postsecondary student financial aid programs, and other data included in a state's SLDS. Such data sharing would allow the data to be assigned PIKs, integrated into the administrative data infrastructure, and provided to researchers working in the FSRDC environment; states would require funding so that they can adopt systems and processes to comply with reporting requirements.

As discussed in Chapter 2, information about important events such as births, deaths, marriages, and divorce is essential in evaluating mobility. The data infrastructure for studying economic and social mobility will be strengthened if state agencies provide to the National Center for Health Statistics (NCHS) both current and past data that are part of the National Vital Statistics System. This would include the data already being reported to NCHS, as well as data on dates and locations of marriages, divorces, births, and deaths. States would require funding for adopting systems and processes to comply with the reporting requirements. The committee agrees with Recommendation 11-2 in a National Academies report (2023d) that calls for expanding the ability of agencies to share data across agencies and with researchers.

> **Recommendation 6-1:** Building on the Foundations for Evidence-Based Policymaking Act of 2018 (Evidence Act), the chief statistician of the United States should work with federal agencies to advise legislators and policymakers to address the need for revisions to regulations to improve data sharing across federal statistical agencies, including
> a. revisiting U.S. Code Title 26 to allow the Internal Revenue Service to expand the ability to share tax data with the U.S. Census Bureau that are needed to create more comprehensive measures of household income and wealth;
> b. issuing the Presumption of Access rule that was part of the 2018 Evidence Act, thus ensuring that federal agencies share data among themselves; and
> c. requiring nonstatistical federal agencies to provide annual data to the U.S. Census Bureau so that it can conduct an annual administrative record census.

Conclusion 6-2: The data structure for studying economic and social mobility will be strengthened if state agencies provide (1) the U.S. Census Bureau with data on all programs that receive federal funding, and (2) the National Center for Health Statistics with both current and past data that are part of the National Vital Statistics System. States would require funding to adopt systems and processes to comply with reporting requirements.

Conclusion 6-3: The data infrastructure for studying economic and social mobility will be strengthened if the ban prohibiting the federal government from tracking students and from maintaining a national database of student records is repealed.

Beyond sharing across agencies, it is important to improve data access for researchers. Data access laws, such as U.S. Code Titles 13 and 26, need to be modernized to facilitate research, as they have proven to be inadequate amid the recent growth of research using linked administrative data. Furthermore, the application process to obtain these data in secure facilities (FSRDCs) is cumbersome and time consuming. Introducing the SAP could reduce the burden involved in applying for Special Sworn Status, but oversight is needed to ensure its effectiveness. Finally, a key advantage of emerging linked administrative datasets is the option for researchers to obtain data from multiple sources and agencies. Efforts such as the NSDS facilitate interagency data sharing and reduce the need to negotiate individual data use agreements. Streamlining processes for combining private data with state and federal datasets will also be crucial.

Recommendation 6-2: In order to evaluate the policies surrounding economic and social mobility, researchers require tiered access to new blended data. The chief statistician of the United States should work with the federal agencies to review and revise policies concerning external data sharing with the broader research community, including (1) revisiting the missions of federal statistical agencies to formally acknowledge the need for data sharing and the broader benefits to society of research itself; (2) using tiered access to support access for qualified external researchers; (3) expanding the Standard Application Process to ensure that all proposals are evaluated within 3 months; and (4) providing remote access to Federal Statistical Research Data Centers to facilitate data sharing with more researchers. The National Secure Data Service should also work with federal agencies to ensure that these improved data access, analysis, and linking mechanisms are implemented.

Recommendation 6-3: To increase the value of data for studying economic and social mobility, federal agencies should collaborate with the National Secure Data Service to improve the data acquisition and linking process by assigning protected identification keys (PIKs) to federal surveys:
    a. The U.S. Census Bureau should improve the person identification validation system (PVS), which should serve as the

standard for linking all individual-level data held by all federal agencies.
   b. The U.S. Bureau of Labor Statistics and the U.S. Census Bureau should assign PIKs to all records that are part of the (i) monthly Current Population Survey back to 1963, (ii) Consumer Expenditure Survey, (iii) American Time Use Survey, and (iv) National Longitudinal Surveys.
   c. The U.S. Department of Education and the U.S. Census Bureau should assign a PIK to individual Free Application for Federal Student Aid forms, as well as to individual-level administrative data on federal financial aid receipt.

Some impediments to data access are neither legal nor regulative, but financial in nature. It is important to adequately fund agencies to allow them to provide data. Current funding is inadequate in a variety of areas, which impedes the development of evidence-based policy on mobility. Although the United States has multiple longitudinal surveys, they are not refreshed with new cohorts frequently enough because funding is difficult to secure. This means that recent changes in the composition of the U.S. population (e.g., immigration-induced changes) cannot be studied adequately. The NLSY is addressing this data problem (as well as many others) with new data collection efforts and plans for a new cohort in 2027. Understanding intergenerational mobility in the future requires new surveys or significantly enhanced versions of existing surveys to address the changing population of the United States. Resources are also required for (a) streamlining the data application process; (b) improving the person identification validation system (PVS) and allowing it to serve as the standard for linking all individual-level data; (c) subsidizing the institutional costs associated with having an FSRDC, which would allow researchers at a wider range of institutions to access restricted administrative data; and (d) expanding support for qualitative research on intergenerational mobility and incorporating this information into the FSRDC infrastructure.

Conclusion 6-4: In order to facilitate data access for studying economic and social mobility, funding is required for streamlining the data application process, improving linking, supporting Federal Statistical Research Data Centers, enhancing the survey infrastructure, and expanding qualitative research.

The U.S. research infrastructure (e.g., National Science Foundation, National Institutes of Health) does not single out mobility research as an important zone of inquiry that—like defense research, climate research, or cancer research—deserves special organizational support or funding.

Because research on mobility is central to understanding the functioning of the U.S. economy and society, this committee believes that it is important that the United States commit resources to the task of monitoring mobility and facilitating research to understand the processes of intergenerational mobility.

The United States does have many government agencies, research centers, and research initiatives that are relevant to research on mobility and opportunity (e.g., U.S. Department of Health and Human Services [HHS], Institute for Research on Poverty, Upward Mobility Initiative). The HHS (via the Office of the Assistant Secretary for Planning and Evaluation) currently funds a national research center—the National Center on Poverty and Economic Mobility—that fuses the objectives of reducing poverty and increasing mobility. These two objectives are, however, very distinct and may be secured through very different types of initiatives. It is important to recognize this distinction by setting up two research centers—one that addresses poverty and another that addresses economic and social mobility and opportunity.

A new National Mobility Center (NMC) would be designed to assist and organize the country's research on economic and social opportunity. The NMC's constituency would be, first and foremost, *mobility researchers*. The United States already has important and very successful organizations focused on assisting local leaders (e.g., the Upward Mobility Initiative), as well as organizations focused on issues relevant to service delivery (e.g., HHS). However, the United States does not have an organization targeted to support and organize research on trends in mobility, the causes of mobility, and the most effective interventions affecting the amount and type of mobility.

The purpose of the NMC would thus be to assist researchers in meeting the many challenges laid out throughout this report. The NMC would help researchers identify the key unresolved research questions in the mobility field, identify the existing programs and new interventions that would most benefit from a careful evaluation, sort through the hundreds of available datasets and settle on the most useful ones, garner access to datasets that are currently very difficult to access, negotiate the organizational complications of carrying out research in the secure settings (e.g., FSRDCs) that are increasingly central to the field, master the many discipline-specific models and measures for examining the many different types of mobility (e.g., earnings, income, wealth, occupation), and access the various tools (e.g., occupation crosswalks, contextual data) needed to carry out mobility research. For each of these challenges, the NMC would take on the short-term goal of assisting researchers with overcoming them, and the long-term goal of working with agencies and constituencies to reduce the number of such challenges and thereby build a better research infrastructure for the future.

The main functions of the NMC may be divided into six zones:

Clearinghouse on Research and Evaluation Needs Because the mobility field remains balkanized into disciplinary subfields focusing on particular types of mobility (e.g., economic, occupational, educational), it is difficult for researchers to understand the cross-cutting challenges facing the field as a whole. The first goal of the NMC would be to overcome these barriers by identifying unexploited opportunities for high-quality monitoring, model-building, and program evaluation. This requires distinguishing among zones (a) in which much research is available and further effort is probably unnecessary, (b) in which much research is available but key questions remain unresolved, and (c) that are wholly unexplored but might well warrant exploration. The field relies increasingly on quasi-experimental methods, and the results pertaining to the delimited zones in which natural experiments happen become a complicated patchwork. The goal of the NMC, in part, would be to ferret out when limited-scope experiments and quasi-experiments provide strong and compelling evidence and when additional work is needed before one can stitch together a compelling model. The simple goal is to direct energy and effort (especially among new entrants to the field) toward solving the field's most important unresolved problems.

High-Priority Pilots The NMC would also identify zones in which new pilots are warranted. The present report has noted, for example, that some of the most promising systemic and institutional interventions have been deprioritized because they are not amenable to randomized controlled trials, because of the lure of cheap nudges, or because no program already exists to render them testable via quasi-experiments. The NMC would be charged with identifying all interventions—systemic and otherwise—that are promising and would benefit from pilots.

Data Clearinghouse and Data Access Support The NMC would provide a one-stop center for scholars seeking to learn about available surveys, administrative data, proprietary data, and qualitative datasets. It would also facilitate the process of accessing these data. As has been documented throughout this report, research on U.S. mobility has been hampered by impediments to accessing, linking, and analyzing data. The NMC would provide workshops and training on overcoming these impediments and work closely with the NSDS in reducing them. The NMC would additionally identify surveys and other datasets that need to be updated as well as new types of mobility data that are currently undersupported (e.g., qualitative datasets on mobility).

Research Resources To carry out mobility research, scholars rely on a host of resources that are widely scattered, such as occupational crosswalks, contextual datasets, calculators for adjusting for inflation (e.g., CPI-U-RS,[18] PCE,[19] chained-weighted CPI), and much more. The NMC would provide links to these widely used resources for mobility research. It could also become a hub for rigorous qualitative research of mobility—training students and junior scholars in qualitative methods from formulating questions to sampling, data collection, and analysis.

Workshops and Conferences The NMC would also bring together the many disciplines engaged in mobility research by providing workshops on key topics of interest (e.g., data access, new statistical quantitative methods, qualitative research methods) and hosting interdisciplinary conferences on key developments in the mobility field.

Monitoring Mobility Trends in Real Time With the emergence of new linked administrative data, it is now possible to deliver real-time annual reporting of trends in mobility, much like trends in the Official Poverty and Supplemental Poverty measures are monitored annually in the *Poverty in the United States* series (authored by the U.S. Census Bureau). The NMC would, for example, collaborate with the NCES and MOVS initiatives to provide annual reports on (a) the effects of family economic background on college access (for the incoming cohort of college entrants), (b) the effects of family economic background on first jobs (for the incoming cohort of labor market entrants), and (c) the effects of family economic background on transitions to subsequent jobs (again by cohort). These reports would, just like the existing annual assessment of poverty, identify points of progress as well as problem areas that need to be targeted or watched.

The NMC, via these six functions, would not just have a symbolic function (i.e., symbolize the commitment of the United States to promoting opportunity) but would also assist in developing an evidence-based road map for promoting opportunity. The NMC, which would be a nongovernmental research center, could be funded by government agencies and private foundations.

Conclusion 6-5: The United States lacks an institutional body charged with ensuring that the country's commitment to equal opportunity is properly considered when policy is developed and evaluated. A National Mobility Center could serve as a key resource for facilitating data access, reporting on current mobility statistics and analyzing trends, identifying promising systemic and institutional interventions, developing viable approaches for evaluation, and building an interdisciplinary research community to study economic and social mobility.

---

[18] Consumer Price Index research series using current methods.
[19] Personal Consumption Expenditures Price Index.

ANNEX TABLE 6-1 Surveys Frequently Used for Mobility Research

Survey	Type	Birth Cohorts	Sample Size	Key Assets for Mobility Research	Key Liabilities
Panel Study of Income Dynamics (PSID)	Panel	Children of original PSID households: 1950–1968 birth cohorts	~5,000 households (in original PSID sample), many supplemental samples	Sample grows "naturally" as children and grandchildren from initial families form their own households; rich and extensive data collection and data supplements; multigenerational interviews (i.e., grandparent, parent, adult child)	Small sample size
National Longitudinal Survey of Youth (NLSY79 and NLSY97)	Panel	NLSY79: 1957–1964 birth cohorts; NLSY97: 1980–1984 birth cohorts	NLSY79: ~13,000 young adults; NLSY97: ~9,000 young adults	Rich and extensive follow-up surveys; new NLSY planned for 2026	Limited number of birth cohorts covered; small sample size
Wisconsin Longitudinal Study	Panel	1938–1940 birth cohorts	~10,000 Wisconsin high school graduates	Long-running coverage of full life course of Wisconsin high school graduates	Limited geographic coverage; limited number of birth cohorts covered
Future of Families and Child Wellbeing Study	Panel	1998–2000 birth cohorts	~5,000 children born in large cities	Rich and comprehensive interviews with parents and children	Small sample; limited number of birth cohorts; young age of children
National Longitudinal Study of Adolescent to Adult Health	Panel	1975–1983	~20,000 adolescents	Initial wave in 1995 secured educational, income, and occupational data for one of the parents of each of the adolescent participants; comprehensive health data (including genetic markers)	Limited coverage of birth cohorts

continued

ANNEX TABLE 6-1 Continued

Survey	Type	Birth Cohorts	Sample Size	Key Assets for Mobility Research	Key Liabilities
Survey of Income and Program Participation (SIPP)	Panel	1910–present day	~14,000–52,000 households per year	Comprehensive measurement of program participation; SIPP survey data can be matched to administrative earnings records (to carry out intergenerational analyses)	Intragenerational panels are relatively short in duration (up to 4 years)
Health and Retirement Study (HRS)	Panel	1890–1971 (new birth cohorts added every 6 years)	~40,000 respondents (~5,000 cases added every 6 years)	Extensive coverage of birth cohorts; retrospective data on childhood family life of HRS respondents; linked to earnings records, Medicare records, and other administrative data; extensive genetic data	Delayed availability of evidence on trends (respondents do not "age into" HRS until they are ~50 years old)
New Immigrant Survey (NIS)	Panel	1938–2004	First wave: ~9,000 adults and 1,000 children	Nationally representative samples of adult immigrants admitted to legal permanent residence (as well as child supplements)	Only provides information on intragenerational mobility
Children of Immigrants Survey (CIS)	Panel	1977–1978	First wave: ~5,000 8th- and 9th-grade students	Sample of second-generation immigrant children attending 8th and 9th grades in Miami/Ft. Lauderdale and San Diego	Only pertains to two birth cohorts and two metropolitan areas
High School and Beyond	Panel	~1962–1965 (high school sophomores and seniors in 1980)	~58,000 high school students	Rich coverage of secondary and postsecondary experiences (including transcripts and financial aid records); parent questionnaires available for sample of parents; extensive follow-up data	Limited coverage of birth cohorts
National Educational Longitudinal Study of 1988	Panel	~1974–1975 (8th graders in 1987–1988 school year)	~25,000 8th graders (with subsequent sample freshening)	Rich coverage of middle school, secondary, and postsecondary experiences; students' teachers, parents, and school administrators were also interviewed; extensive follow-up data	Limited coverage of birth cohorts

Study	Type	Years	Sample	Description	Limitations
Educational Longitudinal Study of 2002	Panel	~1986–1987 (high school sophomores in 2002)	~15,000 high school sophomores	Rich coverage of secondary and postsecondary experiences (including transcripts); students' teachers, parents, and school administrators were also interviewed; extensive follow-up data	Limited coverage of birth cohorts
High School Longitudinal Study of 2009	Panel	~1994–1995 (9th graders in 2009)	~23,000 9th graders	Rich coverage of secondary and postsecondary experiences (including transcripts); students' teachers, parents, and school administrators were also interviewed; extensive follow-up data	Limited coverage of birth cohorts
Occupational Changes in a Generation (OCGI and OCGII)	Cross-section	OCGI: 1898–1942; OCGII: 1908–1953	OCGI: ~20,000 adults; OCGII: ~34,000 adults	High-quality intergenerational occupation data (i.e., parental occupations secured retrospectively)	Only available for men
General Social Survey (GSS)	Cross-section	1897–2005	1972–1993: ~1,500 adults/year; 1994–2004: ~3,000 adults biannually; 2006–present: ~4,500 adults biannually	Standardized interview protocol delivered biannually via face-to-face interviews; high-quality occupational information (parental occupations secured retrospectively)	Small per-year sample size
American Voices Project	Cross-section	1944–2003	~2,700 adults	Nationally representative immersive interviews on one's "life arc"	Small sample size

ANNEX TABLE 6-2 Illustrative Aggregate and Contextual Datasets

Name	Context	Data Type	Unit of Analysis	Illustrative Variables
National Neighborhood Data Archive	Spatial	Physical, economic, demographic, and social attributes of neighborhoods	Wide range of neighborhood-level spatial units (e.g., Census tract, zip code, county)	Health care, housing, partisanship, public transit, education, demographics, social services, stores, traffic, crime, civics
National Neighborhood Data Archive	Spatial	Physical, economic, demographic, and social attributes of neighborhoods	Wide range of neighborhood-level spatial units (e.g., Census tract, zip code, county)	Health care, housing, partisanship, public transit, education, demographics, social services, stores, traffic, crime, civics
Opportunity Atlas (opportunityatlas.org)	Spatial	Tract-level social mobility (and a range of other neighborhood characteristics)	Census tract	Adult income of children raised in neighborhood (by race, gender, parent income) and many other neighborhood characteristics (e.g., incarceration rate, poverty rate, job density)
Social Explorer (socialexplorer.com)	Spatial	Social and demographic attributes of neighborhoods and other spatial units	Wide range of spatial units (e.g., Census block group, zip code, congressional district, state)	Population, income, occupation, poverty, marital status, age, race, education, house value, crime, health, immigration status (for block groups, school districts, and other spatial units)
Segregation Explorer (edopportunity.org)	Spatial	Racial and economic segregation	X	X
Safegraph Places (safegraph.com)	Spatial	Human mobility within towns, cities, and rural areas	Neighborhoods, parks, restaurants, and other "points of interest"	Number of visitors to points of interest (at a given time)

Justice Outcomes Explorer Within the Criminal Justice Administrative Records System (cjars.org)	Spatial	Criminal justice outcomes by state, county, and commuting zone	States, counties, commuting zones	Per capita rate of prison inmates, misdemeanor charge rate, annual employment rate of felony defendants, Medicaid take-up rates of parolees
Stanford Education Data Archive (edopportunity.org)	Educational institution	Test scores and changes in test scores	Schools (aggregated by school district, county, state, and other attributes)	Average test scores by county and school type (e.g., regular, charter, magnet)
Common Core of Data (nces.ed.gov)	Educational institution	Descriptive data on public elementary and secondary institutions	Elementary and secondary schools (aggregated by school type, state, and other attributes)	School enrollment, graduation rates
College Scorecard (collegescorecard.ed.gov)	Educational institution	Performance assessments of postsecondary institutions	Postsecondary educational institutions	Graduation rate, median earnings of attendees, other variables (many drawn from Integrated Postsecondary Education Data System)
Integrated Postsecondary Education Data System (nces.ed.gov/ipeds)	Educational institution	Descriptive data on postsecondary institution attributes	Postsecondary educational institutions	Tuition, admission rates, enrollment, financial aid, degrees conferred, student success, institutional resources
National Student Clearinghouse (nscresearchcenter.org)	Educational institution	Descriptive data on postsecondary institution attributes	Postsecondary educational institutions	Enrollment, program of study, retention rate, transfer rate, completers, time to credential, age, gender, race and ethnicity
Post-Secondary Employment Outcomes (https://lehd.ces.census.gov/data/pseo_experimental.html)	Educational institution	Descriptive data for postsecondary institutions, degree levels, and majors	Postsecondary educational institutions, degree levels, majors	Earnings and employment outcomes (via experimental tabulations developed by the Longitudinal Employer-Household Dynamics program at the U.S. Census Bureau)

continued

195

ANNEX TABLE 6-2 Illustrative Aggregate and Contextual Datasets

Name	Context	Data Type	Unit of Analysis	Illustrative Variables
Bureau of Labor Statistics (bls.gov)	Labor market	Labor market conditions	Assortment of labor market contexts (e.g., national, industry, occupation, state)	Employment, compensation, productivity
Occupational Information Network (O*NET) (onetonline.org)	Labor market	Occupational activities, skills, values, and conditions	Detailed occupations	Working conditions (e.g., hazards, scheduling, arduousness), writing skills, educational requirements
Longitudinal Employer-Household Dynamics (lehd.ces.census.gov)	Labor market	Employment conditions and outcomes at the firm level	Firms (aggregated spatially or by firm characteristics)	Hires, separations, job creation, earnings (by detailed firm characteristics)
Veteran Employment Outcomes (https://lehd.ces.census.gov/data/veo_experimental.html)	Labor market	Employment outcomes for veterans at the industry and spatial level	Industries and states	Earnings (by years of service, military occupation, Armed Forces Qualification Test range, and more)
Fiscally Standardized Cities (lincolninst.edu)	Policy	Local government finances	Large U.S. cities (~200)	City-level revenues, expenditures, debt, assets
State Laws Related to Structural Racism (https://doi.org/10.1177/00335492920984168)	Policy	State laws affecting health of racial and ethnic groups	State (i.e., state-level laws linked to structural racism)	Stand-your-ground laws, mandatory minimum sentencing laws, voting rights laws

	Policy	State
Correlates of State Policy (ippsr.msu.edu/public-policy/correlates-state-policy)	State laws relevant to fiscal policy, elections, criminal justice, education, welfare, health, labor, and environment	Minimum wage rates, concealed carry laws, environmental building standards, discrimination law, homeschooling law

ANNEX: GLOSSARY OF SELECTED TERMS

Advisory Committee on Data for Evidence Building
Established as part of the Foundations for Evidence-Based Policymaking Act "to review, analyze, and make recommendations to the White House Office of Management and Budget (OMB) Director on how to promote the use of federal data for evidence building" (Advisory Committee on Data for Evidence Building, 2022, p. 1).

Blended data
When at least two data assets are combined to produce statistical information. Careful blending of data from multiple, complementary sources, such as combining or linking statistical surveys and censuses with data from administrative agencies, offers a way to generate more detailed, timely, and useful statistical information than is currently available (see National Academies, 2023a).

Commission on Evidence-Based Policymaking
The Evidence-Based Policymaking Commission Act created the Commission on Evidence-Based Policymaking (CEP). The commission was tasked with examining ways to increase the availability and use of government data to build evidence while protecting data privacy and confidentiality. The commission's report (CEP, 2017) informed the Foundations for Evidence-Based Policymaking Act (2018).

Confidential Information Protection and Statistical Efficiency Act
Combined sources of previously collected data, including data in non-tabular formats. The Confidential Information Protection and Statistical Efficiency Act (CIPSEA) was first enacted as Title V of the E-Government Act and was recodified as part of the Foundations for Evidence-Based Policymaking Act (2018). CIPSEA provides a strong statutory basis for the statistical system with regard to confidentiality protection and data sharing.

Data infrastructure
Includes data assets; the technologies used to discover, access, share, process, use, analyze, manage, store, preserve, protect, and secure those assets; the people, capacity, and expertise needed to manage, use, interpret, and understand data; the guidance, standards, policies, and rules that govern data access, use, and protection; the organizations and entities that manage, oversee, and govern the data infrastructure; and the communities and data subjects whose data are shared and used for statistical purposes and may be impacted by decisions made using those data assets (National Academies, 2023c).

Federal statistical agencies

The principal U.S. federal statistical agencies are Bureau of Economic Analysis (Department of Commerce); Bureau of Justice Statistics (Department of Justice); Bureau of Labor Statistics (Department of Labor); Bureau of Transportation Statistics (Department of Transportation); Census Bureau (Department of Commerce); Economic Research Service (Department of Agriculture); Energy Information Agency (Department of Energy); National Agricultural Statistics Service (Department of Agriculture); National Center for Education Statistics (Department of Education); National Center for Health Statistics (Department of Health and Human Services); National Center for Science and Engineering Statistics (National Science Foundation); Office of Research, Evaluation, and Statistics (Social Security Administration); and Statistics of Income (Department of Treasury). There are also three recognized federal statistical units: Microeconomic Surveys Unit (Federal Reserve Board), Center for Behavioral Health Statistics and Quality (Substance Abuse and Mental Health Services Administration, Department of Health and Human Services), and National Animal Health Monitoring System (Animal and Plant Health Inspection Service, Department of Agriculture).

Federal Statistical Research Data Centers

Partnerships between federal statistical agencies and leading research institutions that provide secure environments to support qualified researchers using restricted-access data while protecting respondent confidentiality.

Foundations for Evidence-Based Policymaking Act of 2018

This statute requires agency data to be accessible and requires agencies to plan to develop statistical evidence to support policymaking (Foundations for Evidence-Based Policymaking Act, 2018).

Inter-university Consortium for Political and Social Research

An international consortium of more than 810 academic institutions and research organizations that maintains a data archive of more than 350,000 files and provides leadership and training in data access, curation, and methods of analysis for the social science research community.

IPUMS

Provides census and survey data from around the world integrated across time and space. IPUMS integration and documentation makes it easy to study change, conduct comparative research, merge information across data types, and analyze individuals within family and community context. Data and services are available free of charge.

National Secure Data Service (NSDS)

Recommended by the Commission on Evidence-based Policymaking to facilitate access to data for evidence-building while ensuring privacy and transparency in how those data are used. The NSDS is envisioned as an added capacity for the federal statistical system to support (not supplant) ongoing work within the individual agencies and to provide a system-wide capacity to aid coordination, data sharing, data linkage, shared research and development, and other functions.

Person Identification Validation System

The Census Bureau's Person Identification Validation System (PVS) assigns unique person identifiers to federal, commercial, Census, and survey data to facilitate linkages across and within files. PVS uses probabilistic matching to assign a unique Census Bureau identifier for each person.

Protected identification key

A unique identifier for a person in a dataset, the protected identification key (PIK) is an anonymous identifier as unique as a Social Security number. The PIK links across all files that have been processed using PVS.

Standard Application Process

A uniform method for accessing federal confidential data assets to systematically provide permission to use protected data from any of the 16 federal statistical agencies and designated units for evidence-building.

U.S. Code Title 13

Includes the major legal provisions related to the Census Bureau, including strict provisions for protecting the confidentiality of population and business information.

U.S. Code Title 26

Applies to the statistical work conducted by the Census Bureau's collection of data from the Internal Revenue Service (IRS) about households and businesses. Title 26 provides for the conditions under which the IRS may disclose federal tax returns and return information to other agencies, including the Census Bureau.

7

New Directions for Research and Policy

This report has reviewed a diverse body of research in an effort to build a nuanced understanding of the trends, patterns, and factors that shape economic and social mobility with a focus on intergenerational mobility—the chances that people have to achieve economic prosperity regardless of their family background. In doing so, the committee has drawn a series of conclusions about the state of knowledge on mobility with an eye toward informing a forward-looking, evidence-based, policy-relevant research agenda. As discussed in Chapter 1, this report focuses on a set of key correlates and drivers of mobility in an effort to detail actionable recommendations for new research to understand mobility and ideas for shaping policy to enhance it.

A research agenda on economic and social mobility is relevant to policymakers at every level of government—federal, state, county, and local. When thinking about safety net approaches to reducing poverty and enhancing mobility, the federal government plays a disproportionate role in part because of its substantially larger tax base. However, states and localities can also shape policies related to education, housing, labor markets, financial institutions, and health care, among other domains. State governments play an important role in establishing policies on family planning and formation, education, financial institutions, and spatial issues. Counties and local governments share authority to enact zoning laws and design public transportation and other transportation policy, and they also have some authority regarding education and social welfare program policy. Thus, all levels of government can innovate and evaluate policies tied directly and indirectly to economic and social mobility and the specific domains described herein.

This report also makes clear that policymakers can take a variety of approaches to promote economic and social mobility. In fact, the findings in this report indicate that there is no single solution, "silver bullet," or pathway to enhancing mobility that is sufficient because of the multiple channels that support or prevent mobility. Policy levers will differ depending on the level of the policy actors (federal, state, local) and may have different effects on absolute and relative mobility. Many of the policies considered by the committee focus on improving the well-being of disadvantaged families, which would support both absolute upward mobility and relative mobility, by detaching individuals from their disadvantaged origins. Alternatively, policies reducing tax, educational, or other benefits for higher-income households may improve relative mobility because they would reduce the ability of high-income parents to pass resources to their children. While the committee acknowledges that some channels for intergenerational economic persistence may be difficult or undesirable to alter via social policy, we argue that there is great opportunity to promote mobility in the United States by dismantling economic and institutional barriers to economic prosperity and instability through policy intervention.

With that said, types of policy approaches to enhance mobility may be categorized into three broad strategies. The first, a safety net approach that seeks to puts a floor on the level of deprivation experienced by members of society, is the most common—it generally focuses on repairing deficits and compensating for disadvantages within low-income populations. This sometimes involves setting up subsidiary institutions to serve low-income populations, operating in parallel to mainstream institutions. Examples include Head Start, public housing or subsidized housing vouchers, workforce development centers, or financial instruments available only to lower-income families. The primary goal and stated purpose of these programs may be to reduce poverty rather than enhance mobility, but in providing resources that support families such policies can have a positive direct effect on upward mobility. They could also support relative mobility by detaching young people growing up in poor households from disadvantages of birth. A side effect of the safety net approach is a one-sided focus on the mobility challenges faced by low-income populations, with little focus on the effects of disproportionate opportunities among those born at the top of the resource distribution. The focus of "supplementary" programs is on increasing opportunity among those born into the bottom of the class system, rather than building mainstream institutions that broaden opportunities for mobility across the entire population.

A second strategy, then, is reforming mainstream institutions to make them work better for all Americans. Such a strategy could change the policy landscape to make such institutions as banks, schools, and housing developments more inclusive. This might mean, for example, making bank accounts or lending at financial institutions more accessible to low-income families or making a more concerted effort to integrate new housing developments by household income to reduce economic segregation. The evidence base on this type of approach is more limited and more difficult to collect, so comparatively less is known about how to reform mainstream institutions or what the outcomes of such changes would be.

A final strategy is forging new ideas for policy and instead rolling back policies that constrict mobility or support the persistence of advantage across generations. Many policies thought of as enhancing economic and social mobility have been used for the opposite purpose. Indeed, many of the mechanisms by which opportunity has been restricted—especially by characteristics such as race, ethnicity, and gender—have been aided and abetted by social policy. More attention could be paid to the impacts of rolling back policies that limit the mobility of certain groups, whether absolutely or relative to others. This might include housing (e.g., zoning laws that reduce the availability of affordable housing), assets (e.g., tax policies that favor certain types of assets or sources of income primarily owned by wealthy families), educational (e.g., tax benefits that disproportionately help higher-income families save for college), or other policies that disproportionately favor high-income groups by providing subsidies or resources that further support the persistence of advantage across generations.

The conclusions and recommendations presented in this report can be used to inform and advance all three policy strategies. The next sections walk through the key domains that drive economic and social mobility as discussed in this report (early life and family; space and place; postsecondary education; wealth, credit, and debt), followed by a section that reviews the needs for a new data infrastructure to measure and study these key pathways. Each section lists the key conclusions and recommendations, numbered according to the report chapter in which they were developed. The final section reviews the report's discussion of a National Mobility Center and highlights the importance of combining different sources of data and methodological approaches to understand mobility dynamics.

EARLY LIFE AND FAMILY

Considerable evidence makes it clear that what happens in early life shapes people's life trajectories. Thus, it is imperative for any research agenda on mobility to include expanded understanding of the intersection of circumstances in early life with long-term economic and social mobility. Family—however constructed—is the fundamental unit of social organization during the early life period. It is clear that how families function is critical to such outcomes as cognitive and socioemotional development, educational attainment, human capital formation, and individual and family health and well-being in the next generation. As such, families are the central unit of intergenerational mobility. Naturally, families do not operate in a vacuum, so their role in the mobility process depends on how they are shaped by institutional and economic resources and constraints. The committee therefore spent considerable time reviewing the evidence on early life and family as it relates to mobility, arriving at the following key conclusions:

Conclusion 2-1: Unintended pregnancies and childbirth are adversely associated with multiple determinants of upward mobility from poverty and persistence of advantage, in domains such as infant and maternal health, cognitive and socioemotional development, human capital formation, and economic well-being.

Conclusion 2-2: Socioeconomic disparities in parenting behaviors and resources are associated with disparities in the social and economic well-being of children throughout the life course, thus providing a mechanism for the persistence of advantage and disadvantage across generations.

Conclusion 2-3: Early childhood education programs, and reproductive health policies and programs that increase access to contraception and abortion, show promise for increasing upward intergenerational mobility. Economic support policies and programs that increase access to financial resources, food, and health care also show promise for increasing upward mobility. In contrast, the evidence on other pregnancy risk reduction, abstinence education, and parenting intervention programs is less encouraging.

Policy strategies that build on the existing evidence on early life and family could be based on any of the three approaches described at the start of this chapter. Conclusions 2-1 and 2-3 support reproductive health, early childhood education, and economic support programs and policies that may be either narrowly targeted or be more universal in design. Conclusion 2-2 highlights the importance of considering the broader forces and institutions that produce and perpetuate socioeconomic and racial/ethnic disparities. With each approach, a more robust evidence base will further inform the development of policies in this domain. The committee offers two research recommendations on early life and family:

Recommendation 2-1: The vast majority of research linking early life and family experiences to intergenerational mobility is descriptive in nature. Researchers should expand the use of existing longitudinal, administrative, and survey data and, when possible, further employ quasi-experimental and experimental approaches to obtain a better understanding of the causal mechanisms through which family context (pregnancy intendedness, family formation, family structure and stability), parenting behaviors and the caregiving environment, and child development affect economic and social mobility, as well as potential heterogeneity in such relationships for demographic subpopulations.

Recommendation 2-2: Existing survey and administrative data are not fully adequate to support comprehensive research on intergenerational economic and social mobility and the range of mechanisms through which mobility may occur. Existing longitudinal surveys, such as the Panel Study of Income Dynamics and the Future of Families and Child Wellbeing Study—currently the only long-term ongoing U.S. panel studies to follow multiple generations of family members—should be maintained and expanded to include detailed information on pregnancy intention and the circumstances of pregnancies, parenting, and child development for all children born to current sample members. In addition, the samples that support these surveys should be refreshed with respondents that represent the contemporary population, especially Latino/Hispanic and immigrant subgroups. The children should be followed in utero and onward and assessed regularly at intervals representing key developmental stages of childhood, adolescence, and young adulthood. In addition, these surveys should be linked to administrative data from the U.S. Census Bureau, the Internal Revenue Service, and state and federal agencies that administer core social welfare programs.

These recommendations—and those from the other chapters—demonstrate the benefits of the growing data infrastructure that is revolutionizing mobility-related research (discussed in Chapter 6) presently underway.

SPACE AND PLACE

There is perhaps no area of research on intergenerational mobility that has seen more development in recent years than the role of space and place. Drawing on this scholarship, the committee arrived at four key conclusions on current scholarly consensus and the best focus for a forward-looking, policy-relevant research agenda.

Conclusion 3-1: Recent evidence suggests that residential environments have a causal impact on economic and social mobility (measured by income, earnings, or occupation) and on intermediate outcomes related to mobility, such as cognitive development and educational attainment. The link between place and individual outcomes has now moved beyond the question of whether neighborhoods matter and toward questions of when, where, why, and for whom residential contexts matter.

Conclusion 3-2: At the neighborhood level, the mechanisms linking the local residential environment with economic and social mobility include schools, community violence, and local social networks. At larger levels of analysis—such as cities, counties, and commuting zones—the forces that influence economic and social mobility include segregation and local labor market conditions.

Conclusion 3-3: Most spatial policy strategies are either housing mobility policies, which relocate families to higher-opportunity areas, or place-conscious investments, which aim to bring opportunity and investment into disadvantaged communities. Although both have the potential to boost economic and social mobility, evidence on the effectiveness of place-based programs that do not target people in disadvantaged communities and do not provide a range of supports is mixed.

Conclusion 3-4: In addition to new housing mobility initiatives and place-based investments, it is important to consider approaches that focus on ending existing programs and policies that have historically amplified spatial and racial inequality and continue to do so.

These conclusions identify the need to move beyond scholarly inquiry about whether place matters, to discuss more about why and how and in what circumstances it matters. Per Conclusion 3-2, there are already some key insights about the mechanisms that affect mobility at the neighborhood and larger levels of geographic analysis; the former may underpin policy interventions that are more targeted in nature, while the latter may inform policies that address larger societal forces and mainstream institutions. In Conclusion 3-4, the committee calls for addressing existing policies that amplify spatial and racial inequalities, such as zoning, discriminatory housing practices, and some regressive federal housing programs (such as the mortgage interest deduction, property tax deduction, and exclusion of capital gains on the sales of homes) that reinforce residential segregation and constrain residential mobility.

The efficacy of strategies implemented at scale to move people to opportunities as opposed to improving the quality of the communities in which they live remains a key question for the field. As noted in Conclusion 3-3, some housing mobility interventions have shown promise, but there is a lack of clarity about the general equilibrium effects of implementing such interventions at scale. At the same time, the overall record of place-conscious investments for improving outcomes that are proximate to social mobility is mixed at best. Place-conscious programs—such as New Hope, the Harlem Children's Zone, and Jobs Plus—that target residents of disadvantaged communities with employment opportunities, training, and support services and/or provide resources to foster job creation and economic development have shown success in improving employment, earnings, and academic outcomes for participants. However, evidence on the effectiveness of broader place-based programs that have not targeted people in disadvantaged communities and have not provided a range of supports has been mixed. Thus, additional research and policy experimentation is needed to develop actionable policies that rigorously address the relationship between space and place and economic and social mobility.

Continued research (in at least the seven areas listed in Recommendation 3-1 below) needs to use a wide range of methods to deepen the understanding of these and other mechanisms and dynamics at play. Perhaps most importantly, the committee highlights that, from a policy standpoint, the understanding of how to combat the deep relationships between space and place and economic and social mobility is still in its infancy. Although existing research has demonstrated that schooling, public funding, community violence, social capital, and racial and economic segregation are all strongly associated with economic mobility, a better understanding is needed of the processes by which these factors lead to mobility. Foregrounding heterogeneity (e.g., who takes up housing vouchers, the characteristics of neighborhoods in which families start and end up, the age and gender of children who move) enables an understanding of which groups are most likely to benefit from social policies designed to reduce spatial inequality or increase economic and social mobility. Qualitative research can further assist in generating insights and hypotheses about the mechanisms by which place shapes mobility, using ethnographic observation and semistructured interviews; these insights can then be integrated into further quantitative tests and policy development.

> Recommendation 3-1: Researchers should strengthen the evidence base on space and place in the following areas: (1) causal impacts of the key mechanisms that link place with economic and social mobility; (2) heterogeneity in the relationship between place and economic and social mobility; (3) qualitative approaches to understanding the mechanisms that undergird the causal effects of place, as well as the mechanisms that explain evidence on effective policy; (4) causal impacts of various

types of place-based investments; (5) existing policies and interventions that amplify spatial inequality; (6) general equilibrium effects of social policies and the feasibility and costs of different approaches; and (7) neighborhood contexts of disadvantaged rural, small town, and suburban areas.

POSTSECONDARY EDUCATION

Elementary and secondary education (i.e., K–12) and postsecondary education both matter for economic and social mobility. The committee decided to focus on postsecondary education because it has received less attention from research and policy than K–12. Postsecondary education is also increasingly on the minds of the public and policymakers when they think about pathways to enhance economic and social mobility. How does a system of postsecondary education build ladders to economic success for anyone, from any starting point? While what happens to individuals before they reach this stage is of critical importance, *access to* and *persistence in* postsecondary education is highly stratified by income, location of residence, and racial minority status. Even among those who enroll in higher education, the probability of graduating, the amount of debt taken, and the quality of education received strongly depends on social background. Understanding these sources of stratification is crucial when shaping systems to become engines of economic and social mobility.

Conclusion 4-1: Postsecondary education in the United States is a very strong predictor of economic well-being and is a critical determinant of intergenerational mobility. However, there are considerable disparities in college enrollment and completion by family income, location of residence, and race and ethnicity. There are also growing disparities by gender, favoring women, the consequences of which are poorly understood.

Conclusion 4-2: Existing data sources cannot be used to properly evaluate current changes in the association between parent's income and bachelor's degree attainment. This data limitation can be addressed by linking survey data with administrative data.

Conclusion 4-3: Although the attainment of a 4-year bachelor's degree is a very strong predictor of economic well-being and security, postsecondary education has become an increasingly risky proposition for many adults and families, especially those who have low incomes and are racial minorities. Broad-access institutions, certificate programs, and the growth of for-profit schools and other educational providers has increased the menu of options but has not necessarily increased completion rates or returns.

Conclusion 4-4: People transition between school and work and between careers throughout their lives and in different ways. Economic and social mobility can be enhanced by recognizing the need for multiple pathways to mobility beyond a college degree, commensurate with people's many starting points and transitions.

Recommendation 4-1: Researchers should examine the implications for economic and social mobility of growing gender differences in college completion.

Recommendation 4-2: Researchers should conduct comprehensive, distributive analyses of the economic costs, benefits, and risks of college and explore the question of the extent to which U.S. postsecondary education is a replicator of intergenerational inequality rather than an engine for intergenerational mobility. Attention should be paid to variations in returns across the heterogeneous postsecondary sector, with broad-access institutions playing a central role for the vast majority of the population, different from that of more elite and selective universities.

Recommendation 4-3: Researchers should explore whether postsecondary funding models in other countries—especially with regard to sub-baccalaureate education—are more effective in generating economic mobility than the U.S. model.

Recommendation 4-4: Researchers should study ways to stimulate demand for postsecondary education for particular populations and settings. Evidence is needed about specific populations defined by level of academic preparation, race and ethnicity, income levels, residential location, and age.

Recommendation 4-5: Researchers should study the effects of inputs, policies, and practices (e.g., curricula, pedagogical techniques, class size, connections to employment opportunities) on the quality of postsecondary education and the implications for economic and social mobility.

Recommendation 4-6: Researchers should study the effectiveness of programs and policies to support the trajectories of those without bachelor's degrees, as well as multiple transitions and pathways between schooling, training, and work.

Although other parts of the report bring attention to nonmainstream institutions, such as alternative credit providers, this report's conclusions and recommendations on postsecondary education emphasize reforming mainstream institutions. Understanding the outcomes yielded by our current systems of colleges and universities can enable policymakers to build with an eye toward broad-based access to opportunity to promote mobility.

WEALTH, CREDIT, AND DEBT

Individuals and families are subject to a complicated financial services landscape, with the possibility of both risk and reward. Wealth, credit, and debt are each directly linked to the other domains discussed in this report (early life and family, space and place, and postsecondary education). A research agenda for enhancing economic and social mobility includes developing a clearer understanding of the relationships between economic and social mobility and wealth, credit, and debt that can then be built on to test policy responses.

Conclusion 5-1: Wealth is transmitted across generations. This transmission occurs partly directly, through transfers and bequests, but also indirectly, through advantages that accrue to children in their early development, neighborhood, educational, and labor market experiences; these indirect channels of wealth transmission undergird wealth's role in sustaining other forms of economic and social mobility. In addition to monetary advantages, family wealth can provide a safety net or buffer that allows individuals to take risks.

Conclusion 5-2: Wealth accumulation and intergenerational wealth transmission are shaped by multiple institutional and structural features of U.S. society that have not been and are still not race neutral.

Conclusion 5-3: Credit and debt are not monolithic. For many individuals, they provide opportunities to make core long-term investments and take risks that engender wealth accumulation and upward mobility. For others, they are hindrances to upward mobility, if not direct sources of downward mobility.

Conclusion 5-4: Targeted policies can address the intergenerational transmission of wealth at different points of the wealth distribution, from the top (through inheritance and wealth taxation), to the middle (chiefly through housing policies), to the bottom (through credit market regulation and asset-building policies). More universal policies (e.g., universal stakeholder grants, baby bonds, reparations) can build a common stock of wealth for all. However, more needs to be known about the relative promise of each of these approaches and of the mechanisms for funding them.

Wealth is a primary factor in shaping intergenerational mobility in the United States; perhaps its most distinctive feature is that it can be transmitted directly to one's children and even grandchildren. Credit and debt may be regarded as two-edged swords in efforts to enhance economic and social mobility—each can be a vehicle to achieve this goal, but each in turn can also thwart it. Few existing policies explicitly target the intergenerational persistence of wealth, which is striking given its importance to economic and social mobility. Blacks and Hispanics have historically faced major barriers to wealth accumulation, and Conclusion 5-2 calls attention to the structural features of society that may produce such disparities in the accumulation and intergenerational transmission of wealth; Conclusion 5-4 sets forth a framework for policy intervention that is relevant to the full range of the wealth distribution. The committee identified several areas where the existing evidence base needs to be strengthened to better inform the development of policy interventions relating to wealth, credit, and debt.

Recommendation 5-1: Researchers should examine the intergenerational behavioral implications of assets and debt to better understand the indirect channels through which wealth is transmitted.

Recommendation 5-2: Researchers should expand the traditional two-generation mobility framework by considering the role of grandparental wealth and debt.

Recommendation 5-3: Researchers should further examine the ongoing role of institutions, policies, and practices in reproducing racial/ethnic wealth gaps and expand beyond White and Black populations to generate evidence on wealth mobility patterns for other racial/ethnic groups.

Recommendation 5-4: Researchers should study in what circumstances, how, and for whom different forms of credit and debt are helpful or harmful for economic and social mobility.

Recommendation 5-5: Researchers should study the relative costs, benefits, and long-term effects of (1) policies that target the intergenerational transmission of wealth at different points in the wealth distribution (top, middle, and bottom); (2) universal policies that seek to provide wealth transfers to all families or young people or provide reparations for slavery; and (3) broader institutional changes that would reduce the necessity of families to rely on their private wealth to support the success of the next generation. Researchers should also study the potential of the existing taxation system and new tax policies to support these initiatives.

DATA INFRASTRUCTURE

The United States is moving toward having a modern integrated data system based on linked administrative data that will rival the systems in many European countries. Developing sustainable structures that ensure increased and equitable access to new data resources remains a central challenge ahead. Achieving this requires cooperation among the many stakeholders in the data ecosystem, including executive and congressional branches of government, federal statistical agencies, state and local government officials, the research community, potential private funding organizations, and the general public. Chapter 6 outlines a number of conclusions and recommendations that can facilitate this new data infrastructure.

Beyond sharing across agencies, it is important to improve data access for researchers. Data access laws, such as those found in U.S. Code Titles 13 and 26, need to be modernized to facilitate research, as they have proven to be inadequate amid the recent growth of research using linked administrative data. A key advantage of emerging linked administrative datasets is the option for researchers to obtain data from multiple sources and agencies through efforts such as the National Secure Data Service. Additionally, it is important to adequately fund agencies to allow them to provide data.

Finally, the United States lacks an institutional body charged with ensuring that the country's commitment to equal opportunity is taken into account when policy is developed and evaluated. Because research on intergenerational mobility is central to assessing the current and future well-being of the U.S. economy and society, the creation of a nongovernmental research center—a National Mobility Center—is appropriate.

Conclusion 6-1: Research on mobility-relevant programs and policies requires the use of blended, multigenerational data for multiple domains—especially family, place, education, and wealth—including both surveys and administrative data (e.g., tax and benefit data). Also needed is a process for ensuring that qualified researchers can access these blended data within a secure environment; this process needs to explicitly recognize both the risk of using confidential administrative data in research and the benefits to society that can be produced from this research.

Conclusion 6-2: The data structure for studying economic and social mobility will be strengthened if state agencies provide (1) the U.S. Census Bureau with data on all programs that receive federal funding, and (2) the National Center for Health Statistics with both current and past data that are part of the National Vital Statistics System. States would require funding to adopt systems and processes to comply with reporting requirements.

Conclusion 6-3: The data infrastructure for studying economic and social mobility will be strengthened if the ban prohibiting the federal government from tracking students and from maintaining a national database of student records is repealed.

Conclusion 6-4: In order to facilitate data access for studying economic and social mobility, funding is required for streamlining the data application process, improving linking, supporting Federal Statistical Research Data Centers, enhancing the survey infrastructure, and expanding qualitative research.

Conclusion 6-5: The United States lacks an institutional body charged with ensuring that the country's commitment to equal opportunity is properly considered when policy is developed and evaluated. A National Mobility Center could serve as a key resource for facilitating data access, reporting on current mobility statistics and analyzing trends, identifying promising systemic and institutional interventions, developing viable approaches for evaluation, and building an interdisciplinary research community to study economic and social mobility.

Recommendation 6-1: Building on the Foundations for Evidence-Based Policymaking Act of 2018 (Evidence Act), the chief statistician of the United States should work with federal agencies to advise legislators and policymakers to address the need for revisions to regulations to improve data sharing across federal statistical agencies, including
   a. revisiting U.S. Code Title 26 to allow the Internal Revenue Service to expand the ability to share tax data with the U.S. Census Bureau that are needed to create more comprehensive measures of household income and wealth;
   b. issuing the Presumption of Access rule that was part of the 2018 Evidence Act, thus ensuring that federal agencies share data among themselves; and
   c. requiring nonstatistical federal agencies to provide annual data to the U.S. Census Bureau so that it can conduct an annual administrative record census.

Recommendation 6-2: In order to evaluate the policies surrounding economic and social mobility, researchers require tiered access to new blended data. The chief statistician of the United States should work with the federal agencies to review and revise policies concerning external data sharing with the broader research community, including (1) revisiting the missions of federal statistical agencies to formally acknowledge the need for data sharing and the broader benefits to society of research itself; (2) using tiered access to support access for qualified external researchers; (3) expanding the Standard Application Process to ensure that all proposals are evaluated within 3 months; and (4) providing remote access to Federal Statistical Research Data Centers to facilitate data sharing with more researchers. The National Secure Data Service should also work with federal agencies to ensure that these improved data access, analysis, and linking mechanisms are implemented.

Recommendation 6-3: To increase the value of data for studying economic and social mobility, federal agencies should collaborate with the National Secure Data Service to improve the data acquisition and linking process by assigning protected identification keys (PIKs) to federal surveys:
 a. The U.S. Census Bureau should improve the person identification validation system (PVS), which should serve as the standard for linking all individual-level data held by all federal agencies.
 b. The U.S. Bureau of Labor Statistics and the U.S. Census Bureau should assign PIKs to all records that are part of the (i) monthly Current Population Survey back to 1963, (ii) Consumer Expenditure Survey, (iii) American Time Use Survey, and (iv) National Longitudinal Surveys.
 c. The U.S. Department of Education and the U.S. Census Bureau should assign a PIK to individual Free Application for Federal Student Aid forms, as well as to individual-level administrative data on federal financial aid receipt.

NATIONAL MOBILITY CENTER

What can be done to forward the research agenda summarized in this chapter? As discussed in Chapter 6, one of the major barriers to drawing conclusions about policymaking regarding economic and social mobility has been inadequate data. Mobility is difficult to measure and occurs only over extended periods of time, including across generations and over the life course of individuals, thus requiring large-scale longitudinal data for its analysis. However, the nation is on the cusp of revolutionizing the study of mobility, in that many new sources of data from administrative records, such as tax records and decennial censuses, will become more accessible to researchers. Indeed, as delineated by the discussion of data infrastructure in Chapter 6, the United States is moving toward a modern integrated data system linking such administrative sources that is in line with many peer countries. This is now beginning to and will further open a host of new opportunities for research. Never before have scholars and analysts been so well equipped to forward this research agenda. As discussed in Chapter 6, a National Mobility Center could serve as a clearinghouse and resource center for statistics on and analysis of mobility trends and dynamics (see Conclusion 6-5). It could serve as a training ground for new scholars who want to conduct research on economic and social mobility. And it could make the confidential administrative data needed to study mobility more accessible—with proper protections—to a broader group of researchers. Such a center could become an important hub that pushes forward much of the research agenda discussed in this report; it would make this metric of economic well-being a priority commensurate to the concern and goals of the American public. In addition to facilitating access to and training on new sources of linked administrative and blended microdata, such a center could also help in setting standards and training researchers on best practices for a variety of methods—including rigorous qualitative inquiry (discussed in Chapter 3) and helping decision-makers understand how a policy or intervention is perceived and valued by those for whom it is intended.

This report highlights the importance and value of qualitative research to the study of the drivers of economic and social mobility and the development of programs and policies to enhance it. In recent years, there has been a sharp rise in the use of qualitative research in the social sciences and growing acknowledgment of its value (Edin et al., 2024). For example, many researchers and policy evaluation scholars are often far removed from the everyday lives and social settings of people they study and who are likely to be affected by mobility interventions. As a result, they typically operate without enough information to understand exactly how an intervention is working within its sociocultural and historical context. Sometimes they do not even know the right questions to ask. Thus at least one key benefit of qualitative work is that it brings policy researchers and those evaluating programs much closer to the contexts of people who are impacted by these interventions.

For instance, an intervention may have strong efficacy for those who participate, but may have low take-up rates and no impact at scale because of a lack of community buy-in. If a program or intervention provides resources to support upward mobility but fails to attract a broad enough section of the target population, then the scale of its impact will be severely circumscribed. Qualitative research can help build knowledge about why target populations do or do not take up an intervention, and perhaps reveal policy levers that can increase take-up and thus enhance impact (Barnes, 2020; DeLuca & Rosenblatt, 2010; Halpern-Meekin et al., 2015; Romich & Weisner, 2000).

Most importantly, though, qualitative research plays a vital role in the basic science of mobility research, with major implications for mobility policy formation. It allows scholars to interrogate important theoretical and policy assumptions; to generate hypotheses for future data collection, analysis, research design, and intervention development. It is an avenue for identifying potential causal mechanisms (which can be evaluated using survey and administrative data) that are drivers of economic and social mobility and may also be targets for policy intervention; it can also reveal the perceptions and beliefs held by those for whom programs and policies are targeted, which aids in more effective policy designs. This report highlights numerous examples of insights offered to the study of mobility in understanding patterns of family formation, the importance of place in determining mobility, and in understanding how and why higher education may or may not be a path toward upward mobility. Qualitative research with target populations and the communities in which they are embedded is a source of valuable data for making decisions on program efficacy (Andrews et al., 2019) and for building policies and programs that enhance mobility.

CONCLUSION

This report seeks to dive into the evidence base on economic and social mobility and to create a forward-looking, policy-relevant research agenda for the future. Clearly, the lack of available data has slowed progress in building knowledge on this metric of economic well-being in the United States. But standing on the cusp of a mobility data revolution, it will likely be possible to reach new heights in the understanding and design of policy to enhance economic and social mobility.

The charge for this report is motivated by the fact that economic and social mobility is a key measure of well-being, and it underlies a fundamental value held by many Americans: that anyone should be able to succeed economically, regardless of circumstances such as family life, home community, and the assets they start out with. The goal that all Americans will have the opportunity for economic and social mobility has been a fundamental tenet throughout U.S. history, even as many observers may rightly argue that it has been, at times and for many groups, severely circumscribed. There is no question, however, that the economic and social mobility of groups of Americans who were systematically excluded for generations—particularly Black Americans and women—has improved over time, even though the pace has been slow and deep inequalities in opportunity persist. More must be done to enhance mobility broadly if the country is to finally live up to the values espoused by its founding documents and the vast majority of its citizens.

References

Aaronson, D., Faber, J., Hartley, D., Mazumder, B., & Sharkey, P. (2021b). The long-run effects of the 1930s HOLC "redlining" maps on place-based measures of economic opportunity and socioeconomic success. *Regional Science and Urban Economics*, *86*(3), 103622. https://doi.org/10.1016/j.regsciurbeco.2020.103622

Aaronson, D., Hartley, D., & Mazumder, B. (2021a). The effects of the 1930s HOLC "redlining" maps. *American Economic Journal: Economic Policy*, *13*(4), 355–392. https://doi.org/10.1257/pol.20190414

Aaronson, D., & Mazumder, B. (2008). Intergenerational economic mobility in the United States, 1940 to 2000. *Journal of Human Resources*, *43*(1), 139–172. https://jhr.uwpress.org/content/wpjhr/43/1/139.full.pdf

Abramitzky, R., & Boustan, L. (2022). Streets of gold: America's untold story of immigrant success. *The Journal of Economic History*, *82*(3), 913–914. https://doi.org/10.1017/S0022050722000298

Ackerman, B. (1999). Taxation and the constitution. *Columbia Law Review*, *99*(1), 1–58. https://doi.org/10.2307/1123596

Ackerman, B., & Alstott, A. (1999). *The stakeholder society*. Yale University Press.

Adamsons, K., & Johnson, S. K. (2013). An updated and expanded meta-analysis of nonresident fathering and child well-being. *Journal of Family Psychology*, *27*(4), 589–599. https://doi.org/10.1037/a0033786

Addo, F. R., Darity, W. A., Jr., & Myers, S. L., Jr. (2024). Setting the record straight on racial wealth inequality. *AEA Papers and Proceedings*, *114*, 169–173. https://doi.org/10.1257/pandp.20241102

Adermon, A., Lindahl, M., & Waldenström, D. (2018). Intergenerational wealth mobility and the role of inheritance: Evidence from multiple generations. *The Economic Journal*, *128*(612), 482–513. https://doi.org/10.1111/ecoj.12535

Advisory Committee on Data for Evidence Building. (2022). *Year 2 report*. Bureau of Economic Analysis. https://www.bea.gov/system/files/2022-10/acdeb-year-2-report.pdf

Aeppli, C., & Wilmers, N. (2022). Rapid wage growth at the bottom has offset rising U.S. inequality. *Proceedings of the National Academy of Sciences, 119*(42), e2204305119. https://doi.org/10.1073/pnas.2204305119

Agarwal, S., Chomsisengphet, S., Mahoney, N., & Stroebel, J. (2015). Regulating consumer financial products: Evidence from credit cards. *The Quarterly Journal of Economics, 130*(1), 111–164. https://www.jstor.org/stable/26372597

Agbai, C. O. (2022). *Wealth begins at home: The GI Bill of 1944 and the making of the racial wealth gap in homeownership and home value.* https://doi.org/10.31235/osf.io/t5xby

Agénor, M., Perkins, C., Stamoulis, C., Hall, R. D., Samnaliev, M., Berland, S., & Bryn Austin, S. (2021). Developing a database of structural racism-related state laws for health equity research and practice in the United States. *Public Health Reports, 136*(4), 428–440. https://doi.org/0.1177/0033354920984168

Ahn, M., Batty, M., & Meisenzahl, R. R. (2018). *Household debt-to-income ratios in the enhanced financial accounts.* FEDS Notes. Board of Governors of the Federal Reserve System. https://doi.org/10.17016/2380-7172.2138

Aizer, A., & Currie, J. (2014). The intergenerational transmission of inequality: Maternal disadvantage and health at birth. *Science, 344*(6186), 856–861. https://doi.org/10.1126/science.1251872

Aizer, A., Eli, S., Ferrie, J., & Lleras-Muney, A. (2016). The long-run impact of cash transfers to poor families. *American Economic Review, 106*(4), 935–971. https://doi.org/10.1257/aer.20140529

Akee, R. K., Copeland, W. E., Keeler, G., Angold, A., & Costello, E. J. (2010). Parents' incomes and children's outcomes: A quasi-experiment using transfer payments from casino profits. *American Economic Journal: Applied Economics, 2*(1), 86–115. https://doi.org/10.1257/app.2.1.86

Aladangady, A., Bricker, J., Chang, A., Goodman, S., Krimmel, J., Moore, K., Reber, S., Volz, A., & Windle, R. (2023). *Changes in U.S. family finances from 2019 to 2022: Evidence from the survey of consumer finances.* Board of Governors of the Federal Reserve System. https://doi.org/10.17016/8799

Alba, R. (2023). When economists eat sociologists' lunch. *Sociological Forum, 38*(1), 286–290. https://onlinelibrary.wiley.com/doi/abs/10.1111/socf.12878

Alexander, J. T., Bleckley, D., Fisher, J., Genadek, K., Leonard, S. H., & Magganas, A. (2024). *Newly available individual-level U.S. tax data from 1969–1994* (ADEP Working Paper No. 2024-02). U.S. Census Bureau. https://www.census.gov/content/dam/Census/library/working-papers/2024/econ/ADEP_WP_Tax-Data-1969-1994.pdf

Almond, D., & Currie, J. (2011). Killing me softly: The fetal origins hypothesis. *Journal of Economic Perspectives, 25*(3), 153–172. https://doi.org/10.1257/jep.25.3.153

Almond, D., Currie, J., & Duque, V. (2018). Childhood circumstances and adult outcomes: Act II. *Journal of Economic Literature, 56*(4), 1360–1446. https://doi.org/10.1257/jel.20171164

Almond, D., Currie, J., & Herrmann, M. (2012). From infant to mother: Early disease environment and future maternal health. *Labour Economics, 19*(4), 475–483. https://doi.org/10.1016/j.labeco.2012.05.015

Ambrose, B. W., Hendershott, P. H., Ling, D. C., & McGill, G. A. (2022). Homeownership and taxes: How the TCJA altered the tax code's treatment of housing. *Real Estate Economics, 50*(5), 1167–1200. https://doi.org/10.1111/1540-6229.12374

Ananat, E. O., Gassman-Pines, A., & Gibson-Davis, C. M. (2011). The effects of local employment losses on children's educational achievement. In G. Duncan & R. Murnane (Eds.), *Whither opportunity: Rising inequality, schools, and children's life chances* (pp. 299–315). Russell Sage Foundation.

Ananat, E. O., & Hungerman, D. M. (2012). The power of the pill for the next generation: Oral contraception's effects on fertility, abortion, and maternal and child characteristics. *Review of Economics and Statistics, 94*(1), 37–51. https://doi.org/10.1162/REST_a_00230

Anderson, E. (1999). *Code of the street: Decency, violence, and the moral life of the inner city.* W. W. Norton & Company.

Andersson, F., Holzer, H. J., Lane, J. I., Rosenblum, D., & Smith, J. (2024). Does federally funded job training work? Nonexperimental estimates of WIA training impacts using longitudinal data on workers and firms. *Journal of Human Resources, 59*(4), 1244–1283. https://doi.org/10.3368/jhr.0816-8185R1

Andrews, N. C. Z., Pepler, D. J., & Motz, M. (2019). Research and evaluation with community-based projects: Approaches, considerations, and strategies. *American Journal of Evaluation, 40*(4), 548–561. https://doi.org/10.1177/1098214019835821

Anelli, M., & Peri, G. (2019). The effects of high school peers' gender on college major, college performance and income. *The Economic Journal, 129*(618), 553–602. https://doi.org/10.1111/ecoj.12556

Angrist, J. D., & Evans, W. N. (1996). *Children and their parents' labor supply: Evidence from exogenous variation in family size* (NBER Working Paper No. w5778). National Bureau of Economic Research. https://papers.ssrn.com/sol3/papers.cfm?abstract_id=3695

Arum, R., & Roksa, J. (2011). *Academically adrift: Limited learning on college campuses.* University of Chicago Press.

Asch, B. J., Heaton, P., Hosek, J., Martorell, F., Simon, C., & Warner, J. T. (2010). *Cash incentives and military enlistment, attrition, and reenlistment.* RAND National Defense Research Institute, RAND Corporation. https://www.rand.org/pubs/monographs/MG950.html

Atkinson, L., Beitchman, J., Gonzalez, A., Young, A., Wilson, B., Escobar, M., Chisholm, V., Brownlie, E., Khoury, J. E., Ludmer, J., & Villani, V. (2015). Cumulative risk, cumulative outcome: A 20-year longitudinal study. *PLoS One, 10*(6), e0127650. https://doi.org/10.1371/journal.pone.0127650

Austin, B. A., Glaeser, E. L., & Summers, L. H. (2018). *Jobs for the heartland: Place-based policies in 21st-century America* (NBER Working Paper Series No. 24548). National Bureau of Economic Research. https://www.nber.org/system/files/working_papers/w24548/w24548.pdf

Autor, D. H. (2014). Skills, education, and the rise of earnings inequality among the "other 99 percent." *Science, 344*(6186), 843–851. https://doi.org/10.1126/science.1251868

———. (2019). Work of the past, work of the future. *AEA Papers and Proceedings, 109*, 1–32. https://doi.org/10.1257/pandp.20191110

Autor, D. H., & Dorn, D. (2013). The growth of low-skill service jobs and the polarization of the U.S. labor market. *American Economic Review, 103*(5), 1553–1597. https://doi.org/10.1257/aer.103.5.1553

Autor, D. H., Dorn, D., & Hanson, G. (2021). On the persistence of the China shock. *Brookings Papers on Economic Activity, 52*(2), 381–476. http://dx.doi.org/10.2139/ssrn.3973950

Autor, D. H., Figlio, D., Karbownik, K., Roth, J., & Wasserman, M. (2019). Family disadvantage and the gender gap in behavioral and educational outcomes. *American Economic Journal: Applied Economics, 11*(3), 338–381. https://doi.org/10.1257/app.20170571

Autor, D. H., Katz, L. F., & Kearney, M. S. (2008). Trends in U.S. wage inequality: Revising the revisionists. *Review of Economics and Statistics, 90*(2), 300–323. https://doi.org/10.1162/rest.90.2.300

Avellar, S., Covington, R., Moore, Q., Patnaik, A., & Wu, A. (2018). *Parents and children together: Effects of four responsible fatherhood programs for low-income fathers* (OPRE Report No. 2018-50). U.S. Department of Health and Human Services. https://www.acf.hhs.gov/sites/default/files/documents/opre/parents_and_children_together.pdf

Avery, C., Howell, J., Pender, M., & Sacerdote, C. (2019). Policies and payoffs to addressing America's college graduation deficit. *Brookings Papers on Economic Activity*, 93–172. https://www.brookings.edu/articles/policies-and-payoffs-to-addressing-americas-college-graduation-deficit/

Avery, R. B., Brevoort, K. P., & Canner, G. B. (2009). Credit scoring and its effects on the availability and affordability of credit. *Journal of Consumer Affairs*, 43(3), 516–537. https://doi.org/10.1111/j.1745-6606.2009.01151.x

Avtar, R., Chakrabarti, R., & Chatterji-Len, K. (2021). Uneven distribution of household debt by gender, race, and education. *Liberty Street Economics*, Federal Reserve Bank of New York. https://libertystreeteconomics.newyorkfed.org/2021/11/uneven-distribution-of-household-debt-by-gender-race-and-education/

Axinn, W. G, Barber, J. S., & Thornton, A. (1998). The long-term impact of parents' childbearing decisions on children's self-esteem. *Demography*, 35(4), 435–443. https://doi.org/10.2307/3004012

Babiarz, P., Widdows, R., & Yilmazer, T. (2013). Borrowing to cope with adverse health events: Liquidity constraints, insurance coverage, and unsecured debt. *Health Economics*, 22(10), 1177–1198. https://doi.org/10.1002/hec.2877

Bailey, A. K., & Sykes, B. L. (2018). Veteran status, income, and intergenerational mobility across three cohorts of American men. *Population Research and Policy Review*, 37(4), 539–568. https://doi.org/10.1007/s11113-018-9477-1

Bailey, B. (2009). *America's army: Making the all-volunteer force*. Harvard University Press.

Bailey, M. J. (2006). More power to the pill: The impact of contraceptive freedom on Women's lifecycle labor supply. *Quarterly Journal of Economics*, 121(1), 289–320. https://doi.org/10.1093/qje/121.1.289

___. (2013). Fifty years of family planning: New evidence on the long-run effects of increasing access to contraception. *Brookings Papers on Economic Activity*, 2013(1), 341–409. https://doi.org/10.1353/eca.2013.0001

Bailey, M. J., DiNardo, J., & Stuart, B. A. (2021). The economic impact of a high national minimum wage: Evidence from the 1966 Fair Labor Standards Act. *Journal of Labor Economics*, 39(S2), 329–367. https://doi.org/10.1086/712554

Bailey, M. J., & Duquette, N. J. (2014). How the U.S. fought the war on poverty: The economics and politics of funding at the Office of Economic Opportunity. *The Journal of Economic History*, 74(2), 351–388. https://doi.org/10.1017/s0022050714000291

Bailey, M. J., & Dynarski, S. (2011). *Gains and gaps: Changing inequality in U.S. college entry and completion*. National Bureau of Economic Research (NBER Working Paper No. 17633). https://doi.org/10.3386/w17633

Bailey, M. J., Guldi, M., & Hershbein, B. (2014). Is there a case for a "second demographic transition"? Three distinctive features of the post-1960 U.S. fertility decline. In L. P. Boustan, C. Frydman, & R. A. Margo (Eds.), *Human capital and history: The American record* (pp. 273–312). University of Chicago Press.

Bailey, M. J., Hershbein, B. J., & Miller, A. R. (2012). The opt-in revolution? Contraception and the gender gap in wages. *American Economic Journal: Applied Economics*, 4(3), 225–254. https://doi.org/10.1257/app.4.3.225

Bailey, M. J., Hoynes, H. W., Rossin-Slater, M., & Walker, R. (2020). *Is the social safety net a long-term investment? Large-scale evidence from the food stamps program* (NBER Working Paper No. 26942). National Bureau of Economic Research. https://www.nber.org/system/files/working_papers/w26942/w26942.pdf

Bailey, M. J., Lin, P. Z., Mohammed, A. R. S., Mohnen, P., Murray, J., Zhang, M., & Prettyman, A. (2022). *LIFE-M: The longitudinal, intergenerational family electronic micro-database (version v3)*. ISPSR–Inter-university Consortium for Political and Social Research. https://doi.org/10.3886/E155186V3

Bailey, M. J., Malkova, O., & McLaren, Z. (2018). Do family planning programs increase children's opportunities? Evidence from the war on poverty and the early years of Title X. *Journal of Human Resources, 54*(4), 825–856. https://doi.org/10.3368/jhr.54.4.1216-8401R1

Bailey, M. J., Wanner Lang, V., Prettyman, A., Vrioni, I., Bart, L., Eisenberg, D., Fomby, P., Barber, J., & Dalton. V. K. (2023). *How costs limit contraceptive use among uninsured women in the U.S.: A randomized control trial* (NBER Working Paper No. 31397). National Bureau of Economic Research. https://www.nber.org/system/files/working_papers/w31397/w31397.pdf

Bailey, T. R., Jaggars, S. S., & Jenkins, D. (2015). *Redesigning America's community colleges: A clearer path to student success.* Harvard University Press.

Baird, M. D., Engberg, J., Gonzalez, G. C., Goughnour, T., Gutierrez, I. A., & Karam, R. T. (2019). *Effectiveness of screened, demand-driven job training programs for disadvantaged workers.* RAND Research Reports. https://www.rand.org/pubs/research_reports/RR2980.html

Baker, C. E., & Brooks-Gunn, J. (2020). Early parenting and the intergenerational transmission of self-regulation and behavior problems in African American Head Start families. *Child Psychiatry & Human Development, 51*(2), 220–230. https://doi.org/10.1007/s10578-019-00921-5

Baker, R. S. (2022). Ethno-racial variation in single motherhood prevalences and penalties for child poverty in the United States, 1995–2018. *The Annals of the American Academy of Political and Social Science, 702*(1), 20–36. https://doi.org/10.1177/00027162221120759

Ballance, J., Clifford, R., & Shoag, D. (2020). No more credit score: Employer credit check bans and signal substitution. *Labour Economics, 63*(2), 101769. https://doi.org/10.1016/j.labeco.2019.101769

Baradaran, M. (2017). *The color of money: Black banks and the racial wealth gap.* Harvard University Press.

———. (2019). *Jim Crow credit* (UC Irvine School of Law Research Paper No. 2021-51). University of California, Irvine. https://ssrn.com/abstract=3395876

Barber, J. S., Axinn, W. G., & Thornton, A. (1999). Unwanted childbearing, health, and mother-child relationships. *Journal of Health and Social Behavior, 40*(3), 231–257. https://doi.org/10.2307/2676350

Barber, J. S., & East, P. L. (2009). Home and parenting resources available to siblings depending on their birth intention status. *Child Development, 80*(3), 921–939. https://doi.org/10.1111/j.1467-8624.2009.01306.x

———. (2011). Children's experiences after the unintended birth of a sibling. *Demography, 48*(1), 101–125. https://doi.org/10.1007/s13524-010-0011-2

Barnes, C. (2020). *State of empowerment: Low-income families and the new welfare state.* University of Michigan Press.

Barr, A. (2019). Fighting for education: Veterans and financial aid. *Journal of Labor Economics, 37*(2), 509–544. http://dx.doi.org/10.1086/700191

Barr, A., Eggleston, J., & Smith, A. A. (2022). Investing in infants: The lasting effects of cash transfers to new families. *The Quarterly Journal of Economics, 137*(4), 2539–2583. https://doi.org/10.1093/qje/qjac023

Barr, A., & Gibbs, C. R. (2022). Breaking the cycle? Intergenerational effects of an antipoverty program in early childhood. *Journal of Political Economy, 130*(12), 3253–3286. https://doi.org/10.1086/720764

Barr, A., & Smith, A. A. (2023). Fighting crime in the cradle: The effects of early childhood access to nutritional assistance. *Journal of Human Resources, 58*(1), 43–73. https://doi.org/10.3368/jhr.58.3.0619-10276R2

Barr, M. S. (2012). *No slack: The financial lives of low-income Americans.* Brookings Institution Press.

Barr, T., & Roy, U. (2008). The effect of labor market monopsony on economic growth. *Journal of Macroeconomics*, *30*, 1446–1467. http://dx.doi.org/10.1016/j.jmacro.2008.05.001

Bastian, J., & Michelmore, K. (2018). The long-term impact of the earned income tax credit on children's education and employment outcomes. *Journal of Labor Economics*, *36*(4), 1127–1163. https://doi.org/10.1086/697477

Baumrind, D. (1971). Current patterns of parental authority. *Developmental Psychology*, *4*(1, Pt. 2), 1–103. https://doi.org/10.1037/h0030372

Beaver, W. (2017). The rise and fall of for-profit higher education. *Academe*, *103*(1), 32–37. https://www.aaup.org/article/rise-and-fall-profit-higher-education

Beck, A., Corak, M., & Tienda, M. (2012). Age at immigration and the adult attainments of child migrants to the United States. *The Annals of the American Academy of Political and Social Science*, *643*(1), 134–159. https://doi.org/10.1177/0002716212442665

Becker, G. S., & Tomes, N. (1986). Human capital and the rise and fall of families. *Journal of Labor Economics*, *4*(3), S1–S39. https://www.jstor.org/stable/2534952

Beckert, J. (2008). *Inherited wealth*. Princeton University Press.

Behrman, J., & Taubman, P. (1985). Intergenerational earnings mobility in the United States: Some estimates and a test of Becker's intergenerational endowments model. *Review of Economics and Statistics*, *67*(1), 144–151. https://www.jstor.org/stable/1928446?origin=crossref

Beller, E. (2009). Bringing intergenerational social mobility research into the twenty-first century: Why mothers matter. *American Sociological Review*, *74*(4), 507–528. https://doi.org/10.1177/000312240907400401

Belley, P., & Lochner, L. (2007). The changing role of family income and ability in determining educational achievement. *Journal of Human Capital*, *1*(1), 37–89. https://doi.org/10.1086/524674

Ben-Shlomo, Y., & Kuh, D. (2002). A life course approach to chronic disease epidemiology: Conceptual models, empirical challenges, and interdisciplinary perspectives, *International Journal of Epidemiology*, *31*(2), 285–293. https://doi.org/10.1093/ije/31.2.285

Benetton, M., Kudlyak, M., & Mondragon, J., (2024). *Dynastic home equity*. https://papers.ssrn.com/sol3/papers.cfm?abstract_id=4158773

Berger, L. M., & Carlson, M. J. (2020). Family policy and complex contemporary families: A decade in review and implications for the next decade of research and policy practice. *Journal of Marriage and Family*, *82*(1), 478–507. https://doi.org/10.1111/jomf.12650

Berger, L. M., Collins, J. M., & Cuesta, L. (2016). Household debt and adult depressive symptoms in the United States. *Journal of Family and Economic Issues*, *37*(1), 42–57. https://doi.org/10.1007/s10834-015-9443-6

Berger, L. M., & Font, S. A. (2015). The role of the family and family-centered programs and policies. *The Future of Children*, *25*(1), 155–176. https://doi.org/10.1353/foc.2015.0007

Berger, L. M., Font, S. A., Slack, K. S., & Waldfogel, J. (2017). Income and child maltreatment in unmarried families: Evidence from the earned income tax credit. *Review of Economics of the Household*, *15*(4), 1345–1372. https://doi.org/10.1007/s11150-016-9346-9

Berger, L. M., & Houle, J. N. (2016). Parental debt and children's socioemotional well-being. *Pediatrics*, *137*(2), 1–8. https://doi.org/10.1542/peds.2015-3059

___. (2019). Rising household debt and children's socioemotional well-being trajectories. *Demography*, *56*(4), 1273–1301. https://doi.org/10.1007/s13524-019-00800-7

Berger, L. M., & McLanahan, S. (2015). Income, relationship quality, and parenting: Associations with child development in two-parent families. *Journal of Marriage and Family*, *77*(4), 996–1015. https://doi.org/10.1111/jomf.12197

Berger, L. M., Paxson, C., & Waldfogel, J. (2009). Income and child development. *Children and Youth Services Review*, *31*(9), 978–989. https://doi.org/10.1016/j.childyouth.2009.04.013

Berger, T., & Engzell, P. (2022). Industrial automation and intergenerational income mobility in the United States. *Social Science Research*, *104*, 102686. https://doi.org/10.1016/j.ssresearch

Bergman, P., Chetty, R., DeLuca, S., Hendren, N., Katz, L. F., & Palmer, C. (2024). Creating moves to opportunity: Experimental evidence on neighborhood choice. *American Economic Review, 114*(5), 1281–1337. https://doi.org/10.1257/aer.20200407

Berlinski, S., Ferreyra, M. M., Flabbi, L., & Martin, J. D. (2024). Childcare markets, parental labor supply, and child development. *Journal of Political Economy, 132*(6), 2113–2177. https://doi.org/10.1086/728698

Berman, Y. (2022). The long-run evolution of absolute intergenerational mobility. *American Economic Journal: Applied Economics, 14*(3), 61–83. https://doi.org/10.1257/app.20200631

Bhattacharya, D., & Mazumder, B. (2011). A nonparametric analysis of Black–White differences in intergenerational income mobility in the United States. *Quantitative Economics, 2*(3), 335–379. https://doi.org/10.3982/QE69

Bilmes, L. J., & Brooks, C. W. (2024). Normalizing reparations: U.S. precedent, norms, and models for compensating harms and implications for reparations to Black Americans. *The Russell Sage Foundation Journal of the Social Sciences, 10*(2), 30–68. https://doi.org/10.7758/RSF.2024.10.2.02

Binder, A. J., David, D. B., & Bloom, N. (2016). Career funneling: How elite students learn to define and desire prestigious jobs. *Sociology of Education, 89*(1), 20–39. https://doi.org/10.1177/0038040715610883

Bitler, M. P., Hoynes, H. W., & Domina, T. (2014). *Experimental evidence on distributional effects of Head Start* (NBER Working Paper No. 20434). National Bureau of Economic Research. https://www.nber.org/system/files/working_papers/w20434/w20434.pdf

Björklund, A., Lindahl, L., & Lindquist, M. J. (2010). What more than parental income, education, and occupation? An exploration of what Swedish siblings get from their parents. *The B.E. Journal of Economic Analysis & Policy, 10*(1), 102. https://doi.org/10.2202/1935-1682.2449

Black, S. E., & Devereux, P. J. (2011). Recent developments in intergenerational mobility. *Handbook of Labor Economics, 4*(B), 1487–1541. https://www.sciencedirect.com/science/article/abs/pii/S0169721811024142

Black, S. E., Devereux, P. J., Lundborg, P., & Majlesi, K. (2020). Poor little rich kids? The role of nature versus nurture in wealth and other economic outcomes and behaviours. *The Review of Economic Studies, 87*(4), 1683–1725. https://doi.org/10.1093/restud/rdz038

Black, S. E., Devereux, P. J., & Salvanes, K. G. (2013). Under pressure? The effect of peers on outcomes of young adults. *Journal of Labor Economics, 31*(1), 119–153. https://doi.org/10.1086/666872

Blanden, J., Eyles, A., & Machin, S. (2023). Intergenerational home ownership. *The Journal of Economic Inequality, 21*(2), 251–275. https://doi.org/10.1007/s10888-023-09563-z

Blattner, L., & Nelson, S. (2021). *How costly is noise? Data and disparities in consumer credit* (Research Paper No. 3978). Stanford University Graduate School of Business. https://ideas.repec.org/p/ecl/stabus/3978.html

Blau, P. M., & Duncan, O. D. (1967). *The American occupational structure*. John Wiley & Sons.

Bleemer, Z., & Quincy, S. (2024). *Changes in the college mobility pipeline since 1900* (Working Paper).

Bloom, H. S., & Riccio, J. A. (2005). Using place-based random assignment and comparative interrupted time-series analysis to evaluate the jobs-plus employment program for public housing residents. *The Annals of the American Academy of Political and Social Science, 599*(1), 19–51. https://doi.org/10.1177/0002716205274824

Bloom, J. (2007). (Mis)reading social class in the journey towards college: Youth development in urban America. *Teachers College Record, 109*(2), 343–368. https://doi.org/10.1177/016146810710900201

Bloom-Weltman, J., Honey, R., Meholick, S., & Fettro, M. (2021). *Profile of state data capacity in 2018: Statewide Longitudinal Data Systems (SLDS) survey descriptive statistics*. Stats in Brief, NCES 2021-126, National Center for Education Statistics. https://nces.ed.gov/pubs2021/2021126.pdf

Bloome, D. (2015). Income inequality and intergenerational income mobility in the United States. *Social Forces*, *93*(3), 1047–1080. https://doi.org/10.1093/sf/sou092

___. (2017). Childhood family structure and intergenerational income mobility in the United States. *Demography*, *54*(2), 541–569. https://doi.org/10.1007/s13524-017-0564-4

Bloome, D., Dyer, S., & Zhou, X. (2018). Educational inequality, educational expansion, and intergenerational income persistence in the United States. *American Sociological Review*, *83*(6), 1215–1253. https://doi.org/10.1177/0003122418809374

Bloome, D., & Opacic, A. (2024). Absolute income mobility obscures marginalized children's disadvantages. *Proceedings of the National Academy of Sciences*, *112*(25), e2321418121. https://doi.org/10.1073/pnas.2321418121

Bloome, D., & Western, B. (2011). Cohort change and racial differences in educational and income mobility. *Social Forces*, *90*(2), 375–395. https://doi.org/10.1093/sf/sor002

Blouri, Y., Büchler, S., & Schöni, O. (2023). The geography of mortgage interest deductions. *Journal of Urban Economics*, *138*(C), 103604. https://doi.org/10.1016/j.jue.2023.103604

Board of Governors of the Federal Reserve System (2017). *Consumer debt service payments as a percent of disposable personal income [CDSP]*. Federal Reserve Bank of St. Louis. https://fred.stlouisfed.org/series/CDSP

Boel, P., & Zimmerman, P. (2022). Unbanked in America: A review of the literature. *Economic Commentary, Federal Reserve Bank of Cleveland*, *2022*(07), 1–10. https://doi.org/10.26509/frbc-ec-202207

Boen, C., Keister, L. A., & Graetz, N. (2021). Household wealth and child body mass index: Patterns and mechanisms. *The Russell Sage Foundation Journal of the Social Sciences*, *7*(3), 80–100. https://doi.org/10.7758/RSF.2021.7.3.04

Bogliacino, F., Posso, C., & Villaveces, M. J. (2025). Restoring property rights: The effects of land restitution on credit access. *World Development*, *186*, 106830. https://doi.org/10.1016/j.worlddev.2024.106830

Bollinger, C. R., & Troske, K. R. (2023, June 20). *Evaluation of a new job training program: Code Louisville* (Working Paper). University of Kentucky. https://gattonweb.uky.edu/faculty/Troske/Working%20papers/Bollinger%20&%20Troske-Code%20Louisville%20Paper%20with%20Figures%20and%20Tables%20in%20Text.pdf

Bonilla-Silva, E. (1997). Rethinking racism: Toward a structural interpretation. *American Sociological Review*, *62*(3), 465–480. https://doi.org/10.2307/2657316

Bornstein, M. H. (Ed.) (2019). *Handbook of parenting (3rd ed.): Volume I: Children and parenting*. Routledge.

Boserup, S. H., Kopczuk, W., & Kreiner, C. T. (2014). *Stability and persistence of intergenerational wealth formation: Evidence from Danish wealth records of three generations* (Working Paper). https://web2.econ.ku.dk/ctk/Papers/WealthAcrossGen.pdf

___. (2017). *Intergenerational wealth formation over the life cycle: Evidence from Danish wealth records 1984-2013* (Working Paper). https://www.columbia.edu/~wk2110/bin/WealthAcrossGen.pdf

Bourgois, P. (2003). *In search of respect: Selling crack in El Barrio* (2nd ed.). Cambridge University Press.

Bozick, R. (2007). Making it through the first year of college: The role of students' economic resources, employment, and living arrangements. *Sociology of Education*, *80*(3), 261–285. https://doi.org/10.1177/003804070708000304

Bozick, R., & DeLuca, S. (2005). Better late than never? Delayed enrollment in the high school to college transition. *Social Forces*, *84*(1), 531–554. https://doi.org/10.1353/sof.2005.0089

___. (2011). Not making the transition to college: School, work, and opportunities in the lives of American youth. *Social Science Research*, *40*(4), 1249–1262. https://doi.org/10.1016/j.ssresearch.2011.02.003

Bradbury, B., Corak, M., Waldfogel, J., & Washbrook, E. (2015). *Too many children left behind: The U.S. achievement gap in comparative perspective*. Russell Sage Foundation.

Bradbury, B., Waldfogel, J., & Washbrook, E. (2019). Income-related gaps in early child cognitive development: Why are they larger in the United States than in the United Kingdom, Australia, and Canada? *Demography, 56*(1), 367–390. https://doi.org/10.1007/s13524-018-0738-8

Brady, D., Finnigan, R., Kohler, U., & Legewie, J. (2020). The inheritance of race revisited: Childhood wealth and income and Black–White disadvantages in adult life chances. *Sociological Science, 7*, 599–627. https://doi.org/10.15195/v7.a25

Braga, A. A. (2005). Hot spots policing and crime prevention: A systematic review of randomized controlled trials. *Journal of Experimental Criminology, 1*(3), 317–342. https://doi.org/10.1007/s11292-005-8133-z

Brand, J. E. (2015). The far-reaching impact of job loss and unemployment. *Annual Review of Sociology, 41*, 359–375. https://doi.org/10.1146/annurev-soc-071913-043237

___. (2023). *Overcoming the odds. The benefits of completing college for unlikely graduates.* Russell Sage Foundation.

Braxton, J. C., Chikhale, N., Herkenhoff, K. F., & Phillips, G. M. (2024). *Intergenerational mobility and credit* (NBER Working Paper No. 32031). National Bureau of Economic Research. https://www.nber.org/papers/w32031

Brayne, S., & Christin, A. (2021). Technologies of crime prediction: The reception of algorithms in policing and criminal courts. *Social Problems, 68*(3), 608–624. https://doi.org/10.1093/socpro/spaa004

Breen, R., & Whelan, C. (1996). *Social mobility and social class in Ireland.* Dublin: Gill & Macmillan.

Brevoort, K. P., Clarkberg, J., Kambara, M., & Litwin, B. (2018). *The geography of credit invisibility* (CFPB Office of Research Report Series No. 18-6). Consumer Financial Protection Bureau. https://ssrn.com/abstract=3288848

Bridges, S., & Disney, R. (2010). Debt and depression. *Journal of Health Economics, 29*(3), 388–403. https://doi.org/10.1016/j.jhealeco.2010.02.003

Bronfenbrenner, U. (1979). *The ecology of human development: Experiments by nature and design.* Harvard University Press.

___. (Ed.) (2005). *Making human beings human: Bioecological perspectives on human development.* Sage Publications.

Brooks-Gunn, J., & Duncan, G. J. (1997). The effects of poverty on children. *Future Child, 7*(2), 55–71. https://doi.org/10.2307/1602387

Brooks-Gunn, J., & Markman, L. B. (2005). The contribution of parenting to ethnic and racial gaps in school readiness. *The Future of Children, 15*(1), 139–168. https://doi.org/10.1353/foc.2005.0001

Brown, A. R. (2022). Women's union status at first birth. *Family Profiles* (Family Profile No. 21). National Center for Family & Marriage Research. https://doi.org/10.25035/ncfmr/fp-22-21

Brown, D. W., Kowalski, A. E., & Lurie, I. Z. (2020). Long-term impacts of childhood Medicaid expansions on outcomes in adulthood. *The Review of Economic Studies, 87*(2), 792–821. https://doi.org/10.1093/restud/rdz039

Brown, J. D., Cohen, S. R., Denoeux, G., Dorinski, S., Heggeness, M. L., Lieberman, C., McBride, L., Murray-Close, M., Qin, H., Ross, A. E., Sandler, D. H., Warren, L., & Yi, M. (2023). *Real-time 2020 administrative record census simulation: A new design for the 21st century.* U.S. Department of Commerce & U.S. Census Bureau. https://www2.census.gov/programs-surveys/decennial/2020/program-management/evaluate-docs/EAE-2020-admin-records-experiment.pdf

Brown, S., Taylor, K., & Wheatley Price, S. (2005). Debt and distress: Evaluating the psychological cost of credit. *Journal of Economic Psychology, 26*(5), 642–663. https://doi.org/10.1016/j.joep.2005.01.002

Brown, T. H. (2012). The intersection and accumulation of racial and gender inequality: Black women's wealth trajectories. *Review of Black Political Economy*, *39*(2), 239–258. https://doi.org/10.1007/s12114-011-9100-8

___. (2016). Diverging fortunes: Racial/ethnic inequality in wealth trajectories in middle and late life. *Race and Social Problems*, *8*(1), 29–41. https://doi.org/10.1007/s12552-016-9160-2

Brown, T. H., & Homan, P. (2023). The future of social determinants of health: Looking upstream to structural drivers. *The Milbank Quarterly*, *101*(S1), 36–60. https://doi.org/10.1111/1468-0009.12641

___. (2024). Structural racism and health stratification: Connecting theory to measurement. *Journal of Health and Social Behavior*, *65*(1), 141–160. https://doi.org/10.1177/00221465231222924

Brown, T. H., Lee, H. E., Bonilla-Silva, E., Hicken, M. T., & Homan, P. (2025). Conceptualizing and measuring systemic racism. *Annual Review of Public Health*, *46*(1), 69–90. https://doi.org/10.1146/annurev-publhealth-060222-032022

Buchmann, C., & DiPrete, T. A. (2006). The growing female advantage in college completion: The role of family background and academic achievement. *American Sociological Review*, *71*(4), 515–541. https://doi.org/10.1177/000312240607100401

Bullinger, L. R., Packham, A., & Raissian, K. M. (2023). *Effects of universal and unconditional cash transfers on child abuse and neglect* (NBER Working Paper No. w31733). National Bureau of Economic Research. https://www.nber.org/papers/w31733

Bulman, G. B., & Hoxby, C. M. (2015). *The returns to the federal tax credits for higher education* (NBER Working Paper No. 20833). National Bureau of Economic Research. https://www.nber.org/system/files/working_papers/w20833/w20833.pdf

Burdick-Will, J., Ludwig, J., Raudenbush, S., Sampson, R., Sanbonmatsu, L., & Sharkey, P. (2011). Converging evidence for neighborhood effects on children's test scores: An experimental, quasi-experimental, and observational comparison. In G. Duncan & R. Murnane (Eds.), *Whither opportunity? Rising inequality, schools, and children's life chances* (pp. 255–276). Russell Sage Foundation.

Burtless, G., & Jencks, C. (2003). American inequality and its consequences. In H. Aaron, J. Lindsay, & P. Nivola (Eds.), *Agenda for the nation* (pp. 61–108). Brookings Institution Press.

Busso, M., Gregory, J., & Kline, P. (2013). Assessing the incidence and efficiency of a prominent place based policy. *American Economic Review*, *103*(2), 897–947. https://doi.org/10.1257/aer.103.2.897

Cabrera, N. J., Alonso, A., & Chen, Y. (2021). Parenting contributions to Latinx children's development in the early years. *The Annals of the American Academy of Political and Social Science*, *696*(1), 158–178. https://doi.org/10.1177/00027162211049997

Cabrera, N. J., Volling, B. L., & Barr, R. (2018). Fathers are parents, too! Widening the lens on parenting for children's development. *Child Development Perspectives*, *12*(3), 152–157. https://doi.org/10.1111/cdep.12275

Calarco, J. M. (2018). *Negotiating opportunities: How the middle class secures advantages in school*. Oxford University Press.

Camarota, S. A., & Zeigler, K. (2021). *Fertility among immigrants and native-born Americans: Difference between the foreign-born and the native-born continues to grow*. Center for Immigration Studies. https://cis.org/Report/Fertility-Among-Immigrants-and-NativeBorn-Americans

Campante, F. (2011). Redistribution in a model of voting and campaign contributions. *Journal of Public Economics*, *95*(7–8), 646–656. https://doi.org/10.1016/j.jpubeco.2010.11.013

Campbell, J. Y., Jackson, H. E., Madrian, B. C., & Tufano, P. (2011). Consumer financial protection. *Journal of Economic Perspectives*, *25*(1), 91–114. https://doi.org/10.1257/jep.25.1.91

Cancian, M., & Meyer, D. R. (2018). Reforming policy for single-parent families to reduce child poverty. *The Russell Sage Foundation Journal of the Social Sciences, 4*(2), 91–112. https://doi.org/10.7758/RSF.2018.4.2.05

Cancian, M., Yang, M.-Y., & Slack, K. S. (2013). The effect of additional child support income on the risk of child maltreatment. *Social Service Review, 87*(3), 417–437. https://doi.org/10.1086/671929

Card, D., Kluve, J., & Weber, A. (2018). What works? A meta analysis of recent active labor market program evaluations. *Journal of the European Economic Association, 16*(3), 894–931. https://doi.org/10.1093/jeea/jvx028

Card, D., & Krueger, A. B. (1995). Time-series minimum-wage studies: A meta-analysis. *American Economic Review, 85*(2), 238–243. www.jstor.org/stable/2117925

Carillo, L., Pattillo, M., Hardy, E., & Acevedo-Garcia, D., (2016). Housing decisions among low-income Hispanic households in Chicago. *Cityscape: A Journal of Policy Development and Research, 18*(2), 109–150. https://www.huduser.gov/portal/periodicals/cityscpe/vol18num2/article6.html

Carrell, S. E., & Hoekstra, M. L. (2010). Externalities in the classroom: How children exposed to domestic violence affect everyone's kids. *American Economic Journal: Applied Economics, 2*(1), 211–228. https://doi.org/10.1257/app.2.1.211

Carrell, S. E., & Sacerdote, B. (2017). Why do college-going interventions work? *American Economic Journal: Applied Economics, 9*(3), 124–151. https://doi.org/10.1257/app.20150530

Case, A., & Deaton, A. (2020). *Deaths of despair and the future of capitalism.* Princeton University Press.

Case, A., Lubotsky, D., & Paxson, C. (2002). Economic status and health in childhood: The origins of the gradient. *American Economic Review, 92*(5), 1308–1334. https://doi.org/10.1257/000282802762024520

Case, A., & Paxson, C. (2002). Parental behavior and child health. *Health Affairs, 21*(2), 164–178. https://doi.org/10.1377/hlthaff.21.2.164

Caudillo, M. L., & Torche, F. (2014). Exposure to local homicides and early educational achievement in Mexico. *Sociology of Education, 87*(2), 89–105. https://doi.org/10.1177/0038040714523795

Cellini, S. R., & Turner, N. (2019). Gainfully employed? *Journal of Human Resources, 54*(2), 342–370. https://doi.org/10.3368/jhr.54.2.1016.8302R1

Chadwick, L., & Solon, G. (2002). Intergenerational income mobility among daughters. *American Economic Review, 92*(1), 335–344. https://doi.org/10.1257/000282802760015766

Chan Tack, A. M., & Small, A. M. (2017). Making friends in violent neighborhoods: Strategies among elementary school children. *Sociological Science, 4*(10), 2330–6696. https://doi.org/10.15195/v4.a10

Charles, K. K., & Hurst, E. (2003). The correlation of wealth across generations. *Journal of Political Economy, 111*(6), 1155–1182. https://dx.doi.org/10.1086/378526

Chaskin, R. J. (1997). Perspectives on neighborhood and community: A review of the literature. *Social Services Review, 71*(4), 521–547. https://doi.org/10.1177/088541229801300102

Chen, Y.-C., Park, S., & Morrow-Howell, N. (2019). Patterns of wealth trajectory in later life: Critical period, accumulation, and social mobility models. *Innovation in Aging, 3*(Suppl. 1), S382. https://doi.org/10.1093/geroni/igz038.1403

Cherlin, A. J., & Seltzer, J. A. (2014). Family complexity, the family safety net, and public policy. *The Annals of the American Academy of Political and Social Science, 654*(1), 231–239. https://doi.org/10.1177/0002716214530854

Chetty, R., Deming, D. J., & Friedman, J. N. (2023). *Diversifying society's leaders? The determinants and causal effects of admission to highly selective private colleges* (NBER Working Paper No. 31492). National Bureau of Economic Research. https://www.nber.org/system/files/working_papers/w31492/w31492.pdf

Chetty, R., Dobbie, W. S., Goldman, B., Porter, S., & Yang, C. (2024). *Changing opportunity: Sociological mechanisms underlying growing class gaps and and shrinking race gaps in economic mobility* (NBER Working Paper No. 32697). National Bureau of Economic Research. http://www.nber.org/papers/w32697

Chetty, R., Friedman, J. N., Hendren, N., Jones, M. R., & Porter, S. R. (2018). *The opportunity atlas: Mapping the childhood roots of social mobility* (NBER Working Paper No. 25147). National Bureau of Economic Research. https://doi.org/10.3386/w25147

Chetty, R., Friedman, J. N., Hilger, N., Saez, E., Schanzenbach, D. W., & Yagan, D. (2011). How does your kindergarten classroom affect your earnings? Evidence from Project Star. *The Quarterly Journal of Economics*, 126(4), 1593–1660. https://doi.org/10.1093/qje/qjr041

Chetty, R., Grusky, D. B., Hell, M., Hendren, N., Manduca, R., & Narang, J. (2017). The fading American dream: Trends in absolute income mobility since 1940. *Science*, 356(6336), 398–406. https://doi.org/10.1126/science.aal4617

Chetty, R., & Hendren, N. (2018). The impacts of neighborhoods on intergenerational mobility I: Childhood exposure effects. *The Quarterly Journal of Economics*, 133(3), 1107–1162. https://doi.org/10.1093/qje/qjy007

Chetty, R., Hendren, N., Jones, M. R., & Porter, S. R. (2020). Race and economic opportunity in the United States: An intergenerational perspective. *The Quarterly Journal of Economics*, 135(2), 711–783. https://doi.org/10.1093/qje/qjz042

Chetty, R., Hendren, N., & Katz, L. F. (2016). The effects of exposure to better neighborhoods on children: New evidence from the moving to opportunity experiment. *American Economic Review*, 106(4), 855–902. https://doi.org/10.1257/aer.20150572

Chetty, R., Hendren, N., Kline, P., & Saez, E. (2014a). Where is the land of opportunity? The geography of intergenerational mobility in the United States. *Quarterly Journal of Economics*, 129(4), 1553–1623. https://doi.org/10.1093/qje/qju022

Chetty, R., Hendren, N., Kline, P., Saez, E., & Turner, N. (2014b). Is the United States still a land of opportunity? Recent trends in intergenerational mobility. *American Economic Review*, 104(5), 141–147. https://doi.org/10.1257/aer.104.5.141

Chetty, R., Jackson, M. O., Kuchler, T., Stroebel, J., Hendren, N., Fluegge, R. B., Gong, S., Gonzalez, F., Grondin, A., Jacob, M., Johnston, D., Koenen, M., Laguna-Muggenburg, E., Mudekereza, F., Rutter, T., Thor, N., Townsend, W., Zhang, R., Bailey, M., Barberá, P., Bhole, M., & Wernerfelt, N. (2022a). Social capital I: Measurement and associations with economic mobility. *Nature*, 608(7921), 108–121. https://doi.org/10.1038/s41586-022-04996-4

___. (2022b). Social capital II: Determinants of economic connectedness. *Nature*, 608(7921), 122–134. https://doi.org/10.1038/s41586-022-04997-3

Chevan, A. (1989). The growth of home ownership: 1940–1980. *Demography*, 26(2), 249–266. https://doi.org/10.2307/2061523

Chin, H. B., Sipe, T. A., Elder, R., Mercer, S. L., Chattopadhyay, S. K., Jacob, V., Wethington, H. R., Kirby, D., Elliston, D. B., Griffith, M., Chuke, S. O., Briss, S. C., Ericksen, I., Galbraith, J. S., Herbst, J. H., Johnson, R. L., Kraft, J. M., Noar, S. M., Romero, L. M., & Santelli, J. (2012). The effectiveness of group-based comprehensive risk-reduction and abstinence education interventions to prevent or reduce the risk of adolescent pregnancy, human immunodeficiency virus, and sexually transmitted infections: Two systematic reviews for the Guide to Community Preventive Services. *American Journal of Preventive Medicine*, 42(3), 272–294. https://doi.org/10.1016/j.amepre.2011.11.006

Choi, J. H., Zhu, J., & Goodman, L. (2018). *Intergenerational homeownership: The impact of parental homeownership and wealth on young adults' tenure choices*. The Urban Institute. https://www.urban.org/research/publication/intergenerational-homeownership

Choi, K. H., & Tienda, M. (2021). Gender and educational differentials in marital sorting of Hispanic young adults. *The Annals of the American Academy of Political and Social Science*, 696(1), 179–197. https://doi.org/10.1177/00027162211043774

Christensen, F. (2011). The pill and partnerships: The impact of the birth control pill on cohabitation. *Journal of Population Economics*, *25*(1), 29–52. https://doi.org/10.1007/s00148-010-0344-6

Chyn, E. (2018). Moved to opportunity: The long-run effects of public housing demolition on children. *American Economic Review*, *108*(10), 3028–3056. https://doi.org/10.1257/aer.20161352

Chyn, E., Collinson, R., & Sandler, D. (2023). *The long-run effects of residential racial desegregation programs: Evidence from Gautreaux* (Working Paper). https://robcollinson.github.io/RobWebsite/CCS_Gautreaux.pdf

Chyn, E., Haggag, K., & Stuart, B. A. (2022). *The effects of racial segregation on intergenerational mobility: Evidence from historical railroad placement* (NBER Working Paper Series No. 30563). https://www.nber.org/system/files/working_papers/w30563/w30563.pdf

Cilesiz, S., & Drotos, S. M. (2014). High-poverty urban high school students' plans for higher education: Weaving their own safety nets. *Urban Education*, *51*(1), 3–31. https://doi.org/10.1177/0042085914543115

Clampet-Lundquist, S., Edin, K., Kling, J. R., & Duncan, G. J. (2011). Moving teenagers out of high-risk neighborhoods: How girls fare better than boys. *American Journal of Sociology*, *116*(4), 1154–1189. https://doi.org/10.1086/657352

Clayborne, Z. M., Kingsbury, M., Sampasa-Kinyaga, H., Sikora, L., Lalande, K. M., & Colman, I. (2021). Parenting practices in childhood and depression, anxiety, and internalizing symptoms in adolescence: A systematic review. *Social Psychiatry and Psychiatric Epidemiology*, *56*(6), 1–20. https://doi.org/10.1007/s00127-020-01956-z

Coates, T.-N. (2014, June). The case for reparations. *The Atlantic*. https://www.theatlantic.com/magazine/archive/2014/06/the-case-for-reparations/361631/

Cohodes, S. R., Grossman, D. S., Kleiner, S. A., & Lovenheim, M. F. (2016). The effect of child health insurance access on schooling: Evidence from public insurance expansions. *Journal of Human Resources*, *51*(3), 727–759. https://doi.org/10.3368/jhr.51.3.1014-6688R1

Coleman, J. S. (1988). Social capital and the production of human capital. *American Journal of Sociology*, *94*, S95–S120. https://www.jstor.org/stable/2780243

Collins, W. J., & Wanamaker, M. H. (2022). African American intergenerational economic mobility since 1880. *American Economic Journal: Applied Economics*, *14*(3), 84–117. https://doi.org/10.1257/app.20170656

Commission on Evidence-Based Policymaking. (2017). *The promise of evidence-based policymaking.* www2.census.gov/adrm/fesac/2017-12-15/Abraham-CEP-final-report.pdf

Congressional Budget Office. (2019). *The effects on employment and family income of increasing the federal minimum wage.* https://www.cbo.gov/system/files/2019-07/CBO-55410-MinimumWage2019.pdf

Conley, D. (1999). *Being Black, living in the red: Race, wealth, and social policy in America.* University of California Press.

Conley, D., & Glauber, R. (2008). *Wealth mobility and volatility in black and white.* Center for American Progress. https://www.americanprogress.org/article/wealth-mobility-and-volatility-in-black-and-white/

Consumer Financial Protection Bureau Office of Research. (2015). *Data point: Credit invisibles.* https://www.consumerfinance.gov/data-research/research-reports/data-point-credit-invisibles/

Conzelmann, J. G., Hemelt, S. W., Hershbein, B. J., Martin, S., Simon, A., & Stange, K. M. (2023). Grads on the go: Measuring college-specific labor markets for graduates. *Journal of Policy Analysis and Management*, 1–22. https://doi.org/10.1002/pam.22553

Cooper, M., & Pugh, A. J. (2020). Families across the income spectrum: A decade in review. *Journal of Marriage and Family*, *82*(1), 272–299. https://doi.org/10.1111/jomf.12623

Corak, M. (2006). *Do poor children become poor adults? Lessons from a cross country comparison of generational earnings mobility* (IZA Discussion Paper No. 1993). Institute of Labor Economics. https://docs.iza.org/dp1993.pdf

___. (2013a). Income inequality, equality of opportunity, and intergenerational mobility. *Journal of Economic Perspectives*, 27(3), 79–102. https://doi.org/10.1257/jep.27.3.79

___. (2013b). Inequality from generation to generation: The United States in comparison. In R. Rycorft (Ed.), *The economics of inequality, poverty, and discrimination in the 21st century* (pp. 107–123). Praeger.

Corak, M., & Heisz, A. (1999). The intergenerational earnings and income mobility of Canadian men: Evidence from longitudinal income tax data. *Journal of Human Resources*, 34(3), 504–533. https://doi.org/10.2307/146378

Corak, M., Lindquist, M. J., & Mazumder, B. (2014). A comparison of upward and downward intergenerational mobility in Canada, Sweden, and the United States. *Labour Economics*, 30(C), 185–200. https://doi.org/10.1016/j.labeco.2014.03.013

Couch, K., & Lillard, D. R. (2004). Non-linear patterns of intergenerational mobility in Germany and the United States. In M. Corak (Ed.), *Generational mobility in North America and Europe* (pp. 190–206). Cambridge University Press.

Council of Economic Advisors. (2014, June). *The economics of paid and unpaid leave*. Executive Office of the President of the United States. https://archive.org/details/TheEconomicEffectsOfPaidAndUnpaidLeave

Cox, R. D. (2016). Complicating conditions: Obstacles and interruptions to low-income students' college choices. *Journal of Higher Education*, 87(1), 1–26. https://doi.org/10.1080/00221546.2016.11777392

Crnic, K. A., & Coburn, S. S. (2019). Stress and parenting. In M. H. Bornstein (Ed.), *Handbook of parenting* (Vol. 3, pp. 421–448). Routledge.

Cronin, J.-A., DeFilippes, P., & Fisher, R. (2024). Refundable credits by race/Hispanic ethnicity, income, and filing status. *AEA Papers and Proceedings*, 114, 649–654. https://doi.org/10.1257/pandp.20241037

Cross, C. J. (2018). Extended family households among children in the United States: Differences by race/ethnicity and socio-economic status. *Population Studies*, 72(2), 235–251. https://doi.org/10.1080/00324728.2018.1468476

___. (2020). Racial/ethnic differences in the association between family structure and children's education. *Journal of Marriage and Family*, 82(2), 691–712. https://doi.org/10.1111/jomf.12625

___. (2023). Beyond the binary: Intraracial diversity in family organization and black adolescents' educational performance. *Social Problems*, 70(2), 511–532. https://doi.org/10.13140/RG.2.2.36370.58563

Cross, C. J., Fomby, P., & Letiecq, B. (2022). Interlinking structural racism and heteropatriarchy: Rethinking family structure's effects on child outcomes in a racialized, unequal society. *Journal of Family Theory & Review*, 14(3), 482–501. https://doi.org/10.1111/jftr.12458

Cross, C. J., Nguyen, A., Taylor, R. J., & Chatters, L. (2018). Instrumental social support exchanges in African American extended families. *Journal of Family Issues*, 39(13), 3535–3563. https://doi.org/10.1177/0192513X18783805

Cuddy, M., Krysan, M., & Lewis, A. (2020). Choosing homes without choosing schools? How urban parents navigate decisions about neighborhoods and school choice. *Journal of Urban Affairs*, 42(8), 1180–1201. https://doi.org/10.1080/07352166.2020.1739537

Cunha, F., Heckman, J. J., Lochner, L., & Masterov, D. V. (2006). Interpreting the evidence on life cycle skill formation. In E. A. Hanushek & F. Welch (Eds.), *Handbook of the economics of education* (Vol. 1, pp. 697–812). Elsevier.

Cutler, D., & Lleras-Muney, A. (2008). Education and health: Evaluating theories and evidence. In R. F. Schoeni, J. S. House, G. A. Kaplan, & H. Pollack (Eds.), *Making Americans healthier: Social and economic policy as health policy* (pp. 29–61). Russell Sage Foundation.

Daly, M. C., & Bengali, L. (2014). *Is it still worth going to college?* FRBSF Economic Letter. Federal Reserve Bank of San Francisco. https://www.frbsf.org/wp-content/uploads/el2014-13.pdf

Darity, W. A., Jr. (2005). Stratification economics: The role of intergroup inequality. *Journal of Economics and Finance, 29*(2), 144–153. https://doi.org/10.1007/BF02761550

Darity, W. A., Jr., Craemer, T., Berry, D. R., & Francis, D. V. (2024). Black reparations in the United States, 2024: An introduction. *The Russell Sage Foundation Journal of the Social Sciences, 10*(2), 1–28. https://doi.org/10.7758/RSF.2024.10.2.01

Darity, W. A., Jr., & Mullen, K. (2020). *From here to equality: Reparations for Black Americans in the twenty-first century.* University of North Carolina Press.

Darrah, J., & DeLuca, S. (2014). Living here has changed my whole perspective: How escaping inner-city poverty shapes neighborhood and housing choice. *Journal of Policy Analysis and Management, 33*(2), 350–384. https://doi.org/10.1002/pam.21758

David, H. P. (2006). Born unwanted, 35 years later: The Prague study. *Reproductive Health Matters, 14*(27), 181–190. https://doi.org/10.1016/S0968-8080(06)27219-7

Davis, A. M. D. (2023). Is working in college worth it? How hours on the job affect postsecondary outcomes. *Educational Evaluation and Policy Analysis.* https://doi.org/10.3102/01623737231210243

Davis, J., & Mazumder, B. (2022). *The decline in intergenerational mobility after 1980* (FRB of Chicago Working Paper No. WP-2017-5). Federal Reserve Bank of Chicago. https://papers.ssrn.com/sol3/papers.cfm?abstract_id=2944584

Dawson, A. F., Brown, W. W., Anderson, J., Datta, B., Donald, J. N., Hong, K., Allan, S., Mole, T. B., Jones, P. B., & Galante, J. (2020). Mindfulness-based interventions for university students: A systematic review and meta-analysis of randomised controlled trials. *Applied Psychology, Health, and Well Being, 12*(2), 384–410. https://doi.org/10.1111/aphw.12188

Daysal, N. M., Lovenheim, M. F., & Wasser, D. N. (2022). The correlation of net and gross wealth across generations: The role of parent income and child age. *AEA Papers and Proceedings, 112,* 73–77. https://doi.org/10.1257/pandp.20221058

de Souza Briggs, X. (1997). Moving up versus moving out: Neighborhood effects in housing mobility programs. *Housing Policy Debate, 8*(1), 195–234. https://doi.org/10.1080/10511482.1997.9521252

de Souza Briggs, X., Popkin, S. J., & Goering, J. (2010). *Moving to opportunity: The story of an American experiment to fight ghetto poverty.* Oxford University Press.

Deaver, K. D. (2021). *Administrative data used in the 2020 census.* U.S. Census Bureau manuscript. https://www2.census.gov/programs-surveys/decennial/2020/program-management/planning-docs/administrative-data-used-in-the-2020-census.pdf

Deil-Amen, R., & Rosebaum, J. E. (2002). The unintended consequences of stigma-free remediation. *Sociology of Education, 75*(3), 249–268. https://doi.org/10.2307/3090268

———. (2003). The social prerequisites of success: Can college structure reduce the need for social know-how? *The Annals of the American Academy of Political and Social Science, 586*(1), 120–143. https://doi.org/10.1177/0002716202250216

DeLuca, S. (2023). Sample selection matters: Moving toward empirically sound qualitative research. *Sociological Methods & Research, 52*(2), 1073–1085. https://doi.org/10.1177/00491241221140425

DeLuca, S., & Burland, E. (2023). *Weighing risk and reward in the postsecondary choices of low income students.* Paper Presented at the Annual Meeting of the Association for Public Policy and Management, Atlanta, GA.

DeLuca, S., Clampet-Lundquist, S., & Edin, K. (2016). *Coming of age in the other America.* Russell Sage Foundation.

DeLuca, S., & Dayton, E. (2009). Switching social contexts: The effects of housing mobility and school choice programs on youth outcomes. *Annual Review of Sociology, 35*(1), 457–491. https://doi.org/10.1146/annurev-soc-070308-120032

DeLuca, S., Duncan, G. J., Keels, M., & Mendenhall, R. M. (2010). Gautreaux mothers and their children: An update. *Housing Policy Debate, 20*(1), 7–25. https://doi.org/10.1080/10511481003599829

DeLuca, S., Garboden, P. M. E., & Rosenblatt, P. (2013). Segregating shelter: How housing policies shape the residential locations of low-income minority families. *The Annals of the American Academy of Political and Social Science, 647*(1), 268–299. https://doi.org/10.1177/0002716213479310

DeLuca, S., & Jang-Trettien, C. (2020). Not just a lateral move: Residential decisions and the reproduction of urban inequality. *City & Community, 19*(3), 451–488. https://doi.org/10.1111/cico.12515

DeLuca, S., Katz, L. F., & Oppenheimer, S. C. (2023). When someone cares about you, it's priceless: Reducing administrative burdens and boosting housing search confidence to increase opportunity moves for voucher holders. *The Russell Sage Foundation Journal of the Social Sciences, 9*(5), 179–211. https://doi.org/10.7758/RSF.2023.9.5.08

DeLuca, S., Papageorge, N. W., & Boselovic, J. L. (2024). Exploring the trade-off between exploring and thriving: Heterogenous responses to adversity and disruptive events among disadvantaged black youth. *The Russell Sage Foundation Journal of the Social Sciences, 10*(1), 103–131. https://doi.org/org/10.7758/RSF.2024.10.1.05

DeLuca, S., Papageorge, N. W., Boselovic, J. L., Gershenson, S., Gray, A., Nerenberg, K. M., Sausedo, J., & Young, A. (2021). *When anything can happen: Anticipated adversity and postsecondary decision-making* (NBER Working Paper No. 29472). National Bureau of Economic Research. https://www.nber.org/papers/w29472

DeLuca, S., & Rosen, E. (2022). Housing insecurity among the poor today. *Annual Review of Sociology, 48*(1), 343–371. https://doi.org/10.1146/annurev-soc-090921-040646

DeLuca, S., & Rosenblatt, P. (2010). Does moving to better neighborhoods lead to better schooling opportunities? Parental school choice in an experimental housing voucher program. *Teachers College Record, 112*(5), 1443–1491. https://doi.org/10.1177/016146811011200504

___. (2017). Walking away from the wire: Housing mobility and neighborhood opportunity in Baltimore. *Housing Policy Debate, 27*(4), 519–546. https://doi.org/10.1080/10511482.2017.1282884

DeLuca, S., Wood, H., & Rosenblatt, P. (2019). Why poor families move (and where they go): Reactive mobility and residential decisions. *City & Community, 18*(2), 556–593. https://doi.org/10.1111/cico.12386

Deming, D. J. (2017). The growing importance of social skills in the labor market. *The Quarterly Journal of Economics, 132*(4), 1593–1640. https://doi.org/10.1093/qje/qjx022

Derenoncourt, E. (2022). Can you move to opportunity? Evidence from the Great Migration. *American Economic Review, 112*(2), 369–408. https://doi.org/10.1257/aer.20200002

Derenoncourt, E., Kim, C. H., Kuhn, M., & Schularick, M. (2023). Changes in the distribution of Black and White wealth since the U.S. civil war. *Journal of Economic Perspectives, 37*(4), 71–90. https://doi.org/10.1257/jep.37.4.71

Derenoncourt, E., & Montialoux, C. (2021). Minimum wages and racial inequality. *Quarterly Journal of Economics, 136*(1), 169–228. https://doi.org/10.1093/qje/qjaa031

Desmond, M. (2016). *Evicted: Poverty and profit in the American city*. Crown.

Deutscher, N., & Mazumder, B. (2021). *Measuring intergenerational income mobility: A synthesis of approaches* (FRB of Chicago Working Paper No. 2021-09). Federal Reserve Bank of Chicago. http://dx.doi.org/10.21033/wp-2021-09

___. (2023). Measuring intergenerational income mobility: A synthesis of approaches. *Journal of Economic Literature, 61*(3), 988–1036. https://doi.org/10.1257/jel.20211413

Dew, J. (2007). Two sides of the same coin? The differing roles of assets and consumer debt in marriage. *Journal of Family and Economic Issues, 28*(1), 89–104. https://doi.org/10.1007/s10834-006-9051-6

___. (2008). Debt change and marital satisfaction change in recently married couples. *Family Relations, 57*(1), 60–71. https://doi.org/10.1111/j.1741-3729.2007.00483.x

DiNardo, J., & Lee, D. S. (2004). Economic impacts of new unionization on private sector employers: 1984–2001. *The Quarterly Journal of Economics, 119*(4), 1383–1441. https://doi.org/10.1162/0033553042476189

DiPrete, T. A., & Buchmann, C. (2006). Gender-specific trends in the value of education and the emerging gender gap in college completion. *Demography, 43*(1), 1–24. https://doi.org/10.1353/dem.2006.0003

___. (2013). *The rise of women: The growing gender gap in education and what it means for American schools*. Russell Sage Foundation.

Dobbie, W., & Fryer, R. G., Jr. (2011). Are high-quality schools enough to increase achievement among the poor? Evidence from the Harlem children's zone. *American Economic Journal: Applied Economics, 3*(3), 158–187. https://doi.org/10.1257/app.3.3.158

Dobbs v. Jackson Women's Health Organization, 597 U.S. 215 (2022).

Doepke, M., & Zilibotti, F. (2019). *Love, money, and parenting: How economics explains the way we raise our kids*. Princeton University Press.

Doleac, J. L., & Stevenson, M. T. (2020). *Algorithmic risk assessments in the hands of humans*. The Salem Center, The University of Texas at Austin. https://repositories.lib.utexas.edu/items/126f743a-f7c4-4833-b4df-ee621fc40117

Doren, C., & Grodsky, E. (2016). What skills can buy: Transmission of advantage through cognitive and noncognitive skills. *Sociology of Education, 89*(4), 321–342. https://doi.org/10.1177/0038040716667994

Dotti Sani, G. M., & Treas, J. (2016). Educational gradients in parents' child-care time across countries, 1965–2012: Educational gradients in parents' child-care time. *Journal of Marriage and Family, 78*(4), 1083–1096. https://doi.org/10.1111/jomf.12305

Drake, K., Belsky, J., & Fearon, R. M. P. (2014). From early attachment to engagement with learning in school: The role of self-regulation and persistence. *Developmental Psychology, 50*(5), 1350–1361. https://doi.org/10.1037/a0032779

Dreier, P., Mollenkopf, J., & Swanstrom, T. (2014). *Place matters: Metropolitics for the twenty-first century* (3rd rev. ed.). University Press of Kansas.

Drentea, P. (2000). Age, debt, and anxiety. *Journal of Health and Social Behavior, 41*(4), 437–450. https://www.jstor.org/stable/2676296

Drentea, P., & Lavrakas, P. J. (2000). Over the limit: The association among health, race, and debt. *Social Science & Medicine, 50*(4), 517–529. https://doi.org/10.1016/S0277-9536(99)00298-1

Drentea, P., & Reynolds, J. R. (2012). Neither a borrower nor a lender be: The relative importance of debt and SES for mental health among older adults. *Journal of Aging and Health, 24*(4), 673–695. https://doi.org/10.1177/0898264311143130

Dressel, J., & Farid, H. (2018). The accuracy, fairness, and limits of predicting recidivism. *Science Advances, 4*(1), 1–5. https://doi.org/10.1126/sciadv.aao5580

Du Bois, W. E. B. (1898). The study of the Negro problems. *The Annals of the American Academy of Political and Social Science, 11*(1), 1–23. https://doi.org/10.1177/000271629801100101

Duncan, G. J., Bos, H., Gennetian, L. A., & Hill, H. (2009). New hope: A thoughtful and effective approach to "make work pay". *Northwestern Journal of Law and Social Policy, 4*(1), 101–115. https://scholarlycommons.law.northwestern.edu/cgi/viewcontent.cgi?article=1035&context=njlsp

Duncan, G. J., & Brooks-Gunn, J. (Eds.) (1997). *Consequences of growing up poor*. Russell Sage Foundation.

Duncan, G. J., Kalil, A., Mogstad, M., & Rege, M. (2023). Investing in early childhood in preschool and at home. In E. A. Hanushek, L. Woessmann, & S. Machin (Eds.), *Handbook of the economics of education* (Vol. 6, pp. 1–91). Elsevier.

Duncan, G. J., Kalil, A., & Ziol-Guest, K. M. (2017). Increasing inequality in parent incomes and children's schooling. *Demography, 54*(5), 1603–1626. https://doi.org/10.1007/s13524-017-0600-4

Duncan, G. J., Morris, P. A., & Rodrigues, C. (2011). Does money really matter? Estimating impacts of family income on young children's achievement with data from random-assignment experiments. *Developmental Psychology, 47*(5), 1263–1279. https://doi.org/10.1037/a0023875

Duncan, G. J., & Murnane, R. J. (Eds.) (2011). *Whither opportunity? Rising inequality, schools, and children's life chances*. Russell Sage Foundation.

Dunifon, R. (2013). The influence of grandparents on the lives of children and adolescents. *Child Development Perspectives, 7*(1), 55–60. https://doi.org/10.1111/cdep.12016

Duran, C. A. K., Cottone, E., Ruzek, E. A., Mashburn, A. J., & Grissmer, D. W. (2020). Family stress processes and children's self-regulation. *Child Development, 91*(2), 577–595. https://doi.org/10.1111/cdev.13202

Durlauf, S. N. (1996). A theory of persistent income inequality. *Journal of Economic Growth, 1*(1), 75–93. https://www.jstor.org/stable/40215882?origin=JSTOR-pdf

Durlauf, S. N., Kourtellos, A., & Tan, C. M. (2022). The great Gatsby curve. *Annual Review of Economics, 14*, 571–605. https://doi.org/10.1146/annurev-economics-082321-122703

Dvir-Djerassi, A. (2024). Closing the racial wealth gap: A counterfactual historical simulation of universal inheritance. *The Russell Sage Foundation Journal of the Social Sciences, 10*(3), 70–91. https://doi.org/10.7758/RSF.2024.10.3.04

Dwyer, R. E. (2018). Credit, debt, and inequality. *Annual Review of Sociology, 44*(1), 237–261. https://doi.org/10.1146/annurev-soc-060116-053420

Dwyer, R. E., McCloud, L., & Hodson, R. (2011). Youth debt, mastery, and self-esteem: Class-stratified effects of indebtedness on self-concept. *Social Science Research, 40*(3), 727–741. https://doi.org/10.1016/j.ssresearch.2011.02.001

Dwyer, R. E., Neilson, L. A., Nau, M., & Hodson, R. (2016). Mortgage worries: Young adults and the U.S. housing crisis. *Socioeconomic Review, 14*(3), 483–505. https://doi.org/10.1093/ser/mwv018

Dyer, J., Bailey, C., & Tran, N. V. (2008). Ownership characteristics of heir property in a Black Belt county: A quantitative approach. *Journal of Rural Social Sciences, 24*(2), Article 10. https://egrove.olemiss.edu/jrss/vol24/iss2/10

Dynarski, S. (2014). *Building better longitudinal surveys (on the cheap) through links to administrative data.* Paper Presented at the Workshop to Examine Current and Potential Uses of National Center for Education Statistics Longitudinal Surveys by the Education Research Community. https://naeducation.org/wp-content/uploads/2016/10/dynarski-nces-longitudinal-surveys.pdf

Dynarski, S., Libassi, C. J., Michelmore, K., & Owen, S. (2021). Closing the gap: The effect of reducing complexity and uncertainty in college pricing on the choices of low-income students. *American Economic Review, 111*(6), 1721–1756. https://doi.org/10.1257/aer.20200451

Dynarski, S., Nurshatayeva, A., Page. L. C., & Scott-Clayton, J. (2023b). Addressing nonfinancial barriers to college access and success: Evidence and policy implications. In E. Hanushek, S. Machin, & L. Woessmann (Eds.), *Handbook of the economics of education* (Vol. 6, pp. 319–403). Elsevier. https://doi.org/10.1016/bs.hesedu.2022.11.007

Dynarski, S., Page, L. C., & Scott-Clayton, J. (2023a). College costs, financial aid, and student decisions. In E. Hanushek, S. Machin, & L. Woessmann (Eds.), *Handbook of the economics of education* (Vol. 7, pp. 227–285). Elsevier. https://doi.org/10.1016/bs.hesedu.2023.03.006

Dynarski, S., & Scott-Clayton, J. (2016). *Tax benefits for college attendance* (NBER Working Paper No. 22127). National Bureau of Economic Research. https://www.nber.org/system/files/working_papers/w22127/w22127.pdf

East, C. N., Miller, S., Page, M., & Wherry, L. R. (2023). Multigenerational impacts of childhood access to the safety net: Early life exposure to Medicaid and the next generation's health. *American Economic Review*, 113(1), 98–135. https://doi.org/10.1257/aer.20210937

Eberharter, V. V. (2013). *The intergenerational dynamics of social inequality: Empirical evidence from Europe and the United States* (SOEP Paper No. 588). https://papers.ssrn.com/sol3/papers.cfm?abstract_id=2331887

Edin, K. J., Fields, C. D., Grusky, D. B., Leskovec, J., Mattingly, M. J., Olson, K., & Varner, C. (2024). Listening to the voices of America. *The Russell Sage Foundation Journal of the Social Sciences*, 10(5), 1–31. https://doi.org/10.7758/RSF.2024.10.5.01

Edin, K. J., & Kefalas, M. J. (2005). *Promises I can keep: Why poor women put motherhood before marriage*. University of California Press.

Edin, K. J., Rosenblatt, P., & Zhu, Q. (2015). I do me: Young Black men and the struggle to resist the street. In O. Patterson (Ed.), *The cultural matrix: Understanding Black youth* (pp. 229–251). Harvard University Press.

Edin, K. J., Shaefer, H. L., & Nelson, T. J. (2023). *The injustice of place: Uncovering the legacy of poverty in America*. HarperCollins Publishers.

Eide, E. R., & Showalter, M. H. (1999). Factors affecting the transmission of earnings across generations: A quantile regression approach. *Journal of Human Resources*, 34(2), 253–267. https://doi.org/10.2307/146345

Elango, S., García, J. L., Heckman, J. J., & Hojman, A. (2015). Early childhood education. In R. A. Moffitt (Ed.), *Economics of means-tested transfer programs in the United States* (Vol. 2, pp. 235–297). University of Chicago Press.

Elder, G. H., Jr. (1999). *Children of the great depression: Social change in life experience* (25th anniversary ed.). Westview Press.

Elder, G. H., Jr., Johnson, M. K., & Crosnoe, R. (2003). The emergence and development of life course theory. In J. T. Mortimer & M. J. Shanahan (Eds.), *Handbook of the life course* (pp. 3–22). Plenum.

Elder, G. H., Jr., Shanahan, M. J., & Jennings, J. A. (2015). Human development in time and place. In M. H. Bornstein, T. Leventhal, & R. M. Lerner (Eds.), *Handbook of child psychology and developmental science: Ecological settings and processes* (7th ed., pp. 6–54). John Wiley & Sons.

Ellis, B. J., & Boyce, W. T. (2008). Biological sensitivity to context. *Current Directions in Psychological Science*, 17(3), 183–287. https://doi.org/10.1111/j.1467-8721.2008.00571.x

Elvery, J. A. (2009). The impact of enterprise zones on resident employment: An evaluation of the enterprise zone programs of California and Florida. *Economic Development Quarterly*, 23(1), 44–59. https://doi.org/10.1177/0891242408326994

Engzell, P., & Mood, C. (2023). Understanding patterns and trends in income mobility through multiverse analysis. *American Sociological Association*, 88(4), 600–626. https://doi.org/10.1177/00031224231180607

Ermisch, J., Jäntti, M., Smeeding, T., & Wilson, J. A. (2012). Advantage in comparative perspective. In J. Ermisch, M. Jäntti, & T. Smeeding (Eds.), *From parents to children: The intergenerational transmission of advantage* (pp. 3–31). Russell Sage Foundation.

Everett, B. G., Limburg, A., Homan, P., & Philbin, M. M. (2022). Structural heteropatriarchy and birth outcomes in the United States. *Demography*, 59(1), 89–110. https://doi.org/10.1215/00703370-9606030

Evidence-Based Policymaking Act of 2018, Pub. L. No. 115-435, 132 Stat. 5529 (2019).

Faber, J. W. (2020). We built this: Consequences of New Deal era intervention in America's racial geography. *American Sociological Review*, 85(5), 739–775. https://doi.org/10.1177/0003122420948420484

Fagereng, A., Mogstad, M., & Rønning, M. (2021). Why do wealthy parents have wealthy children? *Journal of Political Economy*, 129(3), 703–756. https://doi.org/10.1086/712446

Farber, H. S., Herbst, D., Kuziemko, I., & Naidu, S. (2021). Unions and inequality over the twentieth century: New evidence from survey data. *The Quarterly Journal of Economics*, *136*(3), 1325–1385. https://doi.org/10.1093/qje/qjab012

Federal Reserve Bank of New York. (2017). *Quarterly report on household debt and credit*. https://www.newyorkfed.org/medialibrary/interactives/householdcredit/data/pdf/HHDC_2017Q1.pdf

___. (2023a). *Quarterly report on household debt and credit*. https://www.newyorkfed.org/microeconomics/hhdc

___. (2023b, March). *State level household debt statistics 2003–2022*. https://www.newyorkfed.org/microeconomics/hhdc

Feigenbaum, J. J. (2018). Multiple measures of historical intergenerational mobility: Iowa 1915 to 1940. *The Economic Journal*, *128*(612), F446–F481. https://doi.org/10.1111/ecoj.12525

Feiveson, L., & Sabelhaus, J. E. (2019). *Lifecycle patterns of saving and wealth accumulation* (Finance and Economics Discussion Series 2019–010). Board of Governors of the Federal Reserve System. https://doi.org/10.17016/FEDS.2019.010

Feller, A., Grindal, T., Miratrix, L., & Page, L. C. (2016). Compared to what? Variation in the impacts of early childhood education by alternative care type. *Annuals of Applied Statistics*, *10*(3), 1245–1285. https://doi.org/10.1214/16-AOAS910

Ferrie, J. P. (2005). History lessons: The end of American exceptionalism? Mobility in the United States since 1850. *Journal of Economic Perspectives*, *19*(3), 199–215. https://doi.org/10.1257/089533005774357824

Finer, L. B., & Zolna, M. R. (2016). Declines in unintended pregnancy in the United States, 2008–2011. *New England Journal of Medicine*, *374*(9), 843–852. https://doi.org/10.1056/NEJMsa1506575

Finnigan, R., & Meagher, K. D. (2019). Past due: Combinations of utility and housing hardship in the United States. *Sociological Perspectives*, *62*(1), 96–119. https://doi.org/10.1177/0731121418782927

Fiorini, M., & Keane, M. P. (2014). How the allocation of children's time affects cognitive and noncognitive development. *Journal of Labor Economics*, *32*(4), 787–836. https://doi.org/10.1086/67723

Fischel, W. A. (2005). *The homevoter hypothesis: How home values influence local government taxation, school finance, and land-use policies*. Harvard University Press.

Fischer, W., & Huang, C.-C. (2013). *Mortgage interest deduction is ripe for reform*. Center on Budget and Policy Priorities. https://www.cbpp.org/sites/default/files/atoms/files/4-4-13hous.pdf

Fischer, W., & Sard, B. (2017). *Chart book: Federal housing spending is poorly matched to need*. Center on Budget and Policy Priorities. https://www.cbpp.org/research/chart-book-federal-housing-spending-is-poorly-matched-to-need

Fisher, J., & Johnson, D. S. (2023). *Intergenerational mobility using income, consumption, and wealth* (Working Paper No. 060723). Washington Center for Equitable Growth. https://equitablegrowth.org/working-papers/intergenerational-mobility-using-income-consumption-and-wealth/

Fisher, J., Johnson, D. S., Latner, J. P., Smeeding, T., & Thompson, J. (2016). Inequality and mobility using income, consumption, and wealth for the same individuals. *The Russell Sage Foundation Journal of the Social Sciences*, *2*(6), 44–58. https://doi.org/org/10.7758/rsf.2016.2.6.03

Fitzgerald, S. T., & Leicht, K. T. (2014). Introductory comments: Does the American middle class have a future? *The Sociological Quarterly*, *55*(2), 233–235. http://www.jstor.org/stable/24581858

Fleming, A. (2018). The long history of "truth in lending". *Journal of Policy History*, *30*(2), 236–271. https://doi.org/10.1017/S0898030618000064

Fletcher, J. M., & Wolfe, B. (2016). The importance of family income in the formation and evolution of non-cognitive skills in childhood. *Economics of Education Review*, 54(C), 143–154. https://doi.org/10.1016/j.econedurev.2016.07.004

Flippen, C. (2004). Unequal returns to housing investments? A study of real housing appreciation among Black, White, and Hispanic households. *Social Forces*, 82(4), 1523–1551. https://doi.org/10.1353/sof.2004.0069

Flynn, J. (2023). *Can expanding contraceptive access reduce adverse infant health outcomes?* (SSRN Working Paper No. 4408753). SSRN. https://doi.org/10.2139/ssrn.4408753

Fomby, P. (2024). Prioritize families, not marriage. *Journal of Policy Analysis and Management*, 43(4), 1284–1289. https://doi.org/10.1002/pam.22630

Fomby, P., & Cherlin, A. J. (2007). Family instability and child well-being. *American Sociological Review*, 72(2), 181–204. https://doi.org/10.1177/000312240707200203

Fortson, K., Rotz, D., Burkander, P., Mastri, A., Schochet, P., Rosenberg, L., McConnell, S., & D'Amico, R. (2017). *Providing public workforce services to job seekers: 30-month impact findings on the WIA adult and dislocated worker programs*. Mathematica Policy Research. https://www.mathematica.org/publications/providing-public-workforce-services-to-job-seekers-30-month-impact-findings-on-the-wia-adult

Fourcade, M., & Healy, K. (2013). Classification situations: Life-chances in the neoliberal era. *Accounting, Organizations, and Society*, 38(8), 559–572. https://doi.org/10.1016/j.aos.2013.11.002

Fox, L. E. (2016). Parental wealth and the Black–White mobility gap in the U.S. *Review of Income and Wealth*, 62(4), 706–723. https://doi.org/10.1111/roiw.12200

Fox, L. E., Torche, F., & Waldfogel, J. (2016). Intergenerational mobility. In D. Brady & L. M. Burton (Eds.), *The Oxford handbook of the social science of poverty* (pp. 528–554). Oxford University Press.

Frazier, M. (2021, May 20). When no landlord will rent to you, where do you go? *The New York Times*. https://www.nytimes.com/2021/05/20/magazine/extended-stay-hotels.html

Freeman, R. B., & Medoff, J. L. (1985). What do unions do? *ILR Review*, 38(2), 244–263. https://doi.org/10.1177/001979398503800207

Friedberg, L., Hynes, R. M., & Pattison, N. (2021). Who benefits from bans on employers' credit checks? *The Journal of Law and Economics*, 64(4), 675–703. http://dx.doi.org/10.1086/714352

Fry, R., & Cilluffo, A. (2019). *A rising share of undergraduates are from poor families, especially at less selective colleges*. Pew Research Center. https://www.pewresearch.org/wp-content/uploads/sites/20/2019/05/Pew-Research-Center-Undergrad-report-FINAL-05.22.19.pdf

Furstenberg, F. F., Jr., Cook, T. D., Eccles, J., Elder, G. H., Jr., & Sameroff, A. (1999). *Managing to make it: Urban families and adolescent success*. Chicago University Press.

Galor, O., & Tsiddon, D. (1997). Technological progress, mobility, and economic growth. *American Economic Review*, 87(3), 363–382. https://econpapers.repec.org/article/aeaaecrev/v_3a87_3ay_3a1997_3ai_3a3_3ap_3a363-82.htm

Galster, G. C. (2012). The mechanism(s) of neighbourhood effects: Theory, evidence, and policy implications. In M. van Ham, D. Manley, N. Bailey, L. Simpson, & D. Maclennan (Eds.), *Neighbourhood effects research: New perspectives* (pp. 23–56). Springer.

Galster, G. C., Santiago, A., Stack, L., & Cutsinger, J. (2016). Neighborhood effects on secondary school performance of Latino and African American youth: Evidence from a natural experiment in Denver. *Journal of Urban Economics*, 93(C), 30–48. https://doi.org/10.1016/j.jue.2016.02.004

Galster, G. C., & Sharkey, P. (2017). Spatial foundations of inequality: A conceptual model and empirical overview. *The Russell Sage Foundation Journal of the Social Sciences*, 3(2), 1–33. https://doi.org/10.7758/RSF.2017.3.2.01

Galvez, M. M. (2010). *What do we know about housing choice voucher program location outcomes? A review of recent literature*. What Works Collaborative, The Urban Institute. https://www.urban.org/sites/default/files/publication/29176/412218-What-Do-We-Know-About-Housing-Choice-Voucher-Program-Location-Outcomes-.PDF

Gardyan, A., Mwase, G., Sigelman, M., Trumbore, A., & Stevens, M. (2024). *Education and learning for longer lives: Building a national vision for human capital development and shared prosperity*. Stanford Center on Longevity & Center for Advanced Study in the Behavioral Sciences. https://longevity.stanford.edu/wp-content/uploads/2024/11/Education-and-Learning-for-Longer-Lives.pdf

Gelbgiser, D. (2018). College for all, degrees for few: For-profit colleges and socioeconomic differences in degree attainment. *Social Force*, 96(4), 1785–1824. https://doi.org/10.1093/sf/soy022

Genadek, K. R., & Alexander, J. T. (2019). *The decennial census digitization and linkage project* (ADEP Working Paper Series No. 2019–01). U.S. Census Bureau. https://www.census.gov/content/dam/Census/library/working-papers/2019/econ/dcdl-workingpaper.pdf

Genschel, P., Limberg, J., & Seelkopf, L. (2023). Revenue, redistribution, and the rise and fall of inheritance taxation. *Comparative Political Studies*, 57(9), 1–31. https://doi.org/10.1177/00104140231194065

Gershenson, S., & Tekin, E. (2018). The effect of community traumatic events on student achievement: Evidence from the Beltway Sniper attacks. *Education Finance and Policy*, 13(4), 513–544. https://doi.org/10.1162/edfp_a_00234

Ghaffary S. (2019, September 6). It looks like Uber is getting into the small loan business for its drivers. *Vox*. https://www.vox.com/2019/9/6/20853357/uber-driver-direct-loans-payday-small-lorena-gonzalez-ab5

Gibbs, B. G., & Downey, D. (2020). The Black/White skill gap in early childhood: The role of parenting. *Sociological Perspectives*, 63(6), 525–551. https://doi.org/10.1177/0731121419896812

Gibson-Davis, C., & Hill, H. D. (2021). Childhood wealth inequality in the United States: Implications for social stratification and well-being. *The Russell Sage Foundation Journal of the Social Sciences*, 7(3), 1–26. https://doi.org/10.7758/rsf.2021.7.3.01

Gipson, J. D., Koenig, M. A., & Hindin, M. J. (2008). The effects of unintended pregnancy on infant, child, and parental health: A review of the literature. *Studies in Family Planning*, 39(1), 18–38. https://doi.org/10.1111/j.1728-4465.2008.00148.x

Glaeser, E. L., & Gottlieb, J. D. (2008). The economics of place-making policies. *Brookings Papers on Economic Activity*, 39(1), 155–253. https://doi.org/10.2139/ssrn.1299046

Glaeser, E. L., & Gyourko, J., (2002). *The impact of zoning on housing affordability* (NBER Working Paper No. 8835). National Bureau of Economic Research. https://www.nber.org/system/files/working_papers/w8835/w8835.pdf

Glass, T. A., & McAtee, M. J. (2006). Behavioral science at the crossroads in public health: Extending horizons, envisioning the future. *Social Science & Medicine*, 62(7), 1650–1671. https://doi.org/10.1016/j.socscimed.2005.08.044

Goda, G. S., & Streeter, J. L. (2021). *Wealth trajectories across key milestones: Longitudinal evidence from life-course transitions* (NBER Working Paper No. 28329). National Bureau of Economic Research. https://www.nber.org/system/files/working_papers/w28329/w28329.pdf

Goering, J. M., & Feins, J. D. (Eds.) (2003). *Choosing a better life? Evaluating the moving to opportunity social experiment*. The Urban Institute.

Gold, S., & Edin, K. J. (2021). Re-thinking stepfathers' contributions: Fathers, stepfathers, and child wellbeing. *Journal of Family Issues*, 44(3), 745–765. https://doi.org/10.1177/0192513X211054471

Golden, D. (2007). *The price of admission: How America's ruling class buys its way into elite colleges — and who gets left outside the gates*. Crown Publishing Group/Random House.

Goldin, C., & Katz, L. F. (2002). The power of the pill: Oral contraceptives and women's career and marriage decisions. *Journal of Political Economy*, *110*(4), 730–770. https://doi.org/10.1111/j.1728-4465.2008.00148.x

___. (2008). *The race between education and technology*. Harvard University Press.

Goldin, C., Katz, L. F., & Kuziemko, I. (2006). The homecoming of American college women: The reversal of the college gender gap. *Journal of Economic Perspectives*, *20*(4), 133–156. https://doi.org/10.1257/jep.20.4.133

Goldrick-Rab, S., Richardson, J., Schneider, J., Hernandez, A., & Cady, C. (2018). *Still hungry and homeless in college*. Wisconsin Hope Lab. https://www.pdx.edu/basic-needs-hub/sites/studentaccesscenter.web.wdt.pdx.edu/files/2020-08/Wisconsin-HOPE-Lab-Still-Hungry-and-Homeless_0.pdf

Goldstein, A., & Hastings. O. P. (2019). Buying in: Positional competition, schools, income inequality, and housing consumption. *Sociological Sciences*, *6*(16), 416–445. https://doi.org/10.15195/v6.a16

Goodman, J., Hurwitz, M., & Smith, J. (2017). Access to 4-year public colleges and degree completion. *Journal of Labor Economics*, *35*(3), 829–867. https://doi.org/10.1086/690818

Goodman, S., Mezza, A., & Volz, A. H. (2020). On intergenerational immobility: Evidence that adult credit health reflects the childhood environment. *Economic Inquiry*, *Western Economic Association International*, *58*(2), 780–801. https://ideas.repec.org/a/bla/ecinqu/v58y2020i2p780-801.html

Goodman-Bacon, A. (2021). The long-run effects of childhood insurance coverage: Medicaid implementation, adult health, and labor market outcomes. *American Economic Review*, *111*(8), 2550–2593. https://doi.org/10.1257/aer.20171671

Gorostiaga, A., Aliri, J., Balluerka, N., & Lameirinhas, J. (2019). Parenting styles and internalizing symptoms in adolescence: A systematic literature review. *International Journal of Environmental Research and Public Health*, *16*(17), 3192. https://doi.org/10.3390/ijerph16173192

Graham, B., & Sharkey, P. (2013). *Mobility and the metropolis: The relationship between inequality in urban communities and economic mobility*. The Economic Mobility Project, an initiative of The Pew Charitable Trusts. https://nyuscholars.nyu.edu/en/publications/mobility-and-the-metropolis-the-relationship-between-inequality-i

Graham, M., McEntarfer, E., McKinney, K., Tibbets, S., & Tucker, L. (2022). *LEHD Snapshot Documentation* (Working Paper No. 22-51). Center for Economic Studies & U.S. Census Bureau. https://www.census.gov/library/working-papers/2022/adrm/CES-WP-22-51.html

Grall, T. (2020). *Custodial mothers and fathers and their child support: 2017* (Current Population Reports, P60-269). U.S. Census Bureau. https://www.census.gov/library/publications/2020/demo/p60-269.html

Granovetter, M. S. (1973). The strength of weak ties. *American Journal of Sociology*, *78*(6), 1360–1380. https://doi.org/10.1086/225469

Green, G. P., & Sanchez, L. (2007). Does manufacturing still matter? *Population Research and Policy Review*, *26*(5), 529–551. https://doi.org/10.1007/s11113-007-9043-8

Greenberg, K., Gudgeon, M., Isen, A., Miller, C., & Patterson, R. (2022). Army Service in the all-volunteer era. *The Quarterly Journal of Economics*, *137*(4), 2363–2418. https://doi.org/10.1093/qje/qjac026

Gregg, P., & Kanabar, R. (2022). Intergenerational wealth transmission in Great Britain. *Review of Income and Wealth*, *69*(4), 807–837. https://doi.org/10.1111/roiw.12620

Grusky, D. B., Hall, P. A., & Markus, H. R. (2019). The rise of opportunity markets: How did it happen & what can we do? *Daedalus*, *148*(3), 19–45. https://doi.org/10.1162/daed_a_01749

Grusky, D. B., Smeeding, T. M., & Snipp, C. M. (2015). A new infrastructure for monitoring social mobility in the United States. *The Annals of the American Academy of Political and Social Science*, 657(1), 63–82. https://doi.org/10.1177/0002716214549941

Guerrero, D. (2023). *Revisiting the intergenerational effects of the earned income tax credit on the long-run income of children* (SSRN Working Paper No. 4603903). SSRN. https://ssrn.com/abstract=4603903

Guldi, M. (2008). Fertility effects of abortion and birth control pill access for minors. *Demography*, 45(4), 817–827. https://doi.org/10.1353/dem.0.0026

Guryan, J., Hurst, E., & Kearney, M. (2008). Parental education and parental time with children. *Journal of Economic Perspectives*, 22(3), 23–46. https://doi.org/10.1257/jep.22.3.23

Guzman, G., & Kollar, M. (2023). *Income in the United States: 2022* (Current Population Reports, P60-279). U.S. Census Bureau. U.S. Department of Commerce, Government Publishing Office. https://www.census.gov/content/dam/Census/library/publications/2023/demo/p60-279.pdf

Guzzo, K. B. (2021). *Thirty years of change in unintended births* (Family Profiles, FP-21-01). National Center for Family & Marriage Research. https://doi.org/10.25035/ncfmr/fp-21-01

Guzzo, K. B., & Hayford, S. R. (2020). Pathways to parenthood in social and family contexts: Decade in review, 2020. *Journal of Marriage and Family*, 82(1), 117–144. https://doi.org/10.1111/jomf.12618

Gyourko, J., Mayer, C., & Sinai, T. (2013). Superstar cities. *American Economic Journal: Economic Policy*, 5(4), 167–199. https://doi.org/10.1257/pol.5.4.167

Hacker, J. S. (2019). *The great risk shift: The new economic insecurity and the decline of the American dream.* Oxford University Press.

Hacker, J. S., & Pierson, P. (2002). Business power and social policy: Employers and the formation of the American welfare state. *Politics & Society*, 30(2), 277–325. https://doi.org/10.1177/0032329202030002004

Hackworth, J. (2007). *The neoliberal city: Governance, ideology, and development in American urbanism.* Cornell University Press.

Hällsten, M. (2024). The intergenerational transmission of wealth. In M. Albertini (Ed.), *Handbook on intergenerational relations.* Edward Elgar.

Hällsten, M., & Pfeffer, F. T. (2017). Grand advantage: Family wealth and grandchildren's educational achievement in Sweden. *American Sociological Review*, 82(2), 328–360. https://doi.org/10.1177/0003122417695791

Halpern-Meekin, S. (2019). *Social poverty: Low-income parents and the struggle for family and community ties.* NYU Press.

Halpern-Meekin, S., Edin, K., Sykes, J., & Tach, L. (2015). *It's not like I'm poor: How working families make ends meet in a post-welfare world.* University of California Press.

Hamilton, B. E., Martin, J. A., & Osterman, M. J. K. (2023). *Births: Provisional data for 2022* (Vital Statistics Rapid Release Report No. 28). Centers for Disease Control and Prevention, National Center for Health Statistics. https://www.cdc.gov/nchs/data/vsrr/vsrr028.pdf

Hamilton, D., & Darity, W., Jr. (2010). Can 'baby bonds' eliminate the racial wealth gap in putative post-racial America? *Review of Black Political Economy*, 37(3–4), 207–216. https://doi.org/10.1007/s12114-010- 9063-1

Hamilton, L., Roksa, J., & Nielsen, K. (2018). Providing a leg-up: Parental involvement and opportunity hoarding in college. *Sociology of Education*, 91(2), 111–131. https://doi.org/10.1177/0038040718759557

Hamilton, L. T. (2016). *Parenting to a degree: How family matters for college women's success.* University of Chicago Press.

Hamilton, L. T., Dawson, C. E., Armstrong, E. A., & Waller-Bey, A. (2024). Racialized horizontal stratification in U.S. higher education: Politics, process, and consequences. *Annual Review of Sociology*, 50, 475–499. https://doi.org/10.1146/annurev-soc-083123-035938

Hanushek, E. A., & Woessmann, L. (2008). The role of cognitive skills in economic development. *Journal of Economic Literature*, 46(3), 607–668. https://doi.org/10.1257/jel.46.3.607

Harding, D. J. (2009). Collateral consequences of violence in disadvantaged neighborhoods. *Social Forces*, 88(2), 757–782. https://doi.org/10.1353/sof.0.0281

___. (2010). *Living the drama: Community, conflict, and culture among inner-city boys.* University of Chicago Press.

Harding, D. J., Gennetian, L., Winship, C., Sanbonmatsu, L., & Kling, J. (2011). Unpacking neighborhood influences on education outcomes: Setting the stage for future research. In G. Duncan & R. Murnane (Eds.), *Whither opportunity: Rising inequality, schools, and children's life chances* (pp. 277–296). Russell Sage Foundation, Spencer Foundation.

Harris, A. (2016). *A pound of flesh: Monetary sanctions as punishment for the poor.* Russell Sage Foundation.

Harris, K. M., Halpern, C. T., Whitsel, E. A., Hussey, J. M., Killeya-Jones, L. A., Tabor, J. W., & Dean, S. C. (2019). Cohort profile: The National Longitudinal Study of Adolescent to Adult Health (Add Health). *International Journal of Epidemiology*, 48(5), 1415–1415k. https://doi.org/10.1093/ije/dyz115

Hart, B. A. (2019). Hanging in, stopping out, dropping out: Community college students in an era of precarity. *Teachers College Record*, 121(1), 1–30. https://doi.org/10.1177/016146811912100105

Hartley, D., Mazumdar, B., & Rajan, A. (2019). How similar are credit scores across generations? (Chicago Fed Letter, No. 424). *Federal Reserve Bank of Chicago*. https://www.chicagofed.org/publications/chicago-fed-letter/2019/424

Harvey, H., Dunifon, R., & Pilkauskas, N. (2021). Under whose roof? Understanding the living arrangements of children in doubled-up households. *Demography*, 58(3), 821–846. https://doi.org/10.1215/00703370-9101102

Harvey, H., Fong, K., Edin, K., & DeLuca, S. (2020). Forever homes and temporary stops: Housing search logics and residential selection. *Social Forces*, 98(4), 1498–1523. https://doi.org/10.1093/sf/soz110

Hatzenbuehler, M. L. (2016). Structural stigma: Research evidence and implications for psychological science. *American Psychologist*, 71(8), 742–751. https://doi.org/10.1037/amp0000068

Hauser, R. M. (2010). Intergenerational economic mobility in the United States: Measures, differentials, and trends. *Euramerica*, 40(3), 635–681. https://www.ea.sinica.edu.tw/eu_file/128506421414.pdf

Hauser, R. M., Dickinson, P. J., Travis, H. P., & Koffel, J. N. (1975). Structural changes in occupational mobility among men in the United States. *American Sociological Review*, 40(5), 585–598. https://doi.org/10.2307/2094517

Hayes, S. (2020). Special purpose credit programs. *SSRN*. https://papers.ssrn.com/sol3/papers.cfm?abstract_id=3749610

Heckman, J. J. (2006). Skill formation and the economics of investing in disadvantaged children. *Science*, 312(5782), 1900–1902. https://doi.org/10.1126/science.1128898

___. (2008). Schools, skills, and synapses. *Economic Inquiry*, 46(3), 289. https://doi.org/10.1111/j.1465-7295.2008.00163.x

Heckman, J. J., & Landersø, R. (2022). Lessons for Americans from Denmark about inequality and social mobility. *Labour Economics*, 77(C), 101999. https://doi.org/10.1016/j.labeco.2021.101999

Heckman, J. J., Stixrud, J., & Urzua, S. (2006). The effects of cognitive and noncognitive abilities on labor market outcomes and social behavior. *Journal of Labor Economics*, 24(3), 411–482. https://doi.org/10.1086/504455

Heinrich, C. J., Mueser, P. R., & Troske, K. R. (2008). *Workforce investment act non-experimental net impact evaluation.* IMPAQ International. https://wdr.doleta.gov/research/FullText_Documents/Workforce%20Investment%20Act%20Non-Experimental%20Net%20Impact%20Evaluation%20-%20Final%20Report.pdf

Heinrich, C. J., Mueser, P. R., Troske, K. R., Jeon, K.-S., & Kahvecioglu, D. C. (2013). Do public employment and training programs work? *IZA Journal of Labor Economics, 2*(1), 1–23. https://doi.org/10.1186/2193-8997-2-6

Heinz, W. R., & Marshall, V. W. (Eds.). (2003). *Social dynamics of the life course: Transitions, institutions, and interrelations.* Aldine de Gruyter.

Helgertz, J., Price, J., Wellington, J., Thompson, K. J., Ruggles, S., & Fitch, C. A. (2022). A new strategy for linking U.S. historical censuses: A case study for the IPUMS multigenerational longitudinal panel. *Historical Methods: A Journal of Quantitative and Interdisciplinary History, 55*(1), 12–29. https://doi.org/10.1080/01615440.2021.1985027

Heller, S. B. (2014). Summer jobs reduce violence among disadvantaged youth. *Science, 346*(6214), 1219–1223. https://doi.org/10.1126/science.1257809

Heller, S. B., Pollack, H. A., Ander, R., & Ludwig, J. (2013). *Preventing youth violence and dropout: A randomized field experiment* (NBER Working Paper No. w19014). National Bureau of Economic Research. https://www.nber.org/system/files/working_papers/w19014/w19014.pdf

Hendra, R., Greenberg, D. H., Hamilton, G., Oppenheim, A., Pennington, A., Schaberg, K., & Tessler, B. L. (2016). *Encouraging evidence on a sector-focused advancement strategy: Two-year impacts from the WorkAdvance demonstration.* MDRC. https://www.mdrc.org/work/publications/encouraging-evidence-sector-focused-advancement-strategy-0

Hendren, N., & Sprung-Keyser, B. (2020). A unified welfare analysis of government policies. *The Quarterly Journal of Economics, 135*(3), 1209–1318. https://doi.org/10.1093/qje/qjaa006

Henshaw, S. K., & Kost, K. (2008). *Trends in the characteristics of women obtaining abortions, 1974 to 2004.* Guttmacher Institute. https://www.guttmacher.org/sites/default/files/report_pdf/trendswomenabortions-wtables.pdf

Hertz, T. (2007). Trends in the intergenerational elasticity of family income in the United States. *Industrial Relations, 46*(1), 22–50. https://doi.org/10.1111/j.1468-232X.2007.00456.x

Hertzman, C., & Boyce, T. (2010). How experience gets under the skin to create gradients in developmental health. *Annual Review of Public Health, 31*, 329–347. https://doi.org/10.1146/annurev.publhealth.012809.103538

Hicken, M. T., Miles, L., Haile, S., & Esposito, M. (2021). Linking history to contemporary state-sanctioned slow violence through cultural and structural racism. *The Annals of the American Academy of Political and Social Science, 694*(1), 48–58. https://doi.org/0.1177/00027162211005690

Higher Education Opportunity Act of 2008, Pub. L. No. 110-315, 122 Stat. 3078 (2008).

Hirsch, A. R. (2009). *Making the second ghetto: Race and housing in Chicago 1940–1960.* University of Chicago Press.

Hirschl, N., Schwartz, C. R., & Boschetti, E. (2022). *Eight decades of educational assortative mating* (CDE Working Paper No. 2022-01). Center for Demography and Ecology, University of Wisconsin-Madison. https://cde.wisc.edu/wp-content/uploads/sites/839/2023/02/cde-working-paper-2022-01-1.pdf

Hitlin, S., & Elder, G. H., Jr. (2007). Time, self, and the curiously abstract concept of agency. *Sociological Theory, 25*(2), 170–191. https://doi.org/10.1111/j.1467-9558.2007.00303.x

Hodson, R., Dwyer, R. E., & Neilson, L. A. (2014). Credit card blues: The middle class and the hidden costs of easy credit. *The Sociological Quarterly, 55*(2), 315–340. https://doi.org/10.1111/tsq.12059

Holland, M. M., & DeLuca, S. (2016). Why wait years to become something? Low-income African American youth and the costly career search in for-profit trade schools. *Sociology of Education, 89*(4), 261–278. https://doi.org/10.1177/0038040716666607

Holzer, H. J., & Baum, S. (2017). *Making college work: Pathways to success for disadvantaged students*. Brookings Institution Press.

Homan, P. (2019). Structural sexism and health in the United States: A new perspective on health inequality and the gender system. *American Sociological Review*, 84(3), 486–516. https://doi.org/10.1177/0003122419848723

Homan, P., Brown, T. H., & King, B. (2021). Structural intersectionality as a new direction for health disparities research. *Journal of Health and Social Behavior*, 62(3), 350–370. https://doi.org/10.1177/00221465211032947

Homan, P., Everett, B., & Brown, T. H. (2024). Methods for studying structural oppression in quantitative family research. *Journal of Marriage and Family*, 86(4), 1272–1304. https://doi.org/10.1111/jomf.13003

Horan, P. M. (1978). Is status attainment research atheoretical? *American Sociological Review*, 43(4), 534–541. https://www.jstor.org/stable/2094777

Horn, R. (2017). Policy watch: The consumer financial protection bureau's consumer research: Mission accomplished? *Journal of Public Policy & Marketing*, 36(1), 170–183. https://doi.org/10.1509/jppm.17.037

Hosek, J. R., Asch, B. J., Mattock, M. G., & Smith, T. D. (2018). *Military and civilian pay levels, trends, and recruit quality*. RAND National Security Research Division, RAND Corporation. https://www.rand.org/pubs/research_reports/RR2396.html

Houle, J. N. (2014a). A generation indebted: Young adult debt across three cohorts. *Social Problems*, 61(3), 448–465. https://doi.org/10.1525/sp.2014.12110

———. (2014b). Disparities in debt: Parents' socioeconomic status and young adult student loan debt. *Sociology of Education*, 87(1), 53–69. https://doi.org/10.1177/0038040713512213

Houle, J. N., & Addo, F. R. (2022). *A dream defaulted: The student loan crisis among Black borrowers*. Harvard Education Press.

Houle, J. N., & Keene, D. E. (2015). Getting sick and falling behind: Health and the risk of mortgage default and home foreclosure. *Journal of Epidemiology & Community Health*, 69(4), 382–387. https://doi.org/10.1136/jech-2014-204637

Hout, M. (1988). More universalism, less structural mobility: The American occupational structure in the 1980s. *American Journal of Sociology*, 93(6), 1358–1400. https://www.jstor.org/stable/2780817

———. (2004). How inequality may affect intergenerational mobility. In K. Neckerman (Ed.), *Social inequality* (pp. 969–987). Russell Sage Foundation.

———. (2012). Social and economic returns to college education in the United States. *Annual Review of Sociology*, 38, 379–400. https://doi.org/10.1146/annurev.soc.012809.102503

———. (2015). A summary of what we know about social mobility. *The Annals of the American Academy of Political and Social Science*, 657(1), 27–36. https://doi.org/10.1177/0002716214547174

Hoynes, H., Schanzenbach, D. W., & Almond, D. (2016). Long-run impacts of childhood access to the safety net. *American Economic Review*, 106(4), 903–934. https://doi.org/10.1257/aer.20130375

Humphries, J. E., Mader, N. S., Tannenbaum, D. I., & Van Dijk, W. L. (2019). *Does eviction cause poverty? Quasi-experimental evidence from Cook County, IL* (NBER Working Paper No. 26139). National Bureau of Economic Research. https://dpo:10.3386/w26139

Huston, A. C., Duncan, G. J., Granger, R., Bos, J., McLoyd, V., Mistry, R., Crosby, D., Gibson, C., Magnuson, K., Romich, J., & Ventura, A. (2001). Work-based antipoverty programs for parents can enhance the school performance and social behavior of children. *Child Development*, 72(1), 318–336. https://doi.org/10.1111/1467-8624.00281

Huston, A. C., Miller, C., Richburg-Hayes, L., Duncan, G. J., Eldred, C. A., Weisner, T. S., Lowe, E., McLoyd, V. C., Crosby, D. A., Ripke, M. N., & Redcross, C. (2003). *New hope for families and children: Five-year results of a program to reduce poverty and reform welfare*. MDRC. https://www.mdrc.org/sites/default/files/full_457.pdf

Hwang J., Hankinson M., & Brown K. S. (2015). Racial and spatial targeting: Segregation and subprime lending within and across metropolitan areas. *Social Forces, 93*(3), 1081–1108. https://doi.org/10.1093/sf/sou099

Hyman, L. (2011). *Debtor nation: The history of America in red ink*. Princeton University Press.

Ibsen, K., & Rosholm, M. (2024). *What works? Interventions aimed at reducing student dropout in higher education* (IZA DP No. 16853). Institute of Labor Economics. https://www.iza.org/publications/dp/16853/what-works-interventions-aimed-at-reducing-student-dropout-in-higher-education

Iloh, C. (2018). Toward a new model of college choice for a twenty-first-century context. *Harvard Educational Review, 88*(2), 227–244. https://doi.org/10.17763/1943-5045-88.2.227

Iloh, C., & Tierney, W. G. (2014). Understanding for-profit college and community college choice through rational choice. *Teachers College Record, 116*(8), 1–34. https://doi.org/10.1177/016146811411600808

Isaacs, J. B., Sawhill, I. V, & Haskins, R. (2008). *Getting ahead or losing ground: Economic mobility in America*. Brookings Institution Press.

Islam, T. M. T., Minier, J., & Ziliak, J. P. (2015). On persistent poverty in a rich country. *Southern Economic Journal, 81*(3), 653–678. https://doi.org/10.4284/0038-4038-2012.243

Jack, A. A. (2016). (No) harm in asking: Class, acquired cultural capital, and academic engagement at an elite university. *Sociology of Education, 89*(1), 1–19. https://doi.org/10.1177/0038040715614913

___. (2019). *The privileged poor: How elite colleges are failing disadvantaged students*. Harvard University Press.

Jackson, C. K., Johnson, R. C., & Persico, C. (2016). The effects of school spending on educational and economic outcomes: Evidence from school finance reforms. *The Quarterly Journal of Economics, 131*(1), 157–218. https://doi.org/10.1093/qje/qjv036

Jackson, M., & Holzman, B. (2020). A century of educational inequality in the United States. *Proceedings of the National Academy of Sciences, 117*(32), 19108–19115. https://doi.org/10.1073/pnas.1907258117

Jácome, E., Kuziemko, I., & Naidu, S. (2025). Mobility for all: Representative intergenerational mobility estimates over the twentieth century. *Journal of Political Economy, 133*(1), 306–354. https://doi.org/10.1086/732527

James, S., McLanahan, S., & Brooks-Gunn, J. (2021). Contributions of the fragile families and child wellbeing study to child development. *Annual Review of Developmental Psychology, 3*(1), 187–206. https://doi.org/10.1146/annurev-devpsych-050620-113832

Jang-Trettien, C. (2022). House of cards: Informal housing markets and precarious pathways to homeownership in Baltimore. *Social Problems, 69*(4), 928–951. https://doi.org/10.1093/socpro/spab004

Jäntti, M., & Jenkins, S. P. (2015). Income mobility. In A. B. Atkinson & F. Bourguignon (Eds.), *Handbook of income distribution* (Vol. 2A, pp. 807–935). Elsevier-North Holland.

Jargowsky, P. A. (2015). *The architecture of segregation: Civil unrest, the concentration of poverty, and public policy* [Issue Brief]. The Century Foundation. https://tcf.org/content/report/architecture-of-segregation/

Jencks, C., & Tach, L. (2006). Would equal opportunity mean more mobility? In S. L. Mogan, D. B. Grusky, & G. S. Fields (Eds.), *Mobility and inequality: Frontiers of research in sociology and economics* (pp. 23–58). Stanford University Press. doi.org/10.1515/9781503625495-004

Jenkins, R., Bhugra, D., Bebbington, P., Brugha, T., Farrell, M., Coid, J., Fryers, T., Weich, S., Singleton, N., & Meltzer, H. (2008). Debt, income, and mental disorder in the general population. *Psychological Medicine, 38*(10), 1485–1493. https://doi.org/10.1017/S0033291707002516

Jez, R. J. (2024). Culturally responsive/sustaining transition for at-promise youth. *Career Development and Transition for Exceptional Individuals*, 1–13. https://doi.org/10.1177/21651434241235886

Johnson, D., Massey, C., & O'Hare, A. (2015). The opportunities and challenges of using administrative data linkages to evaluate mobility. *The Annals of the American Academy of Political and Social Science*, 657(1), 247–264. https://doi.org/10.1177/0002716214552780

Johnson, H., & Leary, J. (2017). Policy watch: Research priorities on disclosure at the Consumer Financial Protection Bureau. *Journal of Public Policy & Marketing*, 36(1), 184–191. https://www.jstor.org/stable/44878407

Johnson, K. (2015). Behavioral education in the 21st century. *Journal of Organizational Behavior Management*, 35(1–2), 135–150. https://doi.org/10.1080/01608061.2015.1036152

Johnson, R. C. (2020). The impact of parental wealth on college degree attainment: Evidence from the housing boom and bust. *American Economic Review: Papers & Proceedings*, 110, 405–410. https://doi.org/10.1257/pandp.20201110

Johnson, R. C., & Nazaryan, A. (2019). *Children of the dream: Why school integration works*. Basic Books.

Joint Committee on Taxation. (2015, March 16). *History, present law, and analysis of the federal wealth transfer tax system*. U.S. Congress. https://www.jct.gov/publications/2015/jcx-52-15/

Jones, N. (2009). *Between good and ghetto: African American girls and inner-city violence*. Rutgers University Press.

Juras, R., Tanner-Smith, E., Kelsey, M., Lipsey, M., & Layzer, J. (2019). Adolescent pregnancy prevention: Meta-analysis of federally funded program evaluations. *American Journal of Public Health*, 109(4), e1–e8. https://doi.org/10.2105/AJPH.2018.304925

Kain, J. F. (1992). The spatial mismatch hypothesis: Three decades later. *Housing Policy Debate*, 3(2), 371–460. https://doi.org/10.1080/10511482.1992.9521100

Kahlenberg, R. D. (2010). *Affirmative action for the rich*. Century Foundation Press.

Kalil, A. (2014a). Inequality begins at home: The role of parenting in the diverging destinies of rich and poor children. In P. R. Amato, A. Booth, S. M. McHale, & J. Van Hook (Eds.), *Families in an era of increasing inequality: Diverging destinies* (pp. 63–82). Springer International Publishing Switzerland.

———. (2014b). *Proposal 2: Addressing the parenting divide to promote early childhood development for disadvantaged children* (Policies to Address Poverty in America No. 29). Brookings Institution. https://www.brookings.edu/articles/addressing-the-parenting-divide-to-promote-early-childhood-development-for-disadvantaged-children/

Kalil, A., & Ryan, R. (2020). Parenting practices and socioeconomic gaps in childhood outcomes. *The Future of Children*, 30(1), 29–54. https://doi.org/10.1353/foc.2020.0004

———. (2024). How parenting contributes to intergenerational inequality. In E. Kilpi-Jakonen, J. Blanden, J. Erola, & L. Macmillan (Eds.), *Research handbook on intergenerational inequality* (pp. 306–320). Edward Elgar Publishing.

Kalleberg, A. L. (2011). *Good jobs, bad jobs: The rise of polarized and precarious employment systems in the United States 1970s to 2000s*. Russell Sage Foundation.

Kapelle, N. (2022). Time cannot heal all wounds: Wealth trajectories of divorcees and the married. *Journal of Marriage and Family*, 84(2), 592–611. https://doi.org/10.1111/jomf.12824

Karlson, K. B. (2023). Black-White trends in intergenerational educational mobility: A positional analysis. *American Journal of Sociology*, 128(6), 1597–1649. https://doi.org/10.1086/724884

Katz, L. F., & Autor, D. H. (1999). Changes in the wage structure and earnings inequality. In O. Ashenfelter & D. Card (Eds.), *Handbook of labor economics* (Vol. 3, pp. 1463–1555). Elsevier Science.

Katz, L. F., Roth, J., Hendra, R., & Schaberg, K. (2022). Why do sectoral employment programs work? Lessons from WorkAdvance. *Journal of Labor Economics, 40*(S1), S249–S291. https://doi.org/10.1086/717932

Kaufman, J. E., & Rosenbaum, J. E. (1992). The education and employment of low-income Black youth in White suburbs. *Educational Evaluation and Policy Analysis, 14*(3), 229–240. https://doi.org/10.3102/01623737014003229

Kearney, M. S. (2023). *The two-parent privilege: How the decline in marriage has increased inequality and lowered social mobility, and what we can do about it.* Swift Press.

Keels, M., Duncan, G. J., DeLuca, S., Mendenhall, R., & Rosenbaum, J. (2005). Fifteen years later: Can residential mobility programs provide a long-term escape from neighborhood segregation, crime, and poverty? *Demography, 42*(1), 51–73. https://doi.org/10.1353/dem.2005.0005

Keese, M., & Schmitz, H. (2014). Broke, ill, and obese: Is there an effect of household debt on health? *Review of Income and Wealth, 60*(3), 525–541. https://doi.org/10.1111/roiw.12002

Keister, L. A. (2004). Race, family structure, and wealth. The effect of childhood family on adult asset ownership. *Sociological Perspectives, 47*(2), 161–187. https://doi.org/10.1525/sop.2004.47.2.161

Keister, L. A., & Moller, S. (2000). Wealth inequality in the United States. *Annual Review of Sociology, 26*(1), 63–81. https://doi.org/10.1146/annurev.soc.26.1.63

Keister, L. A., Vallejo, J. A., & Borelli, E. P. (2015). Mexican American mobility: Early life processes and adult wealth ownership. *Social Forces, 93*(3), 1015–1046. https://doi.org/10.1093/sf/sou102

Kelly, A., Lindo, J. M., & Packham, A. (2020). The power of the IUD: Effects of expanding access to contraception through Title X clinics. *Journal of Public Economics, 192*(C), 104288. https://doi.org/10.1016/j.jpubeco.2020.104288

Kelty, R., Kleykamp, M., & Segal, D. R. (2010). The military and the transition to adulthood. *The Future of Children, 20*(1), 181–207. https://doi.org/10.1353/foc.0.0045

Kemple, J. J., & Willner, C. J. (2008). *Career academies: Long-term impacts on labor market outcomes, educational attainment, and transitions to adulthood.* MDRC. https://www.mdrc.org/sites/default/files/full_50.pdf

Kiernan, K. E., & Mensah, F. K. (2011). Poverty, family resources, and children's early educational attainment: The mediating role of parenting. *British Educational Research Journal, 37*(2), 317–336. https://doi.org/10.1080/01411921003596911

Killewald, A., & Bryan, B. (2016). Does your home make you wealthy? *The Russell Sage Foundation Journal of the Social Sciences, 2*(6), 110–128. https://doi.org/10.7758/RSF.2016.2.6.06

___. (2018). Falling behind: The role of inter- and intragenerational processes in widening racial and ethnic wealth gaps through early and middle adulthood. *Social Forces, 97*(2), 705–740. https://doi.org/10.1093/sf/soy060

Killewald, A., Pfeffer, F. T., & Schachner, J. N. (2017). Wealth inequality and accumulation. *Annual Review of Sociology, 43*, 379–404. https://doi.org/10.1146/annurev-soc-060116-053331

Kim, C., & Tamborini, C. R. (2019). Are they still worth it? The long-run earnings benefits of an associate degree, vocational diploma or certificate, and some college. *RSF: The Russell Sage Foundation Journal of the Social Sciences, 5*(3), 64–85. https://doi.org/10.7758/rsf.2019.5.3.04

Kiviat, B. (2019). The moral limits of predictive practices: The case of credit-based insurance scores. *American Sociological Review, 84*(6), 1134–1158. https://doi.org/10.1177/0003122419884917

Kleykamp, M. (2009). A great place to start? The effect of prior military service on hiring. *Armed Forces & Society, 35*(2), 266–285. https://doi.org/10.1177/0095327X07308631

___. (2013). Labor market outcomes among veterans and military spouses. In J. M. Wilmoth & A. S. London (Eds.), *Life course perspectives on military service* (pp. 144–164). Routledge.

Kline, P., & Moretti, E. (2014). Local economic development, agglomeration economies, and the big push: 100 years of evidence from the Tennessee valley authority. *The Quarterly Journal of Economics*, 129(1), 275–331. https://doi.org/10.1093/qje/qjt034

Kline, P., & Walters, C. R. (2016). Evaluating public programs with close substitutes: The case of head start. *The Quarterly Journal of Economics*, 131(4), 1795–1848. https://doi.org/10.1093/qje/qjw027

Kling, J. R., Liebman, J. B., & Katz, L. F. (2005). *Experimental analysis of neighborhood effects* (NBER Working Paper No. 11577). National Bureau of Economic Research. https://www.nber.org/system/files/working_papers/w11577/w11577.pdf

Kong, J., Riser, Q., Cancian, M., & Meyer, D. R. (2024). The long-term effects of formal child support. *Journal of Marriage and Family*, 86(4), 1034–1052. https://doi.org/10.1111/jomf.12998

Kost, K., & Lindberg, L. (2015). Pregnancy intentions, maternal behaviors, and infant health: Investigating relationships with new measures and propensity score analysis. *Demography*, 52(1), 83–111. https://doi.org/10.1007/s13524-014-0359-9

Kost, K., & Zolna, M. (2019). Challenging unintended pregnancy as an indicator of reproductive autonomy: A response. *Contraception*, 100(1), 5–9. https://doi.org/10.1016/j.contraception.2019.04.010

Kost, K., Zolna, M., & Murro, R. (2023). Pregnancies in the United States by desire for pregnancy: Estimates for 2009, 2011, 2013, and 2015. *Demography*, 60(3), 837–863. https://doi.org/10.1215/00703370-10690005

Krause, E., & Reeves, R. V. (2017). *Rural dreams: Upward mobility in America's countryside*. Center on Children and Families at Brookings Institution. https://www.brookings.edu/wp-content/uploads/2017/08/es_20170905_ruralmobility.pdf

Krieger, N. (2011). *Epidemiology and the people's health: Theory and context*. Oxford University Press.

Krueger, A. (2012, January 12). *The rise and consequences of inequality* [Paper Presentation]. The Center for American Progress. https://www.americanprogress.org/events/the-rise-and-consequences-of-inequality/

Kubisch, A. C., Auspos, P., Brown, P., & Dewar, T. (2010). Community change initiatives from 1990–2010: Accomplishments and implications for future work. *Community Investments*, 22(1), 8–12. https://www.frbsf.org/community-development/wp-content/uploads/sites/3/A_Kubisch.pdf

Labaree, D. F. (2017). *A perfect mess: The unlikely ascendancy of American higher education*. University of Chicago Press.

LaBriola, J. (2024). Housing market appreciation and the White-Black wealth gap. *Social Problems*, spae030. https://doi.org/10.1093/socpro/spae030

Ladd, H. F. (1994). Spatially targeted economic development strategies: Do they work? *Cityscape: A Journal of Policy Development and Research*, 1(1), 193–218. https://www.jstor.org/stable/pdf/20868371.pdf

LaLonde, R. J., Marschke, G., & Troske, K. (1996). Using longitudinal data on establishments to analyze the effects of union organizing campaigns in the United States. *Annals of Economics and Statistics*, 41–42, 155–185. https://gattonweb.uky.edu/faculty/Troske/My%20published%20papers/lalonde_marschke_troske_vol4142-08.pdf

Lareau, A. (2002). Invisible inequality: Social class and childrearing in Black families and White families. *American Sociological Review*, 67(5), 747–776. https://doi.org/10.1177/000312240206700507

———. (2011). *Unequal childhoods: Class, race, and family life*. University of California Press.

Lareau, A., & Goyette, K. (Eds.). (2014). *Choosing homes, choosing schools*. Russell Sage Foundation.

Lavy, V., & Schlosser, A. (2011). Mechanisms and impacts of gender peer effects at school. *American Economic Journal: Applied Economics*, 3(2), 1–33. https://doi.org/10.1257/app.3.2.1

Lea, S. E. G., Mewse, A. J., & Wrapson, W. (2012). The psychology of debt in poor households in Britain. In R. Brubaker, R. M. Lawless, & C. J. Tabb (Eds.), *A debtor world: Interdisciplinary perspectives on debt* (pp. 151–166). Oxford University Press.

Lederman, D. (2011, August 1). The number of colleges continues to shrink. *Inside Higher Ed.*

Lee, C.-I., & Solon, G. (2009). Trends in intergenerational income mobility. *Review of Economics and Statistics*, 91(4), 766–772. https://doi.org/10.1162/rest.91.4.766

Lee, H. (2024). How does structural racism operate (in) the contemporary U.S. criminal justice system? *Annual Review of Criminology*, 7, 233–255. https://doi.org/10.1146/annurev-criminol-022422-015019

Lee, J. C., & Staff, J. (2007). When work matters: The varying impact of work intensity on high school dropout. *Sociology of Education*, 80(2), 158–178. https://doi.org/10.1177/003804070708000204

Lehmann, W. (2014). Habitus transformation and hidden injuries: Successful working-class university students. *Sociology of Education*, 87(1), 1–15. https://doi.org/10.1177/0038040713498777

Lens, M. C. (2022). Zoning, land use, and the reproduction of urban inequality. *Annual Review of Sociology*, 48(1), 421–439. https://doi.org/10.1146/annurev-soc-030420-122027

Lersch, P. M., Longmuir, M., & Schnitzlein, D. D. (2024). Intergenerational persistence of wealth. In E. Kilpi-Jakonen, J. Blanden, J. Erola, & L. Macmillan (Eds.), *Research handbook on intergenerational inequality* (pp. 86–99). Edward Elgar Publishing.

Levine, P., Staiger, D., Kane, T., & Zimmerman, D. (1999). Roe v Wade and American fertility. *American Journal of Public Health*, 89(2), 199–203. https://doi.org/10.2105/ajph.89.2.199

Limberg, J., & Seelkopf, L. (2022). The historical origins of wealth taxation. *Journal of European Public Policy*, 29(5), 670–688. https://doi.org/10.1080/13501763.2021.1992486

Lindo, J. M., & Packham, A. (2017). How much can expanding access to long-acting reversible contraceptives reduce teen birth rates? *American Economic Journal: Economic Policy*, 9(3), 348–376. https://doi.org/10.1257/pol.20160039

Lipset, S. M., & Bendix, R. (1952). Social mobility and occupational career patterns I. Stability of jobholding. *American Journal of Sociology*, 57(4), 366–374. https://www.journals.uchicago.edu/doi/abs/10.1086/220972

Livingston, G. (2016). *Births outside of marriage decline for immigrant women*. Pew Research Center. https://www.pewresearch.org/social-trends/wp-content/uploads/sites/3/2016/10/ST_2016.10.26_fertility_FINAL.pdf

Lochner, L. (2011). Nonproduction benefits of education: Crime, health, and good citizenship. In E. A. Hanushek, S. Machin, & L. Woessmann (Eds.), *Handbook of the economics of education* (Vol. 4, pp. 183–282). Elsevier Science.

Lochner, L., & Monge-Naranjo, A. (2012). Credit constraints in education. *Annual Review of Economics*, 4(1), 225–256. https://doi.org/10.1146/annurev-economics-080511-110920

___. (2016). *Student loans and repayment*. EconPapers. Elsevier. https://econpapers.repec.org/bookchap/eeeeduchp/v_3a5_3ay_3a2016_3ai_3ac_3ap_3a397-478.htm

Loibl, C., Moulton, S., Haurin, D., & Edmunds, C. (2022). The role of consumer and mortgage debt for financial stress. *Aging & Mental Health*, 26(1), 116–129. https://doi.org/10.1080/13607863.2020.1843000

Long, J., & Ferrie, J. (2013). Intergenerational occupational mobility in Great Britain and the United States since 1850. *American Economic Review*, 103(4), 1109–1137. https://doi.org/10.1257/aer.103.4.1109

Looney, A., & Yannelis, C. (2024). *What went wrong with federal student loans?* (NBER Working Paper No. 32469). National Bureau of Economic Research. https://www.nber.org/papers/w32469

Love, J. M., Chazan-Cohen, R., Raikes, H., & Brooks-Gunn, J. (2013). What makes a difference: Early Head Start evaluation findings in a developmental context. *Monographs of the Society for Research in Child Development, 78*(1), 1–173. https://doi.org/10.1111/j.1540-5834.2012.00699.x

Lovenheim, M. F. (2011). The effect of liquid housing wealth on college enrollment. *Journal of Labor Economics, 29*(4), 741–71. http://dx.doi.org/10.1086/660775

Lovenheim, M. F., & Smith, J. (2023). Returns to different postsecondary investments: Institution type, academic programs, and credentials. In E. A. Hanushek, S. Manchin, & L. Woesmann (Eds.), *Handbook of the economics of education* (pp. 187–313). Elsevier.

Lubell, J., Gubits, D., McInnis, D., Fisman, L., Paulen, L., & Levy, D. (2023). *Research design, data collection, and analysis plan (RDDCAP): Evaluation of the community choice demonstration*. U.S. Department of Housing and Urban Development, Office of Policy Development and Research. https://www.huduser.gov/portal/portal/sites/default/files/pdf/Research-Design-Data-Collection-and-Analysis-Plan.pdf

Ludwig, J., Duncan, G. J., Gennetian, L. A., Katz, L. F., Kessler, R. C., Kling, J. R., & Sanbonmatsu, L. (2012). Neighborhood effects on the long-term well-being of low-income adults. *Science, 337*(6101), 1505–1510. https://doi.org/10.1126/science.1224648

Ludwig, J., Jacob, B., Duncan, G., Rosenbaum, J., & Johnson, M. (2010). *Neighborhood effects on low-income families: Evidence from a housing-voucher lottery in Chicago* (Working Paper). University of Chicago.

Ludwig, J., Sanbonmatsu, L., Gennetian, L., Adam, E., Duncan, G., Katz, L. F., Kessler, R. C., Kling, J. R., Lindau, S. T., Whitaker, R. C., & McDade, T. W. (2011). Neighborhoods, obesity, and diabetes—A randomized social experiment. *New England Journal of Medicine, 365*(16), 1509–1519. https://doi.org/10.1056/NEJMsa1103216

Lundberg, S. (2020). Educational gender gaps. *Southern Economic Journal, 87*(2), 416–439. https://doi.org/10.1002/soej.12460

Lundquist, E., Hsueh, J., Lowenstein, A. E., Faucetta, K., Gubits, D., Michalopoulos, C., & Knox, V. (2014). *A family-strengthening program for low-income families: Final impacts from the supporting healthy marriage evaluation* (OPRE Report No. 2014-09A). Office of Planning, Research and Evaluation, Administration for Children and Families, U.S. Department of Health and Human Services. https://www.acf.hhs.gov/sites/default/files/documents/opre/shm2013_30_month_impact_reporttrev2.pdf

MacLeod, J. (1987). *Ain't no makin' it: Aspirations and attainment in a low-income neighborhood*. Westview Press.

Maddow-Zimet, I., & Kost, K. (2020). Effect of changes in response options on reported pregnancy intentions: A natural experiment in the United States. *Public Health Reports, 135*(3), 354–363. https://doi.org/10.1177/0033354920914344

Madigan, S., Prime, H., Graham, S. A., Rodrigues, M., Anderson, N., Khoury, J., & Jenkins, J. M. (2019). Parenting behavior and child language: A meta-analysis. *Pediatrics, 144*(4), e20183556. https://doi.org/10.1542/peds.2018-3556

Majumder, M. A. (2016). The impact of parenting style on children's educational outcomes in the United States. *Journal of Family and Economic Issues, 37*(1), 89–98. https://doi.org/10.1007/s10834-015-9444-5

Manduca, R., Hell, M., Adermon, A., Blanden, J., Bratberg, E., Gielen, A. C., Van Kippersluis, H., Lee, K. B., Machin, S., Munk, M. D., Nybom, M., Ostrovsky, Y., Rahman, S., & Sirniö, O. (2024). Measuring absolute income mobility: Lessons from North America and Europe. *American Economic Journal: Applied Economics, 16*(2), 1–30. https://doi.org/10.1257/app.20210137

Mann, O., Edin, K. J., & Schaefer, H. L. (2024). Understanding the relationship between intergenerational mobility and community violence. *Proceedings of the National Academy of Sciences, 121*(33), e2309066121. https://doi.org/10.1073/pnas.2309066121

Mare, R. D. (2011). A multigenerational view of inequality. *Demography, 48*(1), 1–23. https://doi.org/10.1007/s13524-011-0014-7

___. (2014). Multigenerational aspects of social stratification: Issues for further research. *Research in Social Stratification and Mobility, 35*, 121–128. https://doi.org/10.1016/j.rssm.2014.01.004

Marks, R., Jones, N., & Battle, K. (2024, April 8). What updates to OMB's race/ethnicity standards mean for the Census Bureau. *Random Samplings Blog*. https://www.census.gov/newsroom/blogs/random-samplings/2024/04/updates-race-ethnicity-standards.html

Marseille, E., Mirzazadeh, A., Biggs, M. A., Miller, M. P., Horvath, H., Lightfoot, M., Malekinejad, M., & Kahn, J. G. (2018). Effectiveness of school-based teen pregnancy prevention programs in the USA: A systematic review and meta-analysis. *Prevention Science, 19*(4), 468–489. https://doi.org/10.1007/s11121-017-0861-6

Marshall, V. W., & Mueller. M. M. (2003). Theoretical roots of the life-course perspective. In W. R. Heinz & V. W. Marshall (Eds.), *Social dynamics of the life course* (pp. 3–32). Aldine de Gruyter.

Massey, D. S., Albright, L., Casciano, R., Derickson, E., & Kinsey, D. (2013). *Climbing Mount Laurel: The struggle for affordable housing and social mobility in an American suburb*. Princeton University Press.

Massey, D. S., & Denton, N. (1993). *American apartheid: Segregation and the making of the underclass*. Harvard University Press.

Masud, H., Ahmad, M. S., Cho, K. W., & Fakhr, Z. (2019). Parenting styles and aggression among young adolescents: A systematic review of literature. *Community Mental Health Journal, 55*(6), 1015–1030. https://doi.org/10.1007/s10597-019-00400-0

Masud, H., Thurasamy, R., & Ahmad, M. S. (2015). Parenting styles and academic achievement of young adolescents: A systematic literature review. *Quality & Quantity: International Journal of Methodology, 49*(6), 2411–2433. https://doi.org/10.1007/s11135-014-0120-x

Mayer, E. J. (2021). Big banks, household credit access, and intergenerational economic mobility. *Journal of Financial and Quantitative Analysis, 59*(6), 2933–2969. https://doi.org/10.1017/S0022109023001114

Mayer, S. E., & Lopoo, L. M. (2005). Has the intergenerational transmission of economic status changed? *Journal of Human Resources, 40*(1), 169–185. https://www.jstor.org/stable/4129569

Mazumder, B. (2018). Intergenerational mobility in the United States: What we have learned from the PSID. *The Annals of the American Academy of Political and Social Science, 680*(1), 213–234. https://doi.org/10.1177/0002716218794129

McCabe, B. J. (2016). *No place like home: Wealth, community, and the politics of homeownership*. Oxford University Press.

McCann, A., Walker, A. S., Sasani, A., Johnston, T., Buchanan, L., & Huang, J. (2024, October 1). Tracking the states where abortion is now banned. *The New York Times*. https://www.nytimes.com/interactive/2024/us/abortion-laws-roe-v-wade.html

McCloud, L., & Dwyer, R. E. (2011). The fragile American: Hardship and financial troubles in the 21st century. *The Sociological Quarterly, 52*(1), 13–35. https://doi.org/10.1111/j.1533-8525.2010.01197.x

McDonald, M., Martinez, S., Selekman, R., & Abendroth, E. (2024). *Factors that impact the child support program's role in reducing child poverty: Convening summary* [Issue Brief]. Office of the Assistant Secretary for Planning and Evaluation. https://aspe.hhs.gov/sites/default/files/documents/d3636e92120856f652a0d796d29a886d/factors-impact-child-support-programs.pdf

McInnis, N. S., Michelmore, K., & Pilkauskas, N. (2023). *The intergenerational transmission of poverty and public assistance: Evidence from the earned income tax credit* (NBER Working Paper No. 31429). National Bureau of Economic Research. https://doi.org/10.3386/w31429

McLanahan, S. (2004). Diverging destinies: How children are faring under the second demographic transition. *Demography*, *41*(4), 607–627. https://doi.org/10.1353/dem.2004.0033

McLanahan, S., & Jacobsen, W. (2014). Diverging destinies revisited. In P. Amato, A. Booth, S. McHale, & J. Van Hook (Eds.), *Families in an era of increasing inequality: Diverging destinies* (pp. 3–23). Springer International Publishing.

McLanahan, S., & Sandefur, G. (1994). *Growing up with a single parent: What hurts, what helps*. Harvard University Press.

McLanahan, S., & Sawhill, I. (2015). Marriage and child wellbeing revisited: Introducing the issue. *The Future of Children*, *25*(2), 3–9. https://www.jstor.org/stable/43581969

McLanahan, S., Tach, L., & Schneider, D. (2013). The causal effects of father absence. *Annual Review of Sociology*, *39*(1), 399–427. https://doi.org/10.1146/annurev-soc-071312-145704

Mehrotra, A., Pang, D., Zhu, J., Choi, J. H., & Ratcliffe, J. (2024). *Evidence of disparities in access to mortgage credit*. The Urban Institute. https://www.urban.org/research/publication/evidence-disparities-access-mortgage-credit

Mendenhall, R., DeLuca, S., & Duncan, G. (2006). Neighborhood resources, racial segregation, and economic mobility: Results from the Gautreaux program. *Social Science Research*, *35*(4), 892–923. https://doi.org/10.1016/j.ssresearch.2005.06.007

Meschede, T., Eden, M., Jain, S., Jee, E., Miles, B., Martinez, M., Stewart, S., Jacob, J., & Madison, M. (2022). *Final report from our GI Bill study* [IERE Research Brief]. The Heller School for Social Policy and Management. https://heller.brandeis.edu/iere/pdfs/racial-wealth-equity/racial-wealth-gap/gi-bill-final-report.pdf

Meursault, V., Moulton, D., Santucci, L., & Schor, N. (2022). *One threshold doesn't fit all: Tailoring machine learning predictions of consumer default for lower-income areas* (Working Paper No. 22-39). Federal Reserve Bank of Philadelphia. https://doi.org/10.21799/frbp.wp.2022.39

Miller, S., & Wherry, L. R. (2019). The long-term effects of early life Medicaid coverage. *Journal of Human Resources*, *54*(3), 785–824. https://doi.org/10.3368/jhr.54.3.0816.8173R1

Miller, S., Wherry, L. R., & Foster, D. G. (2020). *The economic consequences of being denied an abortion* (NBER Working Paper No. 26662). National Bureau of Economic Research. https://doi.org/10.3386/w26662

Mills, C. K, Landau, R., Rodriguez, B., & Scally, J. (2022). *The state of low-income America: Credit access & debt payment*. Federal Reserve Bank of New York. https://www.newyorkfed.org/medialibrary/media/press/the-state-of-low-income-america-credit-access-debt-payment-march-2022

Mills, C. W. (1997). *The racial contract*. Cornell University Press.

Mitchell, C., McLanahan, S., Notterman, D., Hobcraft, J., Brooks-Gunn, J., & Garfinkel, I. (2015). Family structure instability, genetic sensitivity, and child well-being. *American Journal of Sociology*, *120*(4), 1195–1225. https://doi.org/10.1086/680681

Mitnik, P. A., Bryant, V. L., & Grusky, D. B. (2023). A very uneven playing field: Economic mobility in the United States. *American Journal of Sociology*, *129*(4), 1216–1276. https://doi.org/10.1086/728737

Modigliani, F. (1988). The role of intergenerational transfers and life cycle saving in the accumulation of wealth. *Journal of Economic Perspectives*, *2*(2), 15–40. https://doi.org/10.1257/jep.2.2.15

Mohai, P., Pellow, D., & Roberts, J. T. (2009). Environmental justice. *Annual Review of Environment and Resources*, *34*, 405–430. https://doi.org/10.1146/annurev-environ-082508-094348

Mohllajee, M. P., Curtis, K. M., Morrow, B., & Marchbanks, P. A. (2007). Pregnancy intention and its relationship to birth and maternal outcomes. *Obstetrics & Gynecology*, *109*(3), 678–686. https://doi.org/10.1097/01.AOG.0000255666.78427.c5

Mollborn, S., Fomby, P., & Dennis, J. A. (2011). Who matters for children's early development? Race/ethnicity and extended household structures in the United States. *Child Indicators Research*, *4*(3), 389–411. https://doi.org/10.1007/s12187-010-9090-2

Monteiro, J., & Rocha, R. (2017). Drug battles and school achievement: Evidence from Rio de Janeiro's favelas. *Review of Economics and Statistics, 99*(2), 213–228. https://doi.org/10.1162/REST_a_00628

Moore, Q., Avellar, S., Patnaik, A., Covington, R., & Wu, A. (2018). *Parents and children together: Effects of two healthy marriage programs for low-income couples* (OPRE Report No. 2018-58). Office of Planning, Research and Evaluation, Administration for Children and Families, U.S. Department of Health and Human Services. https://www.acf.hhs.gov/sites/default/files/documents/opre/pact_hm_impacts_to_opre_b508.pdf

Moran, K. M., Turiano, N. A., & Gentzler, A. L. (2018). Parental warmth during childhood predicts coping and well-being in adulthood. *Journal of Family Psychology, 32*(5), 610–621. https://doi.org/10.1037/fam0000401

Morduch, J., & Schneider, R. (2017). *The financial diaries: How American families cope in a world of uncertainty*. Princeton University Press.

Morris, A. S., Criss, M. M., Silk, J. S., & Houltberg, B. J. (2017). The impact of parenting on emotion regulation during childhood and adolescence. *Child Development Perspectives, 11*(4), 233–238. https://doi.org/10.1111/cdep.12238

Morrissey, T. W. (2017). Child care and parent labor force participation: A review of the research literature. *Review of Economics of the Households, 15*(1), 1–24. https://doi.org/10.1007/s11150-016-9331-3

Mortimer, J. T. (2010). The benefits and risks of adolescent employment. *The Prevention Researcher, 17*(2), 8–11. https://www.ncbi.nlm.nih.gov/pmc/articles/PMC2936460/pdf/nihms220511.pdf

Mosher, W. D., Jones, J., & Abma, J. C. (2012). Intended and unintended births in the United States: 1982–2010. *National Health Statistics Reports, 24*(55), 1–28. https://pubmed.ncbi.nlm.nih.gov/23115878/

Moullin, S., Waldfogel, J., & Washbrook, E. (2018). Parent-child attachment as a mechanism of intergenerational (dis) advantage. *Families, Relationships, and Societies, 7*(2), 265–284. https://doi.org/10.1332/204674317X15071998786492

Moulton, S. (2022). Researching homeownership inequalities: A life-cycle perspective. *Cityscape: A Journal of Policy Development and Research, 24*(2), 153–164. https://www.jstor.org/stable/48680623?seq=1

Moulton, S., Rhodes, A., Haurin, D., & Loibl, C. (2022). Managing the onset of a new disease in older age: Housing wealth, mortgage borrowing, and medication adherence. *Social Science & Medicine, 314*, 115437. https://doi.org/10.1016/j.socscimed.2022.115437

Mountjoy, J. (2022). Community colleges and upward mobility. *American Economic Review, 112*(8), 2580–2630. https://doi.org/10.1257/aer.20181756

___. (2024). *Marginal returns to public universities* (NBER Working Paper No. 32996). National Bureau of Economic Research. https://www.nber.org/papers/w32996

Mouw, T., & Kalleberg, A. L. (2010). Occupations and the structure of wage inequality in the United States, 1980s to 2000s. *American Sociological Review, 75*(3), 402–431. https://doi.org/10.1177/0003122410363564

Mueser, P., Troske, K., & Orrell, B. (2023). *Government-supported job training in the U.S.: Paths toward reforming the workforce*. American Enterprise Institute. https://www.aei.org/wp-content/uploads/2023/07/Government-Supported-Job-Training-in-the-US-Paths-Toward-Reforming-the-Workforce.pdf?x85095

Muller, C., Sampson, R. J., & Winter, A. S. (2018). Environmental inequality: The social causes and consequences of lead exposure. *Annual Review of Sociology, 44*(1), 263–282. https://doi.org/10.1146/annurev-soc-073117-041222

Mulligan, C. B. (1997). *Parental priorities and economic inequality*. University of Chicago Press.

Nadworny, E. (2023, September 28). Feds offer students new protections against programs that lead to high debt, low pay. *National Public Radio*. https://www.nhpr.org/2023-09-28/feds-offer-students-new-protections-against-programs-that-lead-to-high-debt-low-pay

Nagaraj, A., & Tranchero, M. (2023). *How does data access shape science? Evidence from the impact of U.S. Census's research data centers on economics research* (NBER Working Paper No. 31372). National Bureau of Economic Research. https://www.nber.org/system/files/working_papers/w31372/w31372.pdf

Nam, C. B., & Powers, M. G. (1968). Changes in the relative status level of workers in the United States, 1950–1960. *Social Forces*, 47(2), 158–170. https://www.academia.edu/880947/Changes_in_the_relative_status_level_of_workers_in_the_United_States_1950_60

Narayan, A., van der Weide, R., Cojocaru, A., Lakner, C., Redaelli, S., Mahler, D. G., Ramasubbaiah, R. G. N., & Thewissen, S. (2018). *Fair progress? Economic mobility across generations around the world*. World Bank. https://hdl.handle.net/10986/28428

National Academies of Sciences, Engineering, and Medicine (National Academies). (2000). *From neurons to neighborhoods: The science of early childhood development*. The National Academies Press.

———. (2015). *The integration of immigrants into American society*. The National Academies Press.

———. (2019). *Strengthening the military family readiness system for a changing American society*. The National Academies Press.

———. (2023a). *Closing the opportunity gap for young children*. The National Academies Press.

———. (2023b). *Reducing intergenerational poverty*. The National Academies Press.

———. (2023c). *An updated measure of poverty: (Re)Drawing the line*. The National Academies Press.

———. (2023d). *Toward a 21st century national data infrastructure: Enhancing survey programs by using multiple data sources*. The National Academies Press.

———. (2024a). *Creating an integrated system of data and statistics on household income, consumption, and wealth: Time to build*. The National Academies Press.

———. (2024b). *Toward a 21st century national data infrastructure: Managing privacy and confidentiality risks with blended data*. The National Academies Press.

National Center for Education Statistics (NCES). (2022). *Graduation rate from first institution attended within 150 percent of normal time for first-time, full-time degree/certificate-seeking students at 2-year postsecondary institutions, by race/ethnicity, sex, and control of institution: Selected cohort entry years, 2000 through 2018*. Digest of Education Statistics, Table 326.20. https://nces.ed.gov/programs/digest/d22/tables/dt22_326.20.asp?current=yes

———. (2023). *Postsecondary institution expenses*. Condition of Education. https://nces.ed.gov/programs/coe/indicator/cue/postsecondary-institution-expense

National Research Council. (2004). *Measuring racial discrimination*. R. M. Blank, M. Dabady, & C. F. Citro (Eds.). Panel on Methods for Assessing Discrimination, Committee on National Statistics, Division of Behavioral and Social Sciences and Education. The National Academies Press. https://doi.org/10.17226/10887

Neal, D., & Johnson, W. R. (1996). The role of premarket factors in black-white wage differences. *Journal of Political Economy*, 104(5), 869–895. https://doi.org/10.1086/262045

Neckerman, K. M., & Torche, F. (2007). Inequality: Causes and consequences. *Annual Review of Sociology*, 33(1), 335–357. https://doi.org/10.1146/annurev.soc.33.040406.131755

Nekoei, A., & Seim, D. (2023). How do inheritances shape wealth inequality? Theory and evidence from Sweden. *The Review of Economic Studies*, 90(1), 463–498. https://doi.org/10.1093/restud/rdac016

Nepomnyaschy, L. (2007). Child support and father-child contact: Testing reciprocal pathways. *Demography*, 44(1), 93–112. https://www.jstor.org/stable/4137223

Nepomnyaschy, L., Emory, A. D., Eickmeyer, K. J., Waller, M. R., & Miller, D. P. (2021). Parental debt and child well-being: What type of debt matters for child outcomes? *The Russell Sage Foundation Journal of the Social Sciences*, 7(3), 122–151. https://doi.org/10.7758/RSF.2021.7.3.06

Nepomnyaschy, L., Thomas, M., Haralampoudis, A., & Jin, H. (2022). Nonresident fathers and the economic precarity of their children. *The Annals of the American Academy of Political and Social Science*, 702(1), 78–96. https://doi.org/10.1177/00027162221119348

Neumark, D. (2018). Experimental research on labor market discrimination. *Journal of Economic Literature*, 56(3), 799–866. https://doi.org/10.1257/jel.20161309

Neumark, D., Salas, J. M. I., & Wascher, W. (2014). Revisiting the minimum wage employment debate: Throwing out the baby with the bathwater. *Industrial and Labor Relations Review*, 67(3), 608–648. https://journals.sagepub.com/doi/epdf/10.1177/001979391406 70S307?src=getftr&utm_source=wiley&getft_integrator=wiley

Newman, K. S. (1999). *Falling from grace: Downward mobility in the age of affluence*. University of California Press.

Noghanibehambari, H. (2022). Intergenerational health effects of Medicaid. *Economics & Human Biology*, 45(C), 101114. https://doi.org/10.1016/j.ehb.2022.101114

Norvilitis, J. M., Merwin, M. M., Osberg, T. M., Roehling, P. V., Young, P., & Kamas, M. M. (2006). Personality factors, money attitudes, financial knowledge, and credit-card debt in college students. *Journal of Applied Social Psychology*, 36(6), 1395–1413. https://doi.org/10.1111/j.0021-9029.2006.00065.x

Nybom, M., & Stuhler, J. (2024). Interpreting trends in intergenerational mobility. *Journal of Political Economy*, 132(8), 2531–2570. https://doi.org/10.1086/729582

Oakley, D., & Tsao, H.-S. (2006). A new way of revitalizing distressed urban communities? Assessing the impact of the federal empowerment zone program. *Journal of Urban Affairs*, 28(5), 443–471. https://doi.org/10.1111/j.1467-9906.2006.00309.x

O'Brien, R., Neman, T., Seltzer, N., Evans, L., & Venkataramani, A. (2020). Structural racism, economic opportunity, and racial health disparities: Evidence from U.S. counties. *SSM-Population Health*, 11, 100564. https://doi.org/10.1016/j.ssmph.2020.100564

O'Brien, R. L., & Robertson, C. L. (2018). Early-life Medicaid coverage and intergenerational economic mobility. *Journal of Health and Social Behavior*, 59(2), 300–315. https://doi.org/10.1177/0022146518771910

O'Connor, A. (1995). Evaluating comprehensive community initiatives: A view from history. In J. P. Connell, A. C. Kubisch, L. B. Schorr, & C. H. Weiss (Eds.), *New approaches to evaluating community initiatives: Concepts, methods, and contexts* (pp. 23–63). Aspen Institute.

___. (1999). Swimming against the tide: A brief history of federal policy in poor communities. In R. F. Ferguson & W. T. Dickens (Eds.), *Urban problems and community development* (pp. 77–138). Brookings Institution Press.

Ogg, J., & Anthony, C. J. (2020). Process and context: Longitudinal effects of the interactions between parental involvement, parental warmth, and SES on academic achievement. *Journal of School Psychology*, 78, 96–114. https://doi.org/10.1016/j.jsp.2019.11.004

Oh, B., Tilbrook, N., & Shifrer, D. (2024). Shifting tides: The evolution of racial inequality in higher education from the 1980s through the 2010s. *Socius: Sociological Research for a Dynamic World*, 10. https://doi.org/10.1177/23780231231225578

Oliver, M. L., & Shapiro, T. M. (2006). *Black wealth, White wealth. A new perspective on racial inequality* (2nd ed.). Routledge.

Oreopoulos, P., & Salvanes, K. G. (2011). Priceless: The nonpecuniary benefits of schooling. *Journal of Economic Perspectives*, 25(1), 159–184. https://doi.org/10.1257/jep.25.1.159

Organisation for Economic Co-operation and Development. (2021). *Measuring what matters to child well-being and policies*.

Osborne, C., & McLanahan, S. (2007). Partnership instability and child well-being. *Journal of Marriage and Family*, 69(4), 1065–1083. https://doi.org/10.1111/j.1741-3737.2007.00431.x

Owens, A. (2017). Racial residential segregation of school-age children and adults: The role of schooling as a segregating force. *The Russell Sage Foundation Journal of the Social Sciences*, 3(2), 263–280. https://doi.org/10.7758/rsf.2017.3.2.03

Owens, A., & Smith, R. B. (2023). Producing affordable housing in higher-opportunity neighborhoods: Incentives in California's LIHTC program. *Journal of Urban Affairs*, 1–29. https://doi.org/10.1080/07352166.2023.2288582

Pager, D., & Shepherd, H. (2008). The sociology of discrimination: Racial discrimination in employment, housing, credit, and consumer markets. *Annual Review of Sociology*, 34, 181–209. https://doi.org/10.1146/annurev.soc.33.040406.131740

Parman, J. (2011). American mobility and the expansion of public education. *The Journal of Economic History*, 71(1), 105–132. https://doi.org/10.1017/S0022050711000040

Parolin, Z., Pintro-Schmitt, R., Esping-Andersen, G., & Fallesen, P. (2024). Intergenerational persistence of poverty in five high-income countries. *Nature Human Behavior*, 9, 254–267. https://doi.org/10.1038/s41562-024-02029-w

Pastor, M., & Turner, M. A. (2010, March). *Reducing poverty and economic distress after ARRA: Potential roles for place-conscious strategies*. Paper Prepared for the Georgetown University and Urban Institute Conference on Reducing Poverty and Economic Distress after ARRA. https://www.urban.org/sites/default/files/publication/28516/412067-Reducing-Poverty-and-Economic-Distress-after-ARRA.PDF

Pattillo, M. (1999). *Black picket fences: Privilege and peril among the Black middle class*. University of Chicago Press.

Pender, J., & Reeder, R. (2011). *Impact of regional approaches to rural development: Initial evidence on the delta regional authority* (Economic Research Service Report No. 119). U.S. Department of Agriculture. https://www.ers.usda.gov/webdocs/publications/44855/7407_err119.pdf

Persell, C. H., & Cookson, P. W., Jr. (1985). Chartering and bartering: Elite education and reproduction. *Social Problems*, 33(2), 114–129. https://doi.org/10.2307/800556

Peters, H. E. (1992). Patterns of intergenerational mobility in income and earnings. *Review of Economics and Statistics*, 74(3), 456–466. https://doi.org/10.2307/2109490

The Pew Charitable Trusts. (2012). *Economic mobility of the States*. https://www.pewtrusts.org/en/research-and-analysis/reports/0001/01/01/economic-mobility-of-the-states

———. (2019). *Two decades of change in federal and state higher education funding*. https://www.pewtrusts.org/en/research-and-analysis/issue-briefs/2019/10/two-decades-of-change-in-federal-and-state-higher-education-funding

Pfeffer, F. T. (2011). Status attainment and wealth in the United States and Germany. In T. Smeeding, R. Erikson, & M. Jäntti, M. (Eds.), *Persistence, privilege, and parenting* (pp. 109–137). Russell Sage Foundation.

———. (2014). Multigenerational approaches to social mobility. A multifaceted research agenda. *Research in Social Stratification and Mobility*, 35, 1–12. https://doi.org/10.1016/j.rssm.2014.01.001

———. (2018). Growing wealth gaps in education. *Demography*, 55(3), 1033–1068. https://doi.org/10.1007/s13524-018-0666-7

Pfeffer, F. T., & Hertel, F. R. (2015). How has educational expansion shaped social mobility trends in the United States? *Social Forces*, 94(1), 143–180. https://doi.org/10.1093/sf/sov045

Pfeffer, F. T., & Killewald, A. (2018). Generations of advantage. Multigenerational correlations in family wealth. *Social Forces*, 96(4), 1411–1442. https://doi.org/10.1093/sf/sox086

———. (2019). Intergenerational wealth mobility and racial inequality. *Socius: Sociological Research for a Dynamic World*, 5(2), 1–2. https://doi.org/10.1177/2378023119831799

Pfeffer, F. T., & Waitkus, N. (2021). The wealth inequality of nations. *American Sociological Review*, 86(4), 567–602. https://doi.org/10.1177/00031224211027800

Pierson, P. (1994). *Dismantling the welfare state: Reagan, Thatcher, and the politics of retrenchment*. Cambridge University Press.

———. (1996). The new politics of the welfare state. *World Politics*, 48(2), 143–179. https://doi.org/10.1353/wp.1996.0004

Pietila, A. (2010). *Not in my neighborhood: How bigotry shaped a great American city*. Chicago: Ivan R. Dee.
Piketty, T. (2014). *Capital in the twenty-first century*. Harvard University Press.
___. (2020). *Capital and ideology*. Harvard University Press.
Pilkauskas, N. V. (2012). Three-generation family households: Differences by family structure at birth. *Journal of Marriage and Family*, 74(5), 931–943. https://doi.org/10.1111/j.1741-3737.2012.01008.x
___. (2014). Living with a grandparent and parent in early childhood: Associations with school readiness and differences by demographic characteristics. *Developmental Psychology*, 50(12), 2587–2599. https://doi.org/10.1037/a0038179
Pilkauskas, N. V., & Cross, C. (2018). Beyond the nuclear family: Trends in children living in shared households. *Demography*, 55(6), 2283–2297. https://doi.org/10.1007/s13524-018-0719-y
Pirtle, W. N. L., & Wright, T. (2021). Structural gendered racism revealed in pandemic times: Intersectional approaches to understanding race and gender health inequities in COVID-19. *Gender & Society*, 35(2), 168–179. https://doi.org/10.1177/08912432211001302
Pollack, C. E., Blackford, A. L., Du, S., Deluca, S., Thornton, R. L. J., & Herring, B. (2019). Association of receipt of a housing voucher with subsequent hospital utilization and spending. *Journal of the American Medical Association*, 322(21), 2115–2124. https://doi.org/10.1001/jama.2019.17432
Pollack, C. E., Bozzi, D. G., Blackford, A. L., Deluca, S., Thornton, R. L. J., & Herring, B. (2023a). Using the moving to opportunity experiment to investigate the long-term impact of neighborhoods on healthcare use by specific clinical conditions and type of service. *Housing Policy Debate*, 33(1), 269–289. https://doi.org/10.1080/10511482.2021.1951804
Pollack, C. E., Roberts, L. C., Peng, R. D., Cimbolic, P., Judy, D., Balcer-Whaley, S., Grant, T., Rule, A., Deluca, S., Davis, M. F., Wright, R. J., Keet, C. A., & Matsui, E. C. (2023b). Association of a housing mobility program with childhood asthma symptoms and exacerbations. *Journal of the American Medical Association*, 329(19), 1671–1681. https://doi.org/10.1001/jama.2023.6488
Posselt, J. R., & Grodsky, E. (2017). Graduate education and social stratification. *Annual Review of Sociology*, 43(1), 353–378. https://doi.org/10.1146/annurev-soc-081715-074324
Potter, J. E., Stevenson, A. J., Coleman-Minahan, K., Hopkins, K., White, K., Baum, S. E., & Grossman, D. (2019). Challenging unintended pregnancy as an indicator of reproductive autonomy. *Contraception*, 100(1), 1–4. https://doi.org/10.1016/j.contraception.2019.02.005
Price, J., Buckles, K., Haws, A., & Wilbert, H. (2023). *The Census Tree, 1850-1860*. Inter-university Consortium for Political and Social Research. https://doi.org/10.3886/E193225V1
Price, J., Buckles, K., Van Leeuwen, J., & Riley, I. (2021). Combining family history and machine learning to link historical records: The Census Tree data set. *Explorations in Economic History*, 80(3), 101391. https://doi.org/10.1016/j.eeh.2021.101391
Provenzi, L., Brambilla, M., Scotto di Minico, G., Montirosso, R., & Borgatti, R. (2020). Maternal caregiving and DNA methylation in human infants and children: Systematic review. *Genes, Brain, and Behavior*, 19(3), e12616. https://doi.org/10.1111/gbb.12616
Puma, M., Bell, S., Cook, R., Heid, C., Shapiro, G., Broene, P., Jenkins, F., Fletcher, P., Quinn, L., Friedman, J., Ciarico, J., Rohacek, M., Adams, G., & Spier, E. (2010). *Head start impact study: Final report*. U.S. Department of Health and Human Services. https://eric.ed.gov/?id=ED507845
Putnam, R. D. (2000). *Bowling alone: The collapse and revival of American community*. Simon and Schuster.
Quillian, L., Lee, J. J., & Honoré, B. (2020). Racial discrimination in the U.S. housing and mortgage lending markets: A quantitative review of trends, 1976–2016. *Race and Social Problems*, 12(1), 13–28. https://doi.org/10.1007/s12552-019-09276-x

Randles, J. M. (2016). *Proposing prosperity? Marriage education policy and inequality in America*. Columbia University Press.

Rawls, J. (1971). *A theory of justice*. Harvard University Press.

Reading, R., & Reynolds, S. (2001). Debt, social disadvantage, and maternal depression. *Social Science & Medicine, 53*(4), 441–453. https://doi.org/10.1016/S0277-9536(00)00347-6

Ream, R. K., & Gottfried, M. A. (2019). Household wealth and adolescents' social-emotional functioning in schools. *Social Science Research, 83*, 102316. https://doi.org/10.1016/j.ssresearch.2019.06.007

Reardon, S. F., & Bischoff, K. (2011). Income inequality and income segregation. *American Journal of Sociology, 116*(4), 1092–1153. https://doi.org/10.1086/657114

Reber, S., & Smith, E. (2023). *College enrollment disparities: Understanding the role of academic preparation*. Center for Economic Security and Opportunity, Brookings Institution. https://www.brookings.edu/wp-content/uploads/2023/02/20230123_CCF_CollegeEnrollment_FINAL2.pdf

Reeves, R. V. (2018). *Dream hoarders: How the American upper middle class is leaving everyone else in the dust, why that is a problem, and what to do about it*. Brookings Institution Press.

Reeves, R. V., & Howard, K. (2013, September 9). *The parenting gap*. Center for Economic Security and Opportunity, Brookings Institution. https://www.brookings.edu/articles/the-parenting-gap/

Reichman, N. E., & Teitler, J. O. (2013). Lifecourse exposures and socioeconomic disparities in child health. In N. S. Landale, S. M. McHale, & A. Booth (Eds.), *Families and child health* (pp. 107–134). Springer.

Reichman, N. E., Teitler, J. O., Garfinkel, I., & McLanahan, S. S. (2001). Fragile families: Sample and design. *Children and Youth Services Review, 23*(4–5), 303–326. https://doi.org/10.1016/S0190-7409(01)00141-4

Reosti, A. (2021). The costs of seeking shelter for renters with discrediting background records. *City & Community, 20*(3), 235–259. https://doi.org/10.1177/15356841211012483

Rich, P., & Owens, A. (2023). Neighborhood-school structures: A new approach to the joint study of social contexts. *Annual Review of Sociology, 49*, 297–317. https://doi.org/10.1146/annurev-soc-031021-110311

Rigbi, O. (2013). The effects of usury laws: Evidence from the online loan market. *Review of Economics and Statistics, 95*(4), 1238–1248. https://doi.org/10.1162/REST_a_00310

Ringo, D. (2019). Parental credit constraints and child college attendance. *Education Finance and Policy, MIT Press, 14*(4), 548–571. https://ideas.repec.org/a/tpr/edfpol/v14y2019i4p548-571.html

Rittenhouse, K. (2023). *Income and child maltreatment: Evidence from a discontinuity in tax benefits*. Social Science Research Network. https://papers.ssrn.com/sol3/papers.cfm?abstract_id=4349231

Rodems, R., & Pfeffer, F. T. (2021). Avoiding material hardship: The buffer function of health. *Journal of European Social Policy, 31*(5), 517–532. https://doi.org/10.1177/09589287211059043

Roe v. Wade, 410 U.S. 113 (1973).

Roksa, J., & Potter, D. (2011). Parenting and academic achievement: Intergenerational transmission of educational advantage. *Sociology of Education, 84*(4), 299–321. https://doi.org/10.1177/0038040711417013

Roksa, J., & Velez, M. (2010). When studying schooling is not enough: Incorporating employment in models of educational transitions. *Research in Social Stratification and Mobility, 28*(1), 5–21. https://doi.org/10.1016/j.rssm.2009.03.001

Romich, J. L., & Weisner, T. (2000). How families view and use the EITC: Advance payment versus lump sum delivery. *National Tax Journal, 53*(4.2), 1245–1265. https://doi.org/10.17310/ntj.2000.4S1.09

Rosen, E. (2017). Horizontal immobility: How narratives of neighborhood violence shape housing decisions. *American Sociological Review*, 82(2), 270–296. https://doi.org/10.1177/0003122417695841

———. (2020). *The voucher promise: "Section 8" and the fate of an American neighborhood*. Princeton University Press.

Rosen, E., Garboden, P. M. E., & Cossyleon, J. E. (2021). Racial discrimination in housing: How landlords use algorithms and home visits to screen tenants. *American Sociological Review*, 86(5), 787–822. https://doi.org/10.1177/00031224211029618

Rosenbaum, J. E., Deil-Amen, R., & Person, A. E. (2006). *After admission: From college access to college success*. Russell Sage Foundation.

Rosenbaum, J. E., Popkin, S. J., Kaufman, J. E., & Rusin, J. (1991). Social integration of low-income Black adults in middle-class White suburbs. *Social Problems*, 38(4), 448–461. https://doi.org/10.2307/800564

Rosenblatt, P., & DeLuca, S. (2012). We don't live outside, we live in here: Neighborhood and residential mobility decisions among low-income families. *City & Community*, 11(3), 254–284. https://doi.org/10.1111/j.1540-6040.2012.01413.x

———. (2017). What happened in Sandtown-Winchester? Understanding the impacts of a comprehensive community initiative. *Urban Affairs Review*, 53(3), 463–494. https://doi.org/10.1177/1078087415617852

Rothbaum, J., & Hokayem, C. (2021). *How did the pandemic affect survey response: Using administrative data to evaluate nonresponse in the 2021 Current Population Survey annual social and economic supplement*. United States Census Bureau. https://www.census.gov/newsroom/blogs/research-matters/2021/09/pandemic-affect-survey-response.html

Rothstein, R. (2013). *For public schools, segregation then, segregation since: Education and the unfinished march*. Economic Policy Institute. https://files.epi.org/2013/Unfinished-March-School-Segregation.pdf

Rothstein, R. (2017). *The color of law: A forgotten history of how our government segregated America*. Liveright Publishing.

Rothwell, J. T., & Massey, D. S. (2010). Density zoning and class segregation in U.S. metropolitan areas. *Social Science Quarterly*, 91(5), 1123–1143. https://doi.org/10.2139/ssrn.1322128

Rotz, D. (2016). Why have divorce rates fallen? The role of women's age at marriage. *Journal of Human Resources*, 51(4), 961–1002. https://doi.org/10.3368/jhr.51.4.0214-6224R

Rubinowitz, L. S., & Rosenbaum, J. E. (2000). *Crossing the class and color lines: From public housing to White suburbia*. University of Chicago Press.

Ruggles, S. (2006). Linking historical censuses: A new approach. *History and Computing*, 14(1–2), 213–224. https://doi.org/10.3366/hac.2002.14.1-2.213

Rugh, J. S., & Massey, D. S. (2010). Racial segregation and the American foreclosure crisis. *American Sociological Review*, 75(5), 629–651. https://doi.org/10.1177/0003122410380868

Ryan, A., Trumbull, G., & Tufano, P. (2011). A brief postwar history of U.S. consumer finance. *Business History Review*, 85(3), 461–498. https://www.jstor.org/stable/41301431?seq=1

Ryan, R. M., & Padilla, C. (2019). Public policy and family psychology. In B. H. Fiese, M. Celano, K. Deater-Deckard, E. N. Jouriles, & M. A. Whisman (Eds.), *APA handbook of contemporary family psychology: Applications and broad impact of family psychology* (pp. 639–655). American Psychological Association.

Saez, E., & Zucman, G. (2019). Progressive wealth taxation. *Brookings Papers on Economic Activity*, 50(2), 437–533. https://doi.org/10.1353/eca.2019.0017

Sakamoto, A., & Wang, S. X. (2020). The declining significance of occupation in research on intergenerational mobility. *Research in Social Stratification and Mobility*, 70, 100521. https://doi.org/10.1016/j.rssm.2020.100521

Samari, G., Nagle, A., & Coleman-Minahan, K. (2021). Measuring structural xenophobia: U.S. state immigration policy climates over ten years. *SSM - Population Health*, 16, 100938. https://doi.org/10.1016/j.ssmph.2021.100938

Sampson, R. J. (2008). Moving to inequality: Neighborhood effects and experiments meet social structure. *American Journal of Sociology, 114*(1), 189–231. https://doi.org/10.1086/589843

Sampson, R. J., & Laub, J. H. (1996). Socioeconomic achievement in the life course of disadvantaged men: Military service as a turning point, circa 1940–1965. *American Sociological Review, 61*(3), 347–367. https://scholar.harvard.edu/files/sampson/files/1996_asr_laub.pdf

Sampson, R. J., Raudenbush, S. W., & Earls, F. (1997). Neighborhoods and violent crime: A multilevel study of collective efficacy. *Science, 277*(5328), 918–924. https://doi.org/10.1126/science.277.5328.918

Sanbonmatsu, L., Katz, L., Ludwig, J., Gennetian, L., Duncan, G., Kessler, R., Adam, E., McDade, T., & Lindau, S. T. (2011). *Moving to opportunity for fair housing demonstration program: Final impacts evaluation.* U.S. Department of Housing and Urban Development, Office of Policy Development and Research. https://www.huduser.gov/portal/publications/pubasst/MTOFHD.html

Sanbonmatsu, L., Kling, J. R., Duncan, G. J., & Brooks-Gunn, J. (2006). *Neighborhoods and academic achievement: Results from the moving to opportunity experiment* (NBER Working Paper No. 11909). National Bureau of Economic Research. https://econpapers.repec.org/paper/nbrnberwo/11909.htm

Sandel, M. J. (2020). *The tyranny of merit: What's become of the common good?* Penguin UK.

Sassler, S., & Lichter, D. T. (2020). Cohabitation and marriage: Complexity and diversity in union-formation patterns. *Journal of Marriage and Family, 82*(1), 35–61. https://doi.org/10.1111/jomf.12617

Satter, B. (2009). *Family properties: Race, real estate, and the exploitation of Black urban America.* Metropolitan Books.

Sawhill, I. V. (2014). *Generation unbound: Drifting into sex and parenthood without marriage.* Brookings Institution Press.

Schoeni, R. F., Freedman, V. A., Cornman, J. C., & Seltzer, J. A. (2022). The strength of parent–adult child ties in biological families and stepfamilies: Evidence from time diaries from older adults. *Demography, 59*(5), 1821–1842. https://doi.org/10.1215/00703370-10177468

Schoeni, R. F., & Wiemers, E. E. (2015). The implications of selective attrition for estimates of intergenerational elasticity of family income. *The Journal of Economic Inequality, 13*, 351–372. https://doi.org/10.1007/s10888-015-9297-z

Schreiner, M., & Sherraden, M. (2007). *Can the poor save? Saving and asset building in individual development accounts.* Transaction Publishers.

Schwartz, A. (2015). *Housing policy in the United States: An introduction.* Routledge.

Schwartz, C. R. (2010). Earnings inequality and the changing association between spouses' earnings. *American Journal of Sociology, 115*(5), 1524–1557. https://doi.org/10.1086/651373

Schwartz, H. (2010). *Housing policy is school policy: Economically integrative housing promotes academic success in Montgomery County, Maryland.* The Century Foundation. https://tcf.org/content/report/housing-policy-school-policy-economically-integrative-housing-promotes-academic-success-montgomery-county-maryland/

Schochet, P. Z. (2021). Long-run labor market effects of the job corps program: Evidence from a nationally representative experiment. *Journal of Policy Analysis and Management, 40*(1), 128–157. https://doi.org/10.1002/pam.22233

Scott-Clayton, J. (2012). What explains trends in labor supply among U.S. undergraduates? *National Tax Journal, 65*(1), 181–210. https://doi.org/10.17310/ntj.2012.1.07

Scrivener, S., Weiss, M. J., Ratledge, A., Rudd, T., Sommo, C., & Fresques, H. (2015). *Doubling graduation rates: Three-year effects of CUNY's Accelerated Study in Associate Programs (ASAP) for developmental education students.* MDRC. https://files.eric.ed.gov/fulltext/ED558511.pdf

Seamster, L., & Charron-Chénier, R. (2017). Predatory inclusion and education debt: Rethinking the racial wealth gap. *Social Currents, 4*(3), 199–207. https://doi.org/10.1177/2329496516686620

Seira, E., Elizondo, A., & Laguna-Müggenburg, E. (2017). Are information disclosures effective? Evidence from the credit card market. *American Economic Journal: Economic Policy*, *9*(1), 277–307. https://doi.org/10.1257/pol.20140404

Seltzer, J. A. (2019). Family change and changing family demography. *Demography*, *56*(2), 405–426. https://doi.org/10.1007/s13524-019-00766-6

Seltzer, N. (2024). Cohort-specific experiences of industrial decline and intergenerational income mobility. *Social Forces*, *102*(4), 1223–1248. https://doi.org/10.1093/sf/soad145

Servon, L. (2017). *The unbanking of America: How the new middle class survives*. Houghton Mifflin Harcourt.

Sewell, W. H., Haller, A. O., & Portes, A. (1969). The educational and early occupational attainment process. *American Sociological Review*, *34*(1), 82–92. https://doi.org/10.2307/2092789

Shah, A. K., Mullainathan, S., & Shafir, E. (2012). Some consequences of having too little. *Science*, *338*(6107), 682–685. https://doi.org/10.1126/science.1222426

Shanahan, M. J., Mortimer, J. T., & Johnson, M. K. (2016). Introduction: Life course studies—Trends, challenges, and future directions. In M. J. Shanahan, J. T. Mortimer, & M. K. Johnson (Eds.) *Handbook of the life course* (Vol. 2, pp. 1–23). Springer.

Shanks, T. R. (2007). The impacts of household wealth on child development. *Journal of Poverty*, *11*(2), 93–116. https://doi.org/10.1300/J134v11n02_05

Shapiro, T. M. (2004). *The hidden cost of being African American: How wealth perpetuates inequality*. Oxford University Press.

___. (2017). *Toxic inequality: How America's wealth gap destroys mobility, deepens the racial divide, and threatens our future*. Basic Books.

Sharkey, P. (2010). The acute effect of local homicides on children's cognitive performance. *Proceedings of the National Academy of Sciences*, *107*(26), 11733–11738. https://doi.org/10.1073/pnas.1000690107

___. (2013). *Stuck in place: Urban neighborhoods and the end of progress toward racial equality*. University of Chicago Press.

___. (2016). Neighborhoods, cities, and economic mobility. *The Russell Sage Foundation Journal of the Social Sciences*, *2*(2), 159–177. https://doi.org/10.7758/RSF.2016.2.2.07

Sharkey, P., & Faber, J. W. (2014). Where, when, why, and for whom do residential contexts matter? Moving away from the dichotomous understanding of neighborhood effects. *Annual Review of Sociology*, *40*, 559–579. https://doi.org/10.1146/annurev-soc-071913-043350

Sharkey, P., Schwartz, A. E., Ellen, I. G., & Lacoe, J. (2014). High stakes in the classroom, high stakes on the street: The effects of community violence on student's standardized test performance. *Sociological Science*, *1*(14), 199–220. https://doi.org/10.15195/v1.a14

Sharkey, P., Tirado-Strayer, N., Papachristos, A. V., & Raver, C. C. (2012). The effect of local violence on children's attention and impulse control. *American Journal of Public Health*, *102*(12), 2287–2293. https://doi.org/10.2105/AJPH.2012.300789

Sharkey, P., & Torrats-Espinosa, G. (2017). The effect of violent crime on economic mobility. *Journal of Urban Economics*, *102*(C), 22–33. https://doi.org/10.1016/j.jue.2017.07.001

Shaw, Z. A., & Starr, L. R. (2019). Intergenerational transmission of emotion dysregulation: The role of authoritarian parenting style and family chronic stress. *Journal of Child and Family Studies*, *28*(12), 3508–3518. https://doi.org/10.1007/s10826-019-01534-1

Sherraden, M. (1991). *Assets and the poor. A new American welfare policy*. Routledge, Taylor & Francis Group.

Skocpol, T. (1995). *Protecting soldiers and mothers: The political origins of social policy in the United States*. Harvard University Press.

Small, M. L. (2004). *Villa Victoria: The transformation of social capital in a Boston barrio*. University of Chicago Press.

Small, M. L., Harding, D. J., & Lamont, M. (2010). Reconsidering culture and poverty. *The Annals of the American Academy of Political and Social Science*, *629*(1), 6–27. https://doi.org/10.1177/0002716210362077

Smock, P. J., & Schwartz, C. R. (2020). The demography of families: A review of patterns and change. *Journal of Marriage and Family*, *82*(1), 9–34. https://doi.org/10.1111/jomf.12612

Solon, G. (2004). A model of intergenerational mobility variation over time and place. In M. Corak (Ed.), *Generational income mobility* (pp. 38–47). Cambridge University Press.

———. (2008). Intergenerational income mobility. In M. Vernengo, E. P. Caldentey, & B. J. Rosser, Jr. (Eds.), *New Palgrave dictionary of economics* (pp. 1–5). Palgrave Macmillan.

Song, X., Massey, C. G., Rolf, K. A., Ferrie, J. P., Rothbaum, J. L., & Xie, Y. (2020). Long-term decline in intergenerational mobility in the United States since the 1850s. *Proceedings of the National Academy of Sciences*, *117*(1), 251–258. https://doi.org/10.1073/pnas.1905094116

Spera, C. (2005). A review of the relationship among parenting practices, parenting styles, and adolescent school achievement. *Educational Psychology Review*, *17*(2), 125–146. https://doi.org/10.1007/s10648-005-3950-1

Spilerman, S. (2000). Wealth and stratification processes. *Annual Review of Sociology*, *26*, 497–524. https://doi.org/10.1146/annurev.soc.26.1.497

Sroufe, L. A., Coffino, B., & Carlson, E. A. (2010). Conceptualizing the role of early experience: Lessons from the Minnesota longitudinal study. *Developmental Review*, *30*(1), 36–51. https://doi.org/10.1016/j.dr.2009.12.002

Stanley, M., Katz, L. F., & Krueger, A. (1998, October). *Developing skills: What we know about the impact of American employment and training programs on employment, earnings, and educational outcomes*. Report for G8 Economic Summit. https://scholar.harvard.edu/lkatz/publications/developing-skills-what-we-know-about-impact-american-educational-and-training-pro

Starke, P. (2007). *Radical welfare state retrenchment: A comparative analysis*. Palgrave Macmillan London.

Starr, S. B. (2014). Evidence-based sentencing and the scientific rationalization of discrimination. *Stanford Law Review*, *66*(4), 803–872. https://www.researchgate.net/publication/286656685_Evidence-based_sentencing_and_the_scientific_rationalization_of_discrimination

Stevens, M. L., Alston, G. D., Cini, M., Gallagher, S., Horwitz, I., Kazin, C., McCann, P. C., Pardos, Z., Roumell, E. A., Sheffer, H., Zanville, H., & Settersten, R. (2022). *An applied science to support working learners* (A Report to the National Science Foundation Re: Award #2128165). Stanford Graduate School of Education. https://workinglearners.stanford.edu/wp-content/uploads/2022/08/SUGSE-Working-Learners-Report-2022-v07-FINAL.pdf

Stevens, M. L., & Kirst, M. W. (Eds.) (2015). *Remaking college: The changing ecology of higher education*. Stanford University Press.

Streib, J. (2011). Class reproduction by four year olds. *Qualitative Sociology*, *34*, 337–352. https://doi.org/10.1007/s11133-011-9193-1

Stuber, J. M. (2011). *Inside the college gates: How class and culture matter in higher education*. Lexington Books.

Sullivan, J. X. (2008). Borrowing during unemployment unsecured debt as a safety net. *Journal of Human Resources*, *43*(2), 383–412. https://doi.org/10.3368/jhr.43.2.383

Sullivan, T. A., & Kaufman, G. (2012). Debt and the simulation of social class. In R. Brubaker, R. M. Lawless, & C. J. Tabb (Eds.), *A debtor world: Interdisciplinary perspectives on debt* (pp. 36–59). Oxford University Press.

Sullivan, T. A., Warren, E., & Westbrook, J. (2001). *The fragile middle class: Americans in debt*. Yale University Press.

Sun, A. R., & Houle, J. N. (2020). Trajectories of unsecured debt across the life course and mental health at midlife. *Society and Mental Health*, *10*(1), 61–79. https://doi.org/10.1177/2156869318816742

Sun, S. T., & Yannelis, C. (2016). Credit constraints and demand for higher education: Evidence from financial deregulation. *Review of Economics and Statistics*, *98*(1), 12–21. https://doi.org/10.1162/REST_a_00558

Swift, A. (2004). Would perfect mobility be perfect? *European Sociological Review*, *20*(1), 1–11. https://doi.org/10.1093/esr/20.1.1

Tach, L., Edin, K., Harvey, H., & Bryan, B. (2014). The family-go-round: Family complexity and father involvement from a father's perspective. *The Annals of the American Academy of Political and Social Science*, *654*(1), 169–184. https://doi.org/10.1177/0002716214528655

Tach, L., & Wimer, C. (2017). *Evaluating policies to transform distressed urban neighborhoods*. The Urban Institute. https://www.urban.org/sites/default/files/publication/94026/evaluating-policies-to-transform-distressed-urban-neighborhoods.pdf

Tach, L. M., & Greene, S. S. (2014). Robbing Peter to pay Paul: Economic and cultural explanations for how lower-income families manage debt. *Social Problems 61*(1), 1–21. https://doi.org/10.1525/sp.2013.11262

Tax Policy Center. (2024). *How many people pay the estate tax?* Tax Policy Center Briefing Book, Key Elements of the U.S. Tax System. Urban Institute & Brookings Institution https://www.taxpolicycenter.org/briefing-book/how-many-people-pay-estate-tax

Taylor, K.-Y. (2019). *Race for profit: How banks and the real estate industry undermined Black homeownership*. Chapel Hill: University of North Carolina Press.

Teachman, J., & Tedrow, L. M. (2004). Wages, earnings, and occupational status: Did World War II veterans receive a premium? *Social Science Research*, *33*(4), 581–605. https://doi.org/10.1016/j.ssresearch.2003.09.007

Theodos, B., Coulton, C. J., & Pitingolo, R. (2015). Housing unit turnover and the socioeconomic mix of low-income neighborhoods. *The Annals of the American Academy of Political and Social Science*, *660*(1), 117–135. https://doi.org/10.1177/0002716215576112

Thompson, J., & Conley, D. (2016). Health shocks and social drift: Examining the relationship between acute illness and family wealth. *The Russell Sage Foundation Journal of the Social Sciences*, *2*(6), 153–171. https://doi.org/10.7758/rsf.2016.2.6.08

Thompson, R. A. (2014). Stress and child development. *The Future of Children*, *24*(1), 41–59. https://doi.org/10.1353/foc.2014.0004

Toney, J., & Robertson, C. L. (2021). Intergenerational economic mobility and the racial wealth gap. *AEA Papers and Proceedings*, *111*, 206–210. https://doi.org/10.1257/pandp.20211113

Torche, F. (2011). Is a college degree still the great equalizer? Intergenerational mobility across levels of schooling in the US? *American Journal of Sociology*, *117*(3), 763–807. https://www.jstor.org/stable/10.1086/661904

___. (2015a). Analyses of intergenerational mobility: An interdisciplinary review. *The Annals of the American Academy of Political and Social Science*, *657*(1), 37–62. https://doi.org/10.1177/0002716214547476

___. (2015b). Intergenerational mobility and equality of opportunity. *European Journal of Sociology*, *56*(3), 343–371. https://doi.org/10.1017/S0003975615000181

___. (2018). Intergenerational mobility at the top of the educational distribution. *Sociology of Education*, *91*(4), 266–289. https://doi.org/10.1177/0038040718801812

Torche, F., & Abufhele, A. (2021). The normativity of marriage and the marriage premium for children's outcomes. *American Journal of Sociology*, *126*(4), 931–968. https://doi.org/10.1086/713382

Torche, F., & Nobles, J. (2024). Early life exposures and social stratification. *Annual Review of Sociology*, *50*, 407–430. https://doi.org/10.1146/annurev-soc-091523-023313

Torche, F., & Rauf, T. (2021). The transition to fatherhood and the health of men. *Journal of Marriage and Family*, *83*(2), 446–465. https://doi.org/10.1111/jomf.12732

Trosper, R. L. (1994). American-Indian reparations. PRRAC—Poverty & Race Research Action Council. *Poverty and Race Journal*. https://www.prrac.org/american-indian-reparations-by-ronald-l-trosper-november-december-1994-pr-issue/

Turner, M. A., Toder, E., Pendall, R., & Sharygin, C. A. (2013). *How would reforming the mortgage interest deduction affect the housing market?* The Urban Institute. https://www.urban.org/research/publication/how-would-reforming-mortgage-interest-deduction-affect-housing-market

Turner, S. E. (2004). Going to college and finishing college: Explaining different educational outcomes. In C. M. Hoxby (Ed.), *College choices: The economics of where to go, when to go, and how to pay for it* (pp. 13–62). University of Chicago Press.

Turner, S. E., & Bound, J. (2003). Closing the gap or widening the divide: The effects of the GI Bill and World War II on the educational outcomes of Black Americans. *The Journal of Economic History*, *63*(1), 145–177. https://www.jstor.org/stable/3132498

Turney, K., Kissane, R., & Edin, K. (2013). After moving to opportunity: How moving to a low-poverty neighborhood improves mental health among African American women. *Society and Mental Health*, *3*(1), 1–21. https://doi.org/10.1177/2156869312464789

Turunen, E., & Hiilamo, H. (2014). Health effects of indebtedness: A systematic review. *BMC Public Health*, *14*(1), 1–8. https://doi.org/10.1186/1471-2458-14-489

Ulferts, H. (2020). *Why parenting matters for children in the 21st century: An evidence-based framework for understanding parenting and its impact on child development* (OECD Education Working Paper No. 222). Organisation for Economic Co-operation and Development. https://doi.org/10.1787/129a1a59-en

U.S. Bureau of Economic Analysis. (2023). *News release: Gross domestic product (third estimate), corporate profits, and GDP by industry, fourth quarter and year 2022*. U.S. Department of Commerce. https://www.bea.gov/sites/default/files/2023-03/gdp4q22_3rd_0.pdf

U.S. Department of State. (2020). *The JUST act report*. Office of the Special Envoy for Holocaust Issues. https://www.state.gov/wp-content/uploads/2020/02/JUST-Act5.pdf

U.S. Office of Management and Budget. (2024). Revisions to OMB's statistical policy directive No. 15: Standards for maintaining, collecting, and presenting federal data on race and ethnicity. *Federal Register*, *89*(62). https://www.govinfo.gov/content/pkg/FR-2024-03-29/pdf/2024-06469.pdf

Van Bavel, J., Schwartz, C. R., & Esteve, A. (2018). The reversal of the gender gap in education and its consequences for family life. *Annual Review of Sociology*, *44*(1), 341–360. https://doi.org/10.1146/annurev-soc-073117-041215

Wadsworth, M. E., & Ahlkvist, J. A. (2015). Inequality begins outside the home: Putting parental educational investments into context. In P. R. Amato, A. Booth, S. M. McHale, & J. Van Hook (Eds.), *Diverging destinies: Families in an era of increasing inequality* (pp. 3–24). Springer International Publishing.

Walsemann, K. M., Gee, G. C., & Gentile, D. (2015). Sick of our loans: Student borrowing and the mental health of young adults in the United States. *Social Science & Medicine*, *124*, 85–93. https://doi.org/10.1016/j.socscimed.2014.11.027

Ward, Z. (2023). Intergenerational mobility in American history: Accounting for race and measurement error. *American Economic Review*, *113*(12), 3213–3248. https://doi.org/10.1257/aer.20200292

Warren, J. R., & Hauser, R. M. (1997). Social stratification across three generations: New evidence from the Wisconsin Longitudinal Study. *American Sociological Review*, *62*(4), 561–572. https://doi.org/10.2307/2657426

Washbrook, E., Gregg, P., & Propper, C. (2014). A decomposition analysis of the relationship between parental income and multiple child outcomes. *Journal of the Royal Statistical Society: Series A (Statistics in Society)*, *177*(4), 757–782. https://doi.org/10.1111/rssa.12074

Waters, M. C. (1990). *Ethnic options: Choosing identities in America*. University of California Press.
___. (2009). *Black identities: West Indian immigrant dreams and American realities*. Harvard University Press.
Weber, B. A., Fannin, J. M., Cordes, S. M., & Johnson, T. G. (2017). Upward mobility of low-income youth in metropolitan, micropolitan, and rural America. *The Annals of the American Academy of Political and Social Science, 672*(1), 103–122. https://doi.org/10.1177/0002716217713477
Weeden, K. A., Kim, Y.-M., Di Carlo, M., & Grusky, D. B. (2007). Social class and earnings inequality. *American Behavioral Scientist, 50*(5), 702–736. https://doi.org/10.1177/0002764206295015
Welch, F. (1999). In defense of inequality. *American Economic Review, 89*(2), 1–17. https://doi.org/10.1257/aer.89.2.1
Western, B., & Pettit, B. (2010). Incarceration & social inequality. *Daedalus, 139*(3), 8–19. https://doi.org/10.1162/DAED_a_00019
Wherry, F. F., & Chakrabarti, P. (2022). Accounting for credit. *Annual Review of Sociology, 48*(1), 131–147. https://doi.org/10.1146/annurev-soc-030320-114444
Wherry, F. F., & Perry, V. G. (2021). Anti-Black currents in consumer affairs: An introduction to the special issue. *Journal of Consumer Affairs, 55*(2), 356–365. https://doi.org/10.1111/joca.12374
Wherry, F. F., Seefeldt, K. S., & Alvarez, A. S. (2019). *Credit where it's due: Rethinking financial citizenship*. Russell Sage Foundation.
Wikle, J., & Wilson, R. (2023). Access to Head Start and maternal labor supply: Experimental and quasi-experimental evidence. *Journal of Labor Economics, 41*(4), 1081–1127. https://doi.org/10.1086/720980
Wildeman, C., & Fallesen, P. (2017). The effect of lowering welfare payment ceilings on children's risk of out-of-home placement. *Children and Youth Services Review, 72*(C), 82–90. https://doi.org/10.1016/j.childyouth.2016.10.017
Williams, D. T., & Baker, R. S. (2021). Family structure, risks, and racial stratification in poverty. *Social Problems, 68*(2), 964–985. https://doi.org/10.1093/socpro/spab018
Williams, R., Nesiba, R., & McConnell, E. D. (2005). The changing face of inequality in home mortgage lending. *Social Problems, 52*(2), 181–208. https://doi.org/10.1525/sp.2005.52.2.181
Williamson, V. (2020). *Closing the racial wealth gap requires heavy, progressive taxation of wealth*. Brief Prepared for Brookings Blueprints for American Renewal & Prosperity, Brookings Institution. https://www.brookings.edu/articles/closing-the-racial-wealth-gap-requires-heavy-progressive-taxation-of-wealth/
Wilson, N. J., & Kizer, K. W. (1997). The VA health care system: An unrecognized national safety net. *Health Affairs, 16*(4), 200–204. https://doi.org/10.1377/hlthaff.16.4.200
Wilson, W. J. (1987). *The truly disadvantaged: The inner city, the underclass, and public policy*. University of Chicago Press.
___. (1996). *When work disappears: The world of the new urban poor*. Alfred A. Knopf.
Wodtke, G. T., Yildirim, U., Harding, D. J., & Elwert, F. (2023). Are neighborhood effects explained by differences in school quality? *American Journal of Sociology, 128*(5), 1472–1528. https://doi.org/10.1086/724279
Wolfe, B., Jakubowski, J., Haveman, R., & Courey, M. (2012). The income and health effects of tribal casino gaming on American Indians. *Demography, 49*(2), 499–524. https://doi.org/10.1007/s13524-012-0098-8
Wolff, E. N. (2017). *A century of wealth in America*. Belknap Press.
Wong, K. K. (1999). *Funding public schools: Politics and policies*. University Press of Kansas.

Wood, R. G., McConnell, S., Moore, Q., Clarkwest, A., & Hsueh, J. (2012). The effects of building strong families: A healthy marriage and relationship skills education program for unmarried parents. *Journal of Policy Analysis and Management, 31*(2), 228–252. https://doi.org/10.1002/pam.21608

Wood, R. G., Moore, Q., Clarkwest, A., & Killewald, A. (2014). The long-term effects of building strong families: A program for unmarried parents. *Journal of Marriage and Family, 76*(2), 446–463. https://doi.org/10.1111/jomf.12094

Worthington, A. C. (2006). Debt as a source of financial stress in Australian households. *International Journal of Consumer Studies, 30*(1), 2–15. https://hdl.handle.net/10779/uow.27726501.v1

Xiao, J. J., & Yao, R. (2011a). *Consumer debt delinquency over life cycle stages* (Working Paper No. 2011-WP 18). Networks Financial Institute. https://ideas.repec.org/p/nfi/nfiwps/2011-wp-18.html

———. (2011b). *Debt holding and burden by family structure in 1989–2007* (Working Paper No. 2011-WP-04). Networks Financial Institute. https://papers.ssrn.com/sol3/papers.cfm?abstract_id=1799362

Yoshikawa, H., Aber, J. L., & Beardslee, W. R. (2012). The effects of poverty on the mental, emotional, and behavioral health of children and youth: Implications for prevention. *American Psychologist, 67*(4), 272–284. https://doi.org/10.1037/a0028015

Young, A., & DeLuca, S. (2020). *I don't want to rush everything and end up where I started: Disadvantaged youth, college choice, and the reverse life course.* Paper Presented at the Annual Meeting of the American Sociological Association.

Zaidi, B., & Morgan, S. P. (2017). The second demographic transition theory: A review and appraisal. *Annual Review of Sociology, 43*, 473–492. https://doi.org/10.1146/annurev-soc-060116-053442

Zakeri, H., & Karimpour, M. (2011). Parenting styles and self-esteem. *Procedia–Social and Behavioral Sciences, 29*(4), 758–761. https://doi.org/10.1016/j.sbspro.2011.11.302

Zang, E., Gibson-Davis, C., & Li, H. (2024). Beyond parental wealth: Grandparental wealth and the transition to adulthood. *Research in Social Stratification and Mobility, 89*, 100878. https://doi.org/10.1016/j.rssm.2023.100878

Zewde, N. (2020). Universal baby bonds reduce Black-White wealth inequality, progressively raise net worth of all young adults. *Review of Black Political Economy, 47*(1), 3–19. https://doi.org/10.1177/0034644619885321

Zhai, F., Brooks-Gunn, J., & Waldfogel, J. (2014). Head Start's impact is contingent on alternative type of care in comparison group. *Developmental Psychology, 50*(12), 2572–2586. https://doi.org/10.1037/a0038205

Zucman, G. (2019). Global wealth inequality. *Annual Review of Economics, 11*, 109–138. https://doi.org/10.1146/annurev-economics-080218-025852

Appendix

Biographical Sketches of Committee Members

H. LUKE SHAEFER (*Chair*) is the Hermann and Amalie Kohn professor of social policy at the Gerald R. Ford School of Public Policy at the University of Michigan (UM). At UM, he also serves as the inaugural director of Poverty Solutions, an interdisciplinary, presidential initiative that partners with communities and policymakers to find new ways to prevent and alleviate poverty. Shaefer's research centers on poverty and social welfare policy in the United States, and he has published in top peer-reviewed academic journals in the fields of public policy, social work, public health, health services research, and history. His work has been supported by grants from the National Science Foundation, the Gates Foundation, and the U.S. Census Bureau, among others. Shaefer has presented his research at the White House and before numerous federal agencies, and he has testified before the U.S. Senate Finance Committee and advised several of the nation's largest human service providers. He has a Ph.D. in social service administration from the University of Chicago.

FLORENCIA TORCHE (*Vice chair*) is the Edwards S. Sanford professor of sociology and public and international affairs at Princeton University. Her research focuses on social inequality and social mobility, educational disparities, and marriage and family dynamics. Torche's recent scholarship focuses on the influence of early-life exposures and circumstances—starting before birth—on individual health, development, and well-being using natural experiments and causal inference approaches. She has led large data collection projects, including the first national social mobility surveys in Chile and Mexico. Torche has a Ph.D. in sociology from Columbia University. She is an elected member at the National Academy of Sciences, the American Academy of Arts and Sciences, and the American Academy of Political & Social Science. Recently, Torche served as member of the National Academy of Sciences Committee on Addressing the Long-Term Impact of the COVID-19 Pandemic on Children and Families.

MARTHA J. BAILEY is professor of economics in the Department of Economics and the director of the California Center for Population Research at the University of California, Los Angeles. She is also a research associate at the National Bureau of Economic Research. Bailey's research focuses on issues in labor economics, demography, and health in the United States within the long-run perspective of economic history. Her work examines the determinants of the gender gap as well as the short- and long-term effects of Great Society programs. Bailey has written numerous articles and coedited three books. Currently, she leads the National Science Foundation–funded Longitudinal, Intergenerational Family Electronic Micro-data project and the National Institutes of Health-funded Michigan Contraceptive Access Research and Evaluation Study. Bailey has served as an editor for the *Journal of Labor Economics* and *Demography*. She has a Ph.D. in economics from Vanderbilt University.

LAWRENCE (LONNIE) M. BERGER is associate vice chancellor for research in the social sciences, Sheila B. Kamerman and Alfred J. Kahn professor of social policy, and Vilas distinguished achievement professor in the School of Social Work at the University of Wisconsin–Madison (UW). Prior to this, he was director of the Institute for Research on Poverty at UW. Berger's research focuses on the ways in which economic resources, sociodemographic characteristics, and public policies affect parental behaviors and child and family well-being, and it aims to inform public policy by improving its capacity to assist families in accessing resources, improving family functioning and well-being, and ensuring that children can grow and develop in the best possible environments. He is engaged in studies in three primary areas: examining the determinants of substandard parenting, child maltreatment, and out-of-home placement for children; exploring associations among socioeconomic factors (family structure and composition, economic resources, household debt), parenting behaviors, and children's care, development, and well-being; and assessing the influence of public policies on parental behaviors and child and family well-being. Berger has a Ph.D. in social work from Columbia University.

TYSON H. BROWN is associate professor of sociology at Duke University where he holds the W.L.F. endowed chair. His program of research examines the *who, when,* and *how* questions regarding racial inequities in health and wealth. Brown has authored numerous articles in leading journals in the fields of sociology, demography, and population health, and his research contributions have been recognized with awards from the American Sociological Association. He was the inaugural Duke Presidential fellow, the recipient of Duke University's Thomas Langford Award, and a resident fellow at Oxford University. Brown was awarded funding for his training and research from the Robert Wood Johnson Foundation, the Ford Foundation, and the National Institutes of Health. He has served in leadership positions within professional organizations, including on the Board of Directors of the Population Association of America, as well as on the editorial boards of journals such as *Social Forces, Demography, Social Psychology Quarterly*, and the *Journal of Health and Social Behavior*. Brown has a Ph.D. in sociology from the University of North Carolina at Chapel Hill.

JOHNAVAE CAMPBELL is a senior manager in child welfare and education at ICF International, Inc. She has more than 15 years of experience conducting and managing evaluations using mixed-methods data collection strategies. Campbell evaluates antiracist, culturally responsive teaching strategies for educational programs, specifically those focused on efforts to promote awareness in science, technology, engineering, and math careers and among students from underrepresented populations. She also serves as a senior evaluator on the National Science Foundation–funded Inclusion across the Nation of Communities of Learners of Underrepresented Discoverers in Engineering and Science Initiative, which seeks to broaden science, technology, engineering, and mathematics (STEM) participation and retention efforts for first-generation college students, specifically bolstering access and readiness efforts in West Virginia and Arizona. Campbell's research includes program evaluation specializing in collaborative approaches, college access, broadening STEM participation, and issues of equity. She has evaluation expertise in managing Department of Education–funded grants conducting experimental and quasi-experimental impact and fidelity of implementation study designs. Campbell is a graduate of the University of North Carolina and served as an adjunct professor in the School of Education, where she completed her doctoral degree.

STEFANIE A. DeLUCA is the James Coleman professor of sociology and social policy in the Department of Sociology at the Johns Hopkins University Krieger School of Arts & Sciences, director of the Poverty and Inequality Research Lab, and Research Principal at Opportunity Insights at Harvard University. She has written extensively on education, neighborhoods, housing policies, and mobility among low-income families. DeLuca's research has been made possible by support from the Annie E. Casey Foundation, Abell Foundation, Spencer Foundation, National Academy of Education,

William T. Grant Foundation, Gates Foundation, Russell Sage Foundation, the National Science Foundation, and the Department of Education. She serves on a Federal Research Advisory Commission at the Department of Housing and Urban Development and has been invited to share her research to support policy recommendations at the Department of Housing and Urban Development, the Department of Education, the Department of Health and Human Services, and for several state legislatures. DeLuca is an elected member of the Sociological Research Association and received the Publicly Engaged Scholar Award from the American Sociological Association. She has a Ph.D. in human development and social policy from Northwestern University.

SUSAN MARIE DYNARSKI is Patricia Albjerg Graham professor of education at the Harvard Graduate School of Education, a faculty research associate at the National Bureau of Economic Research, and a fellow of the American Academy of Arts and Sciences and the National Academy of Education. Her research focuses on understanding and reducing inequality in education. Dynarski uses large-scale datasets and quantitative methods of causal inference to understand the effects of financial aid, postsecondary schooling, class size, high school reforms, and charter schools on academic achievement and educational attainment. She was selected as a Carnegie fellow, and she has been awarded the Spencer Foundation Award by the Association for Public Policy and Management for excellence in research. The National Association of Student Financial Aid Administrators awarded Dynarski the Robert P. Huff Golden Quill Award for excellence in research on student aid, and she was named a top ten influencer by *The Chronicle of Higher Education*. She has served on the board of editors of the *American Economic Journal/Economic Policy* and *The Journal of Labor Economics and Educational Evaluation and Policy Analysis*; in addition, she has served on the board of the Association for Public Policy and Management and is past president of the Association for Education Finance and Policy and Midwest Economics Association. Dynarski has a B.A. and M.P.P. from Harvard University and a Ph.D. in economics from the Massachusetts Institute of Technology.

DAVID B. GRUSKY is Edward Ames Edmonds professor in the School of Humanities and Sciences at Stanford University, professor of sociology, senior fellow at the Stanford Institute for Economic Policy Research, director of the Stanford Center on Poverty and Inequality, faculty fellow at the Center for Population Health Sciences, and coeditor of *Pathways Magazine*. He carries out research in inequality, poverty, mobility, gender, and quantitative and qualitative methods. Grusky is a fellow of the American Association for the Advancement of Science, corecipient of the Max Weber Award, founder of the Cornell University Center for the Study of Inequality, and a former National Science Foundation Presidential Young Investigator. He is an elected member of the National Academy of Sciences. His recent books include *Inequality in the 21st Century* (with J. Hill, 2017), *Social Stratification* (with K. Weisshaar, 2014), *Occupy the Future* (with D. McAdam, R. Reich, & D. Satz, 2012), *The New Gilded Age* (with T. Kricheli-Katz, 2011), and *The Great Recession* (with B. Western & C. Wimer, 2011). Grusky has a Ph.D. in sociology from the University of Wisconsin–Madison.

KATHLEEN MULLAN HARRIS is the James E. Haar distinguished professor of sociology and adjunct professor of public policy in the Carolina Population Center at the University of North Carolina at Chapel Hill. Her research centers on social inequality and health with a focus on health disparities, biodemography, social science genomics, and life course and aging processes. Harris continues to work with an interdisciplinary set of scholars from sociology, epidemiology, nutrition, economics, cardiology, genetics, and survey methods to publish research on such topics as the health effects of despair, isolation, and stress; social genetic effects; health costs of upward mobility; early life origins of biological aging; and the obesity epidemic and young adult health. She was awarded the Golden Goose Award from the U.S. Congress for major breakthroughs in medicine, social behavior, and technological research and the Irene Taeuber Award from the Population Association of America in recognition of original and important contributions to the scientific study of population. Harris is an elected member of the American Academy of Arts and Sciences as well as a fellow of the American Association for the Advancement of Science. She is an elected member of the National Academies of Sciences, Engineering, and Medicine and has a Ph.D. in demography from the University of Pennsylvania.

FABIAN T. PFEFFER is professor of sociology at the Ludwig-Maximilians-Universität München (LMU Munich) in Germany and founding director of the Munich International Stone Center for Inequality Research. Prior to his appointment at LMU Munich, he served as founding director of the Stone Center for Inequality Dynamics at the University of Michigan. Pfeffer's research investigates social inequality and its maintenance across generations and time. His current projects focus on wealth inequality and its consequences for the next generation as well as the contexts and consequences of social mobility. Pfeffer holds a Ph.D. in sociology from the University of Wisconsin–Madison. Previously, Pfeffer was an invited expert for the 2018 National Academies of Sciences, Engineering, and Medicine's (National Academies') expert meeting on Using Longitudinal Studies of Younger Cohorts for Aging Research and as a steering committee member for the 2022 National Academies' workshop on Strengthening the Evidence Base to Improve Economic and Social Mobility in the United States.

PATRICK SHARKEY is William S. Tod professor of sociology and public affairs in the Princeton School of Public and International Affairs and the Department of Sociology at Princeton University. Prior to this appointment, he served as chair of sociology at New York University and as scientific director at Crime Lab New York. Sharkey is also founder of AmericaViolence.org. His research focuses on urban inequality, violence, and public policy. He is widely published in areas such as community violence, neighborhood crime, economic mobility, and the relationship between child test scores and localized crime. Sharkey received his Ph.D. in sociology and social policy from Harvard University.

MARTA TIENDA is Maurice P. During '22 professor in demographic studies, professor of sociology and public affairs emerita, and a visiting senior scholar at the Center for Research on Child Wellbeing at Princeton University. She is president of the American Academy of Political and Social Science, past president of the Population Association of America, and a member of the American Academy of Arts and Sciences, the National Academy of Education, and the American Academy of Political and Social Sciences. Tienda currently serves on the boards of the Urban Institute, the Holdsworth Center for Excellence in Public Education, and the Robin Hood Foundation. Her research, which has been supported by U.S. Department of Labor, the Department of Health and Human Services, National Institute of Child Health and Human Development, National Science Foundation, and the Mellon, Spencer, and Ford Foundations addresses racial and ethnic differences in various metrics of social inequality, international migration, immigrant integration, and access to higher education. Tienda has a Ph.D. in sociology from the University of Texas at Austin and received honorary doctorates from the Ohio State University, Lehman College, Bank Street College, and her alma mater, Michigan State University.

KENNETH R. TROSKE is Richard W. and Janis H. Furst endowed chair of economics at the University of Kentucky and the chair of the Economics Department. He also serves as research fellow with the Institute for the Study of Labor and chair of the American Economic Association's Committee on Government Relations. Troske's primary research areas are labor and human resource economics. He has authored numerous papers utilizing employer–employee matched data on topics such as education, productivity, technology, and discrimination. Previously, Troske served as a member of the Congressional Oversight Panel, whose task was to assess the existing condition of America's financial markets, as well as a commissioner on the Commission for Evidence-based Policymaking and on the Federal Advisory Committee on Data for Evidence Building. He has a Ph.D. in economics from the University of Chicago.